Spiritual Dimensions of Ageing

Our understandings of both ageing and spirituality are changing rapidly in the twenty-first century, and grasping the significance of later life spirituality is now crucial in the context of extended longevity. *Spiritual Dimensions of Ageing* will inform and engage those who study or practise in all fields that relate to the lives of older people, especially in social, psychological and health-related domains, but also wherever the maintenance and development of spiritual meaning and purpose are recognised as important for human flourishing. Bringing together an international group of leading scholars across the fields of psychology, theology, history, philosophy, sociology and gerontology, the volume distils the latest advances in research on spirituality and ageing, and engages in vigorous discussion about how we can interpret this learning for the benefit of older people and those who seek to serve and support them.

MALCOLM JOHNSON is Visiting Professor of Gerontology and End of Life Care at the University of Bath, and Emeritus Professor of Health and Social Policy at the University of Bristol. From 1984–1995 he was Professor of Health and Social Welfare and first Dean of the School of Health and Social Welfare at the Open University. His research interests include biographical studies, death and dying and his major specialism, ageing and the lifespan. Of his fourteen books and over 160 monographs, chapters and articles, more than half relate to ageing. These include *The Cambridge Handbook of Age & Ageing*. He is a former Secretary of British Society of Gerontology and Founding Editor of the international journal *Ageing and Society* (Cambridge University Press).

JOANNA WALKER is currently engaged in postgraduate research on ageing and spirituality at Southampton University in the UK, following a career in adult education focused on older learners. Whilst a lecturer at Surrey University she led a government-funded project to improve the national quality of pre-retirement education by developing a resource centre, a postgraduate training scheme for practitioners, and publishing related books and papers. She chaired the Association for Education and Ageing from 2005–2012 and is associate editor of its *International Journal of Education and Ageing*. She was an adviser to the Bishop of Guildford concerning adult education for fifteen years, until 2014. A common thread has been a passion for older people's continuing development.

Spiritual Dimensions of Ageing

Malcolm Johnson

Universities of Bath and Bristol

Joanna Walker

University of Southampton

CAMBRIDGE
UNIVERSITY PRESS

CAMBRIDGE
UNIVERSITY PRESS

University Printing House, Cambridge CB2 8BS, United Kingdom

One Liberty Plaza, 20th Floor, New York, NY 10006, USA

477 Williamstown Road, Port Melbourne, VIC 3207, Australia

314-321, 3rd Floor, Plot 3, Splendor Forum, Jasola District Centre, New Delhi - 110025, India

79 Anson Road, #06-04/06, Singapore 079906

Cambridge University Press is part of the University of Cambridge.

It furthers the University's mission by disseminating knowledge in the pursuit of education, learning and research at the highest international levels of excellence.

www.cambridge.org
Information on this title: www.cambridge.org/9781107465848

© Cambridge University Press 2016

First published 2016
First paperback edition 2018

A catalogue record for this publication is available from the British Library

Library of Congress Cataloging in Publication data
Names: Johnson, Malcolm Lewis, editor and Walker, Joanna Kate, editor.
Title: Spiritual dimensions of ageing / [edited by] Malcolm Johnson, University of Bristol and University of Bath, Joanna Walker, University of Southampton.
Description: 1 [edition]. | New York : Cambridge University Press, 2016. | Includes bibliographical references and index.
Identifiers: LCCN 2016026907 | ISBN 9781107092570 (hardback : alk. paper) | ISBN 9781107465848 (pbk. : alk. paper)
Subjects: LCSH: Aging–Religious aspects.
Classification: LCC BL65.A46 S65 2016 | DDC 204/.40846–dc23 LC record available at https://lccn.loc.gov/2016026907

ISBN 978-1-107-09257-0 Hardback
ISBN 978-1-107-46584-8 Paperback

Contents

Contributors

W. ANDREW ACHENBAUM is Professor of History and Social Work at the University of Houston and holds adjunct appointments in the School of Public Health, the McGovern School for the Humanities and Ethics, and the Institute for Spirituality and Health at Texas Medical Center. He has written five books and edited eleven others, most recently, *Older Americans; Vital Communities: A Bold Vision for Ageing Societies.* His biography of Robert Butler (with Harry R. Moody) *Robert N. Butler, MD: Visionary of Healthy Aging,* was published in 2013.

KEITH R. ALBANS is an ordained Methodist minister, with a doctorate in chemical entomology. He is Director of Chaplaincy and Spirituality for Methodist Homes (MHA) and leads an innovative programme of services for residents in more than ninety care homes across the UK. He writes liturgies for older people and on spirituality in old age and with Malcolm Johnson he co-edited *God, Me and Being Very Old: Stories and Spirituality in Later Life.*

ROBERT C. ATCHLEY is Professor Emeritus of Gerontology, Miami University, Oxford, Ohio. He is author of the standard text, *Social Forces and Aging* (ten editions); *Understanding American Society*; *The Sociology of Retirement*; *Aging: Continuity and Change*; *Continuity and Adaptation in Aging: Creating Positive Experiences* and most recently *Spirituality and Aging.*

VERN BENGTSON is Senior Researcher in the Edward R. Roybal Institute on Aging of the School of Social Work, and AARP/University Professor Emeritus of Gerontology, Leonard Davis School of Gerontology, at the University of Southern California, Los Angeles. A former President of the Gerontological Society of America, he has published seventeen books, including *The Changing Contract across Generations* (with Achenbaum); *Intergenerational Linkages: Hidden Connections in American Society*; *How Families Still Matter: A Longitudinal Study* (with Biblarz and Roberts) and *Handbook of Theories of Aging* (third edition, 2016). His most recent book, *Families and Faith: How Religion Is (and Isn't) Passed Down across Generations* (with Putney and Harris) has achieved international recognition.

PETER G. COLEMAN is Professor Emeritus of Psychogerontology, at the University of Southampton, UK. He is interested in the challenges of advanced old age and in quality of late life, as well as in both depression and dementia. He takes a lifespan perspective to the study of ageing and is interested in earlier life antecedents of late life behaviour. His books include *Ageing and Reminiscence Processes: Social and Clinical Implications;* (with Ann O'Hanlon) *Ageing and Development: Theories and Research;* and most recently *Belief and Ageing: Spiritual Pathways in later life.* and *Self and Meaning in the Lives of Older People* (with Ivani-Chalian and Robinson).

SUSAN EISENHANDLER is Professor of Sociology at the University of Connecticut. She has studied ageing and belief as well as social-psychological and contextual features of later life. A unifying motif for work on driving, relationships with adult children and health among community-dwelling elderly is the location of identity within situated and biographical experiences. Facets of everyday life predominate. She and L. Eugene Thomas co-edited *Aging and the Religious Dimension* and *Religion, Belief and Spirituality in Late Life.* Following publication of *Keeping the Faith in Later Life,* a seven-year qualitative study on gardening and well-being was completed.

PAUL HIGGS is Professor of the Sociology of Ageing at University College London. He has published widely in both social gerontology and medical sociology. His research interests in ageing include the third age; embodiment; identity; generations, cohorts and ageing; consumption and later life; and influences of quality of life in early old age and retirement. His books include (with Gilleard) *Cultures of Ageing: Self, Citizenship and the Body; Medical Sociology and Old Age: Towards a Sociology of Health in Later Life; and The Power of Silver: Age and Identity Politics in the 21st Century.*

ELLEN IDLER is Samuel Candler Dobbs Professor in the Department of Sociology at Emory University, Atlanta, USA. She is the Director of Emory's Religion and Public Health Collaborative, and holds faculty appointments in the Graduate Division of Religion, and the Department of Epidemiology in the Rollins School of Public Health. She studies the impact of religious participation on health, the timing of death and end of life decisions among the elderly. She is the editor of *Religion as a Social Determinant of Public Health* 2014.

ALBERT JEWELL has been a Methodist minister for more than fifty years. He was Pastoral Director and Senior Chaplain with MHA Care Group, 1994–2001. He co-ordinated the Sir Halley Stewart Age Awareness Project and established a Centre for Spirituality and Ageing in Leeds. He was editor of the influential *Spirituality and Ageing* and of *Ageing, Spirituality and Wellbeing* and most recently *Spirituality and Personhood in Dementia*. He is a visiting research fellow at Glyndŵr University and is currently researching the importance of faith for the primary carers of persons with dementia.

ELIZABETH MACKINLAY is Professor of Theology, Charles Sturt University, NSW and inaugural Director (until 2012) of the Centre for Ageing and Pastoral Studies at St Mark's National Theological Centre, Canberra. She is author of *The Spiritual Dimension of Ageing; Spiritual Growth and Care in the Fourth Age of Life;* and most recently, *Ageing and Spirituality across Faiths and Cultures;* (with Trevitt) *Finding Meaning in the Experience of Dementia* (Awarded the Australian Journal of Ageing book prize) and *Facilitating Spiritual Reminiscence for People with Dementia: A Learning Guide.* She is also an Anglican priest.

RONALD J. MANHEIMER was the founding director of the North Carolina Center for Creative Retirement, a lifelong learning, leadership and community service institute at the University of North Carolina Asheville where he was also Research Associate Professor of Philosophy. Author in the field of philosophy and aging, his *A Map to the End of Time: Wayfaring with Friends and Philosophers* has been translated into Chinese and Korean. His newest book is *Mirrors of the Mind: Reflecting on Philosophers' Autobiographies.* Manheimer serves on the editorial boards of *The Gerontologist* and *Journal of Aging Studies.* He chairs the Center for Jewish Studies at UNC-Asheville.

HARRY R. MOODY is Visiting Professor at Fielding Graduate University in their Creative Longevity and Wisdom Program. He recently retired as Vice President for Academic Affairs with AARP in Washington, DC and previously served as Chairman of Elderhostel (now Road Scholar). His research is in older adult education, bio-ethics and critical gerontology. His books include *Abundance of Life: Human Development Policies for an Aging Society; Ethics in an Aging Society* and (with David Carroll) *The Five Stages of the Soul.*

ANN MORISY is a London-based Community Theologian and lecturer in the UK and beyond and author of widely regarded books, including *Beyond the Good Samaritan; Journeying Out; Bothered and Bewildered* and most recently *Borrowing from the Future: A Faith Based Approach to Intergenerational Equity.*

JAMES WOODWARD is an Anglican priest, researcher and writer who is presently Principal of Sarum Theological College, Salisbury, UK. Until October 2015 he served as a Canon of St George's Windsor. He has written extensively in the area of pastoral and practical theology including books about illness, old age and death. Before Windsor he was Master of the Foundation of the Lady Katherine Leveson and Director of the Leveson Centre for the Study of Ageing, Spirituality and Social Policy, Temple Balsall. His books include *Befriending Death: Facing Loss; Valuing Age: Pastoral Ministry with Older People; Between Remembering and Forgetting: The Spiritual Dimensions of Dementia.*

The Editors

MALCOLM JOHNSON is currently Visiting Professor of Gerontology and End of Life Care at the University of Bath. He was Professor of Health and Social Policy at the University of Bristol (now Emeritus) from 1995. Between 1984 and 1995 he was Professor of Health and Social Welfare and subsequently first Dean of the School of Health and Social Welfare at the Open University. His research and academic interests are wide, including the social aspects of health and illness, biographical studies, social policy analysis, death and dying and his major specialism, ageing and the lifespan. Of his twelve books and over 160 monographs, chapters and articles, more than half relate to ageing. He is a former Secretary of the BSA Medical Sociology Group and of the British Society of Gerontolgy and was Founding Editor of the international journal *Ageing and Society.* He is Director of the International Institute on Health and Ageing.

His books include: (with Gearing & Heller) *Mental Health Problems in Old Age*; (with Dickenson) *Death, Dying and Bereavement* (two editions); (with Bengtson, Coleman and Kirkwood) *The Cambridge Handbook of Age & Ageing*; (with Albans) *God, Me and Being Very Old: Stories and spirituality in later life.* An elected Fellow of the Academy of Social Sciences (FAcSS), Malcolm is also a Fellow of the Royal Society of Arts (FRSA), a Fellow of the Gerontological Society of America and a Founding Fellow of the British Society of Gerontology who gave him the Outstanding Achievement Award 2014.

JOANNA WALKER is currently a postgraduate researcher in the Centre for Research in Ageing within the Faculty of Social and Human Studies at the University of Southampton, UK. Up until recently she was the

Bishop's Adviser in Adult Education in the Diocese of Guildford, where she had encouraged a focus on lifelong faith development and a special interest in the Church's response to older people's spiritual development. Previously, she held a lectureship at the University of Surrey in the Department of Educational Studies and established the first national educational resource centre for pre-retirement educators. She is a founding member of the Association for Education and Ageing, now in its thirtieth year, and has held roles of Secretary and Chair during this period. She remains Associate Editor (Reviews) for the *International Journal of Education and Ageing*.

In addition to chapters and articles in the educational gerontology field since the mid-eighties, Joanna published *Changing Concepts of Retirement, Educational Implications*, a textbook to support professional and postgraduate students in pre-retirement education and *Preparing for Retirement: The Employer's Guide* to promote good practice within organisations. Trained initially in sociology and psychology, an early interest in older people and later life led to employment as a policy adviser with Age Concern England (now AgeUK) and, following postgraduate studies in medical sociology, professional development work with the Health Education Council. Joanna's current research into spirituality, ageing and lifelong learning reflects her range of interests and experience.

Preface

From a faint glimmer in the eyes of the editors a plan was evolved to bring together international experts on ageing and spirituality and provide them with surroundings and a structure sufficient to enable significant discussion of their current thinking. The vision gained support, sponsorship and interest in a potential publication of the invited papers – all of which we are most grateful to acknowledge, since nothing could have taken place without them. The Symposium on Spiritual Dimensions of Ageing took place in Cumberland Lodge, Windsor Great Park in the UK, with sixteen scholars from Europe, America and Australia.

Abstracts and first drafts of chapters had been received and shared, and the arrangement of the presentations was not dissimilar to the eventual order of appearance in this volume, as their common interests or approaches seemed to suggest. The huge value, as well as the pleasure, of hearing papers delivered lies in the interaction that ensues. This process was orchestrated both on the days of the symposium and extended as far as possible through recording, transcribing and further circulation of responses and suggestions. Participants were asked to identify key points of their own papers, and links with others', and to suggest themes for the book. All of this has fed into the chapters now before the reader.

The accumulation of expertise, combined with long experience and the wisdom that knows the limits of such knowledge, was powerful indeed and has left a lasting impression on those who participated, not least the editors whose dream had come to reality. We were grateful for the continued generosity of the participants, all of whom have subsequently revised their papers in the light of the discussions and made them available for this publication.

We are aware that spirituality and ageing is a field of study that draws on many disciplines, professions and philosophical approaches. It is also becoming more visible as an academic enterprise, though still widely distributed, so it seemed timely to bring together some excellent, but similarly diverse contributions. Our hope for the book is the encouragement and inspiration of contributions yet to come; for the benefit of our ageing societies, and the older people we wish not only to live alongside but also to become.

Acknowledgements

We wish to offer our warmest thanks to all who have assisted in the preparation and development of this book.

Generous support for the Symposium was provided by two important organisations committed to the spiritual wellbeing of older people:

Methodist Homes is a leading provider of care and support to older people in England, Scotland and Wales. In each of its Care Homes, Retirement Living Schemes and Retirement Communities, it employs a Chaplain to nurture the spirituality of its residents and to support staff and relatives, of all faiths and none (Malcolm Johnson is a Member of its Board). Its financial contribution is gratefully acknowledged and our special thanks go to the then Chief Executive, Roger Davies.

The Diocese of Guildford provided grant funding towards the cost of organising and hosting the Symposium at Cumberland Lodge, Windsor. It also sponsored the attendance of two of its Advisers: Joanna Walker (Adult Education) and Tony Oakden (Church and Community) and the use of audio recording facilities and subsequent transcriptions. We are grateful to the Bishop and Diocesan Secretary for supporting the vision of the Symposium in these practical ways.

Revd Dr Keith Albans is the Director of Chaplaincy and Spirituality at Methodist Homes. Keith was a major supporter of the idea of this book and the holding of a Symposium to bring together the chapter authors (of which he is one) in fruitful exchange. Keith has been a colleague and friend to both of the Editors for a long period, sharing the work of listening to the lives and reflections of people at the far end of life. We thank him for his friendship and encouragement.

Caron Staley is the Administrator of the Centre for Death & Society University of Bath. The Centre was the academic sponsor of the Symposium. Caron gave her considerable administrative skills to arranging the Windsor Symposium and the travel arrangements for those who made journeys from other countries. She also shared responsibility for recording the proceedings and providing transcripts to participants.

Tony Oakden, Diocese of Guildford, provided technical assistance at all sessions, recording and subsequently transcribing presentations and discussions. Transcripts formed valuable resources to chapter authors and to editors, since they captured the linkages and discussion topics raised by the individual papers. We thank them both, sincerely.

Hetty Marx and Janka Romero have been our patient and supportive Editors at Cambridge University Press. We hope they will feel this volume rewards their professional and personal efforts to bring it to completion.

It is often the case that books have a long gestation period and this one has been no exception. They claim the time and attention of authors and editors, sometimes to the point of preoccupation. So we want to reserve special thanks and love for Christine Johnson and Chris Walker – our partners for the journey.

1   Spirited Ageing

Malcolm Johnson and Joanna Walker

Introduction

A fundamental underlying theme of this book is that the later years are a significant time for the spiritual dimension of life, both as a resource for facing the challenges of ageing and for the potential it offers for growth and development. Spirituality is, of course, as much a part of human experience as any other normal kind of thought or behaviour, although this has not always been the view of scholars or practitioners. Furthermore, both spirituality and religion are widespread phenomena, being part of many cultures and of the lives of people of all ages and statuses. Spirituality continues to adapt and evolve new forms because it addresses people's human needs to connect meaningfully with themselves, with each other and to a higher power or larger source of meaning and purpose. Thus, the sources of spiritual inspiration and sustenance are internal, drawing on and making sense of experiences and interactions in the world as well as through any perceived transcendent connection.

However, until recently, this inner life of older people has been largely ignored or treated as problematic by gerontologists. Research is heavily directed towards physical and economic well-being and the political economy of ageing populations. The unseen dynamics of living are investigated principally in terms of physical and psychological pathologies within conventional disease paradigms or the policy challenges that they pose. This volume offers a more detailed map of the way individuals in later life experience and manage their psychological and spiritual self-identities, especially when finitude intensifies the process of life review.

Much of the current rise in interest in spirituality is related to its traditional link with health and well-being, making it a potential contributor to interventions or therapies that can improve people's lives. For instance, spiritual experiences and practices that are capable of helping establish an integrated personality are being recognised as playing a part in mental health. Older people with a developed spiritual dimension to their lives are said (in various experimentally established situations) to

1

deal better with negative life events and their attendant stress, and to recover more quickly from illness or trauma (Mohan 2001). Such research is based on, and gives rise to further investigation of, ideas about spirituality being involved in coping, adjusting, social inclusion, mature self-identity and esteem, meaning and purpose, death awareness and so on.

However, whilst much attention is devoted by governments and service providers to older people's health needs, the focus of that attention may not reflect the range of needs that trouble everyday life. Whilst increasing concern is exercised (rightly) in relation to dementia, by contrast the epidemic of depression in older age is widely overlooked and typically treated pharmaceutically. The same can be said generally of research and policy on the rapidly changing experience of ageing. Comparatively little attention is given to the psychosocial aspects of the end of lives. More specifically, the experience of long-lived individuals is only just beginning to be recognised for the unknown territory it represents. As a relatively 'new' stage of life, in terms of mass experience, we do not yet have adequate conceptual frameworks to describe its character and purposes, beyond the model of extended middle age that is the essence of 'successful', 'productive' or 'positive' ageing.

Despite the demographic impacts of ageing societies worldwide becoming well known, even outside the gerontological community, a less-understood aspect of population ageing is the impact of so many more elderly people needing to negotiate meaning and purpose in late life. The absence of a social understanding for this part of the life-course is unhelpful, both for the individuals living it and society's response to it. It adds urgency, and perhaps an additional rationale, to research that hopes to understand the world of older people from *their* point of view, as well as from the viewpoint of researchers or society at large.

Of course, many older people never enter the age of dependency and many have their continued contributions to family and society recognised, but the trend towards longer lives and pressures on families mean increasing numbers will risk entering and surviving longer in a dependency that is less than ideally supported. For their sakes, we do need to rethink our understanding of the life-course and meet the fears of the rising generations of older people concerning being resented as a leisured class in their third age, and as burdens in their fourth (Coleman 2009).

One of the chief roles of research into ageing and spirituality can be to inform policy responses to the demands and challenges of societies that are ageing. However, it should not be the presumption of social policy to cast the role of older age as one of continuing struggle against demise (Howse 1999). Rather, the true root of the 'problem' of old age is the need for a shared value about what is desirable and possible beyond the third age (where older people's social contribution can be more easily recognised). If spirituality can influence the social construction of late life towards it being seen as a time of possibility for growth, service and fulfilment, then it will have contributed significantly to a broader under-standing of old age (McFadden 1995). Thus, appreciation of a spiritual dimension for late life matters less because of how it might inform service provision for older people, and more for the way it shapes the value that is attached to particular stages of life.

The demographic projections for life expectancy and survival rates at increasing ages cannot be overstated for their impact on the scale of the spiritual understanding of later life that will be needed. Simon Biggs (1999) has written about the 'mature imagination' that will be required to re-conceive meaningful lives in old age, whose numbers will extend much further than in previous societies' experience. To borrow the observation that the cost of education is nothing compared to the cost of not educating, research needs to address itself to the (individual and social) costs of neither understanding nor attempting to support mean-ingful living in later life. It is the contention of this volume that spiritual-ity in later life can address both the individual and societal dilemmas concerning the purpose and value of older age.

Aims of 'Spiritual Dimensions of Ageing'

The primary purpose of the book, and the symposium on which it is based, is to bring together an international group of leading researchers and writers on spirituality and ageing; to distil the latest advances in knowledge and thinking; and to engage in vigorous discussion about how we can interpret this learning for the benefit of older people and those who seek to serve and support them.

Despite the involvement of gerontologists in a bewildering array of issues related to age and ageing, researchers – with a few honourable exceptions – have avoided both spirituality and death. Yet the increasing presence of finitude as we grow older is an inescapable fact. Life review and reflection about personal pasts and diminishing futures are both well known to students of later life. Nonetheless, the focus on positive ageing appears to have all but eclipsed study of the inner life, both religious and non-religious. So the literature on ageing and spirituality is still relatively slender, especially outside of North America.

Similarly, the world of theology has witnessed a significant ageing of the membership of faith communities in much of the developed world, but it too has given little attention – other than to regret that the young are conspicuously absent. There is a paucity of theology of age and later life and a continuing belief in the misguided truism that the young are the future of the churches, mosques, or synagogues. Some, however, do see the need not only to understand the way faith and beliefs come under new pressures as life moves into its later stages, but also the potential of the inner journey and later life spirituality. Occasional liturgies and innovative practices appear, but make no headway as faith leaders fail to understand the depth of need as well as spiritual strength amongst older people. Sociologists of religion continue to be observers of what they largely see as unstoppable secularisation.

A co-incidental rise in spirituality in recent times is seen as a related phenomenon, but not one that reverses the decline of traditional faith and religion. We see that in the stimulating accounts provided by Carrette and King (2005) of new spiritualities and their annexation by consumerism and business. Moreover such research appears to have no gerontological perspectives. For unaccountable reasons, one of the most spectacular developments of the twentieth century, the demographic revolution which saw life expectancy increase in developed societies by over half, has escaped attention. On the other hand sociologists have been deeply interested in shifting patterns of belief and unbelief. They have been active in exploring the cultural consequences in socio-political terms and in the search for new forms of spiritual practice. Today's older people are tantalisingly caught up in these changes at both levels, as their own life and faith dynamics move alongside the larger social and cultural changes in faith and spirituality.

Ageing, beliefs and the inner life are long-established features of academic psychology, sociology and the different worlds of clinical and professional practice. Here the literature is much fuller; ranging from the detailed studies of religious belief and psychological well-being, religion as a cause of guilt and anguish, and theorists who have attempted to formulate models, patterns and stages to deal with the exigencies of life as it progresses through the life-course. Chapter authors represent invited individuals from all of these domains. The selection was based on the principle of inviting those whose work has achieved recognition and which has impinged on our own attempts to understand better how human beings negotiate the meaning of their lives.

Themes

We take this opportunity to explore the main, interrelated themes that emerge from the rich resource of the contributed chapters. First, there is the nature of spirituality and its development in later life. This includes the agentic and purposeful seeking of spiritual experience and knowledge, as well as the less consciously apprehended impacts of personal development and the practice of well-loved and meaningful ritual. Then, there is the relationship of later life spirituality to meaning and purpose, which is a key gerontological theme, encompassing psychological, sociological and theological approaches. Last, there is the question of how spirituality and religion respond to the existential issues of later life (such as diminishment and finitude), both at individual and communal levels, in theory as well as in practice. Although these cross-cutting themes are powerful ways of exploring the material, and we recommend you bear them in mind as you read, they are not the easiest way of presenting the material. So a four-part scheme will organise the contributions, as described below.

Personal Encounters with the Meanings of Old Age

We have titled the first part *The Spiritual Journey of Ageing*, since it deals with the inner journey of spirituality, which may become more pressing in later life, but which emerges and finds expression in different ways. The means by which such journeys can be understood are also a challenge when observation of private, or even less-than-conscious, processes are involved. Two 'traditional' scientific approaches are included here, from two of the seminal contributors to this field of study – Robert Atchley and Elizabeth MacKinlay. Based on their many years of research experience, their wisdom allows them to also admit into their discussions the need for humanistic practice and sensitive spiritual insight. They both lay out for the reader the fruits of their own understanding of how spirituality in later life is conceived and operates. The voice of the mind or soul is the focus for the other two chapters, with Harry Moody tapping into the rich 'data' that comes from dreams and Andrew Achenbaum drawing on narratives in the particular form of fables, by way of illustrating the stories we all live by. Tuning into these sources offers an alternative paradigm for the generation of knowledge and understanding on spirituality and ageing which, by its very nature, is a challenge for the earlier positivist approaches that supported gerontology.

Spirituality in a Changing Landscape: Believers, Doubters and Re-constructors

The second part, subtitled *Cultures of the Spirit in Modernity*, articulates the particular intellectual challenge that spirituality and ageing finds itself addressing at this moment in time. The tectonic plates of social and cultural change that have transformed the developed world in recent decades regarding religion, faith and spirituality are providing a changed landscape to today's and tomorrow's older people. Cohort differences are currently apparent in the spiritual understanding of third agers compared to fourth agers. Within societies, the institutions of the family as well as religious communities are struggling to comprehend and act on the changes.

Vern Bengtson presents a broad population approach to exploring these changes, including the generational transmission of spiritual or faith values and practices. His signal study has attracted considerable attention in the US media and has served to undermine established interpretations of decline, such as Putnam and Campbell's (2010) *American Grace*. Drawing as it does on a 35-year-cohort study, his findings are all the more remarkable, in observing religious and spiritual resilience.

Peter Coleman's international experience has recently focused on the impact for spiritual belief and practice of major political and cultural change in Eastern Europe, and the role that older people have played in sustaining and adapting their spirituality, and that of younger generations. Ellen Idler's humane account of religious ritual and practice is woven with the life and ministry story of her father, but with sociological insight on the meaning and value in later life of spiritual practices that are still based in families, communities and institutions.

She illustrates Peter Coleman's often made point that religion is still the bulwark of many older people, providing a framework for life, the glue in many communities, and meanings through which experiences can be interpreted despite the changing landscape.

Paul Higgs, a cultural gerontologist, offers a re-orientation of spirituality in de-religionised modern and postmodern societies. He draws us into the discourses of postmodernity, with its emphasis on individualism and the claimed rejection of the old institutions of social control. Religion falls squarely into this analysis and has led one commentator to conclude that the new culture enables individuals to have 'A God of one's own'. Paul Higgs confronts writers about spirituality in old age with suggestions that the generational rationales of the old are completely at odds with the ego-centric values of later generations.

Grappling with the Inner Self: The Universal Quest for Meaning and Purpose

In this part, subtitled *Searching for Meaning in Later Life*, we have brought together material that features the age-old search for meaning and validation; for forgiveness and regret as well as thankfulness and completion.

Most of the chapters, if not all, also feature the absence of understanding about the fourth age, where dependency and loss may be taking people beyond their established retired or third-age identity and creating further challenges. Susan Eisenhandler takes as her motif the 'full hearted even-song' of the starling in a bleak winter setting who, despite his age and hostile environment, lets loose a wonderful song. Her interpretation of generational disjunctures about religion and belief reflect some of Higgs' analysis, but claims that 'generations and cohorts born after 1939 reflect different, "modern," structures and social worlds that by the mid 1970s, post-Vietnam for the sake of argument, begin to change dramatically at a pace which accelerates (circa the mid-1980s) with advances in cyber-technology. My sense is that present cohorts of older Americans have strong bedrock socialization in terms of religion, faith, and belief; how-ever, the bedrock becomes porous or is not found as uniformly among the "boomer" generation.'

Albert Jewell provides us with a thorough going analysis and account of the way that meaning and purpose has been studied and applied to later life spirituality, not least in his own research on older Methodists, whose resili-ence in later life first drew him to this topic. The challenge of ageing to people's meaning (reflection on the past) and purpose (hope for the future) is considered as a potential but avoidable crisis, through an increased understanding of the fourth age on the part of individuals, their faith communities and researchers developing better concepts and methods.

Malcolm Johnson's analysis of the need for better spiritual awareness and care has a more universal application; the vastly increasing numbers of both older and very old people point to current failings in policy and practice in our dealings with and understandings of late life. He offers a framework for representing the deeply anguished position of some older people at the end of life and counsels greater attention to their spiritual well-being and what he terms 'Biographical Pain'.

Ron Manheimer's exploration of spirituality as a lifelong process is a masterpiece of storytelling, using fictional characters to illustrate how the meanings and purposes that we hear debated are also profoundly influ-enced and played out against social change. Thus ageing itself may or may not reveal the fruits of spiritual development, such as the discovery of meaning, despite a potential 'inner' movement towards spirituality.

Enabling Older People to Address Their Spirituality

The last part, *Meeting Spiritual Needs in Older Age,* is more overtly based in practice rather than theory, although plenty of links to the findings and schemas of others are offered along the way. Applying the benefits of narrative, as discussed earlier, Ann Morisy proposes a particular and tried method for enabling older people to do business with their spirituality.

She makes the case for facilitated group conversation that enables reflection to turn to resilience, through a process of encouragement, helping people to reaffirm or even reassemble their inner lives. Joanna Walker is also interested in the primary role of reflection and the spiritual development and learning what this can lead to, which she expresses in a mapping exercise for the different ways in which this might take place in later life. James Woodward takes a theological approach to exploring what spirituality and ageing have to say to each other, using terms such as redemption and incarnation, but also ones such as metaphor, narrative, fragility and dependency, to which theology has a particular voice to add. Keith Albans writes comprehensively about the derivation and application of a spiritual dimension to planning and delivering a residential care environment, such that the last part of life can be a significant rather than a neglected period. He brings to the reader thinking and practical experience of creating and delivering a service of 'chaplaincy and spirituality' to over 6000 older people.

The Book

The book sets out to provide a kaleidoscopic picture of an emerging field. We hope it will set a benchmark, as it maps the range of interests which are emerging from gerontology. But if it succeeds in enticing other researchers and thinkers it will certainly shift the debate into as yet unexplored areas. Clearly there is a debate to be developed about generations and cultural change; foreshadowed here by Vern Bengtson's research indicating the power of generational transfers of religious values within families and Paul Higgs' scepticism about the survival of these values as new generations take their place as social leaders.

A central area of research by gerontologists in the exploration of spirituality in later life is the documenting and interpreting what spirituality means for people in different cultures and religious dispositions born before the second World War. Social values and ways of thinking are influential throughout life and leave their imprint to the end. But there is strong evidence of varied patterns of re-evaluation over the life course. Beliefs are rarely static in the lives of individuals. These processes will also occur in the members of Generations X and Y as they progress through ages and stages. Sylvia Collins-Mayo's book (2010) *The Faith of Generation Y* reveals an open-minded cohort of people born 1982 onwards, for whom the cultural memory of Christianity is very faint indeed. Simple comparisons at a point in time will inevitably provide marked contrast and may lead some to apocalyptic interpretations. Yet it is not unknown for young adults at later points on the age ladder to re-embrace the values and rationales of their parents, even if presented in novel ways. So we need a greater body of evidence and a wider constituency of researchers to fashion the character of tradition and change.

The authors, their interests and styles of enquiry are a reflection of the many dimensions of spirituality as a realm of human experience and its diverse manifestations in older age. They come from very different societies around the modern world. Such interests are yet to emerge in developing nations where world religions in all their sectarian diversity are still dominant. As better survival rates, improved healthcare, smaller families and globalised practices change population structures, the inevitable foci of attention are on healthcare and pensions. It will be some time before the nations of Africa, South America and parts of Asia turn attention to the inner lives of their longer-lived elders.

The chapters derive from psychology theology, history, philosophy, sociology and gerontology. This mix represents the present state of play. In the near future there might be contributions from computer science, neurology, economics and business studies. Ageing cuts across the whole swathe of academic disciplines, though only some are seriously present now. What links the chapters of this book and the scholars who produced them is the connection between the experiences of growing older and the way these are associated with faith, belief and spirituality. Not surprisingly most of those attracted to the field so far have preexisting interests in one or other form of spirituality or religious affiliation. This experiential foundation to their studies gives them insight, access and prior knowledge alongside their intellectual and professional skills. In turn these qualities will invite some to challenge their independence of view. But students of social class were largely the socially mobile offspring of working class parents' and researchers into family disruption and violence are often led there by experience and a sense of injustice. It would be a pity if serious scholarship was dismissed by ideological discomfort rather than the genuine discourse this volume invites.

Reinventing Spirituality

Ageing societies around the world confront not only unprecedented life extension, but also populations where the numerical balance between the generations is radically reshaped. There are fewer young people and many more who are deemed to be old. Instead of ideas and social movements being in the exclusive hands of rising generations as we have been accustomed to for over half a century, there will be new eras of contested ideas and influence on what we think and believe. Generational differences are already in evidence and our book adds substance to these trends. What should remain in doubt is the thesis that any contest for what constitutes a good and worthwhile life will be trumped by the newer generations. There are no models or templates for a reshaped demography. We shall negotiate our way into an uncharted future all-age society.

As young people themselves age, they will reformulate their estimates of what a good life and a good society should look like, just as their parents and grandparents did. If previous experience is any guide there may well be what statisticians term 'regression to the norm'. Religious and spiritual values and practices will inevitably adapt to cultural change. But it would be an unwise foreteller of the future that presumed that established ideas will be squeezed out in the rationalism and individualism of postmodern society.

There is ample evidence of a desire to embrace spiritualities among the younger adult population. As they encounter ideas and precepts about living that derive from long-recognised philosophies, psychologies and religions, there is some possibility that established ideas about self-worth and the inner life will re-enter social life. In the meantime, growing numbers of already older people need their spiritual concerns to be understood and supported.

References

Biggs, S. (1999). *The Mature Imagination: Dynamics of Identity in Midlife and Beyond*. Buckingham: Open University Press.

Carrette, J. and King, R. (2005). *Selling Spirituality: The Silent Takeover of Religion*. London: Routledge.

Coleman, P.G. (2009). 'Ageing and personhood in twenty-first century Europe: a challenge to religion', *International Journal of Public Theology* 3(1):63–77.

Collins-Mayo, C., Mayo, B., Nash, S., and Cocksworth, C. (2010). *The Faith of Generation Y*. London: Church House Publishing.

Howse, K. (1999). *Religion, Spirituality and Older People*. London: Centre for Policy on Ageing.

McFadden, S. (1995). 'Religion and well-being in aging persons in an aging society', *Journal of Social Issues* 51(2):161–175.

Mohan, K.K. (2001). 'Spirituality and well-being: an overview', in Cornelissen, M. (ed.) *Integral Psychology – Consciousness and Its Transformation*, pp. 227–253. Pondicherry: Sri Aurobindo Ashram Press.

Putnam, R.D. and Campbell, D.E. (2010). *American Grace: How Religion Divides and Unites Us*. New York: Simon & Schuster.

Part I

The Spiritual Journey of Ageing

2 Spirituality and Ageing
Yesterday, Today and Tomorrow

Robert C. Atchley

Introduction

This chapter clarifies and deepens concepts of spirituality, spiritual development, and spiritual journeying. It draws on theory and data from recent gerontology to make the case for a strong relationship between ageing and adult development and various aspects of spirituality. It looks at evolution in the study of spirituality within the field of ageing from the 1960s to the present, particularly the evolution of spiritual seeking and spiritual practice in post-modern culture. Finally, it addresses implications for further study, education, and practice in the area of spirituality and ageing.

Spirituality is primarily an inner experience of being that infuses a person with energy, offers a vantage point for transcending the personal self, opens the experiencer to awareness of a vast inner space, and perhaps offers direct experience of the 'ground of all being' (God, Allah, Jahweh, Nirvana, The Absolute). Spirituality is a very important part of life for most elders.

The essence of spirituality is the capability to experience pure being, an intense sense of presence, unadulterated by concepts, language, and other elements of culture. Pure being is often experienced as inner space, silence, stillness, or peace. It is through the experience of pure being that people report being most likely to experience union with the ground of being. The experience of pure being is a vantage point from which we can see the spiritual aspects of all other experiences.

When accompanied by awareness of pure being, the events of ordinary life have the potential to evoke qualities of experience that we call spiritual – qualities such as wonder and awe, deep insight, mental clarity, compassion, or feeling of direct connection with the ground of being. Spiritual aspects of experience may be seen more easily in some activities than in others. For example, being in nature, engaging in art or music, performing religious devotions, relating with others, or engaging in service are often-mentioned avenues of spiritual experience, but the number of activities that can evoke spiritual experience is very large indeed (Atchley 2009).

Although humans are born with the capacity for spiritual experience (Trimble 2007), we must learn to perceive pure being and its relationship with other experiences if we want to be conscious of them. *Capacity* must be converted to *capability*. Often, a main purpose of age-related religious socialisation is to enable people to perceive the spirituality that is in and all around them.

The gradual unfolding of the capability for spiritual experience is called spiritual development and involves a growing, evolving capacity to perceive the spiritual elements of experience. For most people, spiritual capacity continues to evolve throughout the lifespan and is used to maintain motivation and direction in making life choices. Spiritual experience can have profound effects on individual development, relationships, and performance of various roles in the community. Studies of spiritual experience in childhood have shown that experiences with nature often provide early experiences of awe, wonder, peace, and direct connection with the ground of being (Hoffman 1992). How these experiences are received by family and community can have a profound influence on whether an individual seeks or remains open to such experiences.

Scholars disagree about when ageing begins, but most agree that by middle age ageing becomes noticeable, which begins the existential processing of ageing as part of one's life awareness. The first signs of ageing are usually physical – changes in appearance, dexterity, or endurance, and increased susceptibility to injury and chronic health conditions. Awareness of ageing also comes from a realisation that one's older age is influencing how one is treated. Ageing is a subset of life experience but many life experiences are not conditioned by an awareness of age, either by the individual or the social environment.

The existential aspect of ageing brings an increased awareness of the finitude of each human life and invites reflection on the deeper meaning of our existence. Not only are people aware of their own ageing and death, they observe the ageing and deaths of older generations in their families. Perhaps more than any other stimulus, encounters with the reality and inevitability of death invite grappling with the great meaning questions that have confronted and confounded philosophers and theologians for thousands of years. Who are we really, and why are we here? Why do we have this life and consciousness? How are we related to the universe? For a large majority of ageing people throughout the world, these questions are invitations to begin, or dig deeper into, a spiritual journey.

A spiritual journey is a personal narrative about an individual's spiritual life and its development. These narratives usually include a history of experiences, actions, and insights connected with a search for spiritual meaning. Underlying the spiritual journey is an intentional process of seeking spiritual experiences, using spiritual values and insights to inform life choices, and learning from experience with this process. Spiritual journeys usually involve learning to persist and be content on a journey into imperfectly known territory, where insights are always limited, no matter how profound they seem at the time. Spiritual journeys are seldom linear; they often involve periods of confusion and unclear direction as well as periods of clarity and satisfaction. Most spiritual journeys also involve elements of commitment, self-discipline, and regular spiritual practice.

Most people prefer to journey as part of a convoy of peers who have similar visions of the spiritual journey. People who have been on an intentional spiritual journey for decades usually develop a sense of humor about the contradictions and paradoxes they encounter, even as they use these enigmas as food for contemplation. They also learn not to force the issue. Waiting is often an important spiritual practice; not 'waiting for' but just waiting. In the space created by patient waiting, an experience of direct connection with the sacred or ground of being may be more likely. In my experience, the best way to learn about how spirituality fits into a person's life is by asking them 'How did you come to be the spiritual being you are today?' Be prepared for a short answer, and hope for a long answer. Many people have never thought about this question and have no idea of how to think or speak about it. Some have been waiting years for someone to ask it.

How Are Spiritual Development and the Spiritual Journey Related to Ageing?

Spiritual development and the spiritual journey are related to ageing in several important ways: First, we experience spirituality through a human body, and the body's maturation and ageing influence how effectively it can perceive spirituality. For example, psychobiological ageing usually slows a number of functions and, as people adapt to this slowing, the pace of life slows and some of them become more aware of the contemplative space in their consciousness (Tornstam 2005; Sherman 2010). This can have a strong positive effect on the depth of their spiritual experiences. On the other hand, some people react to ageing by becoming increasingly defensive and psychologically over-habituated, which results in difficulties appreciating the present moment. For them, ageing does not foster spiritual experience.

Second, nearly all cultures have conceptions of a succession of age-related life stages. Socialisation, normative expectations, and access to a wide variety of life experiences are linked to life stages. Having reached an advanced life stage is often a prerequisite for entering into spiritual study and practice. For example, the Hindu concept of life stages prescribes that the spiritually centered lifestyle should begin in earnest after the birth of the first grandson. Such customs recognise that a certain amount of life experience is helpful for the spiritual journey. In the words of Nisargadatta Maharaj (1973), 'You have to be burdened before you can be unburdened.' There are several life course transitions that can invite conscious reflection on spiritual aspects of life: Religious rites of passage such as confirmation or bat mitzvah, marriage, birth of a child, death of a parent, mid-life crisis of meaning, marriage of an adult child, birth of a grandchild, retirement, or onset of disability. All these transitions, and many others, can invite a turning inwards in search of deeper meaning.

Third, there is a more general turning inwards with age. Bernice Neugarten (1973) was early to point out that, in addition to transition-related cycles of turning inwards for reflective assessment, there is also a general turning inwards in later life. Cumming and Henry (1961) mistakenly called this process disengagement. Partly in reaction to disengagement theory, Tornstam (1994) called this turning inwards gero-transcendence. Tornstam asserted that gero-transcendence is a natural phenomenon of turning inwards that steadily increases from middle age onward, unless stifled by social forces such as age expectations or discrimination.

Gero-transcendence involves a shift from a materialistic, role-oriented life philosophy to a transcendent, spiritual perspective in late old age. In its full-blown form, gero-transcendence has three dimensions. In the *cosmic dimension*, concepts such as life, death, space, and time are seen as involving an element of mystery and against a backdrop of infinity. In the *self-transcendent dimension*, the personal self is no longer the center of attention and there is increased honesty and acceptance concerning the personal self. In the *social selectivity dimension*, relationships focus mainly on close friends and family, and much less energy is spent relating with casual acquaintances or strangers, with a consequent increase in solitude and less emphasis on *pro forma* role playing. Attitudes towards material possessions shift from acquisition to maintaining the essentials for a comfortable life. Social selectivity leads to a more thoughtful, contemplative stance towards relationships, activities, and lifestyles.

Mature gero-transcendence makes for a different type of effective participation in the community rather than for disengagement. Gero-transcendence theory successfully reframed turning inwards as a positive development and has received support from numerous studies.

Researchers working in different time periods and cultures have found that turning inwards is a characteristic of later life, and the course of this turning inwards follows the general outlines Tornstam laid out (Hillman 1999; Atchley 2009; Sherman 2010).

This finding of turning inwards with age begs the question: What are these people turning towards? Erikson, Erikson, and Kivnick (1986) wrote that in middle age people start turning away from ego absorption towards what they called generativity – a concern with supporting and nurturing upcoming generations. To be generative, we have to be able to transcend our personal egos. Sherman (2010) wrote that in later adulthood we turn inwards towards an increasingly open inner space. We become more contemplative – we abide in inner space and see the passing world with 'eyes unclouded by longing'. It is not that we drop out of life, we just see it from a greater distance. For example, grandparents are often able to 'just be' with their grandchildren, to create a larger space for the grandchildren to be as they are without the impatience for developmental progress that parents seem obliged to feel. Sherman traced the concept of contemplative ageing back to ancient India and Greece, so it is part of our cultural heritage both Eastern and Western.

Erikson, Erikson, and Kivnick (1986) also wrote that in later life we develop wisdom by confronting the contradictions and paradoxes involved in our experiencing both integrity and despair and realising that each of these qualities is a natural component of a whole person. This process of dwelling in contemplation and acceptance is a key spiritual element of the increased life satisfaction elders show in spite of the many psychological, physical, and social declines associated with ageing. If you are living *in* the brass ring, what do you care how fast the merry-go-round is going?

Fourth, spirituality is an increasingly important resource for coping as we age (Atchley 2009). Most of us hope to learn from our life experiences and actually do so. How and what we learn and how we put our knowledge to use is related to our experiences going through various life stages. The concepts we have of upcoming life stages can have important effects on motivation, preparation, and experiences of life stage transitions. In this view, human development is an open feedback system in which the individual is the scientist and the individual's world is the laboratory and the resulting observations are used to fashion, maintain, and correct a belief/value system, lifestyle, and philosophy of life (Atchley 1999). Also, it does not take most people long to see that learning to cope when things do not turn out as expected is very important. It is in this ongoing developmental context that we learn to interpret, re-interpret, pursue, and give meaning to spiritual experiences. Thus resilience is one outcome of faith in one's coping.

Fifth, spiritual development can strongly influence the vantage points from which we see and respond to physical, psychological, and social ageing. The fact that most elders are happy in the face of all the decrements of ageing and a social world that often responds negatively to ageing does not make sense until we factor in the positive effects of a more contemplative vantage point. Many studies attest to this 'life satisfaction' effect in late life (Atchley and Barusch 2004).

Sixth, for a considerable proportion of people, the spiritual path leads to the capability of serving as a *sage*. As has been recognised for thousands of years, sages are wise elders. Developing the capacity to function as a sage is a process many elders go through, whether or not they are conscious of it. Responding to a call to be a sage is an important stimulus for developing this capacity, but social environments vary widely in terms of whether elders are sought out or encouraged to be sages. Spiritual development is a key element of being a sage.

In an earlier work, I described three stages of becoming a sage: sage-in-training, actualised sage, and transcendent sage (Atchley 2003). The sage-in-training stage begins when a person realises that becoming a sage is a real and attractive possibility. Sages-in-training begin to see the sages in their midst and to observe the abilities they possess that make them different from other older people. These abilities often include deep listening, empathy, compassion, nonadversarial communication skills, and many years of reflected-upon life experience. Most sages-in-training are on an intentional spiritual journey and recognise the link between spiritual development and capability to serve as a sage. Regular spiritual practice is an important aspect of life for most sages-in-training.

Actualised sages are those who have done the inner work that allows them to experience both present-moment awareness and transcendence as they function in the world. They are able to accomplish 'being while doing'. Generativity and wisdom are the hallmarks of the actualised sage. Sages-in-training evolve into actualised sages through practice. Practising as a sage means being willing to respond to requests for generativity or wisdom. Sages are uniquely effective as providers of counsel, mentors, mediators, and conveners. Sages differ from others who perform these roles because sages approach these roles from a spiritual, transpersonal vantage point and with the qualities of a sage.

Transcendent sages are masters of 'being radiantly at peace'. They embody silence, stillness, and equanimity. Their very presence can affect the atmosphere of a gathering. They speak only infrequently and instead serve as 'holders of the field'. In my experience, transcendent sages are mostly in their 80s and 90s. They are akin to super-novas whose light shines brightest just before it goes out. Most transcendent sages have served as actualised sages for many years. Some scholars who have looked at this phenomenon have asserted that transcendent sages are very rare (e.g. Fowler 1981). However, I have observed more than twenty transcendent sages during my fifteen years of observing two spiritual communities in Boulder, Colorado, which leads me to conclude that, among people who are on an intentional spiritual journey and who live to advanced old age, transcendent sages are definitely not rare.

Sage-ing® International is a non-profit organisation that fosters the process of becoming a sage, serving as a sage in the community, and providing opportunities for community amongst those who are pursuing these possibilities (http://sage-ing.org). Sage-ing® International offers training, conferences, and online resources. They are part of the Alliance for Conscious Elderhood, a loose confederation of organisations interested in the intersection of spirituality and ageing.

Why Do So Few People Know about the Link between Ageing and Spirituality?

The study of spirituality and ageing has been hampered by a lack of conventional language for this region of life, scepticism and hostility towards the study of what seems to be a subjective reality, and conflation of religion and spirituality. Nevertheless, in recent years a significant body of scholarship has emerged that includes: 1) the beginnings of a language of spirituality as a topic in its own right and separable from religion, 2) descriptive research about the nature and consequences of spiritual experience for human development and ageing, and 3) concepts and theories of spiritual development in later life that can lead to greater understanding of this neglected topic. We now have the resources needed to teach students about spirituality and ageing and develop programmes of research. We also know enough at this point to be able to help elders see the benefit that spirituality and spiritual development can be in their lives. Our biggest challenge is to remain open and to avoid premature closure. To understand how spirituality and ageing emerged as a topic for research, I will briefly review my own experience with it. As you will see, my experience with spirituality and ageing preceded any opportunity to study it.

Yesterday

In 1963, when I enrolled in a two-semester graduate course in gerontology taught by the noted gerontologist Clark Tibbitts, we used three texts: *Handbook of Social Gerontology* (Tibbitts 1960), *Handbook of Aging and the Individual* (Birren 1959), and *Handbook of Aging in Western Societies* (Burgess 1960). These tomes were the result of a ten-year review of the literature on ageing funded by the U.S. Government. On these more than 2,000 pages, not one word concerned the inner experience of spirituality and how it might interact with ageing. In fact, at that time we did not even have an adequate vocabulary for discussing this aspect of life, which was nevertheless very important to many of the ageing people we were studying.

During my graduate studies, I was also interviewing older women for a study of the effects of retirement on their self-concepts. They spoke about feeling close to nature, the fruits of a life spent trying to maintain integrity, the peace and stillness of contemplation, the challenges and fun of connecting with younger generations in their families, and a host of other topics. I was impressed with these women's 'way of being', although at that time I did not have the vocabulary to put it that way. These individuals were nothing like the used-up, bored, and aimless old people depicted in the stereotypes of the early 1960s.

These respondents piqued my interest and I began to look for research that might deal with positive experiences of ageing. My first glimpses came from Margaret Clark and Barbara Anderson's book, *Culture and Aging* (1969). In their case studies, Clark and Anderson accurately described the vital elders I was interviewing. On reflection, I realised that the 'problem' emphasis of early gerontology – ageing as a universal physical, psychological, and social difficulty to be endured or adapted to – led us to ignore the positive experiences of ageing, including spirituality. Indeed, in one of my early interviews about women's experiences of retirement, I was confronted with my own biases in this regard. I had written an interview protocol and was pre-testing it with a woman in her early seventies. When she had answered my list of questions, I said:

"Thanks very much for talking with me. Your responses will be very helpful."
"Is that it?" she said.
"What do you mean?" I asked.
"When are you going to ask me about the good stuff?" she asked.
"Tell me about the good stuff," I said.

For an hour, I scribbled notes frantically as she described her life in retirement and all its positive aspects. I realised at that point that our entire field was not asking about the good stuff, and this realisation fundamentally reshaped my development as a gerontologist. For the ensuing fifty years, I have consciously tried to balance my research, to look at the opportunities and positive development that occur with ageing as well as its challenges and deficits.

Spirituality is a primary area of development and growth in later life, so this subject has increasingly occupied my interest. Spirituality is a vital region of psychological and social development throughout adulthood, but if we do not have the necessary concepts and language, it is difficult to understand what is happening, or even to see it. Most adults have had experiences they call spiritual, and a large number see themselves as being on a spiritual journey. Yet we struggle to include this subject among the 'fundamentals' of the study of ageing.

The Nature of Spirituality

Spirituality is rooted in our awareness of pure being – our sense of 'aliveness' or unadulterated sense of presence. *Awareness* is a key word here. Evidence shows that we are born with the brain structure needed to experience 'being' (Trimble 2007), but we must learn to *perceive* our experience of being, to become conscious of it. Otherwise being is like a computer programme running in the background; we do not see it on our screens but it is there doing its bit nevertheless. Thus, we can say that spiritual development is cultivating a capability to perceive the spiritual aspects of experience. This development can occur both intentionally and nonintentionally. Spiritual experience occurs before it is put into language, so the language we use to describe it is fabricated and borrowed so we can describe and represent our experiences, but those descriptions should not be confused with actual spiritual experiences.

Conscious spiritual awareness comes in three forms: intense experience of presence (present-moment awareness), self-transcendence (witness-consciousness that transcends the personal self), and contemplative con-sciousness (spacious being, open to direct experience of the sacred). Culti-vating and nurturing all three of these levels of spiritual consciousness is a major theme of many spiritual journeys and a goal of spiritual practices such as prayer or meditation. These three levels are further illustrated below.

In *present-moment awareness*, life is more vivid and perception is opened up to allow us to experience a much fuller and richer array of what is coming through our senses than we usually do when we are on the 'automatic pilot' created by psychological habituation. As elders open to the wonders of the present moment, they can enjoy a much richer life experience without having to change their circumstances or exert add-itional physical effort. This is a definite plus.

I am washing dishes and only that. I feel the hot water on my hands, hear the sounds of the sloshing water, and see the light reflecting off the wet dishes. This is a spiritual experience for me. (Woman, age 80)

Spiritual development depends on our being able *to transcend the personal self*, especially the ego, with its tangles of desire and fear. The personal self often distorts our perceptions of ourselves and the situations we find ourselves in. A key to self-transcendence is to learn to view one's life through 'witness-consciousness'. Humans have the amazing capability of observing themselves, and self-observation is an important source of feedback. But most people stop short and only see themselves through the eyes of the critical, moralist, or perfectionist observer. These observers are still part of the ego; Freud called them the super-ego. Spiritual development requires that we push past these judgmental observers to the 'dispassionate observer', the inner observer that can look unflinchingly at what is happening, acknowledge it, and have compassion for the actor. As Wilber (2001) points out, when we transcend the personal self, we do not destroy it. We transcend to a bigger picture, include our personal self in that bigger picture, and in the process place the personal self in a bigger context, which of course changes how we see that personal self. This is a cyclic process with many iterations and is a major dynamic in the growing self-acceptance and humility that many elders show over time (Atchley 2009).

I had inadvertently said something in a meeting that made my boss very angry. At the end of the meeting, he said through clenched teeth, "I need to chat with you in my office *now!*" Unexpectedly, I felt no fear. It was as though I was outside myself watching. In his office, he threw a major tantrum, shouting as he paced back and forth. I sat there calmly and quietly and did not respond in my usual defensive way. When he finally ran out of steam and sat down, I said, "I understand that you are very angry about what happened, and I will not do that again." He said, "Well, okay". By my being able to stand outside my own feelings about what had happened, a situation that could have been very ugly was neutralized. (Man, age 46)

Contemplative consciousness is the bigger context into which witnessing places the personal self. Heidegger (1966) contrasted two inner worlds: the world of *calculative thinking*, within which we use conceptualisation and logic in our attempts to manipulate ourselves and the circumstances of our lives, and the world of *contemplation*, within which we *abide* in the peaceful vastness of inner space. Many people go through life without experiencing inner space because they are not looking for it. Some are afraid to look into it, for fear of what they might find, but since 1950 there has been a steady rise in the proportion of people who have engaged in contemplative practices such as meditation, centering prayer, yoga, or Tai Chi. Such practices increase the odds that one will experience deep inner space. Numerous investigators have found that there is also a natural tendency for elders to experience contemplative consciousness as a naturally occurring part of a slower-paced life (Tornstam 2005; Sherman 2010). Those who have experienced contemplative consciousness describe it as silent, peaceful, still, liberating, and enlightening. Once people experience these inner qualities, they are usually motivated to abide there as much as possible.

Mrs. E is an eighty-year-old woman who has lived in a nursing home for several years. I visit her regularly.
"There are times when you seem to be in a far-off place in your mind," I said.
"Yes," she said.
"Is it a pleasant place?" I asked.
"Oh my, yes," she said.
"Can you tell me what it is like?" I asked.
"Words don't describe it. It's warm and cozy. Thoughts come and go but are of no importance. I feel completely at peace," she said.
No wonder she enjoyed, and insisted on time for, her afternoon reveries.

Mysticism generally occurs in contemplative consciousness. Mysticism is *direct* experience of the 'ground of being' (Carmody and Carmody 1996). Ground of being is a term used by Aldous Huxley (1944) and later Paul Tillich (1967) to refer to 'the God beyond God', the aspect of the divine that goes beyond any anthropomorphised or specific conception of the ultimate reality. Direct experience means an experience of being fully with and in the ultimate reality that permeates the universe. Direct also means directly available, not needing an intermediary. Direct experience of the sacred is not a concept, although we use concepts to speak about it. Mystics often seek this union by engaging in spiritual practices such as meditation, contemplation, or prayer. These practices encourage abiding in contemplative consciousness, and in that consciousness mystical experience may be more likely. As one mystic put it, 'We call spiritual practices "keeping the room clean". We do them in hope that we will have a visitor, but even if we do not, we still get to enjoy a clean room.' This was said with a lovely smile.

I have argued that ageing can make contemplation and mystical union more likely (Atchley 1996). The mellowing of physical drives and simpler lifestyles of many elders are conducive to contemplation. Many elders intentionally simplify their lifestyles and turn their attention inwards to focus on their experiences of spirituality. Reading scripture and other material about spiritual aspects of life, prayer, and meditation are examples of activities aimed at 'keeping the room clean'. Many elders who lead a spiritually centered life have the comfort of absolute confidence in their spiritual process. But they do not stand out; rather, their main characteristics are their quietness, inwardness, empathy and kindness towards others, capacity to forgive, and gratitude for having life (Moody 1995). Moody wrote, 'Taking mysticism and ageing seriously would mean a very far-reaching reassessment of the possible meaning of old age. One can think of old age as a kind of "natural monastery" in which earlier roles, attachments, and pleasures [are re-imagined].' (p. 96)

These various dimensions of spiritual consciousness usually develop by degrees over a period of years. This development can be intentional, non-intentional, or both. When people write or speak their personal stories of spiritual journeying, they are contemplating and sharing their personal spiritual development (Atchley 2011). Large numbers of people have gone through this process, and we can learn much from reading or listening to these stories. Based on observations of elders, I see the essence of fully developed spirituality as an intense aliveness, self-acceptance, and humility; a deep sense of contemplative understanding; and feeling of interconnectedness with all things. There can also be an experience of direct and deepening connection with the ground of being, which can be experienced and described in many ways.

Spirituality and Ageing Imbedded in Historical Time

In his insightful and useful review of social change in American spiritual thought and behaviour in the last half of the twentieth century, Robert Wuthnow (1998) argues that spirituality shifted from a religion-centered *spirituality of dwelling* towards a person-centered *spirituality of seeking* and later towards a personal *spirituality of practice*. I suspect that this progression occurred in much of the developed world.

Spirituality of dwelling 'emphasises habitation: God occupies a definite place in the universe and creates a sacred space in which humans too can dwell; to inhabit sacred space is to know its territory and feel secure' (Wuthnow 1998, pp. 3–4). A spirituality of dwelling offers the security available from adherence to doctrine and worship primarily in awe-inspiring edifices and rituals. Spirituality of dwelling also provides relatively stable doctrine, ritual, and organisational structure. Comfort, security, and answers to meaning questions come from predictability.

Gerontology began in a time dominated by this spirituality of dwelling, and spirituality was seen as applying mainly in the context of organised religion. What mattered was the person's connection to religion, so early gerontology was concerned primarily with religious affiliation, church attendance, and how elders were ministered to in religious congregations (Maves 1960). There was little consideration of the inner spiritual life of the respondents. In the culture of that time, a person invited spiritual experience by emersion in the spaces and rituals of a specific religion.

By contrast, a spirituality of seeking emphasises openness, journeying, and negotiation. On a journey, we never know exactly what we will encounter and, to make effective decisions, we have to remain aware of our needs and be open to opportunities. Spiritual journeying requires that an individual learn to negotiate a landscape filled with 'complex and confusing meanings of spirituality' (Wuthnow 1998, p. 4). On the spiritual journey, we never have perfect maps, so we need an enduring set of questions that will allow us to discover spirituality in that time and place. Here are examples of the *types* of questions that support the spiritual journey (Atchley 2009):

- What is my spiritual nature?
- What does it mean to grow spiritually?
- How did I become the spiritual being I am today?
- Do I have confidence and trust in my spiritual process?
- How does spirituality manifest in my world?
- How does spirituality relate to my life choices?

Gerontology was slow to pick up on this emerging spirituality of seeking. Bits and pieces appeared beginning in the 1990s. Particularly notable was a scholarly collection, *Aging and the Religious Dimension*, by Thomas and Eisenhandler (1994) that contained contributions by leading gerontologists interested in a spirituality of seeking. My book, *Spirituality and Aging* (Atchley 2009), contains extensive discussion and case examples of a spirituality of seeking. Edmund Sherman's *Contemplative Aging: A Way of Being in Later Life* (2010) has an excellent discussion of the roots of contemplative ageing in classical philosophy, suggesting that ideas about contemplative ageing are by no means new. Sherman also provides a rich discussion of how one seeks contemplative consciousness, how abiding in contemplative consciousness affects us as we age, and how ageing actually encourages spiritual seeking.

Wuthnow argues that most people live a life that balances dwelling and seeking. Both the security of dwelling and openness of seeking are seen as valuable. He also sees an emerging *practice-oriented spirituality* that features a mosaic of regular spiritual practices that, come what may, provides an ongoing, constant commitment to nurturing spirituality. This is based in the idea that we can become what we do (Walsh 1999), and returning to a spiritual practice over and over again creates habits of mind and of being that come to seem natural. If these practices are part of an open context of spiritual attention, these habits can be consistently enlivening and a substantial resource for coping with what life brings.

We are only beginning to study the primary and secondary effects of spiritual practices and how these might intersect with ageing (Atchley 2001). The effects of meditation on stress, physical health, and mental health have been widely studied, but there has been little analysis of patterns of spirituality and ageing over time in longitudinal studies. Some of my best ideas on this subject have come from respondents. For example, I asked a seventy-three-year-old man who had been meditating regularly for more than thirty years, "Can you give me an example of how meditating has affected your life?"

Well, meditation led me to a very calm and peaceful place inside myself. At first it was not a very predictable trip. Some days I would get there, but most days I did not. But over the years I noticed that a faint path had turned into more of a road, and I got there more often than not. Now it's like a freeway, and I can go to that calm place anytime I want, even when I'm not meditating. This was incredibly important when I had to cope with the prospect and aftermath of [coronary artery] bypass surgery.

The overarching cultural process that Wuthnow describes is a movement from 1) a cultural image of actors trying to find spirituality by following a preordained script, to 2) an image of actors guided by their own inner light and spiritual intentions, disciplined by life experience, to 3) an image of actors actively creating mosaics of spiritual practice, lifestyles, and communities specifically designed to nurture their vision of the spiritual journey. The spiritual journey is a much different prospect and experience in the evolving dwelling-seeking-practice framework than that experienced in a more static framework that emphasises authority structures and one-size-fits-all approaches to the spiritual path.

Next Steps

There is no question that we are onto something important. Spirituality, spiritual development, and the spiritual journey are important elements of life for a growing majority of elders. Today, middle-aged adults are the major market for books, workshops, and retreats focused on the spiritual journey. Elders appreciate the qualities that accompany spiritual experience and are motivated to do whatever they can to enjoy these qualities as much as they can.

To advance our study of spirituality and ageing, more of us need to become adept at using what Ken Wilber calls 'the Eye of Contemplation' (Wilber 2001). As Wilber points out, contemplative ways of knowing have been used since ancient times and have been employed by contemplative masters of both Eastern and Western mysticism. Contemplative consciousness is a place to be, but it is also a place from which to see and learn. To understand contemplative, transcendent consciousness requires contemplative methods.

Fortunately, in *Eye to Eye*, Ken Wilber has laid out the fundamentals of contemplative ways of knowing. It begins with St. Bonaventure's identification of three 'eyes' through which we can see and learn. The first is the *eye of the flesh* – the sensory and perceptual capabilities we use to apprehend the external world of space, time, and objects. The second is the *eye of reason*, through which 'we attain knowledge of philosophy, logic, and the mind itself' (Wilber 2001, p. 3). The third is the *eye of contemplation* 'by which we rise to knowledge of transcendent realities' (Wilber 2001, p. 3). The process for each of these eyes involves three steps: following an accepted procedure or injunction, being illuminated by that action, and confirming the results by a social process of peer review. The three ways of knowing differ, however, in the nature of the agreed-upon procedure, the form that illumination takes, and who is qualified to provide peer review. For the sensory/perceptual eye, observation is the agreed-upon procedure, description is the illumination, and intersubjective agreement among experienced observers is the confirmation. For the eye of reason, logic is the procedure, induction is the illumination, and logical proof is the confirmation, verified by experienced peers. For the eye of contemplation, contemplative practice is the procedure, intuition is the illumination, and confirmation comes from peers who are adept at contemplative understanding.

Since spirituality is at its root a contemplative topic, those who would study spirituality would benefit from being experienced contemplatives. Another important point is that these three forms of knowing have a structure. The sensory/perceptual eye gives us descriptive raw materials, but to understand more deeply, we must transcend description to conceptualise and theorise through the eye of reason. To understand even more deeply, we can transcend description and analysis to apprehend through the eye of contemplation. As we go up these levels, transcendence only goes one way – *transcend and include*. When we transcend description we bring that description into our reasoning about what is described, we bring description into a bigger context. When we transcend description and analysis, we bring them into the field of contemplation, a much, much bigger context. Sensory perception and reasoning involve brain functions that deal with manipulating very definite experiences. Contemplation involves awareness of *regions* of inner space (Heidegger 1966). In contemplation, there is no impulse towards manipulation, the province of calculative thinking. There is simply abiding with what is and coming to understand deeper realities within what is.

As this chapter shows, we have the basic sources needed to build a curriculum on spirituality and ageing. We need to begin to educate students about spirituality and ageing. There is always a battle over getting new material into any curriculum, but a very large proportion of students have a self-interest in this topic. They want to know 'the meaning of life', and we have a positive message to teach them about that. They are also hungry for reasons to be positive about ageing.

Spirituality and Ageing for Practitioners

For people who work directly with ageing people, to whom do they respond? Is it the stereotyped feeble older person who has no life and is lonely? Or is it a vitally involved person on a spiritual journey despite the inconveniences and losses that can come with age? Or is it another spiritual being just like them but in a different human form? George Fox, a founder of Quakerism, said we should go joyfully about the world, answering that of God in everyone. Fox's point was to respond to the basic spirituality of each person and not the personality or social background. At the level of basic spirituality, what is there to get into conflict about or to object to? What would happen if we learned to tune into the basic spirituality of the people being served? To tune into the spirituality of those being served, would we need to tune into our own? Would trying to tune into the basic spirituality of another person help us tune into our own?

The expanded view of spirituality presented in this book provides a framework for learning important things about many of the people we work with. There are few things more important to many ageing people than their intentions for their own spiritual journey. But we cannot assume we know anything about those intentions, or even a basic outline of how they see that journey. We have to wait for them to tell us in their own time and in their own way. Some will tell us in words, others in body language, others in the art they make, others through the music they sing. Where does basic spirituality manifest in a person? It can be in any of a hundred places. To see it, we must create a safe place. I gave several examples earlier of questions that might get this conversation started.

Earlier I wrote that to study spirituality, researchers benefit from being able to use their own spiritual capacities and perspectives. So it is with serving the spirituality of clients. *How Can I Help?* (Dass and Gorman 1995) is the best resource I have seen on how to help from a spiritually awakened place. The authors begin with the notion that we all have an impulse to care when faced with others in need. Whether we translate that impulse into action depends on how we deal with barriers to the natural expression of caring. Spiritually grounded caring comes from compassion, not pity.

> Compassion and pity are very different. Whereas compassion reflects the yearning of the heart to merge and take on some of the suffering, pity is a controlled set of thoughts designed to assure separateness. Compassion is the spontaneous response of love; pity, the involuntary reflex of fear. (Dass and Gorman 1995, p. 62)
>
> Who *are* we to ourselves and to one another? It will all come down to that. *Will we look within?* Can we see that to be of most service to others we must face our own doubts, needs, and resistances? (Dass and Gorman 1995, p. 15)

To see situations clearly and dispassionately, we benefit from learning to see things from nonpersonal consciousness, or *witness consciousness* as Ram Dass and Gorman label it.

> [W]itnessing is dispassionate. It's not committed to one result or another; it's open to everything. Because it has ... no axe to grind, it is more able to see truth. As the Tao Te Ching says, "The truth awaits for eyes unclouded by longing." The Witness, however, is not passive, complacent, or indifferent. Indeed, while it's not attached to a particular outcome, its presence turns out to bring about change. As we bring *what is* into the light of clear awareness, we begin to see that the universe is providing us with abundant clues to the nature of the suffering before us, what is being asked, what fears have been inhibiting us, and, finally, *what might really help*. All we have to do is listen—really listen. (Dass and Gorman 1995, pp. 68–69)

Thus, commitment to objectivity turns out to be a spiritual practice that is essential to doing effective service.

> Light from within, that's our illumination
> To dwell in silent peace, that's our meditation
> To see the passing world with clearness and compassion
> And when we clearly see, we are drawn to BE love and to
>   serve. Adapted from Atchley 1996

References

Atchley, B. (1996). *The Journey*. Nashville, TN: Broadcast Music Incorporated.

Atchley, R.C. (2011). 'How spiritual experience and development interact with aging', *Journal of Transpersonal Psychology*, 43(2):156–165.

Atchley, R.C. (2009). *Spirituality and Aging*. Baltimore, MD: Johns Hopkins University Press.

Atchley, R.C. (2003). 'Becoming a spiritual elder', in Kimble, M.A. and McFadden, S.H. (eds.), *Aging, Spirituality and Religion: A Handbook*, pp. 33–46. Minneapolis: Fortress Press.

Atchley, R.C. (2001). 'The influence of spiritual beliefs and practices on the relation between time and aging', in McFadden, S.H. and Atchley, R.C. (eds.), *Aging and the Meaning of Time*, pp. 157–170. New York: Springer Publishing Co.

Atchley, R.C. (1999). *Continuity and Adaptation in Aging: Creating Positive Experiences*. Baltimore, MD: Johns Hopkins University Press.

Atchley, R.C. (1997). 'Everyday mysticism: Spiritual development in later life', *Journal of Adult Development* 4(2):123–134.

Atchley, R.C. and Barusch, A.S. (2004). *Social Forces and Aging*, 10th edn. Belmont, CA: Wadsworth.

Birren, J.E. (1959). *Handbook of Aging and the Individual*. Chicago: University of Chicago Press.

Burgess, E.W. (1960). *Handbook of Aging in Western Societies*. Chicago: University of Chicago Press.

Carmody, D.L. and Carmody, J.T. (1996). *Mysticism: Holiness East and West*. New York: Oxford University Press.

Clark, M.E. and Anderson, B.G. (1969). *Culture and Aging*. Springfield, IL: Charles C. Thomas.

Cumming, E. and Henry, W.E. (1961). *Growing Old: The Process of Disengagement*. New York: Basic Books.

Dass, R. and Gorman, P. (1995). *How Can I Help? Stories and Reflections on Service*. New York: Knopf.

Erikson, E.H., Erikson, J.M., and Kivnick, H.Q. (1986). *Vital Involvement in Old Age: The Experience of Old Age in Our Time*. New York: W.W. Norton & Company Ltd.

Fowler, J.W. (1981). *Stages of Faith*. San Francisco: Harper & Row.

Heidegger, M. (1966). *Discourse on Thinking*. New York: Harper & Row.

Hillman, J. (1999). *The Force of Character and the Lasting Life*. New York: Random House.

Hoffman, E. (1992). *Visions of Innocence: Spiritual and Inspirational Experiences in Childhood*. Boston, MA: Shambhala Publications.

Huxley, A. (1944). *The Perennial Philosophy*. New York: Harper & Row.

Maharaj, N. (1973). *I Am That*. Bombay, India: Chetana.

Maves, P.E. (1960). 'Aging, religion and the church', in Tibbitts, C. (ed.) *Handbook of Social Gerontology*, pp. 678–749. Chicago: University of Chicago Press.

Moody, H.R. (1995). 'Mysticism', in Kimble, M.A. and McFadden, S.H. (eds.) *Aging, Spirituality and Religion: A Handbook*, pp. 87–101. Minneapolis: Fortress Press.

Neugarten, B.L. (1973). 'Personality change in later life: A developmental perspective', in Eisdorfer, C. and Lawton, M.P. (eds.), *The Psychology of Adult Development and Aging*, pp. 311–335. Washington, DC: American Psychological Association.

Sherman, E. (2010). *Contemplative Aging: A Way of Being in Later Life*. New York: Gordian Knot Books.

Thomas, L.E. and Eisenhandler, S.A. (eds.) (1994). *Aging and the Religious Dimension*. Westport, CT: Auburn House.

Tibbitts, C. (ed.) (1960). *Handbook of Social Gerontology*. Chicago: University of Chicago Press.

Tillich, P. (1967). *Systematic Theology: Three Volumes in One*. Chicago: University of Chicago Press.

Tornstam, L. (1994). 'Gero-transcendence: A theoretical and empirical exploration', in Thomas, L.E. and Eisenhandler, S.A. (eds.), *Aging and the Religious Dimension*, pp. 203–225. Westport, CT: Auburn House.

Tornstam, L. (2005). *Gero-transcendence: A Developmental Theory of Positive Aging*. New York: Springer Publications.

Trimble, M.R. (2007). *The Soul in the Brain*. Baltimore, MD: Johns Hopkins University Press.

Walsh, R. (1999). *Essential Spirituality: Seven Central Practices to Awaken Heart and Mind*. New York: John Wiley & Sons.

Wilber, K. (2001). *Eye to Eye: The Quest for a New Paradigm*, 3rd edn. Boston: Shambhala.

Wuthnow, R. (1998). *After Heaven: Spirituality in America since the 1950s*. Berkeley, CA: University of California Press.

3   Ageing and Spirituality across Faiths and Cultures

Elizabeth MacKinlay

Introduction

Spirituality becomes more important for many older people. For many, spirituality is largely associated with life meaning whilst for others, it has a specific religious dimension. Over the last couple of decades this has become an area of great interest, and anecdotes about spirituality in older adults are being replaced with research findings. The importance of understanding how the spiritual dimension is lived out in individual lives in multifaith and multicultural twenty-first century western countries is an important challenge for those who work with older adults. There is also increasing interest from within Asia regarding spirituality and ageing.

The spiritual dimension of life is a vital part of being human. It is from this spiritual dimension that the deepest issues of life meaning and relationship arise. Although people are not always aware of their spirituality, it is likely to come to awareness in times of both great joy and of great trauma and grief. Whilst this is true across the lifespan, matters of the spiritual dimension become more important to many people as they grow older, sometimes for the first time in their lives. For some this is an issue largely associated with finding life meaning and is fulfilled within a secular context; for others, it has a specific religious dimension. Viktor Frankl saw meaning as a crucial factor for survival and hope (1984).

This chapter briefly describes a model of spiritual tasks and process of ageing (MacKinlay 2001) designed to fit both theo-centric and secular modes of meaning-finding. The model recognises a central core of life meaning from which the person responds to life. This core or ultimate meaning is affected by and influences the person's sense of self-sufficiency and vulnerability, their life story, the importance of relationship and finding hope in later life.

The recognition of the universal nature of the spiritual dimension of human beings sets the scene for examination of this dimension, both within a religious and also from a secular perspective. A basic assumption for this chapter is that a person's spiritual dimension lies at the very depths of what it means to be human. The way that culture is experienced and the ways that religions and spirituality are expressed will vary according to regional and specific religious and cultural heritage and custom. However, beneath all the overlay of culture and religion is the common spiritual dimension of all people. It is from this underlying basis that I want to begin.

I will then explore the ways in which the spiritual dimension will be changed in different settings and according to different religious and cultural beliefs. A further assumption behind this chapter is that people have choices, sometimes unrecognised ones, concerning how they will live out their spiritual dimension. These choices are in some ways similar to those that most people make about their life goals. For example, the way they do or do not exercise, and what and how they will eat, depending on the importance that they attach to each of these dimensions of life – physical, mental, social or spiritual.

A Secular Model of Spirituality in Ageing

Working in a largely secular society, such as Australia, it is important to recognise both religious and secular ways of expressing the spiritual dimension (MacKinlay 2001; MacKinlay and Trevitt 2007). In the early 1990s in Australia, there had been little study of the spiritual dimension of older people. MacKinlay's first study was to map the spiritual dimension of older independent-living people (MacKinlay 1998, doctoral thesis[1]). This study used story as the basis for exploring and examining the spirituality of these people. It was considered vital to listen to the words of the older people, rather than to use questionnaires that might foreclose on important aspects of their spiritual lives.

The Importance of Story as a Way of Understanding the Spiritual Journey of Life

Story is closely connected with human identity; in fact, according to Kenyon Clark and de Vries (2001) we don't just have a story, we are story. The Abrahamic faiths have affirmed story as the basis of faith and life, linking God's story with the human story (MacKinlay 2012). From a narrative theological perspective, Lash (1997, p. 120) writes of the story

---

[1] MacKinlay, E.B. (1998) *The Spiritual Dimension of Ageing: Meaning in Life, Response to Meaning, and Well Being in Ageing.* Doctoral Thesis Melbourne: La Trobe University.

of our own faiths, being linked through the autobiographical nature of Christian and Jewish faith narrative.

Stories are said to be co-created with the need for a story-teller and a story-listener (Kenyon Clark and de Vries 2001). The importance of story to understanding humanity is evident in Crites' words: 'Neither disembodied minds nor mindless bodies can appear in stories. The self is given whole, as an activity in time' (Crites 1997, p. 85).

If story is so crucial to being human, then it is crucial to the way we understand ourselves and each other within cultural contexts as well. Story or narrative forms an important context from which to be and to function in any cultural setting. MacIntyre (in Hauerwas and Jones 1997) sees functions of narrative as:

- Intelligible human action is narrative in form;
- Human life has a fundamentally narrative shape;
- Humans are story-tellers by nature;
- People place their lives and arguments in narrative histories;
- Communities and traditions receive their continuities through narrative histories;
- Epistemological progress is marked by the construction and reconstruction of more adequate narrative and forms of narrative (Hauerwas and Jones 1997, p. 8).

These functions of narrative provide a context for exploration of the spiritual dimension of older people and their families and cultures across the major faiths. Story formed the basis for the study of spirituality in the lives of older people conducted by MacKinlay (2001, 2006; MacKinlay and Trevitt 2012) over more than a decade.

A Model of Spiritual Tasks and Process of Ageing

A generic model of spirituality designed by MacKinlay (1998, doctoral thesis), and MacKinlay (2001) is suggested as a way of identifying and assessing the spiritual dimension. This model can be applied to any older person, regardless of culture and religious belief. This model was designed after examination of in-depth interviews that used story to explore meaning in life, first of well older people (MacKinlay 2001), followed by in-depth interviews of frail older people (MacKinlay 2006).

There are certain major life themes that cannot be ignored. For instance, meaning considered as a major theme is a crucial factor of well-being. Without meaning, there can be no sense of well-being; meaning is associated with hope, flourishing and resilience. Lack of meaning leads to hopelessness. For most humans meaning comes largely through relationship with others (MacKinlay 2001, 2006; MacKinlay and Trevitt 2012) and it may even be fair to say that humans are made for relationship. For those who hold a religious faith, their relationships may also be with the God of their understanding. Certain human characteristics are held in common by people of practically every race and creed. It is suggested that, from a spiritual perspective, the need for meaning, for relationship, including love, forgiveness and reconciliation, as well as the need for transcendence, for hope and joy, are central characteristics of human life.

The themes apparent in the study of the stories of independent-living older people (MacKinlay 2001) formed an important beginning for mapping the spiritual dimension of these people. From qualitative analysis of the main themes arising from the participants' stories, the following themes were identified: First, where the participants found ultimate life meaning, for most it was through significant family relationships; second, the ways that participants responded to meaning; third, strong motivation to remain living autonomously in the community versus a fear of losing their independence; fourth, the search for final life meaning through story, including reminiscence; fifth, relationship versus isolation and finally sixth, hope versus despair. The spiritual tasks arising from these themes are described later in the chapter.

The themes identified from the stories of the older people were then examined to develop a model of spirituality and ageing that might guide further study and practice (MacKinlay 2001). The model designed is a developmental model, assuming the potential for continued spiritual growth until life's end. Thus tasks of spiritual development have been identified and a process for these has been suggested. Like Erikson's (Erikson, Erikson, and Kivnick 1986) psychosocial stages of development, it is possible to either continue to grow or to stagnate or despair. The model has been titled the 'spiritual tasks and process of ageing' to give emphasis to the fact that while six tasks have been identified, these are not simply tasks that can be done and ticked off. They are continuing components of the spiritual process of ageing.

This model of the spiritual tasks and process of ageing has six major themes: at the centre lies ultimate or core meaning, from this comes response to meaning, while the remaining four tasks form continuums of relationship versus isolation, self-centeredness versus self-transcendence, provisional versus final meaning and hope versus despair (Figure 1; MacKinlay 2006). These themes were found in both older Christians and older people who claimed no religious faith affiliation.

Therefore, a model of spiritual tasks, based on the findings of the original research, which fits both secular spirituality (MacKinlay and Trevitt 2007) and a religious spirituality (MacKinlay 2001) was

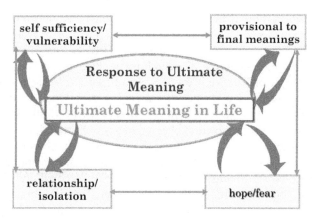

Figure 1. A generic model of the spiritual tasks and process of ageing (from MacKinlay 2006 figure 1.2, p. 23)

developed and is outlined in this chapter. It is noted however, that further modifications to the generic model of spiritual tasks and process of ageing are then desirable for different religious faiths. The model adapted for Christians is shown in this chapter (Figure 2; MacKinlay 2006).

Well-being is based not only on finding individual meaning in life, but also on meaningful connections with others which are crucial for the development of healthy self concepts, and indeed, at a most basic level, for supporting and affirming identity of the self. The need for self-identity, which is found through others as well as self-developed, seems to be culturally based and differs between cultures and religions. It is through stories told and listened to that cultures and religions are taken on and affirmed. We are only affirmed in our identities by others around us; this is well illustrated among those who have dementia, as it is often said that those with dementia have lost their 'self', but as Hughes, Louw, and Sabatt (2006) and Swinton (2012) have written, it is only through relationship that any of us have our identity affirmed.

What is argued here is that, at the most basic of all levels of being human, there are certain spiritual tasks of ageing that are common to all older people. This is not to deny differences between cultures and religion, but to acknowledge that at the greatest depths of being human, there are certain common touching points. Beyond this, it is necessary to consider specific religious and cultural needs and requirements, which are important to those who live within these cultures and religious communities.

Spiritual Tasks of Ageing for Christians:
A Continuing Process

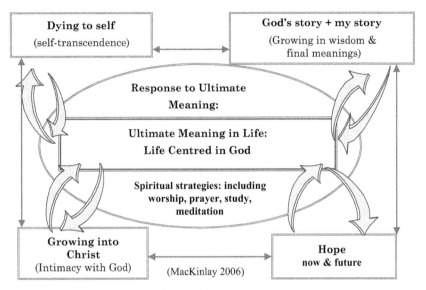

Figure 2. A model of the spiritual tasks and process of ageing for Christians (from MacKinlay 2006 figure 1.3, p. 25)

The Spiritual Tasks of Ageing Described

Ultimate life meaning is used to describe the central, deepest or core meaning held by the person; it is what lies at the heart of the person. It is this meaning, which lies at the depths of one's being, that supports or alternatively rejects life and hope. This is distinguished from the spiritual task and process of moving from provisional to final meanings and finding wisdom. Ultimate life meaning is both an outcome of finding final meanings and at the same time influenced by relationship, the search for transcendence and hope. In my studies of both well older people (MacKinlay 2001) and frail older people (MacKinlay 2006), this core or ultimate meaning was strongly associated with relationship. The well older people mostly found meaning through their relationships, with a life partner, with children, grandchildren or great grandchildren. It was interesting that none of the people in my first study of independent-living old people (MacKinlay 2001) cited work as bringing ultimate meaning to their lives. In subsequent studies of people who had dementia, relationship was almost synonymous with meaning (MacKinlay 2006; MacKinlay and Trevitt 2012).

For frail older Christians, most of whom had lost their most significant human relationships, often God or Jesus was the focus of central life meaning. It was also noted that a sense of hope was affected by the kind of notion of God held by these people. For instance, if God was seen as judgmental and remote, then it was harder for the person to find meaning and hope; or if the concept of God held by the person was of a loving God, then finding the meaning became hope-giving. Those with a well-developed sense of their spiritual dimension (whether in a religious context or not) exhibited a sense of integrity, with associated peace and joy. Those who had not developed their spiritual dimension were found more likely to be denying their ageing process, and struggling to find meaning in the process of growing older. Evidence for this came from analysis of the life stories of these people, who had in some cases retained a very cognitively based faith[2] stage (Fowler 1981) that had not continued to grow and develop over the life span. The searching for and finding of meaning discussed in MacKinlay's model is closely aligned with Erikson's (Erikson, Erikson, and Kivnick 1986) eighth stage of psychosocial development of integrity versus despair; it is the focus on the spiritual dimension rather than the psychosocial dimension which is different.

The task of responding to meaning emerges directly out of where the person finds life meaning. It is from whatever lies at the centre of their being that the person responds to life. If they are able to hold a sense of meaning, whatever the circumstances of life, then they will respond to life with hope. If, on the contrary they cannot find meaning in life, then they are likely to become despondent or depressed and lose hope. For instance, a number of the frail elderly people interviewed (MacKinlay 2006) associated meaning with their close relationship with God, or Jesus. These people expressed a sense of peace and hope and responded to all of life from this outlook on life. On the other hand, those who had a sense of a judgmental God found it hard to be optimistic about their lives and tended to see life through negative lenses. Thus, whatever lies at the heart of one's being will be the impetus for one's view of the world. For some, deep human relationships gave them reason for living, and thus their response to meaning was deeply involved in reaching out to others.

Response to meaning can come through symbols and rituals and the rituals may be of a secular or religious nature. Response to meaning can

---

[2] The way Fowler defines faith is very similar to the way spirituality is defined in this chapter, broadly, as meaning in life, relationship with God and/or others, the search for transcendence, and hope.

be individual or community, or even at a national level, where joy of grief can stir the need to respond to life circumstances.

All faiths use rituals and symbols in their worship. However, there is a wide variety of liturgy and worship even within the same religion, and between different major religious faiths. Culture is important in linking with the meaning that is transported by the symbols and rituals used. Culture carries the meaning of a society (Geertz 1975). Humans are meaning makers; however, meaning is not made in isolation.

The task of moving from self-centredness to self-transcendence or transform-ation comes from the theme of self-sufficiency versus vulnerability. Throughout adulthood people, certainly in western cultures, strive for self-sufficiency and fear vulnerability. In later life as frailty develops, it becomes more difficult to remain self-sufficient. This fear of future vulnerability, of not being able to retain control over one's life, may be either a stimulus for continuing or renewed spiritual growth or it may be a cause of despair. It seems that the move towards self-transcendence and gero-transcendence (Tornstam 2005) is more likely to come with increasing frailty. As older people come to the stage of loss of energy and loss of mobility, so a new struggle begins. This struggle in societies that value youth and not age, involves conflict between a mid-life persona, and a letting go of mid-life goals and desires to embrace the ageing process. Some older people do this naturally, while others fight against these changes, some even becoming depressed in the process.

The task of finding final life meaning is only likely to occur as people become aware of their own mortality, whether it is through the process of increased awareness of growing older, through some major relational loss or through a life-threatening illness. Through the life journey, until this occurs, often people pay little attention to life meaning. Viktor Frankl (1984) describes this search and finding of final life meanings by saying that as we journey through life, we lay down provisional meanings of events, but it is only as we become aware of our own mortality that we begin to process the events of our lives, to come to final meaning. He described this as like shooting a movie, where each event was recorded as it happened, but it is only when the person recognises their own approaching death that they are able, for the first time, to play the entire movie and see the whole story of their lives.

This often results in a re-assigning of meaning when seen in the larger context of the complete life story and is in a real sense, a re-framing of the life story, as new meanings emerge. The process we have used (MacKinlay 2001, 2006; MacKinlay and Trevitt 2012) has been to allow the person, in the context of their story, to find the meanings and reframe as the final meanings emerge. This process of spiritual reminiscence is not a counsellor-focused process, but is person focused. The person themselves through telling the story suddenly sees the meaning of events and comes to new understandings of the meaning of their lives in the present.

The process of spiritual reminiscence has been invaluable in assisting older people to come to a deeper understanding of their identity and to find meaning, not only as individuals, but also in community. This was clearly seen in a group of residents who were displaced persons from Eastern Europe during the Second World War and who many years later were being cared for in the same nursing home in Australia. All members of this small group had at least moderate levels of dementia. Their stories and a shared spirituality, drawn from their early lives in their country of origin, provided a cultural and religious structure for building meaning in the midst of their frailty (MacKinlay 2009).

The task of finding relationship is drawn from the theme of relationship versus isolation, and in later life becomes more challenging, as the most important relationships of life are ultimately lost through death or physical separation of life partners. For many older people, relationship and meaning are closely connected, while at the same time these relationships and life itself become more precarious (Erikson 1997). For some, increasing frailty is associated with increasing awareness of a God in their lives, and this becomes the central focus for relationship (MacKinlay 2006, 2012).

The task of finding hope in the process of growing older is a combination of finding meaning, having healthy relationships and developing transcendence. The theme that underlies this task is hope versus despair. Although hope is central to the Christian faith, it is not confined to a Christian perspective and is part of the other Abrahamic faiths. As well, the concept of hope is now well accepted within secular societies, and the literature from the health professions, especially nursing, affirm the important role of hope in the well-being of older people (Herth and Cutcliffe 2002). Brody and Semel (2006) note the association between hope, hopelessness and suicidal ideation among depressed older people (Brody and Semel 2006, p. 58). Within a secular society we talk about hope and hopelessness and the relation of these to survival. With elderly Christians who were still living independently, hope was mostly centered in relationship, while for those who were more frail and in residential high-level care, the longing for relationship was often present, with loneliness being experienced by many of these people. Numbers of these frail older people, however, came to a sense of the very presence of God, or of Jesus in their lives, and this presence brought hope (MacKinlay 2006).

The Association between Culture and Religion

Having outlined a model of spiritual tasks and process of ageing, I now want to consider culture in the context of spirituality, religion and ageing: 'Culture is the way that a group of people define meaning in their being.' (MacKinlay 2010, p. 12). According to Geertz, taking an anthropological view, culture is:

an historically transmitted pattern of meanings embodied in symbols, a system of inherited conceptions expressed in symbolic forms by means of which men communicate, perpetuate, and develop the knowledge about and attitudes to life. (Geertz 1975, p. 89)

In my writing in 2010, I suggested that from Geertz's view of culture it could be said that 'meaning permeates all that a community is' (MacKinlay 2010, p. 12). Furthermore, the symbols used by the culture to name or point to the meanings held by that culture provide and support the community identity. Culture is therefore seen as a vehicle for 'holding and affirming understandings held by the group, including values and beliefs, while it also presents a view of identity of this community in comparison with any other community' (MacKinlay 2010, p. 12). This view of culture can be applied to either the secular or sacred perspectives, and it is recognised that cultures and their symbols can change and evolve over time. This was well illustrated by Geertz in his study of the place of Islam in two different cultures, Moroccan and Indonesian. He concluded that what changed over the centuries in these cultures was not 'What shall I believe?' but 'How shall I believe it?' (Geertz 1969). It is clear that culture plays an important part in defining the symbols and rituals that carry meaning within the particular religion. It is not so much that religion changes, but the way that it is understood that changes. Therefore, it is important to understand the ways in which meaning is carried for the people of a particular culture or even subculture, perhaps a minority ethnic community, or even a community of older people defined by their residence in a residential aged care organisation; these smaller groupings may too become cultures with their own symbols and rituals that bear meaning.

The Importance of Culture in Later Life

A tension exists between the later part of life and the rest of life, in the context of western ageist attitudes to being older, evidenced at least by the antiageing lobby and, in reality, present right across society. It seems that if there is a culture of ageing, it is a negative one, with a lack of credible symbols of affirmation. It seems that only symbols of decline are generally recognised by the wider society, such as retirement, loss of status, loss of power, loss of security, loss of home, friends and family. Death of course is denied – it is always someone else who dies – so that death is held at a distance. Erikson noted in 1997 that since we lack 'a culturally viable ideal of old age, our civilization does not really harbor a concept of the whole of life' (p. 114).

The Ways Cultures Influence How the Model of Spiritual Tasks and Process of Ageing Is Worked Out

As previously noted, in all cultures and religions, finding meaning is of paramount importance for humans. However, culture and religion will importantly influence the lenses through which particular people view the world. Culture and religion will carry values of the important ways of being and the appropriate roles of members of the particular culture. Culture will influence the way that life is understood by members of the particular group. When I was invited to Singapore and then to Japan to work with people on spirituality and ageing, I was not sure how relevant my work might be to them; I was very conscious of the fact that I had drawn my model from listening to the stories of older people in a Western society. Of course, I could only speak from the perspective that I knew. And I asked, what can I give to older people of a different culture and from different religious backgrounds that I do not know?

However, feedback, first from elderly participants in a workshop in Singapore, and then from participants in different parts of Japan, from aged care providers, members of the Alzheimer's Association and older people all showed that at a basic level, my model of spiritual tasks of ageing worked for these people too. How could this be?

Discussion with the local people and further reflection revealed that it depends very much on the level at which we address issues. There are certain crucial elements of what it means to be human that underlie all cultures and religions. It was apparent that the model was conceptualising the core elements of what it meant to be human.

In the same way that I have adapted the general model to fit with particular Christian tasks of ageing, so further models adapted from the original could be developed to fit with other cultures and religions. In the process of exploring other models, I have approached representatives of other major faiths for responses from their perspectives. This is an area for further work and I acknowledge the importance of working with the other faiths to learn of their perspectives. At the same time, it is important not to try to design one model that fits all faiths and cultures. I suggest that the basic, generic model stimulates relevant and important questions for people of different cultures and religions so that core meaning can be elicited, however it is also important to acknowledge and address the differences of culture and religion.

Culture forms an important aspect affecting the way that religion is expressed. For instance, understanding of the Jewish faith must take account of three major themes: God, Torah and Israel (Zedek 1998, p. 255). Israel connects the Jewish people culturally and with their faith story as spiritual heirs of Abraham, Isaac and Jacob. The Jewish faith has strong connections through a unique history, community and culture. Yet, there are differences in the ways that Judaism is practiced in various countries.

Diversity exists among Muslims in different cultures, however: 'Islam is a discrete cosmology with a number of widely held tenets' (Hodge 2002, p. 6). It is seen as a complete way of life, having a world view that unifies the 'metaphysical and material and gives structure and coherence to personal existence' (Hodge 2002, p. 6). In contrast to the world view of Western secularism, Muslims do not view life as having separate arenas of a secular public sphere and a private religious sphere. 'Islam means "Peace" and "to submit to the will or law of God"' (Husain 1998, p. 279).

The underlying philosophy of Hinduism includes understanding the law of Karma: that all deeds of humans have effects, either good or bad (Juthani 1998). As part of the cycle of reincarnation, the person continues to be recreated in new form until they achieve moksha, which is understood as receiving liberation from the world of illusion (maya), and avidya; the ignorance that keeps people in bondage to the world. Hindus may strive to achieve moksha by three paths: the paths of illumination, action and devotion. Older Hindus may be pursuing one or more of these paths. Dharma is the way of living through rightness, justice, goodness and purpose through selflessness. This brings integrity and harmony to the universe. Brahma (God) is at the centre of the lives of Hindus and they hold to an underlying philosophy by which to live. The Hindu view of God is monotheistic in an ultimate sense, but is also polytheistic, pantheistic and panentheistic. While an afterlife is acknowledged in one way or another in the Abrahamic faiths, there is no concept of that from within Hinduism. Hindus acknowledge the cycle of life and death where reincarnation of the person into different life forms continues until the person achieves moksha (Thursby 2000).

Buddhist adherents are growing older and increasing in number in Western countries. Buddhist belief recognises 'four seals' of belief derived from observations of consciousness. Buddhist thought supports a spiritualistic world where physical reality is merely delusion, constructed by our consciousness. In Buddhism physical reality is a construction of the pancha-khanda – the five instruments of clinging (Palapathwala 2006).

Interactions between Religion and Culture

I would like to use the model of spirituality to describe how it may elicit the questions that are appropriate to understanding spirituality and religion across cultures. Transcendence is one component of the model that readily lends itself to this process. What does transcendence mean? It can mean self-transcendence, meaning to move beyond the focus on self. Frankl (1984) disputes the belief that this state can be arrived at by action on the part of the person, maintaining that people cannot 'self-actualise'. Rather, he would acknowledge that this state of transcendence is one of grace. Frankl has described transcendence as 'self-forgetting', and affirms that: 'Truly, self-transcendence is the essence of life' (Frankl 1997, p. 138).

Tornstam (2005) has coined the term 'gero-transcendence' to denote a sense of cosmic transcendence and a need for solitude, which seem to occur with numbers of older people. Gero-transcendence is an example of secular transcendence, whereby the person becomes more introspective and reflective, seeming to move more into 'being' than engaging in activities. Transcendence is associated with using a new set of lenses to view life and, in that sense, can be described as transformational. MacKinlay (2006) found that increasing losses, frailty and disabilities of ageing sometimes stimulated self-transcendence.

What Shape Does Self-transcendence Take in Different Religions?

Self-transcendence is potentially available to all human beings, whether religious or not. It may have a more overtly spiritual or religious aspect, as understood in the concept of sanctification (Tillich 1963), which for Christians involves growing more into the image of Christ, through prayer, learning and living in the grace of God.

In a Jewish context, Cohen (2010) has written of traditions of meditation and contemplation that involve transformation of the elder and prepares them to bear witness to the coming generation.

Where Christians might speak of transformation, Muslims may speak of purification or transformation of the self or soul. The process of spiritual transformation continues into later life (Abdalla and Patel 2010). In the Islamic faith, spirituality is described by Abdulla and Patel (2010):

... spirituality is a science (*'ilm*) that deals with the cleansing of the heart of all spiritual diseases such as malice, envy, hate and arrogance, to name just a few. A more accurate name for the purification of the self in Arabic and Islamic contexts is *tazkiyat al-nafs*. (Abdalla and Patel 2010, p. 114)

It is this cleansing of the heart that is associated with transcending the self, a process taken over many years. The living out of this involves the observance of external practices such as praying five times a day, fasting during the month of Ramadan and performing the Hajj or pilgrimage once in one's life. Yet, it is the 'inner dimension that one must turn to in order to see, utter and know the One' (Abdalla and Patel 2010, p. 115).

In Buddhist or Hindu terms, the approaching end of life and transformation is a continuing journey through all of life and, as death nears, is looked on as a journey from one life to the next (Rayner and Bilimoria 2010). The final life stage for older Hindus is called *Sannyasa Ashrama*: when the person mentally renounces all worldly ties. The elderly person entering this stage spends all their time in meditation and contemplation, pondering the mysteries of life. Hindus acknowledge the cycle of life and death where reincarnation of the person into different life forms continues until the person achieves moksha. Transcendence forms a part of the spiritual tasks of ageing for Hindus and, to an extent, relationships would involve good works towards others.[3] However, as Thursby notes, the spiritual journey for Hindus constitutes a path of spiritual development towards 'the cessation of a desire-driven identity, toward release, toward nirvana'. Thus release from suffering is not so much the transcendence of it, as it is dissolution of the 'self'. It follows then that 'impermanence is the actual condition of life in the world and the sense of a separate selfhood is inevitably a failing, a false refuge from it' (Thursby 2000, p. 171).

The 'four seals' of Buddhism belief are derived from observations of consciousness. The first seal is dukkha, meaning 'ill'. It recognises that suffering is a universal component of being human. The second is anatta, or 'no-self', and it states that there is no separately existing self:

Buddha's analysis of consciousness concluded that a separate self could not be found in any of the parts of awareness nor in the sum of the parts of awareness. All that could be found to exist was a set of connected events, objects, emotions, and thoughts. (Scotton 1998, p. 264)

---

[3] Personal communication from Ruwan Palapathwala.

Therefore 'reality' and 'self' were only a constantly changing scene of different events, and realising that is an essential step towards release from suffering.

Ways of Responding to Meaning

Although what brings ultimate meaning to people may be at the core of one's being, the ways that groups and individuals respond to meaning differs widely. At one level this is a very individual response but, at another, especially where religion is concerned, there are important community ways of responding to meaning, but even these community responses are coloured by culture. For example, Christians of Western European origins, or Eastern Orthodox, when compared with Christians of Asian, or Indigenous backgrounds will have different ways of using and responding to symbols and rituals and understandings of their religion. In my time in Japan, I was really impressed by the love and respect shown by care staff in a small group home where people with advanced dementia were being cared for. One example of their care, to honour the religious practices of their residents, was of an elderly woman who by this stage was in terminal stages of dementia and confined to bed. Twice every day they took her out of bed to worship at her Buddhist altar in her room; they saw this as being important for the woman, who could no longer speak or walk. Jewish teaching expects that Jews will continue to read the Torah for as long as they are able (Haber 2011). Hindus are likely to have a number of pictures or idols of gods in their homes that will support them in their practice of faith and prayer.

The Importance of Relationship, Spirituality, Culture and a Note of Caution

As in the model of spiritual tasks and process of ageing, MacKinlay (2001) that found relationship so important in later life, this importance is also visible in all the major faiths. The reciprocal nature of child–adult (and adult–child with older parent) relationship and continuing respect is readily apparent. Gratitude, which obviously operates within relationships, is seen as a virtue in Christianity, in Judaism and in Islam. It also features importantly in Buddhism and Hinduism. The Buddhist virtue of gratitude emerges from mutual obligations between generations, where children will willingly care and give to their parents (Ratanakul 2013). Responsibilities of relationship for Jews with their elders are written in the Commandments, which clearly set out the duties towards parents (as for Christians). Jewish scripture teaches respect and care for elders both through scripture and in action (Haber 2011): 'Honour your father and your mother ... that your days may be long, and that it may go well with you' (Deuteronomy 5: 16).

A great deal has been written about the distinctiveness of Jewish families, from the intensity of care-giving to low incidence of alcoholism. However, with increasing secularism in many places, according to Zedek (1998), this seems to be less clearly marked as it perhaps was in previous decades. The nature of relationship and caring in Jewish context arises from the Jewish notion of 'mitzvah of chesed', meaning acts of loving-kindness for Jews. There are a number of ways of working this out through relationship, such as inviting guests into one's home or visiting older people. The act of visiting the sick implies establishing a healing relationship between the sick person and the visitor (Friedman 2001).

During my visit to Japan, and while presenting my work on spiritual reminiscence for people with dementia, I was repeatedly asked by delegates and participants in sessions where I spoke about 'how can one have an intimate relationship with God?' As several of these people explained, they had read my account that was set in a Christian context. From their perspective, as people living in a culture that based its main rituals of life, birth, marriage and death around the practices of Shintoism, they could not understand this concept of relationship with God. My model presupposed a context where such a relationship with God could be present.

In Islamic teaching the importance of relationship is clearly seen in the care and respect shown to elders, especially to one's parents; where Abdulla and Patel say duty to one's parents is second only to prayer. The reciprocal nature of this is shown in these words from the Qur'an 17:23–4 (in Abdalla and Patel 2010, p. 118):

Your Lord has commanded that you worship none but Him, and be kind to your parents. If either or both of them reach old age with you, do not say '*uff*' to them or chide them, but speak to them in terms of honour and kindness. Treat them with humility, and say, 'My Lord! Have mercy on them, for they did care for me when I was little'.

Conclusion

This chapter has explored issues of spirituality of older people, and a model of spiritual tasks and process of ageing, designed from the stories of older people living in Australia. The model is a dynamic one with interactions identified between what lies at the core of one's being; the ways that people respond to life meaning; the relationship with the process of self-transcendence; finding final life meanings; issues of relationship and isolation; and finding hope.

It was asked if this model could be of value to older people from other faiths and cultures. Dialogue and presentation of the model in two different Asians countries showed that, at a very basic level, the spiritual dimension as set out in this model reached into the concerns and needs of older people from these cultures too. Where the main differences were seen was in the ways that culture overlays the core of the greatest depth of being of the individual, and thus the way that rituals and symbols express meaning and connection for people of different cultures and religions. These differences are very important but, at the same time, there is a commonality at the very essence of being, between all human beings.

It is all too easy to be ethnocentric and see only from one's own point of view, as we each have been formed into our culture from birth. We see others through our lenses of our culture, our religion and our society. Sometimes we are blinded to the cultural practices and beliefs of others. An important way forward in this area is surely to hold in tension the differences and similarities between cultures and faiths, listening to each other, respecting and affirming. We too often look only to see differences, instead of the similarities. At the same time, it is also vital not to water down faith differences, with the outcome that no faith is truly honoured because of the desire not to cause offence. For numbers of older people of deep faith, having grown in wisdom, self-acceptance and transcending the griefs and losses of later life, their desire is to reach out in love to others, and thus overcome many of the barriers between peoples.

References

Abdalla, M. and Patel, I. (2010). 'An Islamic perceptive on ageing and spirituality', in MacKinlay, E. (ed.) *Ageing and Spirituality across Faiths and Cultures.* London: Jessica Kingsley Publishers, pp. 112–123.

Brody, C. and Semel, V. (2006). *Strategies for Therapy with the Elderly: Living with Hope and Meaning.* New York: Springer Publishing Company.

Cohen, J. (2010). 'From ageing to sage-ing: Judaism and ageing', in MacKinlay, E. (ed.) *Ageing and Spirituality across Faiths and Cultures.* London: Jessica Kingsley Publishers, pp. 81–94.

Crites, S. (1997). 'The narrative quality of experience', in Hauerwas, S. and Jones, L. (eds.) *Readings in Narrative Theology: Why Narrative?* Eugene, OR: Wipf & Stock Publishers, pp. 65–88.

Erikson, E. (1997). *The Life Cycle Completed: Extended Version.* New York: W.W. Norton.

Erikson, E.H., Erikson, M., and Kivnick, H.Q. (1986). 'Ages and Stages', in *Vital Involvement in Old Age: The Experience of Old Age in our Time*. New York: W.W. Norton.

Frankl, V.E. (1984). *Man's Search for Meaning*. New York: Washington Square Press.

Frankl, V.E. (1997). *Man's Search for Ultimate Meaning*. Reading, MA: Perseus Books.

Fowler, J.W. (1981). *Stages of Faith: The Psychology of Human Development and the Quest for Meaning*. San Francisco: Harper.

Friedman, D.A. (2001). *Jewish Pastoral Care: A Practical Handbook from Traditional and Contemporary Sources*. Woodstock, VT: Jewish Lights Publishing.

Geertz, C. (1969). *Islam Observed: Religious Development in Morocco and Indonesia*. Chicago: Chicago University Press.

Geertz, C. (1975). *The Interpretation of Cultures*. London: Hutchinson.

Haber, D. (2011). 'Jewish aging: Model programs in social service, adult learning, intergenerational exchange and research', *Journal of Religion, Spirituality and Aging* 23: 304–317.

Hauerwas, S. and Jones, L.G. (eds.) (1997). *Readings in Narrative Theology: Why Narrative?* Eugene, OR: Wipf & Stock Publishers.

Herth, K.A. and Cutcliffe, J.R. (2002). 'The concept of hope in nursing 4: hope and gerontological nursing', *British Journal of Nursing* 11(17): 1148–1156.

Hodge, D.R. (2002). 'Working with Muslim youths: Understanding the values and beliefs of Islamic discourse', *Children and Schools* 24(1): 6–21.

Hughes, J.C., Louw, S.J., and Sabat, S.R. (eds.) (2006). *Dementia, Mind, Meaning, and the Person*. Oxford: Oxford University Press.

Husain, S.A. (1998). 'Religion and mental health from the Muslim perspective', in Koenig, H.G. (ed.) *Handbook of Religion and Mental Health*. San Diego: Academic Press.

Juthani, N.V. (1998). 'Understanding and treating Hindu patients', in Koenig, H.G. (ed.) *Handbook of Religion and Mental Health*. San Diego: Academic Press.

Kenyon, G.M., Clark, P., and de Vries, B. (2001) (eds.). *Narrative Gerontology: Theory, Research, and Practice*. New York: Springer.

Lash, N. (1997). 'Ideology, metaphor, and analogy', in Hauerwas, S. and Jones, L.G. (eds.) *Readings in Narrative Theology: Why Narrative?* Eugene OR: Wipf & Stock Publishers, pp. 113–137.

MacKinlay, E.B. (2001). *The Spiritual Dimension of Ageing*. London: Jessica Kingsley Publishers.

MacKinlay, E.B. (2006). *Spiritual Growth and Care in the Fourth Age of Life*. London: Jessica Kingsley Publishers.

MacKinlay, E.B. (2009). 'Using spiritual reminiscence with a small group of Latvian residents with dementia in a nursing home', *Journal of Religion, Spirituality and Aging* 21(4): 318–329.

MacKinlay, E.B. (2010). 'Ageing and spirituality: Living and being in multifaith and multicultural communities', in MacKinlay, E. (ed.) *Ageing and Spirituality across Faiths and Cultures*. London: Jessica Kingsley Publishers, pp. 11–21.

MacKinlay, E.B. (2012). 'Resistance, resilience and change: the person and dementia', *Journal of Religion, Spirituality and Aging* 24(1–2): 80–92.

MacKinlay, E.B. and Trevitt, C. (2007). 'Spiritual care and ageing in a secular society', *The Medical Journal of Australia* 186(10): S74–S76.

MacKinlay, E.B. and Trevitt, C. (2012). *Finding Meaning in the Experience of Dementia: The Place of Spiritual Reminiscence Work*. London: Jessica Kingsley Publishers.

Palapathwala, R. (2006). 'Ageing and death: A Buddhist-Christian conceptual framework for spirituality in later life', *Journal of Religion, Spirituality and Aging* 18 (2–3): 153–168.

Ratanakul, P. (2013). 'Reflections of aging in Buddhist Thailand', *Journal of Religion, Spirituality and Aging* 25: 12–19.

Rayner, A. and Bilimoria, P. (2010). 'Dying: An approach to care from Hindu and Buddhist perspectives', in MacKinlay, E. (ed.) *Ageing and Spirituality across Faiths and Cultures*. London: Jessica Kingsley Publishers, pp. 138–151.

Scotton, B.W. (1998). 'Treating Buddhist patients', in Koenig, H.G. (ed.) *Handbook of Religion and Mental Health*. San Diego: Academic Press, pp. 263–270.

Swinton, J. (2012). *Dementia: Living in the Memories of God*. Grand Rapids: Eerdmans.

Tillich, P. (1963). *Systemic Theology*, vol. 3. Chicago: The University of Chicago Press.

Thursby, G.R. (2000). 'Ageing in eastern religious traditions', in Cole, T.R., Kastenbaum, R., and Ray, R.E. (eds.) *Handbook of the Humanities and Aging*. New York: Springer Publishing Company, pp. 155–180.

Tornstam, L. (2005). *Gerotranscendence: A Developmental Theory of Positive Aging*. New York: Springer Publishing Company.

Zedek, M.R. (1998). 'Religion and mental health from the Jewish perspective', in Koenig, H.G. (ed.) (1998) *Handbook of Religion and Mental Health*. San Diego: Academic Press.

4   Stages of the Soul and Spirituality in Later Life

Harry R. Moody

The second half of life can be a time of growth in spiritual understanding and we can recognize this development if we know what to look for. It is only relatively recently that gerontology has begun to recognize this process (MacKinlay, 2001; Atchley, 2009; Coleman, 2011), and it is time to chart and analyze the process of spiritual development in later life. Building on the idea of stages in spiritual growth (Fowler, 1981), in *The Five Stages of the Soul* I described this process in terms of the Call, Search, Struggle, Breakthrough, and Return (Moody, 1997). Here we offer an approach to these stages not only in conscious experience but also through dreams.

Call

The Call is the moment of awakening of our "soul," the first of the stages of the soul when this inward dimension comes to life. It is that moment when we "come to ourselves" and ask the perennial questions: Who am I? Where am I going? What is this life all about? These questions are painful because, as James Hollis puts it (Hollis, 2006), by midlife the personality we have become is frequently our chief obstacle to listening to the Call. Yet in the second half of life this inner voice demands to be heard. As Jung (1973, 17, par. 307) put it: "Only the man who can consciously assent to the power of the inner voice becomes a personality." Yet this "still small voice" is hard to hear. Everything around us conspires to keep us from hearing the Call, from looking inside ourselves, as Sogyal Rinpoche (1992, p. 52) puts it so well:

Looking in will require of us great subtlety and great courage—nothing less than a complete shift in our attitude to life and to the mind. We are so addicted to looking outside ourselves that we have lost access to our inner being almost completely. We are terrified to look inward, because our culture has given us no idea of what we will find.

One of the simplest, and most powerful, images of the "Call" that appears in a dream is recorded by Sheila Moon, from her autobiography inspired by dreams in the second half of life (Moon, 1983, p. 21).

The Voice

I am walking alone in a deep forest. A voice says, "This way is the Will of God.'

Later in her late forties Moon had another clear and powerful dream (Moon, 1983, p. 97):

A voice says, 'Stop seeking who you are and start asking whom you seek.'

Sheila Moon notes this as part of a series of "religious dreams" in which the Voice of the Other is filled with numinous power and mystery. This dream was literally a Call from On High reminding her, and all of us, of what it means to be lost in unconsciousness, in blind habits, of the danger "of being too ego-centered and negatively self-centered." The Bible has verses where the Call is clearly delineated, as in First Kings (19:11–12): "And behold, the Lord passed by, and a great and strong wind tore into the mountains and broke the rocks in pieces before the Lord, but the Lord was not in the wind; and after the wind an earthquake, but the Lord was not in the earthquake; and after the earthquake a fire, but the Lord was not in the fire; and after the fire a still small voice."

The Call is the first stage of the awakening of the soul, the moment when a spiritual yearning penetrates our ordinary understanding of self and world. The Call challenges us, but we may not know what to make of it. Here is a dream of Helen Luke, at age 59, recorded in her journal in old age (Luke, 2000, p. 221).

Cube Descending

I dreamed there was a great cube of stone which was also pure light, apricot-colored dawn light, that came crashing through the root of a great barn. A small chip from the stone had flown and into me unseen. I was so excited by its beauty that I called urgently to [my friend] Else to come and see it – whereupon immediately the stone began to rise again and disappeared through the roof.

The images of "Cube Descending" are contradictory: the cube is made of stone yet it is also made of light, indeed dawn light, suggesting the beginning of illumination or enlightenment. The experience of the Call, the first stage of the soul, can also be a bona fide experience of the numinous, as in this dream. The stone itself signifies a completely transcendent experience, but here only a small chip from the stone has flown into the dreamer. She thereupon wants to talk about it to her friend, but as soon as she tries to do so, the stone begins to rise and disappear through the roof, moving back into the higher realm from which it descended. The message of the dream is that when we experience the Call it may not be so easily shared with others. Indeed, the very attempt to talk about transpersonal experiences can somehow spoil the experience and make it less accessible to us.

Search

Christopher Bamford, in "The Gift of the Call," writes about the Search that comes after the Call (Bamford, 2005, p. 1): "Answering the call, one becomes a seeker. In my own case, following the call to live otherwise, I sought a different approach. Seeking to awaken from the nightmare of sleep, of egotism run amuck in the world, I studied alternative ways of knowing. I began time-tested practices of meditation, prayer, and attention. I steep myself in esoteric theologies, cosmologies, and philosophies." Bamford, in other words, had entered, the "spiritual marketplace" of our time and of all times (Roof, 1999). But in that marketplace, how to know where to find guidance for nourishing food (Caplan, 2009)?

If we are unsure about what we need or who to trust, then we may feel we have no choice but to rely on ourselves, to try to "see for ourselves." This is not an easy thing to do. The Search may begin with impure or mixed motives. We are still identified with our egos, so why would the Search be any different? Ego enters there, too. But dreams come from another level than the conscious ego, so dreams can give us clues about how to learn to "see for ourselves." Dreams can remind us, too, that this stage of the Search is a time of utmost seriousness. To find guidance, we may need to separate ourselves from people around us, people who, at bottom, are not serious.

This is a dream of Helen Luke, age seventy-three, recorded in her journal (Luke, 2000, p. 140).

Seeing Clearly

> *In my dream I had lost my spectacles, and first my friend Jane offered to lend me a pair of hers but I could see nothing through them. Then my friend Else offered hers and, though I could have seen enough to read through them, they were otherwise no use to me. Then I realized that I had my own glasses all the time but had been looking through them upside down. As soon as I turned them the right way up, I could see perfectly well.*

In the Hindu tradition there is a famous parable of a woman distraught because she has lost a precious jewel. She runs around frantically seeking the lost jewel, until suddenly she discovers it was hanging around her neck the whole time. This is a Vedantic allegory of the process of

Enlightenment. The goal we seek, the jewel we imagine we have lost, is not far off. In fact, we carry it around with us all the time. The problem is that we are looking in the wrong places. Or we are looking at the world through the wrong lenses, as suggested by the dream "Seeing Clearly."

Over a long life, by age seventy-three Helen Luke pursued self-knowledge through a variety of paths, as she tells us in her autobiography. This pursuit is what I describe as the stage of the Search. But, as the dream tells us, the Search is not for something outside of ourselves. Indeed, as long as we adopt another person's point of view, we fail to use our own capacity to see into the nature of things. In "Seeing Clearly" Jane's glasses do not permit the dreamer to see anything while Else's glasses are barely enough to read by. In short, we cannot rely on other people in order to see for ourselves.

Moving into old age, the dreamer struggles with the dynamics of individuation, with the need to stand on one's own feet, see with one's own eyes. In her dream, Helen Luke cannot see without her spectacles. But it is no use borrowing other people's glasses: Jane's glasses give no help and Else's glasses are only partially useful. Finally, the dreamer realizes she is in the same position as the woman looking for the lost jewel but carrying it around her neck: "I had my own glasses all the time." But Helen Luke had been looking through them upside down. Once turned right side up, her vision is perfect.

This image is a wonderful illustration of the psychological situation that persists as long as we try to imitate other people, itself the product of what we commonly call "socialization." This process of internalizing social imperatives may include spiritual beliefs that we borrow from others but do not make genuinely our own. In later life, such "borrowed beliefs," like borrowed glasses, are likely to prove useless and so we can become disillusioned. Erik Erikson spoke of later life as a time of the psychological struggle between what he called ego-integrity versus despair (Erikson & Erikson, 1998). There is no simple answer to the temptation of despair. But the solution must be to see things through our own eyes, demanding help (spectacles) but help uniquely suited to our distinctive vision.

The moment of insight occurs when the dreamer realizes she has had her own glasses all along "but had been looking through them upside down." This moment is a reversal of perspective – like a visual figure-ground shift – that occurs at the moment of insight. Hindu tradition teaches that looking at the world of Maya (illusion) is like looking at a rope which we take to be a snake. We are terrified of the snake until, in a single moment, we realize that it was an illusion all along. This is the moment of enlightenment. So too, as soon as the dreamer turns her glasses right side up, she can see "perfectly well." The message is that she has always had her own glasses, her own means of seeing into the nature of things. The dream is a reminder that the goal is not far off: it requires only a reversal of perspective, for the dreamer and for all of us.

Sometimes it is a Wise Old Woman who offers guidance in dreams, as in the following example (Vaughan-Lee, 1998, pp. 12–13).

Guiding Light

I am reading a book, but the light gets slowly dimmer and dimmer. I bring the light closer to the book, but finally the light goes out. The door opens and on the landing is an old lady with white hair. She beckons and I follow her downstairs. The downstairs room is full of light. There are great trees growing in it.

The stage of the soul called the Search is vividly portrayed in this dream. This dreamer, the Sufi writer Llewellyn Vaughan-Lee, had realized he could not rely on his own sight because the light is gradually getting dimmer and he can no longer read the book in front of him. He needs guidance, he needs to see clearly but he cannot.

At this point in the dream a mysterious figure appears, an old lady with white hair. She is not named or further described, but we recognize her as the archetypal figure Jung called "the Wise Old Woman," the one who can provide guidance to the dreamer. He follows her downstairs: that is, down into a deeper level in himself, where the room is full of light. The last image in the dream is not the illumination of a book but instead an image of "great trees" growing in the "downstairs room." Having descended to this deeper level in himself, the dreamer is now in contact with new energies of growth, symbolized by great trees that grow out of the interior depth to which the Search may lead.

The relationship between therapy and faith is a complex one. Viktor Frankl, creator of logotherapy, cites the case of a dream of a patient in therapy who, on her way to the psychiatrist's office, passed by a particular church. She would often think to herself that she was on her way to God, not through the church directly but instead through psychotherapy. Going to therapy was, in a sense, a "detour" to the church. Then in a dream she found herself entering the very same church she often used to pass by in waking life. Here is her dream (Frankl, 2000, pp. 50–51):

The Deserted Church

The church seems deserted. The church is entirely bombed out; the roof has fallen in, and only the altar remains intact. The blue heavens shine through here; the air is free. But above me is still the remainder of the roof, beams that

*threaten to fall down, and I am afraid of that. And I flee into the open,
somewhat disappointed.*

Frankl notes that the fact that the church in this dream seems deserted
really suggests that it is the dreamer who has deserted the church. The
imagery of the dream begins to tell us why. Her familiar religious faith is
portrayed in the dream as merely a shell, a structure that is "bombed
out," with its "roof fallen in." "Only the altar remains intact." The altar,
of course, is the center of spiritual life, where the divine mystery unfolds.
Above this mysterious center is the path to what is transcendent: the
"blue heavens" and the free air. Frankl suggests that the remaining
beams of the structure threaten to fall down on this dreamer because
she is afraid of once again being trapped in the debris of a religion that is
only a wrecked shell of what it is supposed to be. Religious institutions
have proved disappointing to this dreamer: "I flee into the open, somewhat disappointed." Interestingly, the dreamer in "The Deserted
Church" had actually experienced ecstatic mystical states. Frankl tells
of another dream of hers where she found herself standing in front of the
main door of a great Cathedral, only to find that the door was closed. She
continued: "In the Cathedral it is dark, but I know God is there." As that
dream unfolded, it displayed other symbols of the Search: for example,
the dreamer kept searching for an entrance into the Cathedral, then she
found herself looking through a small window, then again running
through narrow passages, reminding us of the Gospel verse: "Straight is
the gate and narrow the way that leads to Eternal Life."

All of these images of the Search emphasize us that even where the
visible Church seems "deserted" or "dark" or "closed," there is another
side to things. But there is also an underground tradition that Jacob
Needleman (2003) in his book titled *Lost Christianity*, Needleman's book
on this topic was subtitled "a journey of rediscovery." The subtitle is a
fitting description of what for the stage of the Search.

Struggle

In terms of the five stages of the soul, we do not go directly from Call to
Breakthrough. Before reaching Paradise, Dante had to move through
Purgatory: a "dark night of the soul." The stage of Struggle in our dreams
is the realm of Purgatory, as Helen Luke (Luke, 1995, p. 52) observes:
"There are no dreams in Hell; there are no dreams in Heaven; for both
realms are outside time." In Hell, she suggests, "we are possessed by the
archetypes in the unconscious [and] we cannot relate to them, and there
is no process, no dialogue between dream and consciousness; the dream
world has swallowed us up, and we are driven round and round forever at

the mercy of instinctive drives and ego-desires." The state of bliss, in Paradise, is bestowed by "great angelic and human powers of the psyche," in a state beyond time, which is what is conveyed by dreams of Breakthrough. As Dante moves up the mountain of Purgatory, there is an alternation between day and night, for the soul is suffering from the tension between opposites and the long Struggle mirrored in our dreams.

One of the greatest of the Jewish Hassidim was Rabbi Nachman of Bratislav. Nachman is especially to consider here because his spiritual quest centered around the Struggle. In fact, a major biography of Nachman was titled *Tormented Master*. Here is one of Rabbi Nachman's dreams, from the year 1804, reported to his faithful disciple Nathan, who faithfully recorded it (Green, 1992, p. 165). The central image in the dream is a **zaddiq**, a saint or holy man.

The Unclean Saint

I was living in a certain city, which in the dream appeared to be very large. A zaddiq of olden times came along, one who was considered a very great zaddiq. Everyone was going out to him, and I too went along. Then I saw that when they reached him, everyone passed him by and nobody stopped to greet him. It seemed that they were doing so intentionally. I was most astonished at their audacity, for I knew the man to be a great zaddiq. Then I asked how it was that they had the nerve not to greet such a man. I was told that he was indeed a great zaddiq, but that his body was made up of various unclean parts, despite the fact that he himself was a great man. He had taken it upon himself to redeem this body, but since 'one should not greet one's fellowman in an unclean place,' no one offered any greeting to him.

The saint in this dream is a figure of purity and holiness. But what is the "uncleanness" of the saint in Rabbi Nachman's dream? The dream image of the holy man may represent Rabbi Nachman's own sexuality, since we know that he struggled against that, beginning in his adolescence, as Mahatma Gandhi did all his life. This interpretation would be consistent with a traditional Christian, ascetic ideal where the Struggle is understood to be a conflict between the spirit and the flesh.

But another interpretation of Rabbi Nachman's Struggle is possible. In his own words (Green, 1992, p. 164), "The main thing is that one must struggle with all one's strength to be joyous always. It is in the nature of man to be drawn into melancholy and sadness, because of the things that happen to him; every man is filled with sorrow." There are of course countless Jewish jokes about preoccupation with "*tsuris*," a Yiddish word meaning "trouble." Any such preoccupation is understandable in light of long Jewish experience of persecution. But the temptation to incline toward melancholy is not limited to Jewish circles. Rabbi Nachman's dream reminds us that the Struggle is actually much more subtle than it might seem.

The quest of the spiritual seeker is vast, just like the city in Rabbi Nachman's dream which "appeared to be very large." Even a great saint, a **zaddiq**, can be tempted to lose hope: "The main thing is that one must struggle with all one's strength to be joyous always." Perhaps it is not a paradox that this "tormented master" would understand so clearly that the real Struggle is to effort to find joy in life, to "give up suffering." Here is where the genuine Struggle is to be found: to find a way through the "eye of the needle." Dreamwork can be a valuable part of that Struggle.

Rabbi Nachman would go on to use many of his dreams as a basis for his tales and teachings, which have been widely influential down to our own time. Yet it remains true to this day that few in the Jewish mainstream tradition have shown much interest in cultivating dreams, no more so than Christians (Covitz, 1990).

Here is another dream from Helen Luke, this time at age forty-seven (Luke, 2000, p. 107).

The Diamond Dentist

I dreamed that I had been to a dentist for many sessions and that he had now cleaned out all the decay hidden in my teeth, and each one awaited filling. The dentist told me that he was about to fill them with diamonds, but that this would take a very long time and would be exceedingly painful. I must tell him when I wished to begin. I was frightened of the pain and hoped I could wait a day or two, but I knew it couldn't be long delayed.

The diamond is the hardest substance found in nature. But its symbolic meaning points beyond nature toward the Spirit. Thus, in Eastern spiritual traditions the diamond commonly represents an indestructible spiritual reality within us, akin to the "pearl of great price" mentioned in the Gospels, or the "Blessed Pearl" in Islamic tradition. Sometimes also described as the "jewel in the Lotus," the diamond symbolizes a transcendent and immortal substance within the human personality. All of these images are different symbols of the image of God within the soul, or the archetype of the Self, as Jung would put it.

In Helen Luke's dream, she is in the hands of a dentist, a healer who has removed all the decay from her teeth. Our teeth after all are the organ by which we chew our food and get the nutrition we need to live. When teeth decay we may not know about it for a long time. The decay can take place deep below the surface, as the decay of the soul can take place below the level of consciousness. Yet that decay, of teeth or of the soul, if left unchecked will eventually deprive us of our teeth and so prevent us from gaining the nutrition we need to stay alive. The symbolic role of healing and cleaning decay in this dream is very strong and powerful.

Yet there is a puzzle in this dream. The dentist tells Helen Luke that the cleaning is complete. Now he is ready to put in the fillings. But instead of gold or silver, he will put in diamonds and this process "would take a very long time and would be exceedingly painful." What can this warning mean? People of a certain age will remember childhood visits to the dentist – typically without Novocain – when the dentist drilled to teeth to remove decay. This was the painful part, not putting in the fillings. In Helen Luke's dream, the process is exactly reversed. The removal of decay is finished and now the painful part will be putting in the fillings, the diamonds. How can this be? There may be a suggestion here that our ordinary conception of the spiritual Struggle is limited or even mistaken.

We typically imagine that a "Struggle" will be painful and then followed by Enlightenment, perhaps even some kind of happiness or bliss. But "The Diamond Dentist" gives a very different message. If the diamond filling represents Enlightenment, or a spiritual Breakthrough, it evidently will "take a very long time" and will be "exceedingly painful." The Struggle, we begin to surmise, should not be thought of as a discipline capped by "the pursuit of happiness," as Americans often think of it. On the contrary, the spiritual seeker should think long and hard about embarking on this effort, because "right effort," as Buddhism would put, may involve much more than discipline-followed-by-reward (as the ordinary mind thinks of it). When his disciples asked the Buddha about his state and what it was like, he replied, simply, "I am awake." Enlightenment, then, should not be thought of as absence of pain. On the contrary, to have our decayed teeth replaced by this numinous diamond substance may be something painful and frightening. To pursue the Struggle, and to achieve Breakthrough, represents the very highest challenge to our sense of how we are and who we might become.

I conclude this discussion of the Struggle with a dream of my own. My dream invokes the life of Rumi, someone whose life and work had long been a great inspiration to me.

False Teeth

I dreamed I was giving a lecture about the life of Persian poet Jalal ad-din Rumi. I had reached the point in his life story when, at age 37, he was giving a lecture and was interrupted by Shams ad-din at-Tabrizi, an event which totally redirected his life. At that point, I noticed one of my teeth had fallen out. I looked at it, realized it was a false tooth and went to the bathroom to put it back in my mouth. But before I could do that I noticed that all my upper teeth had come out. They were all false. I woke up suddenly and noticed the time on the clock.

To understand the meaning of this dream we need to know something about the life of Rumi. As an academic myself, I naturally identified with Rumi because Rumi during his early career had been trained as a rigorous scholar. He mastered all the fields of learning of his time, but he eventually turned away from scholarship in favour of a spiritual path (Lewis, 2000). The turning point came in Rumi's encounter with Shams, a dramatic moment of midlife transition when Rumi realized that his entire life up to that point had been artificial, based on rationalism: on logic instead of life. In short, Rumi was teaching an "idea" about religion rather than actually living the genuine spiritual experience.

Rumi's encounter with Shams was captured in a famous story told about the two of them. According to this tale, Shams heard Rumi preaching one day and promptly threw all Rumi's cherished books into a pool of water. Rumi expressed outrage, but Shams, miraculously, fetched the books out of the water and handed them back to Rumi, now all completely dry. The miracle changed Rumi's mind in an instant. At that point, Rumi immediately went off with Shams and began a new way of life. His meeting that day was his entry into the Sufi path.

In my dream, while I was giving my lecture about Rumi, I was able to trace his life up to that crucial turning point. But then I discovered that I had a false tooth that fell out – and, in fact, I realized that all my upper teeth, like the upper level of the self, were actually false. Like Rumi's meeting with Shams, my dream was a message about the need to Struggle against falsehood in myself. The encounter with the false self is at the heart of the Struggle and this remains true no matter how far we have seemingly "advanced" on a spiritual path. As James Hollis put it, "Even though we suffer within the constraints of the false self, we cling to it desperately." Like false teeth which help us to chew, there is a way in which we actually need this false self to make our way through the world. As children, we imitate, and then the imitations become a habit, and eventually a false self. To grow up is, in part, to acquire a usable, but false, self that functions well in the world.

The stage of Struggle is the time when we must confront this false self and recognize it for what it is. As in my dream, when we notice that our "false tooth" has fallen out, the first impulse is to put the tooth back in its place, which is what psychological defense mechanisms accomplish. But such defenses only keep us asleep, keep us immune to what Gurdjieff called "the terror of the situation." In the stage of Struggle, we need to wake up, as the dreamer does here when he is shocked to realize that all the upper teeth are in fact false. That is the moment when I, the dreamer, dramatically woke up in my bed and noticed the time on the clock: time is running out. The time for waking up is now.

Breakthrough

The stage of the soul called the Breakthrough is that point which William James recognized as a great awakening, when spiritual forces collecting inside can no longer be held in check. A sudden surge of energy pushes things to the limit and there follows a burst of vision. Something is changed and we are never the same. This inner awakening, or moment of illumination, can come in a dream. But the conviction of the dreamer is that at that time one has truly never been more awake or alive.

We have earlier followed the dreams of Helen Luke and recorded her Search and Struggle. In her old age, at age 85, she had the following Breakthrough dream, recorded in her journal (Luke, 2000, p. 249).

In the Eye of the Storm

I was standing in a sphere, colorless, empty, and moving slowly and calmly from side to side. I was holding out my cupped hand, into which a succession of small spheres, each representing my next task or the next small necessity of my life, was gently put by an unseen giver hidden in the storm clouds surrounding the eye, the calm center. This center space itself moved, as I moved within it, with the movement of the clouds or unseen forces around it – the eye of the storm.

This late-life dream contains an astonishing image of integration of the self and transcendence of the self: it is the numinous symbol of a perfect sphere, empty, like the Buddhist concept of the Void (Sunyata). But this void is also full: it is filled with activity, pure energy. There are "storm clouds," the small necessities of life, and the outstretched hands of the dreamer.

The sphere represents totality and perfection, the unity of the self and of the Divine beyond words ("colorless, empty"), as the medieval mystic Nicholas of Cusa puts it in describing God as "a circle whose circumference is nowhere and whose center is everywhere." The dreamer is here embraced in a perfect sphere and she herself receives in her cupped hand a series of small spheres, symbols of all the multiple tasks of life. The unspoken message is that the life-course itself is contained and guided by a divine "unseen giver." Later life, even amid a storm of losses, moves onward, like the dreamer in this center space. At the calm still point of the circle, in the eye of a storm, the dreamer is embraced by what a late medieval writer called "the Cloud of Unknowing."

Helen Luke kept a journal of dreams throughout her long life. But now, in her ninth decade, she has been given a wonderful gift of seeing how the turbulent storm of life contains a hidden stillness, the Witness that beholds all things from a calm center, deep in the eye of the storm. Here is an example of a contemporary Christian dream that illustrates the Breakthrough stage of the soul. This is the dream, again a very brief one, of an eighty-year old woman, shortly before her own death (Elrod, 1987, in von Franz, p. 134).

Center of the Cross

She saw a cross; at the center stood a radiating sapphire. She knew in the dream she was experiencing a moment of heavenly existence.

This Breakthrough is an anticipation of the bliss of Paradise. If the cross is the symbol of sacrifice, the dream intimates that at the center of sacrifice is a rotating jewel, the radiating sapphire that conveys a transcendent connection with the divine.

Actress Ellen Burstyn's career has seen many triumphant moments, including her performance in "The Last Picture Show" and "The Exorcist," as well as an Academy Award for Best Actress in the film "Alice Doesn't Live Here Anymore." Burstyn went on to become President of Actor's Equity as well as the Actor's Studio. Along with her career success, she has pursued a spiritual quest that led her to explore Jungian psychology and Sufism. At age 63, she had the following dream (Burstyn, 2006, p. 401).

The Pattern in the Room

I had a dream that I was with a group of people in a room and we were working to make the room and everything in it disappear. We succeeded, and when everything—the room, its contents, and the people—had completely dematerialized, there was nothing left except an awareness of the pattern that had been there. Then the awareness spoke: 'Ah, consciousness remains, and that consciousness fills the inner screen with light.' In the dream I thought, 'You need ego to do this.'

The dream represented a culmination of Burstyn's struggle for many years surrounding the idea of individuation. Her autobiography is titled *Lessons in Becoming Myself.* At the same time, the dream points toward a message of self-transcendence – "dropping personal identity," in the words of one of Burstyn's teachers, Carlos Casteneda. Emily Dickinson said something similar in her lines: "I'm nobody. Who are you? Are you nobody, too?" Yet how do we learn to realize that we are "nobody": that is, not the self we think ourselves to be. It is the whole point of spiritual development, of the five stages of the soul.

Following her Breakthrough dream, Burstyn pursued those questions by accompanying Robert Thurman, noted American scholar of Tibetan Buddhism, on a trip to Bhutan. Although that trip was filled with profound insights, it also brought Burstyn back to a sense of her own Return, to her quest as a Sufi and to her roots in Christianity, which she had turned away from earlier. Just as the dream had affirmed the importance of ego as well as transcendence, so Ellen Burstyn's spiritual quest had brought her to an awareness of the essential truth and unity of the teachings of all the great world religions.

A Breakthrough dream carries with it a conviction of revelation, of having been in contact with absolute reality, as in this dream from the renowned scholar of comparative religion, Mircea Eliade (2006, p. 48).

Simplicity

And suddenly, I understood: everything became extraordinarily clear and simple. Everything: life, death, the meaning of existence. And even stronger than this revelation was my surprise: how had no one on earth yet understood this thing, so extraordinarily simple? ... I had the feeling that a message had been transmitted to me, that I should remember [it] so as to be able to communicate it to men. I woke up... with this idea in mind: not to forget what I had seen. A second later, I had forgotten.

One can only remember the lines from the old Shaker hymn: "'Tis a gift to be simple, 'Tis a gift to be free, 'Tis a gift to come down where we ought to be." Yet the dream concludes on a problematic note: "A second later, I had forgotten." The ending poses the great question about Breakthrough dreams: how do we remember them and carry over the message into ordinary waking life?

Return

We cannot remain forever on the mountaintop, in the stage of Breakthrough. As long as we live, we must again return to ordinary life and bring with us that "taste of eternity" which Rumi invokes. As the Sufis understood, our task is to be "in the world but not of it" and this task belongs to the last stage of the soul, the Return. As Jack Kornfeld so memorably phrased it, after Enlightenment, then the laundry.

A Breakthrough dream is a "big dream," but it is not a gift for the dreamer alone. As Joseph Campbell says: "A myth is a public dream; a dream is a private myth." The stage of Return demands that we bring together the public and the private world. Those who disregard dreams forget this challenge. Instead, they follow the aphorism of Heraclitus:

"The waking have one world, while in sleep each man turns in toward his own." But a "private myth" suggests something more, and there lies the challenge. How can we make a transition between private dream and collective reality, between nighttime and daytime? How do we turn from our own private world to the wider world?

Anthony Shafton (1995, p. 81) reminds us that the term "big dream" can be used in several different ways: "Sometimes it refers to archetypal dreams, especially to obvious and numinous ones; sometimes, to any dream of particular vividness or narrative coherence; sometimes, to a dream of notable significance for the dreamer, and sometimes, to dreams of significance for the dreamer's community, dreams dreamt for the benefit of the social collective, especially by prominent individuals and/ or in heightened circumstances." In the stage of the Return, we are concerned with dreams "for the benefit of the social collective" where the lessons of a big dream, a Breakthrough dream, are brought back to ordinary waking consciousness and to the shared world beyond the dreamer.

Those proceeding through the five stages of the soul are faced with a distinctive challenge as they move from a Breakthrough dream into the many problems faced in the Return. The test of the Return may force us to confront what Tibetan Buddhist teacher Trungpa Rinpoche called "spiritual materialism." This temptation was described well by St. John of the Cross in these terms: "The soul that is attached to anything, however much good there may be in it, will not arrive at the liberty of the divine." Breakthrough experiences, including dreams, in short, can be a temptation. Jack Kornfield describes the power of spiritual materialism in terms of what Buddhists call "near enemies." These are qualities in us that are actually only an imitation of spirituality, not the real thing. These states separate us from true feeling instead of connecting us. For example, Buddha spoke about loving-kindness, compassion, sympathetic joy, and equanimity. But each of these states also has a "near enemy" that mimics it, as Christians know from the saying "Satan is the ape of God." For instance, we might respond to other people's pain with pity, but this attitude is not the same as true compassion. Or we might have in our hearts indifference, which is not the same as equanimity, and so on.

The gift of dreams is not for ourselves alone but for others, for "the planet on which I live": in short, on behalf of what the Kabbalah calls **tikkun alam**, or "healing the world," the final task of the Return. We see an evolution toward this wider consciousness in Sheila Moon's lifelong record of dreaming in *The Dreams of a Woman*. Toward the very end of her book, Moon, now in her late sixties, records a series of dreams involving childbirth, where she is pregnant, although in fact Moon was never married and was never a mother in a literal sense. She concluded from these dreams that "much was coming to birth in the psyche" even though her conscious ego could not fully understand its meaning. She titles her last chapter "Not the End" where she explicitly acknowledges an obligation toward future generations, as in this dream (Moon, 1983, p. 188).

The School of Healing

I am in a school where one is taught medicine for healing. It is large, labyrinthine, mostly waterways ... My teachers are two aged women ... I am an experienced student so I am helper to younger ones.

The school of healing represents a prime activity of dreamwork, the encounter with a vast labyrinth of waterways, the interior depths of the self, just as one sees in another of Sheila Moon's dreams, "City Under the Sea." But in "The School of Healing" there is more than a Breakthrough; the dream includes a Return to help young people and successor generations.

Sheila Moon expressed her sense of the Return quite strongly after she had had one particularly vivid dream. Despite the power of that dream, she wrote (Moon, 1983, p. 205), "Such a dream is only valuable as it is enfleshed and lived in the outer world ... If inner experiences remain only inner, no matter how exciting they may be they are only a trip in the worst sense of the word." On the one hand, there is the Breakthrough: "I had then a deep sense of faith of knowing, as if I would never be the same again." On the other hand, there is the Return that points to "healing, both of myself and others, to see humanity naked, scarred, but healable." In the concluding words of her book, Sheila Moon invokes this passage from Breakthrough to Return: "I do know that the religious significance of any existence lies in my working for simplicity, purity of line, leanness. To the degree that I can learn how to do this in myself I can give something to the planet on which I live."

In more recent times, dreams of the Return can bring a message to transform the world. Consider the case of Mahatma Gandhi, who faced many frustrations in his effort to preach a message of nonviolence opposing British colonial rule in India. Over and over again, Gandhi could not find the right method to put his message into practice. For example, after the terrible Rowlett Act riots in India, angry crowds rose up and burned buildings and killed policemen. Gandhi tried to speak out against the violence, but no one listened to him. All his efforts at nonviolence were blocked, and he felt himself isolated and helpless.

At this point he withdrew to enter a period of Struggle through prayer and fasting and then one morning he woke up with the following dream (cited by Taylor, 1992, pp. 118–120).

Interfaith Action

The Congress Party organizers should call upon the leaders of the many diverse and warring religious groups in India—Hindu and Moslem, Parsi and Jain, Buddhist and Sikh—to abandon their respective traditional calendars for public ritual gathering and practice their respective festivals of prayer and public process at the same time.

Gandhi famously said, "Be the change you want to see in the world," and so he understood his dream to be a specific instruction to him, and he acted upon it. He called upon Nehru and the whole Congress party to bring all the religious sects in India together at once where he would impose a nonviolent strategy in practice. It was reported that Gandhi's proposal was greeted with ridicule by Nehru and Gandhi's other advisors. But Gandhi was resolute. His dream had convinced him of the need for Hartal, a Sanskrit word that can be defined as "public prayer and celebration."

Gandhi's dream had very significant consequences: he launched the strike, the first successful general strike, which paralyzed the entire country. His dream had inspired interfaith collaboration, and before long the Colonial Government repealed the hated Rowlett Acts that had triggered the violence. Gandhi's inspired action eventually succeeded in his life-long hope for independence in India. The result came about because Gandhi's dream moved through the cycle of Struggle to Return. Perhaps more than any other modern figure, Gandhi represented the union between ancient spiritual tradition and modern actions to improve the world. A key to his success lay in listening to the message of his dreams.

In conclusion, we offer another dream (Edinger, 1992, p. 218) that presents a powerful image of the transition between individuation, or "becoming the person I was meant to be," and collective action, or leaving a legacy for others.

A Difficult Task

I have been set a task nearly too difficult for me. A log of hard and heavy wood lies covered in the forest. I must uncover it, saw or hew from it a circular piece, and then carve through the piece a design. The result is to be preserved at all cost, as representing something no longer recurring and in danger of being lost. At the same time, a tape recording is to be made describing in detail what it is, what it represents, its whole meaning. At the end, the thing itself and the tape are to be given to the public library. Someone says that only the library will know how to prevent the tape from deteriorating within five years.

The images in this remarkable dream suggest successive moments of the five stages of the soul: Call, Search, Struggle, Breakthrough, and Return. The opening line, "I have been set a task nearly too difficult for me," invokes the Call, and, equally, the dreamer's fear that he may not be up to a task which is "nearly too difficult" for him. The moment of the Search is illustrated by the need to go into the forest to find the covered log and uncover it. The Struggle comes in carving a design "to be preserved at all cost," a precious accomplishment, like finding "the Pearl of Great Price." The Breakthrough comes in the message of the tape recording, which must describe "in detail what it is, what it represents, its whole meaning." Finally, the task of the Return is reflected in the dreamer's obligation to given the "thing itself" and the tape recording to the library, a repository of wisdom for past and future generations.

From another point of view, "A Difficult Task" reflects the duality of the spiritual task in both its active and the reflective sides. The first task is active: to find the covered log in the forest and carve the design, a work of craftsmanship. The second task is reflective: to make a tape recording, a verbal commentary about the whole meaning of what the dreamer has done. These two sides of the challenge also represent two sides of our common human journey: one beginning in the dark forest, the other concluding in a library, symbol of higher civilization. The challenge cannot be completed unless we bring together these two sides of ourselves, forest-dweller and scholar. To do that is indeed "a difficult task" which is possible in the last stage of life.

References

Atchley, Robert C. 2009. *Spirituality and Aging*. Baltimore: The Johns Hopkins University Press.

Bamford, Christopher. 2005. "The Gift of Call," *Parabola (Fall, 2004), reprinted in Philip Zaleski, The Best American Spiritual Writing of 2005*. Boston: Houghton-Mifflin, 2005, p.1

Burstyn, Ellen. 2006. *Lessons in Becoming Myself*. New York: Riverhead Books.

Caplan, Mariana. 2009. *Eyes Wide Open: Cultivating Discernment on the Spiritual Path*. Boulder, CO: Sounds True.

Coleman, Peter. 2011. *Belief and Ageing: Spiritual Pathways in Later Life*. London: Policy Press.

Covitz, Joel. 1990. *Visions of the Night: A Study of Jewish Dream Interpretation*. New York: Shambhala.

Edinger, Edward. 1992. *Ego and Archetype*. Boston: Shambhala.

Eliade, Mircea. 2006. Quoted in *The Sun*, March, 2006.

Elrod, David. 1987. *Psychodynamics of the Dying Process*, p. 171, cited by von Franz, p. 134. Marie-Louise von Franz, *On Dreams and Death: A Jungian Interpretation*. Boston: Shambhala.

Erikson, Erik and Erikson, Joan. 1998. *The Life Cycle Completed*. New York: Norton.

Fowler, John W. 1981. *Stages of Faith: The Psychology of Human Development and the Quest for Meaning*. San Francisco: Harper and Row.

Frankl, Viktor E. 2000. *Man's Search for Ultimate Meaning*. New York: Barnes and Noble Books.

Green, Arthur. 1992. *Tormented Master: The Life and Spiritual Quest of Rabbi Nahman of Bratslav*. Woodstock, VT: Jewish Lights Publishing.

Hollis, James. 2006. *Finding Meaning in the Second Half of Life*. New York: Gotham.

Jung, Carl. 1973. *Collected Works*, vol. 17. Princeton University Press (trans. R.F.C. Hull).

Lewis, Franklin D. 2000. *Rumi: Past and Present, East and West*. London: One World.

Luke, Helen. 1995. *Dark Wood to White Rose: Journey and Transformation in Dante's Divine Comedy*. New York: Parabola Books.

Luke, Helen. 2000. *Such Stuff as Dreams are Made On*. New York: Bell Tower.

MacKinlay, Elizabeth. 2001. *The Spiritual Dimension of Ageing*. London: Jessica Kingsley.

Moody, Harry R. 1997. *The Five Stages of the Soul*. New York: Anchor.

Moon, Sheila. 1983. *Dreams of a Woman: An Analyst's Inner Journey*. Boston: Sigo Press.

Needleman, Jacob. 2003. *Lost Christianity*. New York: Jeremy P. Tarcher.

Rinpoche, Sogyal. 1992. *The Tibetan Book of Living and Dying*. San Francisco: Harper.

Roof, W. Clark. 1999. *Spiritual Marketplace: Baby-Boomers and the Remaking of American Religion*. New Jersey: Princeton University Press.

Shafton, Anthony. 1995. *Dream Reader: Contemporary Approaches to the Understanding of Dreams*. Albany, NY: SUNY Press.

Taylor, Jeremy. 1992. *Where People Fly and Water Runs Uphill: Using Dreams to Tap the Wisdom of the Unconscious*. New York: Warner.

Vaughan-Lee, Llewellyn. 1998. *Catching the Thread*. San Francisco: Golden Sufi Center.

5   Aesop's Fables as Spiritual Touchstones for Ageing

W. Andrew Achenbaum

"When I grew up, I had finished with childish things. Now we see only puzzling reflections in a mirror." I Corinthians 13: 11–12 (New English Bible)

"Spirituality is an abstract, sensitizing concept that refers to a region of human experience involving awareness of being and transcending a purely personal, self-centered viewpoint," writes Robert C. Atchley in *Spirituality and Aging*. "Spiritual experience begins with basic spirituality, an unadorned sense of being. To this is added a sense of 'I' as perceiver and actor" (Atchley, 2009, p. 147). Atchley rightly claims that spirituality manifests itself in the Present, where a receptive "I" embraces both Transcendence and Immanence. Spirituality entails at once all-encompassing and intimate relationships with Ultimate Reality. Experienced in one present moment after another, spiritually inclined persons learn how to balance being and doing. Seekers sustain quests for authentic identities while they go about their business in the world. "Spirituality as the transformation and discovery of the self always happens in encounter ... an activity constantly stirred up and sustained by the other who calls one out of one's self and into the truth of one's mission in life, out of provisionality and into the adventure of incarnation" (McIntosh, 1998, p. 6).

Younger and older seekers usually share certain spiritual traits, such as a history of religiosity and encounters with loss. In most instances, however, spiritual development typically ripens during the second half of life (Clark, 2005). Women and men over forty are the prime consumers and producers of spiritual retreats, workshops, websites, and literature. Promoting spirituality has become big business: Amazon in 2012 offered 132,000 books on spiritual transformation, and 62,000 more under its New Age category. The passage of years nonetheless does not invariably engender spiritual enlightenment. "Developing this capacity is mysterious in that not everyone perceives or accepts the invitation to spiritual consciousness," notes Atchley, acknowledging aging's diverse patterns. "Yet by later life, a large majority of people are in touch with their inner life and can identify elements of their lives that they perceive to be spiritual" (Atchley, 2009, p. 148).

Writers invoke a variety of metaphors to characterize the mysterious, elusive contours of spirituality and aging. One set, focusing on human actors, highlights "spiritual growth" and "self discovery," emphasizing the "mature imagination" of "sages" or "spiritual elders" (Biggs, 1999; Koenig, 1994; Moberg and Ellor, 2001; Schachter-Shalomi and Miller, 1995). Such images of positive aging culminate in expressions of expanded consciousness, which Lars Tornstam (2005) described as "gero-transcendence." A second group of metaphors derive from Nature: Spiritual growth resembles a spider's web or hidden seeds that show their beauty in growing seasons (Palmer, 2004). Hands create nature: piecing together the quilt of life is the analogy proposed by Ruth Ray and Susan McFadden (2001). A third set of spiritual-aging metaphors addresses *process* in terms of stages or pathways. Spiritual aging resembles a journey, calling, pilgrimage, or rowing (Cole, 1992; Erikson and Erikson, 1997; Fowler, 1991; Kimble and McFadden, 2003; Moody and Carroll, 1997). All three metaphorical clusters nurture aging and spirituality; spiritual disciplines can be formalized in exercises learned in adult education classes, gurus' newsletters and videos, or a self-guided *Course in Miracles* as helpfully as on retreats (Shucman and Thetford, 2007).

In "Aesop's Fables as Spiritual Touchstones for Aging," I employ the metaphor of "seeing" to conjoin spirituality with aging. It permits me to put the topic into historical context. A widening gulf between the realms of religion and spirituality in recent decades, argue scholars, has caused a shift in spiritual *sites* from meeting the sacred within traditional religious dwellings to seeking spiritual lights by relying primarily on one's internal resources and convictions (Wuthnow, 1998). Thinking in terms of vision, moreover, serves to remind us that *sight* generally dims with age. Presbyopia refers to changes in the ability to focus with advancing years. Older people often suffer from macular degeneration, glaucoma, and diabetic retinopathy; decreased color vision, loss of peripheral vision, dry eyes, and reduced pupil size also become more pronounced after age fifty (Helting, 2012). Framing spiritual aging in terms of physical site and physiological sight reminds us that this age-old phenomenon varies across historical moments, which often change in manifestations over individuals' life courses.

Ralph Waldo Emerson captured the interrelationship among seeing, aging, and spirituality in two essays entitled "Nature"; "Standing on the bare ground—my head bathed by the blithe air and uplifted into infinite space—all mean egotism vanishes. I become a transparent eyeball; I am nothing; I see all; the currents of Universal Being circulate through me;

I am part or parcel of God," Emerson wrote in the first essay on "Nature" (1836). Eight years later Emerson revisited his ideas about Nature: "We are escorted on every hand through life by spiritual agents, and a beneficent purpose lies in wait for us" (Emerson, 1950, p. 6, 420). The omniscient Eye/I, in Emerson's vision, sees glimpses of divine Transcendence and Immanence amidst Nature. Meanwhile, declares the essayist, spiritual agents facilitate one's ultimate encounter with Destiny.

There are many difference ways of "seeing," of course. My thesaurus lists fifty synonyms, which underscores the validity of complementary modes for observing the world. I start with St. Bonaventure's trilogy (the *eye of flesh*, the *eye of reason*, and the *eye of contemplation*), which theologians, psychologists, and philosophers have incorporated in writing and extended over time to limn three prominent eyes of the soul. "Sensation, reason, and contemplation disclose their own truths in their own realms," observes Ken Wilber in *Eye to Eye*, "and anytime one eye tries to see for another eye, blurred vision results" (Wilber, 2001, pp. 9–10). With a nod to Emerson, who comprehended these various states of visual acuity, I wish to rename the three types of seeing.

Perceiving, which permits people to know and touch at a distance, serves as a means and an end to human understanding. E. F. Schumacher (1977) echoes Frithjof Schuon's claim that "all knowledge originates in sensorial experience" (Schuon, 1975). Ludwig Wittgenstein in contrast focuses on the primacy of sensation itself; discerning the act of perceiving reveals how we dart from object to object through visual senses. Our eyes rarely peer into the eyes of someone with whom we do not want to communicate. Whether consciously or not, nor our eyes remain focused for long on what is before us.

Reflecting, similarly, flashes across levels of understanding. "Seeing is believing" has been idiomatic since Doubting Thomas thrust his finger into Jesus. Engagement in reflecting, however, often involves other senses, such as listening, speaking, and touching. We anticipate a shimmering glow, perhaps an "aha!" moment; these are excitations that result from connecting body and mind. "What is it that you express in your eyes?," Walt Whitman asked in *Leaves of Grass* (1855). "It seems to me more than all the print I have read in my life." Paradoxically, the more rarified reflections are, the more likely that insights capture only a partial, a selective overview of the context. "The aspects that we see at any given moment always indicate further aspects, and so on," declared Emmanuel Levinas (2006, p. 6). "Things are never known in their totality; an essential character of our perception of them is that of being inadequate."

Gazing represents a third way of seeing, an aperçu into the fullness of life. As Will Johnson states in his guide to radical techniques for beholding the Divine, "The practice of gazing at the beloved is like a float trip that takes you down the river of your soul and ends at the ocean of union" (Johnson, 2007, p. 99). Through romancing the Divine, we learn to love others, even strangers. In embracing our beloved, we can turn inward to discover ourselves enmeshed in a cosmic order that simultaneously invites us to discern the spirit within. David Levin affirmed the resiliency and courage that may arise from addressing the vicissitudes of later years. "It is the strength of our being affected by what we see," declaimed Levin in *Opening of Vision* (Levin, 1988, pp. 179–180), "and is the strength of a first understanding, the possibility of a deeper, more adequate and more appropriate understanding essentially depends on this initial realization." The vulnerabilities and decrements of age – no less than the joys and blessings that can come with advancing years – assist us in deepening our sensitivity to essential meanings of life.

Through spiritual exercises that illumine the journey of life, in short, people have opportunities (not always realized) to espy that Transcendent Reality which (spiritual insights reveal) dwells within every living creature. Spirituality neither reverses nor suspends time, but whatever truly matters (past and future) animates the present, albeit partially. On such insights I interpret St. Paul's message in this essay's epigraph: at an advanced age, as I accept the inevitability of my own death, I recognize how dimly that I still perceive life's meanings. This does not mean that I am hopelessly blind to my true nature or to the forces transforming the world around me. I rely on many resources (including traditional meditations, spiritual guides, symbols, stories, and myths) to help me to make sense of what I have seen and sensed.

In order to see where I have been and to envision where I am heading, I choose spiritual touchstones with care. I turned earlier in my life to Aesop for lenses; I still depend on that sixth-century-BCE Greek slave (Shipley et al., 2008, p. 17). Aesop, whose storytelling won him freedom and readers for centuries, has been a constant soul mate. (Nevertheless I must admit that I did not always appreciate the importance of his fables to forming my spiritual development.) Besides shaping my childhood memories, Aesop's fables stirred midlife imaginations. Now, well into the Third Age, I treasure how they ignite spiritual embers, almost serendipitously, through little-noticed details.

Another reason for using Aesop's fables in this essay is their affinity to familiar religious and spiritual sensibilities. "God helps those who help themselves," for instance, is found not in the Bible; it comes from Aesop's "Hercules and the Waggoner" (Gibbs, 2002, p. 222). Martin Luther translated twenty fables while he was doing Scriptural exegesis. Samuel Richardson's *Aesop's fables. With instructive morals and reflections, abstracted from all party considerations, adapted to all capacities; and design'd to promote religion, morality, and universal benevolence* (1753) testifies to Aesop's perduring didactic worth valued over the ages. Anglican minister George Fyler Townsend's 1867 collection of 350 fables remains the standard translation. William Cleary, an ex-Jesuit poet and musician, more recently put fifty fables into verse (Cleary, 1997). Spiritual writers invoke Aesop on the internet. The Indigo Society (a forum for Spirituality, New Age, Lightworkers and General Topics) includes blog posts about "The Fox and the Grapes."

That Aesop offers sojourners like me a window into spirituality and aging introduces a third point: the fables challenge ordinary ways of seeing by revealing fresh, straightforward interpretations of life's perplexities and mysteries through farcical, seemingly aimless, premises (Kotre, 1984, p. 26). Although his best-known fables are usually narrated by animals, plants, or inanimate objects, Aesop did not compose morals primarily for children (Gibbs, 2002, pp. xi–xii). Aesop's messages also captivated elite audiences in ancient Greece because they illuminated popular culture. So, too, Aesop appeals to modern-day audiences insofar as his stories lance the seemingly prosaic with practical wisdom (Kurke, 2011).

After sharing a few critical moments in my life history, I will use three of Aesop's fables to serve as touchstones for reviewing my spiritual journey to date. These focus my mind's eye on (1) perceiving legacy work, (2) reflecting on uses of memories, and (3) gazing at death in the face. Leaving a legacy, reviewing key developments in an open-ended biography, and preparing for finitude are critical challenges of aging. They have been especially significant to me insofar as they engage my mind and heart in a transcendent, imminent here and now.

* * * * * * * * * * *

At forty I found myself in the modern-day equivalent of Dante's dark woods. I was overwhelmed by the deaths of a brother, a mentor, and a dear friend. Doctors first attributed my melancholy to severe depression; they then settled on a diagnosis of bipolar disorder. Hard knocks deflated my sense of control, pride in my charmed standing as a Boomer; suddenly I was transformed into the Other. Unexpectedly, the stigma liberated me from people's expectations, freeing me reluctantly from my own relentless ambitions. "If you have nothing to lose," a Yiddish proverb puts it, "you can try everything." I decided to create a more authentic Self.

Transformative moments in the midst of crisis shifted my priorities in midlife, but I did not know how to proceed with these unwelcome insights, much less adapt to a troubling new identity. Many paths were available; friends encouraged me to look around. Buddhist prayer circles satisfied several colleagues. Some acquaintances had Hindu gurus, another studied Kabbalah. None of these options seemed right for me, however.

Instead, I fashioned a routine of prayer and praise that fit my compartmentalized *modus operandi*. I lit upon beacons in the Anglo-Catholic tradition. I visited Henri Nouwen; this wise and compassionate spiritual director advised hanging icons in my meditation space. Reading Rumi, as a friend recommended, became a way to refocus my sights – though at the outset I wondered whether a thirteenth-century Turk really could speak to me in my current situation.

Much to my surprise, Rumi's earthy, sensual verse illumined a way to romance God. I entered a sacred canopy in which a tavern served as a mosque, where mentors were students, and in which outsiders were welcomed as kin. Rumi prompted new visions of spirituality for me, yet I confess that I rarely witnessed many sparks of the Divine around me. Taking tentative steps, I tried listening to people's woes without rushing (as was my style) to fix things. I weathered students' skepticism and visible dismay each time that I assigned Rumi in social-work classes on "spirituality and aging" (Banks, 2004).

A fresh set of setbacks clouded my passage into the Third Quarter of Life. In addition to weathering a divorce, my mother's death, and a failed deanship, I began a long battle with prostate cancer. Meditating sustained hope amidst pain and suffering, though I must acknowledge that working intensely as I had in graduate school afforded me greater comfort than praying. I wrote a monograph on societal aging to tie up a gerontology project begun two decades earlier (Achenbaum, 1986, 2005). I then decided to prepare a popular book for aging Boomers; I do not recall why I chose to offer guidance to peers through a collection of essays based on Aesop's fables. Even more than Scripture, I considered this familiar body of stories to be accessible vehicles for imparting practical insights to persons my age who (like me) appeared ill-prepared for the challenges and choices of late life. In early drafts of *Boomers Listen to Aesop* I confided experiences, doubts and uncertainties as if I were speaking to close friends. It fascinates me upon reflection that, a decade ago, I did not see terribly much value in Aesop's fables as signposts for spiritual growth – certainly not to the extent that I do now. Was Aesop so familiar that I was blind to its centrality to my aging spirit?

The brush with death made me greatly thankful for life, mindful of the potentialities in each breath. I began to live as if I understood that I were on borrowed time. I remained conscientiously duty-bound in how I performed on the job and in the community, but more and more

I gave precedence to essential relationships that truly matter to me. I intentionally orchestrated moments with Transcendance – and not simply when I meditated (Erikson and Erikson, 1997, p. 127). Spiritual peregrinations now affected "wayfarings with friends and philosophers" (Manheimer, 1999). At every chance I joined kindred spirits in casting aside childish thoughts to pierce mysteries that shape our common destiny. I take the opportunity now to look again at issues surrounding legacies, memories, and dying; these are concerns that have engaged me as a gerontologist and, at last, as one conscious of aging. I seek strength from Aesop whose insights I now see to be more enlightening than I previously imagined. More than ever before I see how the rays of spiritual truths that emanate from Aesop light my approach to finitude. With advancing years my appreciation for the power of familiar spiritual touchstones widens.

Perceiving Legacy Work

"The Farmer and His Sons"

A farmer close to death wanted to share his knowledge with his sons on the best way to keep the farm. He called them to his bedside and said, "My children, all that I have to leave you can be found in the vineyards." The sons, thinking their father was referring to a hidden treasure, set to work with their spades and ploughs and overturned the soil again and again. They found no treasure, but the vines, strengthened by the thorough tillage, repaid their labor with an extraordinarily abundant crop.

Industry in itself is a treasure.

The moral of this fable, I have long perceived, jibes with my father's example and repeated exhortations. A child of the Great Depression and World War II hero, Dad worked hard to become a success. That meant in his view being a faithful steward in the vineyard. "To those to whom much has been given," he constantly admonished his sons, "much is expected." Turning in sloppy homework or earning poor grades, as he saw it, would sully family honor. As the eldest, I was expected to pick my career carefully – and then to do well and do good (in that order). I understood Dad's marching orders but, like the old farmer, his direct-ives seemed vague. Had my father insisted that I become a physician, I would have complied. Instead, my career choice to become a professor – a school teacher is how he he put it – disappointed Dad; my father died before he could ever tell me that he might have changed his mind.

My parents' emphasis on work had deep roots. They quoted St. Paul's injunction: "The man who will not work shall not eat" (2 Thessalonians 3:10). Ben Franklin exemplified for them industriousness. The message from childhood was reinforced in early adulthood: each day that I went to my office in Pittsburgh, I looked at Andrew Carnegie's statue bearing the declaration that "my heart is in the work." My daughters assure me that they did not resent my long hours; they knew that work paid the bills and energized me. Thus was the ethic transmitted from generation to generation. Work itself was the *sine qua non* of life.

I first invoked "The Farmer and His Sons" to write about legacy work in my book for Boomers. Dealing with cancer roughly the age at which my father had died, I insistently urged readers in my cohort to reap the rewards of productive aging. Working and volunteering, I felt, would enable them to create options and pursue dreams unavailable to our parents and grandparents at our age. In retrospect I realize that I discounted stressors (impairment of cognitive functions, age discrimination, disillusionment, and health issues) that beset many mature workers at the end of their careers. These very stressors blinded me to my own illusion – to become Ulysses or (as a fall-back) an aging Icarus.

My attitude toward "work" has changed over the past decade. So have my thoughts about legacy-building. I treasure being an effective teacher, and I am proud of what I have accomplished, but I also am cognizant of limits to patience and stamina. I concentrate on mentoring those I really think that I can assist; they are the ones whom I count on contributing spiritual as well as intellectual dimensions to our work together. "The work of the soul transcends our work in the world" (Cameron, 2008, p. 313). Soul work inspires me whether I am collaborating on books about the Longevity Revolution or conversing about wisdom at the Institute for Spirituality and Health in Houston, Texas, or meditating under a tree ablaze in autumn. Unlike the Old Farmer, however, Death's proximity does not motivate me. No serious legacy work I plan to undertake will ever be completed. To build a future for my grandchildren and their grandchildren, I try to focus on articulating and actualizing by example essential aspects of living authentically and meaningfully. That is what matters.

Reflecting on Memories in Reviewing a Life

"The Old Woman and the Wine-Jar"

An old woman found an empty jar which had lately been full of prime old wine and which still retained the fragrant smell of its former contents. She greedily placed it several times to her nose, and drawing it backwards and forwards said, "O most delicious! How nice must the Wine itself have been, when it leaves behind the very vessel which contained it so sweet a perfume!"

The memory of a good deed lives.

I cannot imagine that my parents ever read this fable to my brothers and me at bedtime. Most working memories from childhood involve learning how to read, pitch a ball, or set a table (Gathercole et al., 2004; Seigneuric and Ehrlich, 2005). And yet, "The Woman and the Wine Jar" invites reflections on how reminiscences from individual's formative years buttress and buffet women and men in the third quarter of life and beyond.

Psychologists of aging taught me that touching, hearing, or revisiting places evoke memories. Yet reminiscences do not depend solely on physical artifacts. How we retrieve, reconstruct, and remember past moments in our memory bank is influenced by the stories that we tell, and frequently invent, about ourselves in order to represent ourselves in the present (Kenyon et al., 2010). Shared memories, like recounting JFK's assassination, reinforce collective identities among peers (Schillinger, 2012). Memories of the Holocaust serve an analogous purpose. Accepting the Nobel Peace Prize, Elie Wiesel summoned "the mystical power of memory" to help people remember evil along with good: "Hope without memory is like memory without hope" (Wiesel, 1986).

Once again, my impressions of this particular fable change though the touchstone remains the same. The pertinence of "The Old Woman and the Wine-Jar" to aging and spirituality delights me. In a vessel still containing "sweet perfume" from a "prime old wine," The Old Woman tries to smell nectar by "greedily" shaking it "backwards and forwards" several times. Her action anticipates Dr. Robert N. Butler's theme in "The Life Review," which "participates in the evolution of such characteristics as candor, serenity, and wisdom among certain of the aged" (Butler, 1963). Neither bitter over things she has lost nor depressed by the futility of her quest, the Old Woman swigs the fragrant wine, according to Aesop, by reminiscing about a good deed.

That Aesop portrays his protagonist as elderly invites further reflections on perennial attributes of growing older, aspects not fully realized by me and other Boomers. "Old age is a disguise that no one but the old themselves see through," observes May Sarton. "I feel exactly as I always did, as young inside as when I was twenty-one, but the outward shell conceals the real me—sometimes even from itself—and betrays that person deep down inside, under wrinkles and liver spots and all the horrors of decay" (Sarton, 1973, p. 74). We ripen into true selves mainly by stumbling along the way. If we are fortunate, Emerson's spiritual agents lighten our paths.

Dr. Butler modified his earlier definitions of "the Life Review" while taking pulse of his own challenges in senescence. "Probably at no other time in life is there as potent a force toward self awareness operating as in old age," America's foremost gero-psychiatrist wrote a week before his death at age eighty-three. "Those who lead us through the valley of the shadow of death have the responsibility to help us deal with disillusion and help us hold a vision of the larger world that links us with others and with the universe" (Butler, 2013). Dregs transported the Old Woman back to instances in her life when full-bodied wine was abundant. The fragrant cask restored the protagonist's sense of wholeness, refreshing her resilience and optimism in late life. Perhaps the Old Woman remembered that she once was a vessel that held exquisite wine.

"The Old Woman and the Wine-Jar" exults in a Presence, in a sacred moment of connection, right under her nose. The protagonist's spiritual gesture is worthy of William Blake (1803):

> To see a world in a grain of sand,
> And a heaven in a wild flower,
> Hold infinity in the palm of your hand,
> And eternity in an hour.

The Old Woman's passionate effort to quaff the Mystery of Life prompted memories of my own concerning a precious moment in my spiritual journey: holding my first grandchild, surrounded by my daughters, I conjured an image of my beloved Nana holding my youngest brother as an infant. Did my grandmother's thoughts complement mine? Who knows, and does the memory have to be detailed? We both saw our future Self in that tiny bundle. As I write, my mind suffuses emotions of joy and gratitude, for this is partly how memories gird spiritual aging.

So what happens if and when memory fails? Is it similar to other short-term losses and long-term decrements, like HIV and strokes, which affect daily living (Dass, 2011; Vance et al., 2011)? How does permanent memory loss compare to other forms of Biographical Pain (Johnson, 2013)? For many elders, Alzheimer's Disease and other dementias prove to be a debilitating bio-medical problem that undermine their sense of selfhood and ability to relate to others. One in eight Americans over the age of sixty-five currently suffer from this scourge, at a cost of $183 billion per annum (Alzheimer's Association, 2014). Since prevalence rates increase among the long-lived, the incidence of Alzheimer's is expected to double by 2050 in the United States. "Can courage [grow] larger in the face of diminishments, I wonder, [with a] sense of human possibility in the midst of limitation?" (Fischer, 1985, p. 5).

Advances have been made in care giving, especially for participants who glimpse hope in the shadows. "For some sufferers who become vegetative—who not only have failed minds, but whose postures in some cases have regressed to near-fetal positions—a 'hidden' self or mind can be socially preserved against ageing and death through the interpretive efforts of caregivers and significant others" (Gubrium, 2005, p. 313). Singing a hymn or reciting a psalm can be helpful. "The experience of loving a person with dementia is a unique, mutual spiritual path," observe Jane Marie Thibault and Richard C. Morgan (2009, p. 33). "It is a spiritual path in which we learn to love generously, without constraint, without praise of thanks, sometimes despite a slap in the face." Acts of spiritual aging teach us in difficult situations, observed Theodore Roethke, that "love is not love until love is vulnerable."

Gazing Death in the Face

"The Old Man and Death"

An Old Man was employed in cutting wood in the forest, and, in carrying the pile of wood to the city for sale one day, became very wearied with his long journey. He sat down by the wayside, and throwing down his load, besought "Death" to come. "Death" immediately appeared in answer to his summons and asked for what reason he had called him. The Old Man hurriedly replied, "That lifting up the load, you may place it again upon my shoulders."

Although this fable never was one of my bedtime stories in childhood, I have had to gaze death in the face – in nightmares, emergency rooms, at wakes, and facing surgery. Looking back on these situations, I first thought Aesop was portraying Finitude as a physical transition. Now, I envision the fable's full spiritual dimensions – as powerfully as I behold "The Angel Prevents the Sacrifice of Isaac," Rembrandt's rendition of an old man choosing life over duty (Goodman, 2013). Aesop's simple narration guides me into deep meditation, one grounded in the twists and turns of my spiritual journey. I more clearly see the end of the road, and I sense that I will have to face it alone. "When you see me/Sitting quietly like a sack/Left on a shelf," wrote Maya Angelou (2008), "Don't think I need your chattering/I'm listening to myself."

The Old Man in the fable carries wood, which represented in Classical times an inexhaustible source of life, a superhuman element of knowledge and wisdom. Aesop depicts the protagonist as a poor man doing menial tasks, a wise elder meeting Death on the way. The protagonist summoned death without hesitation or fear; he took for granted that this was the natural thing to do.

The Old Man's negotiation with Death probably took place in an equivalent of Dante's dark woods. Exhausted by his journey – he seems ready to be freed from earthly troubles – the protagonist nonetheless was not quite ready to give up his burden. He had things to do before Charon greeted him in Hades. Hence the Old Man asked Death to place the wood back on his shoulders.

My peers and I, like the Old Man, are poised to transmogrify the meanings and experiences of death – just as we redefined conventions and expectations associated with schooling and working. Boomers (like Aesop's protagonist) can choose in our last act, an extended curtain call, to meet Death at a bend of the road. (Many of us remain haunted by loved ones who transpired comatose in a nursing home or intensive care unit.) "The greatest dignity to be found in death is the dignity of the life that preceded it," Sherwin Nuland postulated in *How We Die* (Nuland, 1994, p. 242). "There is a form of hope that we can all achieve, and it is the most abiding of all. Hope resides in the meaning of what our lives have been."

Like Aesop's Old Man, having gleaned and accepted the inevitability of my own death, I intend get on with the business of living. Ideally I will still be reinventing myself to the very end, for this can prove to be one of the gifts of extra years. "Maturity is largely a combination of hard-earned savvy, the habit of thinking ahead, and the patience to see long-term projects through" (Brand, 1999, p. 199) I hope to negotiate the terms of dying in accordance with my spiritual direction, not just in accordance with legal-medical advanced directives. May *kairos*, a divinely given, supremely opportune moment that surpasses chronological, sequential time, bathe me in a Light as bright as Henry Wadsworth Longfellow sang in his "Psalm of Life:"

> Life is real! Life is earnest!
> And the grave is not its goal
> 'Dust thou art, to dust returnest,' Was not spoken of the soul
> (Longfellow, 1838).

* * * * * * * * * * * *

"It's not what you look at that matters, it's what you see." –Henry David Thoreau

Spirituality is a mature way of seeing – perceiving, reflecting, and gazing. Aging sojourners seek to embrace in the here and now an understanding of an Ineffable Power that transcends the universe as it penetrates within and animates thoughtout all living things. Some see what is encapsulated in love, while others focus on legacy or material gain. Still others blink. Few of us can sustain any perspective for long. Life's mysteries leave us puzzling, as St. Paul observed in the epigraph, at reflections in the mirror.

We need touchstones, icons, and mantras to rivet our mind's eye on the spirit that permeates within as it flows beyond ourselves. Aesop's fables are such spiritual touchstones, deceptively safe and familiar. As these touchstones illuminate spirituality and aging, they reflect a pair of overarching patterns not immediately apparent to me, insights that radiate my thoughts towards larger vistas. On the one hand I once thought that the "Old Woman and the Wine-Jar" looked backward, that "The Farmer and the Sons" looked forward, and "The Old Man and Death" met in the present. I see things differently now: Past, present, and future converge in all three fables. This perception undercut any linear sense of time, with which I usually review my life story. On the other hand, none of Aesop's protagonists is truly alone. Each relates to an inner self, kin, or cosmic force. Through these connections, the Old Woman, the Father, and the Old Man compose lives, ripened by experience to attain a unique authenticity. "Individual improvisations can sometimes be shared as models of possibility for men and women in the future" (Bateson, 1990, p. 232) Struggle, false steps, loneliness, and longing inevitably color the improvisations that shadow spiritual aging. Nevertheless, shadows do not necessarily diminish the hope that, if we choose life, we can continue to find purpose and meaning in the shadows. "Everything exposed to the light," St. Paul wrote to the Ephesians (5:13)

> Light dwells within, that's our illumination.
> To dwell in silent peace, that's our meditation
> To see the passing world, with clearness and compassion,
> And when we clearly see, we are drawn to BE love and to serve.

References

Achenbaum, W. A. (1986) The Aging of the First New Nation. In Pifer, A. & Bronte, D. L. (eds.) *Our Aging Society*. New York: W. W. Norton.

Achenbaum, W. A. (2005) *Older Americans, Vital Communities*. Baltimore: Johns Hopkins University Press.

Atchley, R. C. (2009) *Spirituality and Aging*. Baltimore: Johns Hopkins University Press.

Angelou, M. (2008) "Growing Older by Design." Available from: septuagenarian-sarah.blogspot.it/2009_or_01. Archive.html (Accessed September 21, 2014).

Banks, C. (trans.) (2004) *The Essential Rumi*. New York: HarperCollins.

Bateson, M. C. (1990) *Composing a Life*. New York: Plume Penguin.

Biggs, S. (1999) *The Mature Imagination*. Buckingham, England: Open University Press.

Blake, W. (1803) Auguries of innocence. Available from: www.artofeurope.com/blake/bla3.htm (Accessed: February 5, 2012).

Brand, S. (1999) *The Clock of the Long Now*. New York: Basic Books.

Butler, R. N. (1963) The Life Review. *Psychiatry*, 26:655–676.

Butler, R. N. (2013) Prologue or Introduction: Life Review. In Achenbaum, W. A. (ed.) *Robert N. Butler, M.D.* New York: Columbia University Press.

Cameron, J. A. (2008) *Prayers to the Great Creator*. New York: Tarcher Penguin.

Clark, S. (2005) *Religiosity and Spirituality in Younger and Older Adults.* Unpublished PhD dissertation, University of North Texas.

Cleary, W. H. (1997) *Prayers and Fables: Meditating on Aesop's Wisdom.* New York: Rowan and Littlefield.

Cole, T. R. (1992) *The Journey of Life.* New York: Cambridge University Press.

Emerson, R. W. (1950) Nature (1836/1844). In Atkinson, B. (ed.) *The Selected Writings of Ralph Waldo Emerson.* New York: The Modern Library.

Erikson, E. and Erikson, J. W. (1997) *The Life Cycle Completed, Expanded Edition.* New York: W. W. Norton.

Fischer, K. (1985) *Winter Grace: Spirituality for the Later Years.* New York: Paulist Press.

Fowler, J. W. (1991) *Stages of Faith.* San Francisco: Harper & Row.

Gathercole, S. E. et al. (2004) The Structure of Working Memory from 4 to 15 Years of Age. *Developmental Psychology,* 40:177–190.

Gibbs, L. (2002) *Aesop's Fables.* New York: Oxford University Press.

Goodman, J. (2013) *But Where Is the Lamb?* New York: Schocken Books.

Gubrium, J. F. (2005) The Social Words of Old Age. In Johnson, M. L. et al. (eds.) *The Cambridge Handbook of Age and Ageing.* Cambridge: Cambridge University Press.

Helting, G. (2012) How Your Vision Changes as You Age. Available from: http://allaboutvision.com/over60/vision-changes.htm (Accessed: August 13, 2012).

Johnson, M. L. et al. (eds.) (2005) *The Cambridge Handbook of Age and Ageing.* Cambridge: Cambridge University Press.

Johnson, M. L. (2013) 'Biography and Generation : Spirituality and Biographical Pain at the end of life in old age'. in Merril Silverstein, and Roseann Giarrusso (eds) *Kinship and Cohort: From Generation to Generation.* Baltimore: The Johns Hopkins University Press, pp. 176–189.

Johnson, W. (2007) *The Spiritual Practices of Rumi.* Rochester, VT: Inner Traditions.

Kenyon, G., Bohlmeijer, J., and Randall, W. L. (2010) *Storying Later Life.* New York: Oxford University Press.

Kimble, M. A. and McFadden, S. (eds.) (2003) *Aging, Religion, and Spirituality.* Minneapolis: Fortress Press.

Koenig, H. G. (1994) *Aging and God.* New York: Haworth.

Kotre, J. (1984) *Outliving the Self: Generativity and the Interpretation of Lives.* Baltimore: Johns Hopkins University Press.

Kurke, L. (2011) *Aesopic Conversations.* Princeton: Princeton University Press.

Levin, D. (1988) *Opening of Vision.* New York: Routledge.

Levinas, E. (2006) In Purcell, M. (ed.) *Levinas and Theology.* Cambridge: Cambridge University Press.

Manheimer, R. J. (1999) *A Map to the End of Time.* New York: W. W. Norton.

Marvell, A. (ca. 1650) Eyes and Tears Available from: www.luminarium.org/Sevenlit/marvell/eyesandtears (Accessed: August 13, 2012).

McIntosh, M. A. (1998) *Mystical Theology: The Integrity of Spirituality and Theology.* Malden, MA: Blackwell.

Moberg, D. and Ellor, J. (2001) *Aging and Spirituality.* Philadelphia: Taylor & Francis.

Moody, H. R. and Carroll, D. (1997) *The Five Stages of the Soul*. New York: Anchor Books.

Nuland, S. B. (1994) *How We Die*. New York: Knopf.

Palmer, P. J. (2004) *A Hidden Wholeness*. San Francisco: Jossey-Bass.

Ray, R. and McFadden, S. (2001) The Web and The Quilt. *Journal of Adult Development*, 8:201–211.

Sarton, M. (1973) *As We Are Now*. New York: W. W. Norton.

Schachter-Shalomi, Z. and Miller, R. S. (1995) *From Age-ing to Sage-ing*. New York: Warner Books.

Schillinger, L. (2012, February 5) Smoldering Subversive. *The New York Review of Books*.

Schuon, F. (1975) *Logic and Transcendence*. 1975, Perennial Books, 1984 New translation, World Wisdom, 2009.

Schumacher, E. F. (1977) *A Guide for the Perplexed*. New York: Harper & Row.

Seigneuric, A. and Ehrlich, M-F. (2005) Contributions of Working Memory Capacity to Children's Reading Comprehension. *Reading and Writing*, 18:617–656.

Shipley, G. et al. (eds.) (2008) *The Cambridge Dictionary of Classical Civilization*. Cambridge: Cambridge University Press.

Shucman, H. and Thetford, W. (2007) *A Course in Miracles*. New York: Course in Miracles Society.

Thibault, J. M. and Morgan, R. (2009) *No Act of Love Is Wasted*. Nashville: Upper Room Books.

Tornstam, L. (2005) *Gerotranscendence: A Developmental Theory of Positive Aging*. New York: Springer.

Vance, D. E. et al. (2011) Religion, Spirituality, and Older Adults with HIV. *Clinical Interventions in Aging*, 6:101–109.

Whitman, W. (1855) Song of Myself. *Leaves of Grass*. On Line Available from: http://poetry.about.com/od/poems/l/blwhitmansong.htm (Accessed: August 13, 2012).

Wiesel, E. (1986, December 11) Nobel Peace Prize Speech.

Wilber, K. (2001) *Eye to Eye*. Boston: Shambhala.

Wuthnow, R. (1998) *Spirituality in America Since the 1950s*. Berkeley: University of California Press.

Part II

Cultures of the Spirit in Modernity

6   Religion, Belief and Spirituality in Old Age: How They Change

Vern Bengtson and Malcolm Johnson

Do people become more religious as they move into old age? We see differences between older and younger adults in religiousness; how much are these due to processes of ageing, and how much to differences between age cohorts? When people from different age groups speak about their religious and spiritual lives, do we see cohort contrasts related to their having different historical experiences? Is there a "retirement surge" in religiosity?

There is an uncertain assumption, encouraged by biographies, biopics, fictional literature and accounts of the great and the good, that as they faced death their certainty about the love of God, their place in the world beyond and the warming prospect of meeting their loved ones in heaven, remains strong. As McConnell and Lang (2001) put it in their book *Heaven: A history*, 'The expectation of being re-united with family and friends in heaven is so prevalent throughout Christian history that it is not surprising that contemporaries see it as the "natural" notion of life everlasting' (p.xiv). Theological writings continue to cite extensive Biblical and Quranic references to heaven and the life beyond 'if you have faith'.

Everlasting life in all the world religions is conditional, on the one hand, on having lived a good and faithful life and on the other the boundless mercy and forgiveness of God. So being among the faithful and the observant (within or beyond a worshipping community) is a known prerequisite. In this chapter the focus is on if, and in what ways, current older people continue to practice religious belief; how they have re-formulated those beliefs as they have lived their lives and how those that have left religion behind feel about life and death.

Many writings on these topics are informed by examining writings about religion and belief from a personal, theological or psychoanalytic basis. Others draw on findings from small interpretive studies. Comparatively few have used findings from large-scale investigations, which enable a more cultural and population based analysis. Here we are able to draw upon 35 years of repeated enquiries which examine the lives of individuals and families as they have aged. The latest of these lifespan studies has focused on the significance of belief to older people and how religion is transmitted across generations. The wider body of findings are reported in Bengtson, Putney and Harris (2013). In that book, *Families and Faith*, there is compelling evidence that despite the changes in American civic and religious life in the decades between 1970 and 2005 ... The extent to which religious families are successful in passing on their faith to younger generations appears to have remained stable over time' (p.185).

So, our research has challenged the conventional wisdom of the times over religious belief and its enduring presence in families. This chapter, drawing on the same body of data, examines another mantra, that even those who continue to believe into old age allow their religious beliefs to decline and become uncertain.

Age Differences in Religiosity

Sociological research has indicated that there are strong age differences in religiosity, and that that the elderly have higher overall religious involvement compared to younger adults (Ellison & Hummer, 2010; Sherkat & Ellison, 1999; Wuthnow, 2007). Older people maintain regular church attendance, reflecting patterns established earlier in life. It is only near the end of their lives when they become frail that religious participation declines (Idler, 2006; Idler, McLaughlin & Kasl, 2009; Krause, 2010; Hayward & Krause, 2013). Other facets of religiosity, such as subjective religiousness and the strength of religious beliefs, have been shown not to decline in old age (Moody, 2006,) and Chaves recently summarized trends in American religion by asserting that "... there is much continuity". Chaves, Dillon and Wink (2007) found similar age patterns of religious affiliation across seven decades within two cohorts (both born in the 1920s) in the Institute of Human Development longitudinal study at UC Berkeley. While the period between late adolescence and early adulthood is a time of greater variability in religious beliefs and practices, individual religiosity remains highly stable across the later phases of adulthood. When they looked at the effects of bereavement and health declines on religiosity in late life, they found these effects were quite variable. This contrasts with the findings of Ferraro and Kelley-Moore (2000) showing that bereavement and poor health prompt individuals to become more religious in later years compared to middle age, Dillon and Wink (2007) did note that in their study they could not rule out cohort effects.

However, age differences in religiosity – the fact that older adults show higher religious involvement than younger adults – may not be due to individuals growing older, or changes across the course of life. There are also cohort differences, and these may translate into higher religious involvement among older adults compared to younger adults. Younger adults today are less actively involved in religious organizations than younger adults were a generation ago (Wuthnow, 2007). One reason may be demographic: delays in the completion of college, a time in the life course when religious commitment is weaker (Myers, 1996), as well as changes in decisions about marriage and children. Sociologists have long noted that marriage and parenthood make religion more important to people and increase their participation in local congregations (Edgell, 2006; Sherkat, 2010; Sherkat & Ellison, 1999; Stolzenberg, Blair-Loy & Waite, 1995). Today's young adults are marrying later, and having fewer children at later ages (Casper & Bianchi, 2002).

A second reason may be the differential impact of historical trends on different age groups. Younger adults today appear to feel less compelled by tradition to attend religious services or events, or even to affiliate with a specific denomination, as was true for previous generations (Putnam & Campbell, 2010; Wuthnow, 2007). While there is certainly a significant segment of younger adults who are very religious and have high religious involvement (Smith & Denton, 2005), an increasing number are religious "nones." Given the powerful influence and direction of the demographic, social and cultural changes that have occurred over recent decades in American and European societies – changes which have affected different age groups in different ways depending on their developmental stage when they experienced these changes – we might expect today's older adults to have greater religious involvement than younger adults.

Thus, historical changes can influence age differences in religious involvement. Historical events or conditions such as economic recessions or expansionary periods, or wars, or dramatic cultural changes such as the civil rights and feminist movements of the 1960s, will affect all age cohorts or generations, but to different degrees. The "baby boom" generation (born between 1946 and 1964) exemplifies the imprint of historical change on the ageing experience (their sheer size affecting all institutions and cohorts as they passed through each succeeding life stage). Three decades ago Wuthnow (1978) reported what he saw as a "generation gap" in religiosity between baby boomers and their parents' generation, whereas he saw no such age group contrast in data collected in previous decades. His conclusion was that the "gap" was the result of younger people having been involved in the counterculture of the 1960s. Other scholars (Roof 1993, 1999), in describing the "spiritual journeys" of his baby boom group of adults, described its members' movement away from mainline religious institutions toward a more fluid and personal spirituality.

This trend has been picked up by more recent studies (Flory & Miller; 2009) that have focused on today's young adults. Young adults tend to opt for personal experience over church doctrines, while older adults are about equally likely to choose one or the other. One consequence is that young adults are missing from many churches and synagogues (Belzer, Flory, Roumani & Loskota, 2007). To explain their absence from organized religious life, young adults are seen as professing and acting out "spiritual but not religious." Repeated surveys by the US-based Pew Research, on the topic of Religion and Public Life, document the marked decline of religious involvement in younger age groups, but also record a high level of regard for religious values and spiritual practices (Pew Research, 2013). Carrette and King (2005) see these shifts as 'what amounts to a silent takeover of 'the religious' by contemporary capitalist ideologies by means of the increasingly popular discourse of 'spirituality' (p.2). Indicating that corporations are annexing youthful interest in health and spiritual practices – and use it in marketing – they observe threatening distortions of what being religious might mean. A set of messages that have yet to penetrate the thinking of older believers.

As this brief review suggests, assessing whether individuals become more religious as they move through the life course and into in their later years is complex. It requires that we take into account not only individual development or biographical ageing, but also the often unique effects associated with cohort membership: being born and growing up within a particular historical interval. Moreover, there are historical contexts and cultural changes that can affect all age groups, but not always to the same degree. There are many examples of all-age cultural/religious shifts throughout history. Across medieval and post – Reformation Europe, monarchs, Christian, Jewish and Muslim leaders have moved the boundaries of accepted beliefs. McDonnell and Lang (2001) in their comprehensive history of heaven and ideas about it, provide a template of the manner in which wider populations of the powerless faithful have seen central religious ideas reformulated. In turn, these pieces of ecclesiastical revisionism cause uncertainty and sometimes anguish, particularly in the old.

Research Findings from a 35-Year Longitudinal Study

Do people get more religious as they age, with the approach of the end of life? To what extent are there cohort differences in this? And what about historical or period effects, reflecting that broad cultural trends such as increased secularization may influence age changes and age differences in religion? These issues have been examined empirically (Bengtson, Silverstein, Putney, and Harris, 2015) using a set of unique data from the 35-year Longitudinal Study of Generations. This analysis used growth curve estimations across eight waves of data collection, from 1970 to 2005, to trace age and period changes in dimensions of religiosity among family members representing four generations. The goal was to examine ageing effects and cohort influences on religiosity across adulthood, especially in later life.

The study design is described in detail in Bengtson, Putney, and Harris (2013). To briefly summarize, the Longitudinal Study of Generations was started in 1970 and has involved 3,500 individuals from an original sample of over 400 three- and four-generation families. The sample was drawn from a southern California medical group of 840,000 members serving labor unions; its design required families that included grandparents, parents, and young adult grandchildren. Because eight waves of data have been collected between 1970 and 2005, analyses can be conducted to trace individuals' pathways on religiousness over 35 years or until death, and to compare generations in religious practices and orientations. Two cautions should be noted in interpreting results. First, this is an American study, from a nation which is more highly religious by many standards than other industrialized societies; its applications may be less relevant to European and other nations. Second, because it is not based on a nationally representative sample, results may be more characteristic of Southern California than, say, the American South where religious involvement is higher.

To examine how religiosity may change with ageing, or differ between age groups, we will focus on two dimensions of religiosity from this study: *religious intensity*, the degree to which individuals define themselves as having religious commitment; and *religious participation*, the frequency with which they attend services at a church or synagogue. The statistical analysis estimated intraindividual ageing effects and differentiated those effects by cohort membership using a two-level growth curve model using HLM (v6.08) with observations nested within individuals, and all available data were used under the assumptions of FIML maximum likelihood estimation (see Bengtson, Silverstein, Putney, and Harris, 2015, for details of the analysis).

Changes in Religiousness Associated with Ageing

First, let us consider religious intensity. This is a self-report response ('How religious would you say you are?') In Figure 1 age trends are shown for each generation (G1s are the oldest; G4s are youth) as the

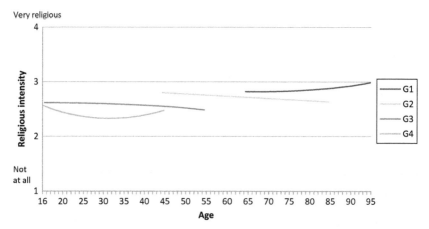

Figure 1. Age Trends for Religious Intensity by Generation, with Period Trend, Gender and Education Controlled (Source: Bengtson, Silverstein, Putney and Harris, 2015)

scores progress over the ageing of respondents. This figure also shows that intensity of belief is not, as some may think, a sharp gradient at the end of life, but a sustained progression over the second half of the lifespan. To the extent that we see significant changes in trajectories for generations as they age, we would conclude that these reflect aging effects. Differences in the trajectories of each generation as they age suggest cohort effects.

In Figure 1 we see the demonstration of ageing effects in the trajectories shown within and across age groups. Looking first at the oldest generation (G1s) at the right of the figure, we see that, late in life, there is an increase in self-reported religious intensity. (This is a true ageing effect since period effects are controlled in this analysis). For the next younger age group, the G2s and G3s, religious intensity is generally stable across the life course, though trending slightly downward across midlife into later adulthood. For the youngest generation, the G4s, there is a curvilinear pattern by age, with religious intensity declining in their twenties (leaving home, going to university) before swinging slightly higher in their thirties (as they marry and have children). Looking over the lifetime of the oldest individuals in this study, religious intensity tends to increase; whether this will occur for the more recently born generations will require the passage of more years to assess.

Religiosity is multidimensional, involving several aspects of belief and practice, and to assess age changes requires us to look at both inward and outward aspects of religion. The outward and more objectively measured

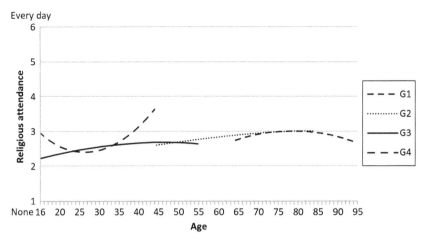

Figure 2. Age Trends for Religious Service Attendance with Period Trend, Gender and Education Controlled. (Source: Bengtson, Silverstein, Putney and Harris, 2015)

aspect of religiosity is participation in religious activities, for example, frequency of attendance at religious services (Figure 2). Here we see that the ageing trajectory for the G1s curves downward (from when they are in their late 70s to very old age), undoubtedly because declining health makes getting to church or synagogue increasingly difficult. For the G2s and G3s, the pattern is fairly stable as they age (but bending slightly downward with advancing age). The G4s show a curvilinear pattern for frequency of religious service, just as we saw for religious intensity, trending downward after leaving home and then moving upward through early adulthood.

Generations: Age Differences Associated with Cohort Membership

So far we have examined these data in terms of aging effects, the degree to which religious expression may change as individuals grow up and grow old. Next we look to another explanation for religious differences between older and younger persons, the degree of cohort, or generational, contrasts in religion. We look again to the two figures, but this time we focus not only on the trajectory over time for each generation but also on the height of the line, indicating the relative position of each generation to each other.

In religious intensity (Figure 1), the trajectory or line of predicted values for the oldest (G1) generation trends higher than that of the younger cohorts. That is to say, in terms of cohort differences, the G1s display somewhat higher levels of religious intensity than do the other generations. For subsequent generations the patterns show progressively lower trajectories for the G2s and G3s, though these differences are not large. The trajectory for G4s, while slightly lower on average, fluctuates such that the cohort average approaches that of the G3s. These data suggest that there are cohort differences in self-rated religiosity, with the oldest generation having the highest scores compared to the others. But within the cohorts there is considerable variability, particularly within the youngest generation showing a curvilinear trend. This means we should be cautious in making statements about a particular cohort – first the younger generation through the adult life course; second, variations within an age cohort can be as significant as differences between age groups.

For religious service attendance (Figure 2), there appears to be relatively little difference between the older three generations in their trajectories across their life course. While the trajectory pattern of the G4s is dissimilar, the overall level is not that different. The G4s show a curvilinear trajectory – in keeping with a family cycle explanation – but at an overall level they are not very different than the G3s or G2s, once we follow this cohort across time.

These results may seem to conflict with other much-publicized findings from public opinion polls, showing for example that people aged 18–35 are significantly less likely to attend church and be religious 'nones' than are older cohorts (Pew, 2012). However, those studies are based on cross-sectional data, based on responses at one point in time grouped by age categories. In this study we have longitudinal data that show responses from the same individuals, grouped by age cohorts, as they develop and grow older over time. Taking a longitudinal perspective we can see the trajectories of cohort members over time, and this leads to more nuanced perspectives of generational differences.

Narrative Accounts of Ageing and Cohort Trends

The survey data reported above are useful in demonstrating that both ageing and cohort membership are effects that influence religiosity. For many people there is something of an upswing in religious intensity, though a downswing in religious participation, in the later years of life. In addition, we see cohort or generational differences in both aspects of religiosity. But survey data are limited in advancing understanding of the meanings underlying such differences and the variation in their expression. To examine these we turn next to narrative data from a variety of sources collected by the authors: interviews conducted in a pilot investigation of religious change in later life; in-depth interviews with a subset of the LSOG respondents:

The "Retirement Surge" in Religiosity

For most individuals the pattern of religious practices and beliefs is relatively stable throughout adulthood and into the last stages of life, with many having no religious involvement at all. But a significant number of individuals evidence an increase in religious interest and practice after age 65 or so. An example is David, age 73. A successful dentist and a lifelong agnostic, he began going back to church a few years after his retirement. It wasn't something he had expected:

There was this sort of ah-ha experience. I just realized something was missing in my life, and now I had the time to pursue it. I was brought up in a Christian home, made to go to Sunday school every Sunday, say prayers, learn the Bible. When I got into my teens it stopped making sense to me, so I quit. But I took some Bible courses in college, so something must have stuck with me. Then I went to church for many years – I wanted my children to have a Christian background – but I didn't believe. Then after retirement I started going more often, and they started a class on the Book of Job, and that hooked me. Got me more involved, and then I started feeling different. It was like a light bulb had gone on inside.

The story of Dora, age 75, is somewhat different. She has been a lifelong Presbyterian, taught Sunday school when her children were young, and served on the church's governing board. She says:

I feel God has always been with me. My church has always meant a lot to me. But I was always so busy with other things in life. And I was going through the motions but never stopping to think what they meant...Then I retired, and I started getting more involved. I joined a Bible study group, and that got me to thinking about what I believed, and what was important. Then my husband's health failed and he died. I don't know what I would have done without my faith and without my Bible study group. And there were others there who had similar losses...They helped pull me thorough.

Dora says she is more active in church activities than ever before. 'It's more that the strength of my conviction is greater. I believe more intensely in Jesus, I guess.'

For those individuals who become more religiously intense in the later years, what are some reasons? David mentions greater time flexibility that retirement afforded which allowed him to reengage with church. For Dora also it was more time to become involved as well as a supportive environment that helped her through difficult times associated with her husband's decline and death. Other respondents provided additional reasons. Michael, age 71, mentioned a health crisis: 'I almost died, there on the operating table. And when I pulled through, I had a new perspective on life. And death. I thought, "I might not be around much more. I'd better pay attention to my spiritual side."' Yvonne, age 59, said that having grandchildren brought her back to church; since her daughter did not attend, 'I was the only one available to bring them up in God's way.' Ralph, 79, who had been a lapsed Roman Catholic, talked about 'the Judgment Day, the Great Reckoning. I didn't want to die without the sacrament. But then you have to keep the other sacraments too. So I reformed.'

These individuals reflect a group within the elderly for whom there has been an increase in religiosity in the later years. And it must be emphasized that for others in their age category, undoubtedly the majority, the pattern of religious and spiritual expression does not represent change but rather stability, neither upward or downward, as they approach the end of life. But a third possibility involves decrease in religious faith or practice. It would be impossible to say how many exhibit such a trajectory of disbelief at the end, for the progression would be less evident than for those who re-engage in religion or engage for the first time toward the end of life. But the story of Marie provides one example:

For Marie, who died at age 82, God had been the very center of her life. She was the wife of a minister and in young adulthood had prepared to be a missionary in Alaska to Native Americans. In her middle years she had labored ceaselessly to share her testimony, bringing the Gospel to those who were in need of faith and hope in Christ. Every Sunday afternoon she would go to a nursing home to sing hymns and pray with the elderly residents. At the age of 75 she fractured a hip, which caused much pain, and at age 77 she had a stroke; she herself hospitalized temporarily in the nursing home. She prayed to God to take her to heaven, to be with her husband and released from pain. At the age of 79, with her dementia symptoms progressing rapidly, she was moved to the nursing home permanently. For the last two years of her life she lay there, often curled in a fetal position, responding only to feeding. Her son recalls visiting her one day during her 80th year when she was suddenly cogent. She clutched his hand and said, so softly he could hardly hear: "You know, I think I'm losing my faith." God had not answered her calls to be taken home to heaven. These were the last words anyone heard her speak.

In the Hebrew Bible the suffering Job's friends advised him to 'Curse God, and die.' We have little firm evidence of how frequently this happens, but it is an instance that theories regarding ageing and spirituality should be able to address.

Sociologist of death, Allan Kellehear in his insightful book, *The inner life of the dying person (2014)*, after presenting an extensive body of evidence from many sources, argues that transformations in late dying are common. These might involve reports that individuals simply experience, that their perceptions of the world have altered in rather radical ways as a result of 'conversations with their dead' (p.195). Others have biographical or religious visions. He goes on to point out that the prevalence of deathbed visions is estimated to occur to about one third of all dying people. He concludes: "despite popular and academic beliefs to the contrary, the matter of the ultimate meaning of these experiences in not settled" (p.202).

In his chapter in this volume, Harry Moody extensively explores the nature and meanings of late life dreams, where individuals encounter their earlier selves in situations that are either revelatory of previously hidden truths – some affirmatory and some deeply painful. In his reflections in a further chapter in the book, Andrew Achenbaum draws out the deeper meanings for old age of this stories of Aesop. They remind us that quantitative empirical enquiry delivers only one portion of our developing understanding.

The Ways Religious Expression May Differ Between Age Cohorts

The examples we have listed are indicators of ageing effects, the ways that individuals may change in religious orientations during their later years. But there are also generational or cohort differences in religious practices and beliefs, for example in perceptions of 'religion' and 'spirituality'. In what ways have social and cultural trends over the past century left their imprint on the religious and spiritual experiences of different age cohorts – individuals who were born and grew up in a particular historical period? Here we summarize data from interviews with a subsample of the LSOG families (Bengtson, Silverstein, Putney, and Harris, 2015) who were asked about the meanings of religion and spirituality in their lives. Responses were analyzed by cohorts defined by year of birth; for example, those born between 1909 and 1915 were identified as the 'WWI Generation' – those born 1955–64 as 'younger Boomers'.

These interviews indicate that expressions of religion and spirituality vary by generational cohort. The 'WWI Generation' members in this sample tended to describe God as a relatively abstract, external influence that controls individuals' lives from on high. For some this was an omnipotent God; for others it was a powerful force in nature. Myrna Jackson, age 95, described her beliefs this way:

I know that there's another power above us. All I have to do is look out in the morning and see the sunshine and, all the different– The birds singing and all that. You can – It's just there. . . . I don't know how to express it. It's just there.

Only six individuals from this cohort could be interviewed, and as their average age was 95, it is not surprising that they often appeared to have difficulty in articulating their religious beliefs. Members of the next younger age groups – the 'Depression Era' and the 'Silent Generation' (born between 1916–1931 and 1932–1945, respectively) – provided more clear, straight-forward descriptions of the role God plays in their lives. As Ken, 88 years old, put it:

I believe there is a higher entity, sort of bird-dogging you, watching you, and you've got to be a good person. I just think that to me is my idea of being a helpful, responsible, good person to help others in life. That's maybe not 'religion,' but that's what I try to practice.

Also evident in Kenneth's comments is another pattern: a distinction between believing in God and being 'religious', as well as the separation of religious practice from religious institutions. Many in this age group talked about God as an internal force – a higher power that dwells within the human spirit – and many described the 'personal relationship' they have with God. For most, this relationship is facilitated by religious institutions; for some, it is not. Brigitte, age 73, was asked, 'What role does religion play in your life?'

None, so far as an organized religion. [But] so far as me communicating with my God, or my maker or a supreme being, a lot, a great deal. . . . I think it helps me stay focused on who I am, and how I need to react with others, for the [benefit] of myself and them. . . . So I ask for guidance in that, and to please lead me to the correct path. I just communicate every day.

The Baby Boomers (born 1946–1964) seemed to differ from the older generational cohorts in important ways. Many respondents made an explicit distinction between 'religion' and 'spirituality': religion is linked to institutional practices, while spirituality is a feeling of personal connection to God. Susan, 53, contrasted them as follows:

Religion seems to be, to me, more of an institutionalized practice, where you go to church and you believe certain things that have to do with the Christian faith. Spirituality, being a spiritual person means you're in connection. You're in communication and connection with God on an ongoing basis, every day; not just once a week when you go to church.

Many of the younger Boomers (born 1955–64) expressed a preference for the spiritual over the religious – a personal connection with God over going to church and participating in institutional religious practices. The phrase 'I'm not religious, I'm spiritual' captures the perspective of many in this group, as evident in the comments of 51-year-old Mary:

To me religion is about what building you go to, what day you go to, what time you go [to] it, and who's telling you what to believe. And spirituality is your connection you feel with God. But when they tell me that certain people aren't going to heaven, or you have to be such and such or you'll go to Hell, then I feel that religion is too invested in perpetuating its own lies. So I don't feel religious in that way, because I don't feel like – I don't think God looks at how often people go to church.

The youngest age groups in this sample (born 1965–1988) were more difficult to categorize; these members of Generation X and the Millennial Generation describe a much wider array of religious beliefs and practices than do the older cohorts. Some were highly religious; others anti-religious. There is much variation by age within this cohort. Many seem to have temporarily set aside religion – at least the institutional aspects of it – because of the demands of work or family. But the tendency to set aside religion when life gets in the way may be due more to their current life stage (for example, many are the parents of young children) than their membership in Generation X or the Millennial Generation. What is perhaps most characteristic of the Millennials who were interviewed is an open-minded approach to religion and the tendency to draw from a wide range of religious perspectives or to selectively choose from the tenets of a particular religion. Diane, a 25-year-old lapsed Catholic, explained it this way:

If you pigeonhole the universe in God, into one – I think that it's closed-minded to do that, and that's another reason why I've kind of, I'm not really into church and stuff like that. Because I don't know what's right, and I don't know what's wrong. . . I believe in God and I do believe that He created [the world]. But I don't know if it's necessarily the Christian perspective, or the Buddhist perspective, or the Muslim perspective, or the Jewish perspective [that is right]. I think there's truth in all of it.

These narratives provide insight concerning differences in the religious and spiritual experiences of members of different cohorts. The themes noted, while not exclusive to one age group, appear more frequently in members of one cohort compared to another; and these can be linked to show trends across age generational cohorts (Bengtson, Silverstein, Putney and Harris, 2015). They are persuasive evidence of historical events interacting with time of birth to influence religious and spiritual experiences.

Dying, Death, and Spirituality

We have seen that there are age changes in religiosity, with some individuals becoming more religious as they move from mid-life into the later years, and that there are age differences in religiosity, with older cohorts less likely to cite 'spirituality' in contrast to organized 'religion'. But what about as death approaches? Is there evidence that people become more religious as they are dying, or in the presence of mortality?

As Kellehear, above, indicates there is much literature that scholars are sceptical of, which report profound and transforming experiences, in the liminal stages prior to death. Clearly not all of it deserves serious attention, but its sheer volume and historical duration (Davies, 2005) suggest that it be re-appraised. In doing so we should consider the enduring influence of the writings of Jung (1970), Frankel (1981), Erikson (1982) and Fowler (1981) among many others who have investigated the existential and religious realities of facing death after a long life. Johnson (2013) has more recently revealed what he calls 'Biographical Pain' which results from deeply anguished life review, under the pressure of finitude. For some the end of life is a welcome and eagerly anticipated conclusion of a life which will transform into a promised nirvana. For all too many it is accompanied by guilt, uncertainty and fear.

Conclusions

Assessing research on religious participation across the life span, Ellen Idler (2006) writes: 'A one-sentence summary of the research ... would be that religious involvement remains stable or increasing until late life' (p. 283). She found that it is only in late life that religious participation drops because of declines in health and increasing fragility. Subjective religiousness, however, does not decline but remains stable across life. Our results qualify and extend these findings.

Drawing from the 35-year Longitudinal Study of Generations, we use multilevel growth curve modeling to examine the effects of age, cohort membership and historical factors on changing religiosity into old age. In many respects there is considerable stability across the life course for the older generation, particularly in subjective religiousness. Church attendance also demonstrates stability, except for the oldest generation, who show a slight *increase* with age before declining in very old age, after age 77. There are also differences between generations (cohort effects). Even after controlling on historical effects, the G1s showed higher trajectories than the younger three generations. On the other hand, with age effects controlled we found stability across time for two dimensions of religiosity (attendance and subjective religiousness). Yet, support of beliefs concerning Biblical inerrancy and civic religiosity showed a slight but significant decline between 1971 and 2005 for all generations. This decline was due to historical change, not individual ageing effects. We were able to extend existing research because we were able to compare today's very old adults with successive age cohorts of adults.

In the narrative data, we found some intriguing patterns associated with the religious and spiritual perceptions of members of different cohorts. As we examined the interview data, three central themes emerged: (1) changing conceptualizations of God; (2) the increasing separation of religious practice from religious institutions; and (3) the growing differentiation between 'religion', particularly organized religion, and 'spirituality'. In many ways these themes are in accord with trends described earlier in the literature review, although we were able to add a more in-depth understanding of some of these changing aspects of religion and spirituality. While not exclusive to one age cohort, the themes appear to be far more prevalent in one cohort, or appear first in the interviews of the members of a particular group, then in either earlier or later born cohorts.

One theme concerns differences between older and younger adults in their *conceptualizations of God*. The oldest cohort who came of age during World War I were more likely to perceive of God as transcendent and omniscient ('out there, up there'). A view of God as an imminent, internalized higher power ('in me, with me') was much more common among the younger adults in our study.

Another theme relates to the *increasing separation of religious practice from religious institutions*. For the G1s, the oldest adults in our study, most associated religious practice exclusively with a house of worship; they were apologetic when illness or difficulty with walking forced them to give up churchgoing. In the next age group, the older G2s, individuals began to distinguish between a conceptualization that being religious meant going to church, and an evolving understanding that leading a religious life did not require regular churchgoing. The younger G2s, the Silent Generation, increasingly saw 'God' and religion as being expressed outside of the institutional context, residing primarily within the human spirit. Thus for the older cohorts in our qualitative study, we see a gradually changing image of God, from the transcendental to the internal.

The third trend we observed in the narratives was the growing differentiation between 'religion', particularly organized religion, and 'spirituality', emphasizing an internal, personal relationship with God. Emerging first in interviews with older Boomers, the emphasis on spirituality served to further separate religious practice from institutionalized religious contexts. Baby Boomers provide a conceptual framework for understanding the personal and highly individualized 'relationships' with God later developed by Generation Xers and Millennials.

These quantitative analyses of trajectories of change in three aspects of religiosity for multiple generations across age and historical period provide new insights into the changing patterns of religious involvement in American society. Further, we suggest that issues such as the changing *perceptions* and *meanings* concerning religion and spirituality are central to our understanding of religiosity among different age groups as they grow older. The qualitative results demonstrate the increasing complexity of religious and spiritual experience over time and the departure from more clearly defined institutional boundaries of religion in the past by successive cohorts. As the accounts of the youngest age group, the Millennials, most notably suggest, older terms for religion may no longer work for younger individuals, who with others in their cohort develop new concepts and contexts for religious and spiritual practice. At the same time, our findings indicate that religion is still highly relevant to individuals in our fast-changing society. Time will tell how these diverse generational cohorts, and younger ones to follow, will continue to modify the religious practices and institutions of American religion, and what this implies for adults in late life.

Our purpose in this chapter has been to bring data and empirical evidence to a subject that is often obscured by competing claims in a contest between modernist secularists and those who are deemed to be traditionalist believers. What our findings reveal is that these dichotomies are unhelpful and contrary to the evidence. The picture is more nuanced and more interesting as a set of social trends. Religious beliefs are dynamic across the lifecourse and subject to revision in the light of experience and the pressing of finitude. People in different cohorts will be experiencing the distinctive influences of their own life journeys, whilst others have yet to travel that path and whilst others have been there and moved on. So it is inevitable that generations and cohorts will express their spirituality and beliefs differently. Such differences will be based on age and stage and may, of course, represent fractures in social values. Out in the public square, the presumption is that older people are the last refuges of religion. But this is more an ideological position than one based upon an understanding of the proper reflexivity of people of faith. Refining what you believe is a lifelong task. It is part of the maturation of human beings in their understanding of human existence and what it is for. To assume that uncertainty and new understandings are a sign of faltering or of being overwhelmed by doubt is to fail to comprehend the essence of ageing.

References

Belzer, T., Flory, R. W., Roumani, N., & Loskota, B. (2006). Congregations that get it: Understanding religious identities in the next generation. In J. L. Heft, S.M. (Ed.). *Passing on the faith: Transforming traditions for the next generation of Jews, Christians, and Muslins* (pp. 103–122). New York: Fordham University Press.

Bengtson, V. L., Biblarz, T. J., & Roberts, R. E. L. (2002). *How families still matter: A longitudinal study of youth in two generations*. New York: Cambridge University Press.

Bengtson, V.L., with Putney, N.M. and Harris, S. (2013) *Families and faith: How religion is passed down across the generations*. Oxford & New York: Oxford University Press.

Bengtson, V., Silverstein, M., Putney, N, & Harris, S. (2015). *Does religiousness increase with age?* Age changes and generational differences over 35 years. *Journal for the Scientific Study of Religion*. 54, 363–379.

Carrette, J. and King, R. (2005) *Selling Spirituality: The silent takeover of religion*. London: Routledge.

Casper L., & Bianchi, S. M. (2002). *Continuity and change in the American family*. Thousand Oaks, CA: Sage.

Chaves, M (2011). *American Religion: Contemporary Trends*. Princeton, NJ: Princeton University Press. 14, 50–51.

Comrey, A.L. & Newmeyer, J.A. (1965). Measurement of radicalism-conservatism. *Journal of Social Psychology*, 67, 357–69.

Davies, D.J. (2005) *A brief history of death*. Oxford: Blackwell.

Dillon, M., & Wink, P. (2005). Religiousness and spirituality: Trajectories and vital involvement in late adulthood. In M. Dillon (Ed.). *Handbook of the sociology of religion* (pp. 179–189). New York: Cambridge University Press.

Dillon, M., & Wink, P. (2007). *In the course of a lifetime: Tracing religious beliefs, practice, and change*. Berkeley: University of California Press.

Edgell, P. (2006). *Religion and the family in a changing society*. Princeton, NJ: Princeton University Press.

Ellison, C. G., & Hummer, R. A. (Eds.). (2010). *Religion, families, and health: Population-based research in the United States*. New Brunswick, NJ: Rutgers University Press.

Erikson, E.H. (1982) *The life cycle completed*. New York: W.W. Norton.

Flory, R. W., & Miller, D. E. (2008). *Finding faith: The spiritual quest of the post-boomergeneration*. New Brunswick, NJ: Rutgers University Press.

Ferraro, K. F., & Kelley-Moore, J. (2000). Religious consolation among men and women: Do health problems spur seeking? *Journal for the Scientific Study of Religion*, 39, 220–234.

Fowler, J.W. (1981) *Stages of faith*. San Francisco, CA: HarperCollins.

Glass, J., Bengtson, V. L., & Dunham, C. (1986). Attitude similarity in three-generation families. Socialization, status inheritance or reciprocal influence? *American Sociological Review 51*, 685–698.

Hout, M. & Fischer, C. S. (2002). Why more Americans have no religious preference: Politics and generations. *American Sociological Review 65*, 1655–190.

Idler, E. (2006). Religion and aging. In R.H. Binstock & L.K. George (Eds.). *Handbook of aging and the social sciences*, Sixth Edition (pp. 277–300). New York: Elsevier.

Idler, E., McLaughlin, J., & Kasl, S. (2009). Religion and the quality of life in the last year of life. *Journal of Gerontology: Social Sciences 64B(4)*, 528–537.

Inglehart, R., & Baker, W. (2000). Modernization, cultural change, and the persistence of traditional values. *American Sociological Review*, 65, 19–51.

Johnson, M.L. (2013) Biography and generation: Spirituality and Biographical Pain at the end life in old age. In, Silverstein, M and Giarrusso, R. (editors) *Kinship and cohort in an aging society: from generation to generation*. Baltimore: The Johns Hopkins University Press. 176–190.

Jung, C. (1970) The stages of life in *The structure and dynamics of the Psyche: Vol. 8, The collected works of C.G. Jung*. 2nd Edition Princeton, NJ: Princeton University Press.

Kellehear, A. (2014) *The inner life of the dying person*. New York: Columbia University Press.

McDonnell, C. and Lang, B. (2001) *Heaven: A history*. New Haven: Yale University Press.

Moody, H.R. (2006). Is religion good for your health? *The Gerontologist*, 46, 147–149.

Pew Forum on Religion & Public Life (2008). U.S. Religion Landscape Survey. Retrieved from http://pewforum.org/reports.

Myers, S. M. (1996). An interactive model of religiosity inheritance: The importance of family context. *American Sociological Review*, 61, 858–866.

Pew Research (2013) *Growth of the non-religious*, July 2013 pewforum.org/2013/07/02/growth-of-the-nonreligious-many-say-trend-is-bad-for-american-society/ (viewed November 20, 2014).

Presser, S. & Chaves, M. (2007). Is religious service attendance declining? *Journal for the Scientific Study of Religion*, 46, 417–424.

Putnam, R., & Campbell, D. (2010). *American Grace: How Religion Divides and Unites Us*. New York: Simon and Schuster.

Roof, W.C. (1993). *A generation of seekers: The spiritual journeys of the baby boom generation*. San Francisco: Harper Collins.

Roof, W.C. (1999). *Spiritual marketplace: Baby boomers and the remaking of American religion*. Princeton, NJ: Princeton University Press.

Sherkat, D.E. (1998). Counterculture or continuity? Competing influences on baby boomers' religious orientations and participation. *Social Forces*, 76, 1087–1114.

Sherkat, D. E. (2010). The religious demography of the United States: dynamics of affiliation, participation, and belief. In C. G. Ellison & R. A. Hummer (Eds.). *Religion, families, and health: Population-based research in the United States* (pp. 403–430). New Brunswick, NJ: Rutgers University Press.

Smith, C., & Denton, M. (2005). *Soul searching: The religious and spiritual lives of American teenagers*. New York: Oxford University Press.

Smith, E. & Snell, P. (2009). *Souls in transition: The religious and spiritual lives of emerging adults*. New York: Oxford University Press.

Stolzenberg, R., M., Blair-Loy, M., & Waite, L. J. (1995). Religious participation in early adulthood: Age and family life cycle effects on church membership. *American Sociological Review*, 60, 84–103.

Warner, R. S. (2005). *A church of our own. Disestablishment and diversity in American religion*. New Brunswick, NJ: Rutgers University Press.

Wink, P., Dillon, M., & Fay, K. (2005) Spiritual seeking, narcissism, and psychotherapy: How are they related? *Journal for the Scientific Study of Religion*, 44, 143–158.

Wuthnow, R. (1978). Recent patterns of secularization: A problem of generations? *American Sociological Review, 41,* 850–67.

Wuthnow, R. (1988). *The restructuring of American religion: Society and faith since World War II.* Princeton, NJ: Princeton University Press.

Wuthnow, R. (1998). *After heaven: Spirituality in America since the 1950s.* Berkeley, CA: University of California Press.

Wuthnow, R. (2007). *After the baby boomers: How twenty- and thirty-somethings are shaping the future of American religion.* Princeton, NJ: Princeton University Press.

7 Ritual and Memories of Ritual in Older People's Lives
Contrasts between Eastern and Western Europe

Peter G. Coleman

Religion is one of human culture's major sources of support for ageing. It provides well understood forms of ritualised meaning and belonging at key points in later life, particularly at times of bereavement as well as of life threatening illness, but also at joyous family events such as marriages and births. In her chapter in this volume, Ellen Idler (2016) refers to the essential role of ritual in religion and describes the benefits it brings to older people, arising out of the consistency of its performance over a lifetime, its physical and sensory nature, and the fact that it brings groups of people together in shared practice. Religious ritual is predictable, familiar and held in common. However, during the twentieth century, attendance at traditional communal religious ritual has declined in many parts of the Western world. New secular forms of ritual have emerged, sometimes intended to take the place of religious ritual, but it is questionable whether they yet provide equivalent psychological support to older people.

The European experience of religion varies considerably. Some countries are much more religious in attitudes and practice than others and there are no very clear geographical patterns (Eurobarometer 2005). There are particularly religious societies in the north as well as in the south of Europe, and more secularised societies in the east as well as the west. The historical experience of persecution by and of religious people also varies greatly between nations, and seems to have some relationship with the current status of religious practice within them.

In Russia from the time of the 1917 revolution, and in most parts of Eastern Europe following the installation of communist regimes after WWII, religious practice was discouraged and religious practitioners persecuted by explicitly atheist governments (Froese 2008). But religious practice survived, and since 1989 has been recovering some of its former position in society, including marking important occasions in the life of the nation, family and individual. In much of Western Europe, by contrast, religion remained an influential social force until the middle of the twentieth century. In the United Kingdom secularisation occurred more slowly and over a longer period of time, but it gathered particular pace in the 1960s and accelerated towards the end of the century (Brown 2001). Similar changes occurred in neighbouring countries, such as the Netherlands (Rooden 2010). Religion, however, has come to increased public attention again in the first decade of the twenty-first century as a result of globalisation, immigration from more religious parts of the world and the religious fundamentalism implicated in Islamic terrorist attacks on Western society.

As part of a project funded by the UK research councils' 'Religion and Society' programme (2007–2012) older people's (seventy-five years and over) attitudes to ritual, both religious and secular, were studied in two contrasting parts of Europe, England and Bulgaria/Romania. A personal life history approach to data collection was employed, in which interviewees were asked about their experience of ritual throughout their lives, from childhood to the present. Our Eastern European participants' attitudes to religious ritual appear to have remained relatively untouched by communism. Although the communist regime in Bulgaria, in particular, went to great trouble to provide substitute secular rituals, only religious rituals now seem to be seen as appropriate at key moments in life. Thus older people in Bulgaria and Romania tend to want religious rituals for births, marriages and death, even when they do not hold religious beliefs. For many, religious ritual remains an important sign of community belonging (Koleva 2013). By contrast, in England there appears to be an increase, even among older people, in preference for individually chosen ritual, whether religious, spiritual or secular, to mark key life events, rather than traditional religious ritual.

In this account I shall restrict the case illustrations of this project to those aged over eighty-five years at the time of interviews in 2010–2011. This has the advantage that these Bulgarian and Romanian participants can all be considered to have reached adulthood before the consequent social and political changes of the post-war period. Therefore their initial religious socialisation would not have been affected by the post-war changes. Those in England would have been brought up in a still predominantly religious society and one in which there was in fact a resurgence of church going in the initial post-war period (Brown 2001).

For each of these persons of advanced age I have considered the evidence for the importance attributed to religious belief and practice in the way they recounted both their life stories and their present situation. Consideration has also been given to alternative secular and humanistic themes that have provided a sense of meaning and value in our participants' lives. The study as a whole has focused on ritual, both religious and secular, by which we understand a shared outward form of behaviour which in its performance expresses a communally held belief or attitude. Of course it is possible to enact ritual without faith, to act as if one held such a religious or secular belief, while in fact not holding to such belief. But the ritual would soon become empty of meaning if few or no people held to the underlying belief expressed. In reality, of course, there is likely to be a huge variation in the extent to which a person's ritual actions are consonant with their inner disposition to believe what is expressed.

The following sections provide very brief portraits of eight of the oldest and typically frailest women and men in our sample (all names used are pseudonyms). Their significant memories and experience of religious ritual throughout the course of their lives, and especially in childhood are highlighted, as well as their attitudes to religious belief and practice in relation to their current health situation. In the concluding discussion possible explanations are considered for the differences between our oldest participants in Eastern and Western Europe.

The Oldest Participants in Bulgaria and Romania

Interviews were conducted in different areas, around the capital cities of Sofia and Bucharest but also around Varna on the Black Sea coast of Bulgaria and Cluj-Napoca in Transylvania.

The oldest man in our sample was *Aurelian* living near Cluj. He gave a remarkably detailed interview just before his ninety-seventh birthday in which he stressed the importance of his religious faith throughout his life, particularly in some of the important choices he made, including the 'fateful' decision to join the nationalist movement of the 'Iron Guard' in pre-war Romania which had led to his long periods of imprisonment and persecution in the communist period. The Iron Guard had appealed to his religious sensitivities in exhorting a cleansing of the moral character of the country. As the son of a priest his religious socialisation has been very strong. He described himself as very religious since childhood, although he referred to his sister who died young and inspired his father's building of a monastery as even more religious.

Although mentally alert for his age, he was physically frail, still mobile inside the house but not outside, and spent his time lying down much of the day. He had to be very careful walking, having fallen and fractured his leg already twice. His sight was very poor and he was unable to read. He could only attend religious services by listening to the television or radio. His attitude to his present health condition was marked by religious faith, consistent with the rest of his life story: 'I know that nothing happens without the will of God, and if God let this happen, then we shall bear it.'

His situation and that of his wife was vulnerable. She was ten years his junior, but also frail, and he was concerned how she would manage without him, but had been reassured by a monk that they would not be separated for long. He said that they were 'also dependent spiritually upon one another'. Night was a difficult time, feeling how 'powerless' their situation was, but night was also the time he repeated phrases from memory, poems and prayers, and began to recite: 'May Your gaze descend upon us, O most pure and eternally virgin Mother Mary.'

Dimana, at ninety-one years, had been fortunate in her health for most of her life and was still very active for her age. Dressed in simple clothes and thin due to her ascetic lifestyle, she still kept the Orthodox fasts on Wednesdays and Fridays, and additionally on Mondays. She was brought up in a village in North East Bulgaria. Dimana had been brought up religiously by her parents but, after she came to Varna following her marriage, her mother-in-law's practice had had an even stronger influence on her.

We were brought up to fear God. Our mother and father taught us not to steal and not to lie because grandpa God was watching. And we feared God; there might be nobody watching us, but we didn't dare steal or lie ... It happened so that the family here (after her marriage) was even better, very good Christians. My husband was an only child and my mother-in-law, she lived for God only ... I was constantly with my mother-in-law. My husband was a military person and he travelled all the time. So hand in hand, the two of us, we'd go to church.

During the communist period Dimana had been given special permission, as a woman in the absence of available men, to serve the priests behind the iconostasis during the celebration of the holy liturgy. Her sight and hearing were now deteriorated but she remained fixed on the example her mother and her mother-in-law had given her:

'Whatever I've asked, God has always given me it ... That's how my mother used to teach us. Those who ask God for help and go to church, God helps in all enterprises and now I'm thankful. I worked in the church, I baptized my children, and I wed them. Every morning when I get up, the first thing I do is to cross myself in front of the icon, I wash and I say my prayer and then, 'Dear Lord, you first, I follow'. Now that I can't see so well and I can't hear I say, 'Dear Lord, send me guidance'. There's always a person and they'd tell me where to go – come on, my girl, my boy, no one has refused to take me to the other side (of the road).

Andon was eighty-seven years of age and living in Sofia at the time of his interview. He had been recovering from a major operation carried out earlier in the year, and now had to use a walking stick. Nevertheless, he attended church every Sunday and visited his wife's grave afterwards.

He had come from a strongly religious background. His grandfather on his father's side was a priest and, as his mother was also very religious, he grew up in a strictly practising setting:

We'd go to church, fast – not only in the family, but also at school. I can even say that, as far as I can remember, we felt even less hungry, fuller in the time of fasting. The food they gave us was varied. We'd always go to receive communion in new shoes, new clothes as the tradition has it. We'd often receive communion.

His early life was spent in the Sredna Gora, the Valley of the Roses, and he enjoyed hiking in the nearby mountains, before he was attracted to navy school on the Black Sea. He served in the Bulgarian navy during WWII but his religious behaviour (reading prayers on ship and lighting candles) led to his dismissal after Bulgaria's alliance with the Soviet Union in the later stages of the war. He subsequently served on fishing vessels. As a result of the surveillance of church attendance by the authorities he had felt obliged to organise his religious wedding ceremony in secret with a priest at home. He was particularly proud of the fact that he had been successful in passing on his religious faith to his son.

Although Andon thought a more rational approach should be applied to the conflicts of everyday life including within the churches, he realised that not everything could be explained. He felt that 'mysticism intensified' in him as he grew older, and that this had a meaning in God's will for him. He had thought a lot on these issues and was able to respond to the question 'what he understood by God and how he experienced Him':

He cannot be described, he can only be felt, sensed, I can feel Him – all the questions I can't explain to myself, the entire existence, the circle of life, all this is a kind of power – be it God, be it Lord, be it Allah. The realization of these things leads to different attitudes. I can feel He's with me, I can feel it.

Sometimes it's cold, I say, "Dear Lord, when will the bus come?" And in a minute it comes. He helps me, it's again God that helps me. Thank you Lord! I'm on the bus! Besides, every morning I wake up, I believe it's the first day of the rest of my life – my life that belongs to God. That's the truth.

Ioana, a widow of eighty-six years living in Bucharest, described herself as a happy person, pleased especially with her children. Heart problems had led her to retire from work at the age of forty-four, and she was now awaiting her tenth hospital operation. For the last two years she had been unable to walk outside. Heavy or difficult housework was out of the question and even simple cooking, like making a soup, took her a long time. But she did not complain.

You know something? I am very sick, but still I am very healthy … I have to have all sorts of tests done, but as long as you don't complain, 'Oh my God what is happening to me', and you take life as it is … I think it's normal when you are 86 years old and you don't have the strength you used to have or the health you used to have.

Ioana herself made the connection between her serenity, despite her difficult life experiences, and her religious practice. She described the 'inner peace' she felt also as an old person when she was in church, and especially in the monasteries she had visited. At the time of the interview she was intending to ask again for the priest to come to perform the Prayers of St Basil which were:

a special religious service carried out to protect the house, for breaking spells, bad things and that sort of stuff. Last time I did it was three years ago. I believe in this, that I need a protector who watches over this house.

In her life she had witnessed many upheavals. She was orphaned at the early age of twelve when her mother died (her father having died when she was very little) and her older brother became her guardian. His early death in a motorcycle accident was a further traumatic event, which she described to the interviewer in great detail. And yet she appeared to have adjusted well to the difficult experiences in her life. Most remarkable of all was her response to her husband's desertion of her and their two children when she was aged thirty-seven years. She remained living with her mother-in-law. But sixteen years later her husband's new house was irreparably damaged in an earthquake and she accepted him and also his second wife back in his previous house living together with her. So they continued to live for twenty-six years. Her husband's second wife died of breast cancer the year after his own death, and in that last year Ioana and the second wife cared for each other.

People asked me how was I ever able to live in the same house with my former husband and his wife. I said we are Christians, civilized people. We too care for one another. For example after my husband died I started to have problems with my heart, they found a blood clot in my heart. His wife, they discovered that she had breast cancer, she had chemotherapy. She went to the market and she did not let me carry because she knew I wasn't allowed to bend down. So we took care of one another, as much as we could.

I taught my children to respect their father, because he's their father and to respect her as well, because she was his wife. She appreciated this greatly and she said: 'My children, if it were the case, wouldn't have respected me like yours did!'

She had strong beliefs in a life beyond death and that throughout her life she could call on the help not only of God but of loved ones, especially her mother and her brother. At the same time, and despite her extensive knowledge of religious related ritual, she taught a balanced approach to its use. For her own death she had told her daughter to pay more attention to almsgiving, also required by the Orthodox tradition, than spending money on elaborate meals.

The Oldest Participants in England

Within England interviews were conducted in the Borough of Hackney in North East London and also in Southampton, like Varna, a port city, on the south coast.

Kitty at ninety-six years was the oldest British woman we interviewed. Never married, she was still living independently in the apartment her parents had also inhabited in London. Her health had been remarkably good until relatively recently when she had begun to experience 'horrible turns', including pains in her head, which her doctor had not been able to diagnose, but which had begun to stop her going outside the house.

Religion had only started playing an important part in her life after the age of sixty years when she started attending the church near her home. Subsequently she had also become a 'friend' of St Paul's Cathedral in the City of London, helping with visitors to the church. Neither her father nor mother had attended church regularly when she was young. In fact, her mother was hostile from her experience of working in service as a cook.

Mum always said that she'd had so much drummed into her as a young woman ... one of the houses where she was they had to go three times (to church) on a Sunday and she said that they were the most unchristian people.

But she had memories of things her father had said that indicated he was religious, for example, disapproving of her dressmaking on Good Friday. He had also taken her to St Paul's to visit as a child, which had remained for her an important memory. However, Sunday school had made the biggest impression. She had enjoyed it immensely and what she had been taught had made a lasting influence.

Well I wouldn't say I was a religious person ... but I do believe in what our religion is. I do believe that. Even when I didn't go to church, it was there, what I'd been taught in Sunday school. That, you know, was so deeply put into me though, as I say, I didn't go to church.

She had found her way back to church, after her mother died, on the invitation of her friend, and she continued to attend. A day trip to St Paul's had awakened her interests in the cathedral and the possibility of offering to serve as a volunteer behind the shop counter there. She was sad that the cathedral was getting so commercialised, that the 'friends' were now less involved. She wished that more people would attend church and in particular that families would go as in the past (though her own family had not). She made comparisons with the Jewish community in the area of London where she lived.

I think it's lovely when you do see a family because personally I think that is really what should happen. That's why, as I say, you must admire the Jews. Sabbath is the Sabbath and the whole family go to synagogue. I think that's a great deal to be admired and I think it's very sad how few of our young men go to church.

Derek, at eighty-nine years, was the oldest man in our British sample. His health was good for his age, although he had to take hormone injections for testicular cancer for which he received surgery four years previously. He has virtually retired from his role as a church reader and also given up, because of tiredness, active involvement in amateur dramatics, which has been a much enjoyed feature of all his adult life. His hearing has also deteriorated and despite his hearing aid he could not hear church services well anymore. His interview took place in stages as he needed some breaks.

He was brought up by his parents as an Anglican and has remained so all his life. Most important to his religious formation was attending Sunday school. He found bible classes very interesting, and followed them through for a number of years, at the end receiving a certificate as a 'knight of the grand cross'. In 1939 at the age of seventeen he was confirmed as a member of the Church of England, a relatively late age at the time. He described his becoming a Christian as a gradual development. His growing religious interests influenced his parents. After his confirmation they began attending church again, and even took on roles in the church community, his father as treasurer of the church council and his mother chairperson of the women's group.

He had lived in North London all his life, apart from war service in the Middle East where he was captured by the German army in 1942 and imprisoned in a POW camp first in Italy and after 1943 in Germany. During his time as a prisoner of war he discovered his talent for acting, taking the part of St Mark as narrator in a passion play describing the arrest and crucifixion of Jesus, and enjoying in particular comedy and character impersonations. After the war he became a Sunday school teacher himself and took an active role in church services, singing in the choir. In 1950 at the age of twenty-nine years he became a lay minister or 'lay reader'. An only child and a single man, he continued to live with his mother after his father died. He worked in sales all his life, travelling for a time as a representative of his firm, but later in his career working back in the office as a sales office manager.

His main beliefs had remained stable since youth. He prayed every morning and evening and read the Bible every day following guidelines he has used for many years. Moreover his identification with the Anglican Church had not wavered. The one girl to whom he came closest to proposing marriage was Roman Catholic and he spoke to her openly about the difficulties there would be because he would want any children brought up as Anglicans whereas she would want them as Catholics.

Although he still officiated at services on occasions when the vicar was not there during the week, he was now a 'reader emeritus'. At present he attended two churches, his own church during the week and a different church on Sundays, which was 'high church' with more ceremony, including more elaborate use of robes, incense and bells. Difficult for him (as for many older people) were changes in liturgical form, experienced both within the Anglican and Roman Catholic churches since the 1960s, but also as a result of shifting population, with in and out migration, particularly evident in the north London area in which we interviewed.

Our minister, our vicar, is a Nigerian and we've only got two or three white people left in the church now. Now I've nothing against coloureds, it's not that, but it's that they love this 'happy clappy' stuff. They wave their arms and they move up and down. And they go on and on with this, and to me that puts me off. I go to church, to a communion service, to say my prayers and to sing a few hymns and all the rest of it. But all this – and it goes on and on and on – and what put me off was we had a harvest festival service, which went on for four hours. I mean a normal service is an hour, an hour and a half at the most and this went on for four hours. And what infuriated me was that our vicar – he's got three churches to look after ... and he wasn't (at our church) he was at one of the other churches, well he came in after this service had been going on about a couple of hours or so and he said 'Oh well we haven't got time for the communion, we'll cut that out'. And that's, I mean I couldn't believe it, because that is a communion service, the Eucharist is what you go to it for.

Nevertheless, he showed understanding for such changes in the character and length of worship that immigrants brought with them.

But of course you see these people they would go on all day. Out in Africa the churches are few and far between and so they go for miles and miles and they make a day of it and that sort of mentality still applies here I think, you see.

Generally he seems to have coped well with changes in the churches, and shown a willingness to accommodate to the different needs of the present day.

I was a reader and I felt it was a privilege to do it. When they said anybody can do it I thought 'Well' I wasn't very happy about that. But then I suppose when I think about it, it's a good thing. You get more and more people involved in doing more and more things in the church... And of course they've got all this problem in the Church of England about women bishops and ... I wasn't very happy at first because, I mean, I've always been a bit of a traditionalist at heart. But when you think about it I'm sure if Jesus was alive today he would welcome them. I know he didn't (have women apostles) in his day but things were very different. But he did have women followers.

Jennifer, aged eighty-six years, had been brought up in the East End of London. Married twice and with four children, she had vivid memories of the community events and traditions which were special to the area, including the magnificent funerals with their elaborate hearses and plumed horses, and also of the devastation caused by wartime bombing which she experienced first hand as she had refused to be evacuated to the countryside. Although non-religious, she had a positive view of the Catholic school she went to (she had been accepted with some reluctance as a non-Catholic attender), and of the colourful Catholic processions she eagerly awaited as a child.

Magnificent. It was all entertainment, a freebie. You only had to be able to know where it was and be able to get there ... The churches used to bring out their regalia and their statues of Mary with Jesus or Jesus on the cross. You would get men with their green braids across and hats too – they would play quite solemn music. The kids would all be dressed ... The girls would have blue ribbons round their hair. And this procession could be anything up to about half a mile long and it'd trail through the streets. And various houses would have opened up their window or pulled down their window and decorated their front window, so it was like an altar.

But it was not the religious meaning that was important to onlookers like her.

Well we knew that this lot believed in something. Whether we believed in it or not I don't think it really mattered. I just think we thought it was the ceremonial, how nice it was to see ... in the summer you could see a procession every Sunday (in different parishes) ... But mainly I think we went to the churches because things were happening. Not about God, but like cinema, you know, 'see it on there!', 'coming up'!

However, she could not bring herself to believe in the Christian faith as it had been presented to her.

The only time I was religious was when I used to get sent to Sunday school and they used to give you a card and they'd stamp your card, and if you had a full card you got to go on the outing which was in the summer. I can't get over this bit of seeing a bloke on a throne with cherubs and angels all swizzeling about and him ordering the state of the world. Because what makes me cross is he allows awful things to happen.

She disapproved of the 'ease' of confession. Her conscience was her judge.

She described her health as reasonable. She had had a heart attack three years previously but had not let it 'get her down'. Her head, she said, was the 'most brilliant bit'. There were things she still wanted to do but her body wouldn't let her do it.

Lewis was aged eighty-five years and living in the Southampton area. He had a number of health problems and could not walk far. At the time of interviewing his wife was also recovering from an accident, but he was hoping that they would be able to return to Fabian (socialist intellectual) group meetings. Political beliefs were important to him and these were issues, rather than religious beliefs, that he spoke about with his children.

He had gone to Roman Catholic primary and grammar schools. He was sent there by his mother who was half Irish and a Catholic. He described her as 'an uneducated Irish Catholic' with a 'nonthinking religious belief', who went to Mass every Sunday but otherwise did not display her beliefs. He remembered no images, crucifixes or statues in the house. However, she was ambitious for her children and an active member both of the Labour party and of the Catholic women's league, and for a time was chairperson of the local branches of both. His father was irreligious but had promised on his marriage that their children would be brought up as Catholics, according to the Catholic Church's requirement for permitting the marriage of Catholics and non-Catholics within the Catholic Church. Lewis remembered being told that his father had said (prophetically) 'you can bring them up as however you like but they'll just be like me by the time they're my age'.

Lewis remained at school until he was sixteen years old and learned to serve Mass there and continued to do this also when he was a member of the boy scouts. During the latter part of the war and afterwards, he served in France and Singapore. He remembered the comfort he felt when he walked into a Catholic church in France during the war and listened to exactly the same words being said (in Latin) there as he would have heard in his own church back home. On his return to England, he applied for teaching training, and as a Catholic thought he stood better chances of admission if he applied to a Catholic college and was successful. Up to that time he described himself also as an 'unthinking' Catholic, but the experience of teaching the Catholic catechism changed him.

I had one discussion with one of the priests that left me very doubtful. It was the idea that we all got our bodies back with the resurrection of the body. And fairly obviously I was having a certain amount of basic study of religion because that's what I was supposed to be teaching. I've got a Catholic teacher's certificate somewhere in the house. And so the resurrection of the body. And I said 'If we're all being given our bodies, or given bodies back, which body is it? I don't know that I want the one that I've got now for example. Where are they all going to go? If you're talking about these being physical, and you are, then when on earth is this place going to be ...'. He could have waffled, but he said something bloody stupid, he said 'Oh well there are all sorts of unexplored planets out there'. And I thought 'Well that's a load of old rubbish'. And I mean that is not to say I hadn't ever doubted before, but that planted that.

He did not take action on his doubts until much later in his life for fear of upsetting his mother, whom he lived near also after he was married (to a Catholic French woman whom he had met at the end of the war). The first school he taught at was run by nuns, and he continued to attend Mass with his mother on Sundays. He said that he 'played the part of the Catholic teacher' in the community. His three children also went to Catholic schools. But after he left his wife at the age of thirty-six and married again, he stopped attending. The conflict between the Catholic Church's teaching on divorce and remarriage and his own views on the matter made that impossible, and he no longer needed to please his mother as he was not living nearby. He said that his mother remained convinced that 'some day he would go back' to the Church.

Later in life he joined a group of Humanists. He was impressed by the way they held funerals and contrasted this with the 'insult to his intelligence' of the sentimental talk he had heard recently at a Catholic funeral of a past colleague's husband 'waiting for' her. It also seemed inconsistent to lament the death of a person who died early if you really believed a better life was awaiting them. Surely they should be more fortunate than those who had to live a long life. When asked to describe his beliefs, he said he was agnostic about the existence of a 'supreme spirit' but found unacceptable the idea that this God could be all knowing and 'aware of us all' or that there could be some form of afterlife. He repeated a number of times during the interview the difficulties he experienced with Christian teaching on bodily resurrection.

Reflection on Differences in Religious Attitudes between the Oldest Participants in Eastern and Western Europe

A focus on the oldest age group in our samples, those aged over eighty-five years, has brought out some marked differences in religiosity between our Eastern and Western European participants. Those we interviewed in Bulgaria and Romania who grew to adulthood during or just before the Second World War appear to have been a traditionally religious generation who with few exceptions have kept to the religious norms with which they were socialised, despite the anti-religious discrimination practised in their societies in the post-war years. This is less true of our British participants. We met a number of non-religious persons, including Jennifer and Lewis, in the oldest age groups we interviewed in England.

Much of the discussion on differences in religiosity between Western and Eastern Europe have focused on the greater influence of modernity, in the shape of the influences stemming from both the Reformation and the Enlightenment periods, on questioning of religious beliefs in Western Europe. However, there has been less discussion on the changing character of religious transmission in the transition to modernity. Our interview data suggest interesting differences in modes of religious socialisation in childhood between our samples, which may have contributed to the greater durability of religious commitment in the oldest participants in Romania and Bulgaria.

Early religious experience provides the emotional basis for the subsequent interpretation of religious experience. One of the most powerful theories of psychological development is that of attachment, which postulates the need for a secure base with a parental figure on which to rely for stability of emotional well-being. This expresses itself first strongly in early infancy but remains evident throughout the vicissitudes of life, especially in the building of subsequent intimate relationships but also in late life attitudes to care and dependency. Early life variations in parental experience lead to differences in attachment style, which appear to distinguish persons until the end of their lives. As religion is one of the main cultural providers of emotional security, it is no surprise that attachment theory has also been applied to the psychology of religious development (Kirkpatrick 2004). Religious socialisation also typically occurs in the context of family life in which concepts and images of parental and divine love and authority are often juxtaposed and intermingled.

However, whereas the family appears to have remained the main source of religious socialisation in our Eastern European countries throughout the pre-war and war period – and indeed even more so after the removal of religious education from schools and the limitations on the teaching function of religious organisations imposed during the communist period – the situation was already different in England. In fact formal religious education and in particular the role of the 'Sunday school' formal religious education appears as a much more significant feature of religious socialisation in our English sample. The importance to children in England, and also in other parts of the United Kingdom, of attending classes of religious education separated from their parents, typically on a Sunday late morning or afternoon, often as a preparation for receiving sacraments of initiation as Eucharist and Confirmation, has been pointed out by others. Davies (2004) for example has argued it to be a major source in the making of the British moral character. The institution was widespread through the first part of the twentieth century up to the 1950s and often led to young people attending church two or even three times a day on Sunday.

Mention of Sunday school comes up often in interviews with older people on their religious history (Coleman 2011). It is often remembered positively and could have lasting influence (as in the cases of Derek and Kitty) but this is not always so. As the sole or principal basis of religious education its discursive and rationalistic character could also lead to questioning of paradoxical, illogical and poorly represented doctrines of Christian faith. This also applies to religious teaching received in schools and later. When Lewis did begin to pay close attention to religious doctrine at his Catholic Teaching Training College, where he was expected to learn to teach religious education, he found unacceptable the responses he received to his questioning of church doctrine.

Our Romanian and Bulgarian elders' memories of religion are richly intertwined with the religious practices of their parents, grandparents and other members of their extended families. As a result the emotional ties with their faith of our Eastern European participants appear stronger than their counterparts in England. All of the former participants of eighty-five years and over had been brought up in predominantly Orthodox Christian families, generally in rural settings. The strength of religious practice in the family appeared to be the major influence on their subsequent religiosity as a young adult. Some of them (including Aurelian and Andon) had priests in their families. Generally, however, the mother's and grandmother's influence on the young person's religion appeared more evident than the father's or grandfather's. The strong emphasis on physical enactment of religious faith from early childhood, particular strong in the Eastern Christian tradition (kissing icons and lighting candles), may also be a factor in that faith's durability (Coleman, Koleva and Bornat 2013).

It is interesting that, also in the English sample, associations with the faith of parents and other members of the family were seen as especially significant, for example in Kitty's belief in her father's intrinsic religiosity despite his lack of churchgoing. Even among the non-religious and atheists, the more affective ties with religion could leave a lasting impression as Jennifer's happy memories of Catholic processions in her childhood in Poplar in the East End of London. Even Lewis whose mother was, in his own words, a 'non-thinking Catholic', appeared to regret the loss of the Latin mass and remembered how in war service in France in 1944 it made him 'feel part of something'.

To live a long life is to experience much change in the world around. Adaptation is required of ageing persons but successful adjustment (in the sense of acceptance of change) can be difficult if the changes also affect a person's sense of identity. The religious changes in the post-war years, both in Western and Eastern Europe, have been of this character (Coleman 2011). In Western Europe, surprisingly little investigation has been carried out into older people's experience of the sometimes massive changes that have occurred, for example the sudden disappearance of the traditional liturgical form of the Roman Catholic Mass. Kitty and Derek both regretted the changes they experienced as older persons within their Anglican parishes. Derek described himself as 'bitterly disappointed' that his goddaughter never decided to become confirmed as a Christian.

Our data also provided additional evidence on the impressive response to state persecution among many religious believers in Eastern Europe. All of our Bulgarian and Romanian participants in the oldest age group had arrived at adulthood as religiously practising individuals and therefore were liable to encounter potential problems under the new communist regime. Aurelian was an extreme example of suffering long years of imprisonment associated with his political activities which were connected in his own mind to his religious faith. But also Andon was adversely affected in his career by his open displays of religious practice. Many of the women also behaved heroically, or were called by the circumstances of the time to undertake unusual tasks, as in Dimana's case within the church's liturgy. English older persons had also preserved their faith despite the advance of a secular society. But often this was accompanied by regret at the extent of falling away of faith within the succeeding generation.

In old age, our religious participants kept up their religious activities as best they could, the Orthodox continuing to confess, receive communion and fast where appropriate. Aurelian and his wife articulated in striking detail the frailty of their situation, particularly their powerlessness at night. Their belief that 'nothing happens without the will of God' sustained them. They were content that they could still walk. All Aurelian asked for was that he would not go blind completely. Many acknowledged their experience of God helping them in their daily life. If this faith appeared stronger among our Eastern European participants it may be because of its practice within the family context from childhood onwards and through the period of state persecution. Failure of transmission of faith was a painful aspect of interviews with older people in England. Some of our Eastern European participants were aware that further trials lay ahead for their peoples as a result of European integration. As another of our Romanian participants over the age of eighty-five years commented: 'I think that communist atheism was less dangerous than the western one'.

Prediction of the future is always a highly uncertain matter. However, greater awareness of cultural and generational differences can alert us to possibilities. For example, Vern Bengtson's analysis of the differences between successive cohorts born throughout the twentieth century show a decline in religious allegiance in those born in the post Second World War years but also suggest that the latest 'millenial' generation may be transcending the active antagonism of their parents towards religious authority and showing more interest in what religious traditions have to offer (Bengtson and Johnson 2016). Increasing access to the faith practices of other cultures, also as the result of the immigration of Eastern Europeans to Western Europe, may encourage greater respect not only for these new forms of religious life but also for native traditions. As Paul Higgs (2016) stresses in his contribution to this volume, personal ownership of religious practice is a supreme value in contemporary society. But this does not exclude belonging to a shared tradition. In later life, in particular, sharing practice of a common faith offers huge, perhaps incomparable, benefits in terms of providing both emotional security and a sense of generativity towards future generations.

References

Bengtson, V. and Johnson, M. (2016). 'Religion, belief and spirituality in old age: how they change'. In Johnson, M. and Walker, J. (eds.) *Spiritual Dimensions of Ageing*. Cambridge: Cambridge University Press.

Brown, C. (2001). *The Death of Christian Britain*. London: Routledge.

Coleman, P.G. (2011). *Belief and Ageing. Spiritual Pathways in Later Life*. Bristol: Policy Press.

Coleman, P.G., Koleva, D. and Bornat, J. (eds.) (2013). *Ageing, Ritual and Social Change: Comparing the Secular and Religious in Eastern and Western Europe*. Farnham: Ashgate.

Davies, C. (2004). *The Strange Death of Moral Britain*. New Brunswick, NJ: Transaction.

Eurobarometer. (2005). *Social Values, Science and Technology. Report 225*. Brussels: European Commission.

Froese, P. (2008). *The Plot to Kill God. Findings from the Soviet Experiment in Secularization*. Berkeley, CA: University of California Press.

Higgs, P. (2016). 'New cultures of ageing: the impact of the third age on issues of spirituality and religion'. In Johnson, M. and Walker, J. (eds.) *Spiritual Dimensions of Ageing*. Cambridge: Cambridge University Press.

Idler, E. (2016). 'Religious ritual and practice in old age'. In Johnson, M. and Walker, J. (eds.) *Spiritual Dimensions of Ageing*. Cambridge: Cambridge University Press.

Kirkpatrick, L.A. (2004). *Attachment, Evolution and the Psychology of Religion*. New York: Guilford Press.

Koleva, D. (2013). 'Performing social normativity: religious rituals in secular lives'. In Coleman, P., Koleva, D. and Bornat, J. (eds.) *Ageing, Ritual and Social Change*, pp. 111–132. Farnham: Ashgate.

Rooden, P. van. (2010). 'The strange death of Dutch Christendom'. In Brown, C. and Snape, M. (eds.) *Secularisation in the Christian World*, pp. 175–195. Farnham: Ashgate.

8 Religious Ritual and Practice in Old Age

Ellen Idler

Introduction

All religions have the dimension of rituals or religious practices that define them. Some rituals, like the repetition of the rosary or a yoga mantra, are primarily spoken. Others, like meditation, or the practice of t'ai chi, may be mostly nonverbal. Some rituals, such as infant circumcision, are performed only once in a lifetime; others, such as the Muslim five-times-daily prayers, are performed numerous times per day, every day. Over the course of a long life, the number of times a ritual is performed and experienced can become an unbroken thread that ties together the cycles of days, weeks and years. The ritual dimension of religious experience was a profound part of the thinking of the classical sociologists, but fell out of favour by the latter part of the twentieth century, when the word ritual took on the meaning of being rote, unconscious, meaningless or empty. More recently, there has been a new burst of scholarship in cognitive science and religious studies on religious ritual and practice, although none of it has made the (obvious) connection with ageing and the life course. In this chapter I will attempt to show the connections between the new research and existing literature on religion, ageing and health. I will illustrate some of these issues with examples from the long life of my father, a Presbyterian clergyman, who died in August 2011.

My Father's Story

My father died at the age of eighty-three. He was a Presbyterian minister and for most of his career he pastored several small and medium-sized congregations in Pittsburgh and Harrisburg, Pennsylvania. When he did not have a church of his own (while in academic administration at Pittsburgh Theological Seminary, and even well into his official retirement) he was a 'supply' or 'interim' preacher, who travelled to churches that needed someone to fill the pulpit. As a little girl, I would visit his office with its walls of books and the black robe hanging on the back of the door. On one of the shelves was a small brown box that became an object of intense fascination for me. I thought of it as Daddy's little tea set. The box opened with a snap. Inside, it was lined with purple velvet. There were six tiny glasses with heavy bottoms and a flared shape, a small plastic bottle with a cap, and a little ivory-coloured plate that had a cover. The only time I ever saw the inside was at home when my mother was washing the contents – in the office I knew it was serious, and mysterious, and not to be played with, as much as I might want to. It was a child's perception of the sacred.

This box was my father's Communion visitation kit, used to take consecrated bread and wine (well, grape juice – we were Presbyterians) to the 'shut-ins'. These were members of the congregation, almost always elderly, who were too ill or disabled to worship and take Communion with the congregation. For Christians, Communion, or the Eucharist, is the sacrament that commemorates the Lord's Supper, the final meal that Jesus ate with his disciples the night before he was crucified. The wine symbolises the blood, and the bread the body of Christ. By eating and drinking together, modern Christians, like the disciples two thousand years ago, become bound to each other and to their belief in Jesus Christ as the Son of God. In this ritual act, members of a congregation them-selves become – in the language of the liturgy – the body of Christ, a living thing that transcends the time and space of the rite, bringing together Christians all over the globe.

In the Reformed tradition, by comparison with the Anglican or Roman Catholic churches, Communion is celebrated relatively infrequently – as rarely as quarterly, but usually not more often than once per month. After each one of these services was held, my father took Communion to those who could not attend the worship service because they were ill. Although he might visit the sick in their homes at other times as well, he would not take Communion – in the special brown box – with him unless the congregation had celebrated the sacrament first. Thus the ritual was not a symbol of the need of the particular sick person, but much more a statement about the larger congregation. The timing underscored the belonging of the 'shut-in' to the congregation – remembering them, including them, showing them that the celebration of the sacrament by the congregation was incomplete without them.

For many years during his long life, my father took Communion to the shut-ins. After his stroke in 2008, the tide turned. From that moment on, my father was the one who could not walk or care for himself. The minister who had replaced him after his retirement became the one who reached out to include him in the circle of the congregation. Revd

Roach had his own Communion visitation kit, of course – my father's was never used again.

I tell this story to give an example of a religious ritual and its role in old age. The purpose of this chapter will be to contextualise this single example of religious practice in old age in a broader view of new scholarship on religious ritual; scholarship that draws our attention away from intrinsic, subjective, belief-based dimensions of religion and spirituality – what people think – to focus instead on religious acts – what people do. A second purpose is to bring a life course perspective to this research, to initiate thinking about the meaning and significance of lifelong religious practices.

Rituals and Religious Practices

A ritual, according to the late, brilliant anthropologist Roy Rappaport (1999), is a prescribed 'performance of more or less invariant sequences of formal acts and utterances not entirely encoded by the performers'. This definition is a good one because it does not make any assumptions about the content or the function of ritual, it simply characterises its structure. Rappaport, in his important work *Ritual and religion in the making of humanity*, argues that ritual is 'the ground from which religion grows'. (Rappaport 1999, p. 26) He calls religious rituals 'liturgical orders'; they are unvarying, formalised, elaborated sets of words and linked actions that perform, or enact, the performer's relationship to the sacred.

Several aspects of this definition are important to our understanding of the meaning of ritual in old age. The first is that the ritual doesn't exist unless it is performed; liturgical orders can be written – the words that must be said and the actions that must coincide with them can be described in text – but the ritual itself is the combination of the actual 'saying' and the actual 'doing'. Second, the words and acts are formal in the sense that they must be done in the same way, time after time; the performer strives for sameness and consistency, not originality or innovation. The words and acts have a sequence along two parallel tracks; each leads to the next in an invariant order, although the words do not always narrate the acts. This invariant sequence, then, has a beginning and an end, which leads us to a third important aspect: a ritual experience is a binary, an on-off. One either is participating in a ritual, immersed in its time and place, or not. Within the space of the ritual, the structure of fused-together words and acts brings us finally to one of ritual's most important aspects, and that is its capacity for creating sensory experiences in the participants.

Rituals require that the performer has the cognitive capacity, or memory, for a competent performance, as well as the physical capacity for the motions, gestures, and postures that are required. Frequently, rituals are performed in groups, where individuals are simultaneously entrained in a synchrony of sound, sight, touch, and even taste and smell. Music, drumming, chanting and dance are all powerful methods for producing experiences that may memorably unify the minds, bodies and spirits of ritual performers, moving them through the performance as if they are caught up in a powerful wave. It is in this space of ritual that human beings may come to perceive their relationship to the sacred, be it in the form of ancestors, spirits, gods or God. That it is a predictable, familiar, continuous practice is critical for its relevance in old age.

Rappaport's intellectual progenitors were the great social and anthropological minds of the early twentieth century, chief among them Emile Durkheim (Durkheim 1915/1965). They sought to understand not only the formal structure of religious ritual, but also the ritual's functions for the human groups who performed it. They noted that religious rituals were called on in times of crisis, or at moments of transition or change. They noted that they took place in accordance with the changing of the seasons or when births or deaths occurred. They noted especially that rituals were performed in social groups, and that the performance brought the group together with feelings of solidarity and unity. They concluded that the primary function of religious ritual was to create, re-create, and enhance social structure, by resolving social conflict and reinforcing the social order. In performing religious rituals, Durkheim argued, social groups represent themselves to themselves. Each individual sees him or herself as one person immersed in a larger group, and belonging to it, being a constituent part of it. Anthropologist Victor Turner called this the sense of *communitas* (Turner 1969). It is exactly this sense that was transmitted every time my father took Communion to an elderly woman in a nursing home, or his pastor brought it to him. As we noted earlier, Christian clergy make many visits to the sick, only a small proportion of which include the ritual of Communion. Each visit symbolises the connection of the congregation to the sick person, but the ritual practice of Communion *enacts* that connection, by linking the whole congregation with the body and blood of Christ.

The Timing and Cycles of Religious Rituals over the Life Course

When and *how often* rituals are performed – their timing – is a critical feature. Some, like a *bar mitzvah*, occur only once in a lifetime. Others

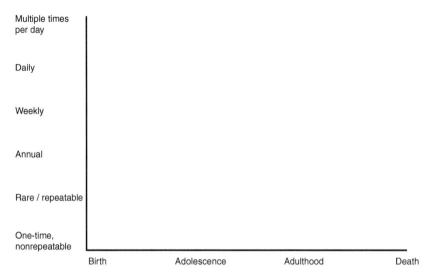

Figure 1. Potential for religious ritual performance over the life course

occur once every year, at the same time. Others may take place weekly, or every day, or even several times a day. Rituals have been described as being either calendrical or non-calendrical (Wallace 1966). Calendrical rituals are based on the day of the week, or the season or the time of year. Calendrical rituals are performed regularly, on a schedule that is known and can be anticipated, and they involve all members of the religious community. Non-calendrical rituals, on the other hand, are performed 'as needed' – when a baby is born, or a couple wants to marry, or someone dies. These non-calendrical rituals would involve a smaller group of people who are personally related to the subject(s) of the ritual.

Imagine the space of a person's religious life as an area with X and Y axes graphing the intersection of the two dimensions of time and frequency. Along the bottom of the graph, on the X axis, we could measure the person's age from birth to death. Along the Y axis we could measure the frequency of religious ritual performance. That graph would look like Figure 1, allowing us to depict the frequency of ritual repetition over the course of a long life.

This empty space could be filled in a number of ways. Figure 2 shows us what the maximum performance of religious ritual over the life course would look like. This maximum could be reached only for an individual who was born into a religious community and who began participating in religious rituals in early life, continued through adolescence and midlife

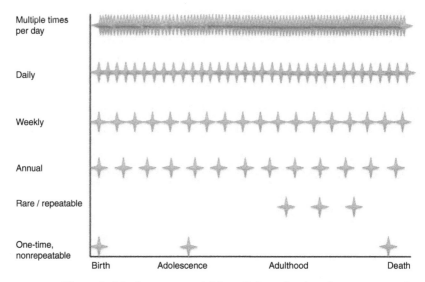

Figure 2. Maximum potential for religious ritual performance over the life course

and into old age. To see the potential accumulation of ritual experiences over the life course, we would multiply the cyclical frequency of the ritual performance by the number of years or weeks or days that a person has lived. So a ninety-five-year-old Hindu man could have celebrated Diwali – the festival of the goddess Lakshmi – ninety-five times but not ninety-six. A twenty-five-year-old woman could have said grace before her meals 3 (times per day) × 365 (days per year) × 25 (years of life) = 27,375 times. Muslim prayers said five times per day would multiply even faster. Some rituals, such as a *bris*, the Jewish ceremony for infant circumcision, or a funeral mass, occur only once for a person. The graph includes some rituals that may or may occur, and that could theoretically be repeated. These would be tied to moments in the adult life course, such as ordination into the priesthood, or the sacrament of marriage, which might not occur at all in some lives; marriage, in particular, might be repeated more than once in others. We would note that this graph takes the perspective of the subject of the ritual – one might participate as an observer in a large number of *bar* or *bat mitzvahs*, for example, but one can experience one's own only once.

As we said, Figure 2 represents the theoretical maximum for the number of times rituals could be performed during the course of a life. But it is unlikely that a person would ever participate in the maximum number possible, even in the strictest and most observant religious communities. Moreover, the periods of non-observance might form specific patterns; in Figure 2 those patterns might appear as white spaces, or gaps, where there are currently stars. Individuals who have had a religious upbringing, for example, might cease being observant when they become adults. In this case a vertical line could be drawn and all stars to the right of that line eliminated. Another configuration might be found for individuals who participate with their family in the one-time-only life course rituals, and perhaps annual religious holiday celebrations, but none of those that take place more frequently. This case would include the stars in the lower half of the graph but none of those at the top. To be sure, the individual's faith tradition plays a role in determining the frequency of ritual performance. Our recent research in a religiously diverse sample found that conservative Protestants (Baptists, Pentecostals) and Muslims were significantly more likely than mainline Protestants, Jews, Roman Catholics or Hindus to participate in daily devotional activities (Idler et al. 2009).

On a graph like Figure 2, my father, a mainline Protestant, would have had many stars. He was born into an observant family of German Presbyterians living in Philadelphia. He said grace silently or aloud before most meals; led two worship services on many Sundays; led spiritual retreats for and with other clergy; and as far as I know never had a period of non-observance.

Rituals and Ageing

One-Time-Only Rituals

The rituals represented in Figure 2 can be thought of as occurring in cycles. For some, the cycle is made just once in a life. Baptism, circumcision, confirmation, *bar mitzvah* – these are the familiar Judeo-Christian rituals that take place in infancy, childhood or at the time of puberty. Hinduism has as many as forty distinct rites (*sansakars*) prescribed for different moments of the life course. Salamone (2010, p. 173) lists the sixteen most important; fourteen of these Hindu rites (such as naming, and giving the child's first haircut) take place in infancy, childhood and youth. The remaining two are marriage and cremation, leaving the later years of the life course fairly free of religious ritual markers by comparison with the early part of the life course.

One reason for this may be that the rituals of the major world religions draw their origins back to a period when few members of a society reached old age. The life course transition points marked by religious ritual – birth, puberty, marriage, childbearing – mark and celebrate the survival and growth of the society itself. Thus the *end* of fertility (for a woman), for example, was a biological transition point not reached by many women in early societies, and would not have been seen as a cause for celebration in any case. Thus none of the life course rituals in any of the world's religions commemorate old age or take place specifically during that period of the life course. Today we think of rituals for the dying and at the time of death as being particularly relevant to old age, but in fact they are the same no matter what the age of the dying person is.

A similar argument could be made for the optional rituals of marriage or ordination. While they *could* take place in old age, they rarely would. Both rituals mark the start of a new role for the individual, with new status, responsibilities and privileges. The person has usually passed through a period of training, or engagement, and the ritual marks their transition into a new position of leadership for a social institution, be it a family or a religious group. One might argue that the installation of a Pope would disprove the statement, especially in recent times when the papacy has been held by very elderly men. But actually one could not become Pope unless one had already spent a career in the priesthood, beginning in young adulthood. My father was ordained and married in the same year, when he was twenty-three. Within a week of his wedding, while he was still travelling to a Presbyterian mission in Arizona, his own father died suddenly of a heart attack. As the oldest son, he became at that moment the male head of both his natal and procreative families, and the religious rituals of his ordination and marriage were followed very closely by the funeral rites for his father.

It is easy to link the singular, once-only or rarely occurring rituals to the life course (Reynolds and Tanner 1995). They mark the process of growth and maturation of the individual. They create and recognise the ritual subject's new status in his or her community. They legitimise the individual's assumption of roles that have new powers and privileges. These rites of passage move the individual from one stage of the life course to the next (Van Gennep 1908/1960). In the moment of the puberty ritual a boy becomes a man and a girl becomes a woman – everything prior to that was childhood, and everything from now on is adulthood. For the older members of the religious group, their own experience of this ritual will have taken place long in the past. But the repeated participation in it as an observer for successive generations, particularly one's own children and grandchildren, signals the ongoing, vital persistence of the religious group itself. Particularly those for whom death is near, the visible renewing of the community may be a comforting reminder that one's own life was part of something greater that will live on for many more generations. Death threatens both individuals and communities. As individuals, we will all die; but those who participate in the religious rituals of ongoing religious communities may have the cognitive and emotional comfort that the something larger that they are a part of, and which is meaningful to them, will continue without them.

Annual Rituals

Next in terms of frequency would be the annual rituals, the once-a-year observances that often commemorate some of the most significant events of the faith. They provide an opportunity to tell and retell the central narratives of the religious tradition. Annual rituals are a feature of nearly all religions around the world, although some observe more yearly festivals or holidays than others do. Some of the most significant would be: Yom Kippur (Judaism), Easter (Christianity), Ramadan (Islam), Diwali (Hinduism) and Wesak (Buddhism). The celebration of the most important annual holidays may involve a period of preparation (both material and spiritual), time off from work, attendance at religious rituals and, frequently in modern societies, travel to participate in family festivities – in other words, significant amounts of time are given each year to the observance of these once-per-year religious holidays. For many in secular societies these observances are the only prominent marker of one's religious identity and group membership, which may be of little personal significance on a daily or weekly basis. Observing these holidays often involves preparing the home (and church or temple) by cleaning and/or placing special decorations, preparing special foods eaten only on that occasion, wearing special clothes, performing special music, giving gifts.

As annual celebrations, these rituals 'mark time' in the lives of individuals and families. The level of sensory pageantry is high (McCauley and Lawson 2002). Their repetition is widely spaced, but frequent enough that a child can remember the experience from the past and anticipate it accurately in their future. In fact, children often play a key role in these observances, as they learn and even enact the stories of their religious tradition. Across the life course, the string of these annual observances grows. In middle age, an individual with a lifetime of holiday rituals will be able to recall their own childhood observances with family members who have since died. In old age, a religiously observant individual will have celebrated eighty or more such holidays, with two generations of family and religious group members now dead, and two or even three who come after.

There is evidence that the significance of the holiday continues to the moment of death. Our study of the timing of deaths of elderly Christians and Jews around annual holidays found that both were significantly more likely to die in the thirty days following their own annual holidays of Christmas, Easter, Yom Kippur, Passover or Rosh Hashanah than they were in the thirty days preceding it (Idler and Kasl 1992). This was not a significant delay in the sense of increasing life expectancy through religious participation; the subjects in the study were very elderly people who were near the end of their lives. What the study tells us is that the opportunity to experience a religious ritual, and probably a family gathering as well, provided some additional 'will to live' that was enough to enable them to have that meaningful religious experience just one more time.

Weekly Rituals

Moving even further up the Y axis in Figure 2, we come to the far more frequently celebrated weekly rituals. The weekly cycle of a day of worship and rest, or Sabbath, is more a feature of the monotheistic religions, especially Judaism and Christianity, than it is of Hinduism or Buddhism. Notably, the 'seven-day circle' is an entirely human invention; nothing in nature provides a model (Zerubavel 1985). The weekly religious observance takes place in the sacred space of a church, temple or mosque. The congregation, even in the most staid Protestant church, does not simply observe passively; it participates actively by kneeling, singing, reading, praying or even clapping, swaying and dancing. The words and actions of the ritual focus the consciousness and emotions of the participants on the moment, including even their breathing, when speaking and singing in unison. This simultaneous participation of many individuals in the rituals of their faith entrains them, fuses them, unites them into one larger living thing that is performing acts and words as they have been performed for centuries.

Over the life course, the repeated experience of weekly religious ritual observances such as the mass, or Friday prayers, builds up many memories. I have often noted that the weekly worship service is the most age-integrated social experience that people attend on a regular basis. Every other social institution that we are a part of is either actively or passively age-segregated in some way – nuclear families, the work place, schools, doctors' offices. The youngest and oldest members of our societies are excluded from many of these settings. But weekly religious services welcome and even celebrate the newborn and the centenarian, and everyone in between, and all are there for the same purpose and are equally valued for their membership and participation. It is true that older persons may become disabled and unable to attend without assistance, but many congregations provide transportation to services and clergy visit those who are truly unable to attend, just as my father did.

In our study of the religious attendance of community residents in their last year of life, we found that attendance at services did not decline significantly until the last six months of life, and even then it was on average still once per month (Idler, Kasl and Hays 2001). For elderly persons who live alone or who have limited mobility, the ritual of the religious service may be the highlight of their week, a social and spiritual event to anticipate with pleasure. In fact, a study of the timing of death in Israel showed the same before – after pattern of deaths that we saw with the annual holidays in New Haven, Connecticut: older Jews were less likely to die in the three days prior to the Sabbath than they were the three days following (Anson and Anson 2001). In this very short space at the end of life, religious ritual plays a significant role.

Daily or Multiple Daily Rituals

Finally, at the top of Figure 2, we have religious rituals that are engaged in every day, or even multiple times per day. The most common daily practices would be prayer, meditation, contemplation, yoga and other spiritual disciplines that likely take place in the home or other private space, although some Roman Catholics may attend a Mass every single day, and a Muslim may go to the mosque to say prayers every day, not only on Friday. We should distinguish ritual prayers – said in the same way every time, often with performative gestures or postures – from other types of spontaneous, supplicative or intercessory prayers. The 2008 General Social Survey found that 58 percent of US residents reported that they prayed at least once per day; Protestants and Catholics prayed more often, Jews less often. The involvement of the physical body is an important feature of ritual prayer. Morning prayers for Orthodox Jews may include the binding of phylacteries to the forehead and arms. Muslims pray five times per day and each instance of *Salat* is preceded by washing of the face, hands, neck and feet, and is accompanied by eleven different postures. Roman Catholic Christians perform the sign of the Cross before praying the Our Father. This gesture of touching the forehead and chest in four places invokes in an instant the story of the Crucifixion, Christ's suffering and the complex symbol of the Trinity – Father, Son and Holy Ghost. The elderly person who prays repeatedly each day and who has done so for most of his or her life has immersed in a unified experience of the spiritual and the physical, a 'level of body awareness that can operate below the level of consciousness' (Orsi 2005, p. 108). The spiritual disciplines of Eastern religions such as yoga, t'ai chi and meditation would provide this integrated experience of mind, body and spirit even more profoundly (d'Aquili, Laughlin and McManus 1979).

Let us return to Figure 2. This 'maximum performance potential' would in fact be an accurate representation of the religious ritual participation of my father. With his religious upbringing, theological training, marriage to an equally observant woman of the same faith, membership of the clergy and active practitioner of contemplation, he was about as soaked in religious ritual as a twentieth century, politically liberal mainline Presbyterian could be. My father was not a saint. He liked to tell dirty jokes (very embarrassing), and while able to give up his single malt whiskey for the forty days of Lent every year, he was always happy to have a second or third at other times. He was a lot of fun to be with.

Why Ritual Got a Bad Name

So if ritual was such an important aspect of the thinking of early and mid-twentieth century thinkers, how did it come to get a bad name? The works of Emile Durkheim (1956), Arnold Van Gennep (1960), Victor Turner (1969), Anthony Wallace (1966) or Mary Douglas (1966) are classics that place ritual at the centre of what religion is. By the 1980s, however, a notable shift had taken place, and scholarship that still engaged the concept had to contend with the now-widespread perception that the term itself was a pejorative. Ritual now, to most people's ears, connotes rote actions that are unthinking, empty, meaningless. This change in the understanding of the concept coincided with the increasingly rapid secularisation that picked up steam in the second half of the twentieth century in western Europe, and in the United States to a lesser extent. To many Europeans, ritual was empty and meaningless because religion itself was empty and meaningless. To some European academics, ritual carried the extra stigma of being a focus of the structural-functional school of anthropology, and therefore a tool of conservative privilege to maintain inequality and unjust social arrangements.

The reasons for the casting of aspersion on the concept in the much more religiously observant US are different and more interesting. Here the critique of ritual comes partially from the religious quarter itself. Adam Seligman and colleagues, in a fascinating book entitled *Ritual and its consequences: An essay on the limits of sincerity* (Seligman et al. 2008), argue that evangelical Protestantism, which has been growing in market share as the mainline Protestant churches have declined, has had an undue influence on our thinking about ritual. In its emphasis on 'sincerity' – by which Seligman et al. mean the search for inner certainty and for a personal relationship with Christ – evangelical Protestantism privileges the inner spirit over the outward practice. Seligman argues that the quest for this 'truth-standard' is perfectionistic, deriving from the need to know if one is saved or damned. In this view, only by attending to the 'still, small' inner voice, can one be sure of one's salvation. In Tanya Luhrmann's insightful book *When God talks back* (Luhrmann 2012) she describes the distinctly unritualised practices that US Christian Evangelicals use to learn to hear the voice of God in their everyday lives. They do this by writing their prayers and dreams in notebooks, participating in study groups and, with the help of the group, refining their powers of discernment to know if it is really God talking. Because the goal is a personal, intimate relationship with God, the formal practice of ritual (that anyone can do, and that all do in the same way) may not be seen as the way to achieve the unique relationship that is sought. Christian Evangelicals Luhrmann interviewed desired to live in the continual presence of God, in which prayer was a spontaneous, two-way conversation. In fact, I think we see this US influence in much of the research to date on religion and health, where the emphasis has been on developing survey measures that probe the individual's inner life, while ignoring the public, social dimensions of religious involvement (Idler et al. 2009). Thus, for a confluence of social, political and religious reasons, the term ritual had become a dirty word by the end of the twentieth century, in common conversation as well as in academe.

Why the Study of Ritual Is Now the Cutting Edge of the Cognitive Science of Religion

This is all background to say why it is so amazing to see the recent upsurge of research in the cognitive science of religion. Back in 1966, A.F.C. Wallace wrote that 'Ritual is religion in action: it is the cutting edge of the tool' (Wallace 1966, p. 102). And in fact ritual does seem to be the new cutting edge of the tool for cognitive scientists such as Pascal Boyer (2001), Roy Rappaport (1999), Catherine Bell (2009), Robert McCauley (2002), Adam Seligman (2008) and Justin Barrett (2004). Despite being labelled 'cognitive', this new wave of scholarship has taken a special interest in the *practice* of religion – its outward performances – rather than the structure of its *beliefs*. Rappaport (1999) argues that liturgical orders are *public* orders, and performing them implies accepting them. In a sense it does not matter what you believe; the outward performance, particularly for the once-only rituals, is all that counts. If you undergo the sacrament of marriage in a Roman Catholic Church, you are married. If you take the vows of priesthood you are a priest. If you are circumcised by a mohel, you are a Jewish male; there is nothing you can do about it – your status in the eyes of the group has been permanently changed. But as a whole this new work actually turns the critique of 'meaningless ritualism' on its head. Ritual can actually do all that it says it can do, whether the people doing it 'believe' in it or not! This makes ritual a pretty powerful thing. Even the more frequently performed rituals take one out of the 'profane' sphere of everyday life, and transport one to the 'sacred' time of the ritual for those few moments, marking out a distinct before and after.

Practice-based religions may pursue and aspire to perfectionism, but the daily and weekly repetition of rituals implies acceptance of the limits and foibles of ordinary human beings. One of Seligman et al.'s memorable examples is that participating in regular religious rituals is like brushing your teeth (2008). You do it, and it is done well and your teeth are clean, but no one would say that you only have to do it once, that it will not be necessary again. In his amusing book *Religion for atheists*, Alain de Botton (2012) observes that religions have a certain genius to them, in perceiving that mere humans need frequent reminding and reinforcement. The liturgical calendar in the Christian Church assures that the important narratives of scripture are returned to on a regular basis. As he notes, this is a much wiser approach than that of most educational institutions, which blithely assume that the words a teacher says in class a single time will be remembered forever, even after the test.

Ritual makes religion into a visible, material thing. It makes it available to the senses (Feierman 2009). We smell the incense of the Greek Orthodox service; we taste the bitter herbs at a Seder; we feel the touch of hands when they are laid on us in a Christian healing ritual; we hear the chanting of the Tibetan Buddhist priests; we see the millions of Muslim pilgrims making the Hajj to Mecca. The new and popular interest in 'embodied spirituality' comes, perhaps not surprisingly, from many religious traditions that are reappreciating their own embodiedness and also sometimes adopting practices from other traditions. The effect and the purpose of the ritual practice is to bring the individual into a collective state with the transcendent. It does this through every sensory pathway that the body has, and repeats the experience throughout our lifetimes.

Why the New Research Needs to Consider the Importance of the Repetition of Ritual over the Life Span

Although it seems incredibly relevant to me, the new scholarship has paid very little attention to the intersection of religious ritual with the processes of ageing and the life course. For example, Pascal Boyer calls rituals 'snares for thought' that collapse incredibly complex sets of symbols and meanings into familiar forms that can be learned and performed by individuals of varying levels of cognitive capacity (Boyer 2001). Justin Barrett (2004) writes about human agency detection devices (HADD) that human beings are evolutionarily 'wired' with, because awareness of others (with agency) in the environment – both those who threaten and those who protect – was critical for the survival of our human ancestors. So he contends that we are wired to anthropomorphise the cosmos, and to attribute motive and agency to forces we cannot necessarily see or perceive directly. Some of his most interesting research (Barrett 2004) is about the ability of young children to differentiate their concepts of God from those of other figures of authority by using the Theory of Mind. In his experiments, three-year-olds attribute superhuman knowledge to both God and their mothers, but by age four they report that their mother will not know what has happened in the room while she was outside, but that God will.

Barrett's and Boyer's work is on the acquisition of cognitive facility in early life, or in the widespread participation in religion of people throughout history, regardless of their level of literacy or intellectual ability. The application of their thinking to the performance of religious ritual throughout the life course seems profound to me, although they themselves do not make this connection. From earliest, pre-literate, even pre-verbal life, religious ritual carries meaning and portent. At every stage of life there are appropriate rituals that mark and dignify transitions and provide a map or a guide for behaviour in new or confusing circumstances that one is facing for the first time. And in old age, when cognitive facility may be waning, familiar religious rituals may be a substantial source for continued cognitive functioning when recent memories are fleeting and unreliable. While there has been rather little research on the topic of religion and dementia, Koenig and colleagues (Koenig, King and Carson 2012) speculate that religion and spirituality may be especially related to procedural memory (that is based on habits and skills that do not have to be consciously recalled) and priming memory (that would be evoked by familiar religious symbols). For those with lifelong religious practice as depicted in Figure 2, the availability of well-learned religious practice from the past may be an important resource for maintaining personhood and identity in the face of confusion and impairment in the present.

Religious ritual is *practice*, and as such it has an impact on the physical, emotional, cognitive and spiritual and religious state of the individual. The world's religions have certain structural similarities, and one of them is the coinciding of their rituals with particular moments of the life course. Rituals link the physical body with the social body, each of which has timetables. Every year as we celebrate another birthday in our personal timetable, there is the potential for exactly one celebration of an annual religious holiday, fifty-two celebrations of weekly observances, and 365 or more daily practices. As we return to them in more or less frequent cycles, their meaning is confronted with the fresh perspective of the present moment, as well as the past perspectives of all of those previous moments. Our physical bodies have timetables of eating, sleeping, having babies and, eventually, getting old and dying. When we participate with others in these life course transition ritual practices, we anticipate our own future transition or remember our past. For the final transition, whether or not one believes in an afterlife, the knowledge that one's life will be commemorated by one's community can give dignity, grace, and comfort to the end of life.

My father died in August 2011 in a nursing home run by the Church of the Brethren, a prominent denomination in central Pennsylvania, where there are also many Amish and Mennonite communities. It was ecumenical: he had a Jewish nurse, a Muslim nurse and many Church of the Brethren nurses. He would go to the worship services on Sunday morning in the nursing home's chapel if my mother took him, but she did not like the conservative theology of the pastor, so they more often sat in the room and watched the broadcast from the large Presbyterian church in downtown Harrisburg where they had both worked for many years in the soup kitchen and homeless shelter. His memorial service was held at the church he had served for twenty-five years. Nearly three hundred people attended. An astonishing number of these people had been married by him – including my husband and me, but also my aunt and uncle, cousins and many members of the church. The same could be said for their baptisms and confirmations. We placed his ashes in the ground near the sanctuary, in the memorial garden that he had drawn up plans for many years before. His life closed in the dignified, embodied, embedded way that it had begun, in the circle of a religious community, bound together by religious practice and the continuous thread of religious ritual.

References

Anson, J. and Anson, O. (2001). 'Death rests a while: Holy day and Sabbath effects of Jewish mortality in Israel', *Social Science and Medicine* 52: 83–97.

Barrett, J. L. (2004). *Why would anyone believe in God?* Lanham, MD: Altamira Press.

Bell, C. (2009). *Ritual theory, ritual practice.* New York: Oxford University Press.

Boyer, P. (2001). *Religion explained: The evolutionary origins of religious thought.* New York: Basic Books.

d'Aquili, E. G., Laughlin, C. D. and McManus, J. (1979). *The spectrum of ritual: A biogenetic structural analysis.* New York: Columbia University Press.

de Botton, A. (2012). *Religion for atheists: A non-believer's guide to the uses of religion.* New York: Pantheon Books.

Douglas, M. (1966). *Purity and danger: An analysis of the concepts of pollution and taboo.* London: Routledge & Kegan Paul.

Durkheim, E. (1956). *Education and society.* California: Free Press.

Durkheim, E. (1915/1965). *The elementary forms of the religious life.* New York, NY: Free Press.

Feierman, J. R., (ed.) (2009). *The biology of religious behavior: The evolutionary origins of faith and religion.* Santa Barbara, CA: Praeger.

Idler, E. L. (2011). 'Religion and adult mortality', in Rogers, R. and Crimmins, E. (eds.) *International Handbook of Adult Mortality*, pp. 345–377. Dordrecht: Springer.

Idler, E. L. and Kasl, S. V. (1992). 'Religion, disability, depression, and the timing of death', *American Journal of Sociology* 97: 1052–1079.

Idler, E. L., Kasl, S. V. and Hays, J. C. (2001). 'Patterns of religious practice and belief in the last year of life', *Journal of Gerontology: Social Science* 56B: S326–S334.

Idler, E. L., Boulifard, D. A., Labouvie, E., Chen, Y., Krause, T. J. and Contrada. R. J. (2009). 'Looking inside the black box of "attendance at services": New measures for exploring an old dimension in religion and health research', *The International Journal for the Psychology of Religion* 19(1): 1–20.

Koenig, H. G., King, D. E. and Carson V. B. (2012). *Handbook of religion and health*, 2nd Edition. New York: Oxford University Press.

Luhrmann, T. (2012). *When God talks back: Understanding the American Evangelical relationship with God.* New York: Knopf.

McCauley, R. N. and Lawson, E. T. (2002). *Bringing ritual to mind: Psychological foundations of cultural forms.* Cambridge: Cambridge University Press.

Orsi, R. A. (2005). *Between heaven and earth: The religious worlds people make and the scholars who study them.* Princeton, NJ: Princeton University Press.

Rappaport, R. (1999). *Ritual and religion in the making of humanity.* New York: Cambridge University Press.

Reynolds, V. and Tanner, R. (1995). *The social ecology of religion.* London: Oxford University Press.

Salamone, F. (2010). *Routledge encyclopedia of religious rites, rituals and festivals.* New York: Routledge.

Seligman, A. B., Weller, R. P., Puett, M. J. and Simon, B. (2008). *Ritual and its consequences: An essay on the limits of sincerity*. New York: Oxford University Press.

Turner, V. (1967/1976). *The ritual process: Structure and anti-structure*. Ithaca, NY: Cornell University Press.

Turner, V. (1969). *The ritual process: Structure and anti-structure*. Chicago: Aldine Publishing Co.

Van Gennep, A. (1908/1960). *The rites of passage*. London: Routledge and Kegan Paul.

Wallace, A.F.C. (1966). *Religion: An anthropological view*. New York: Random House.

Zerubavel, E. (1985). *Hidden rhythms: Schedules and calendars in social life*. Berkeley, CA: University of California Press.

9 New Cultures of Ageing

The Impact of the Third Age on Issues of Spirituality and Religion

Paul Higgs

Contemporary later life, as viewed in the context of recent social and cultural changes, has taken on the designation of 'old age problematic'. In particular this perspective argues that the social space that older people now exist in is substantially removed from the worlds of old age that have previously provided the coordinates for organised religion. Utilising the 'Cultures of Ageing' approach as a lens to understand the impact of the generationally based culture of the third age on religious and spiritual practices, it argues that many of the assumptions that held together both the 'natural' and standardised life course have been transformed by the emphasis on agency, choice and lifestyle which now constitute the desirable objectives of post-work life. Individual participation in the cultural field of the third age can vary considerably as it is dependent on resources and circumstances as well as on predispositions of individuals. However, it is also the case that the generations now entering retirement are marked most fully by their engagement with consumer society and consumer culture.

In preferring to be living in an 'ageless' later life rather than experiencing a more ascriptive old age, members of these cohorts have put a distance between themselves and those who they identify as frail, dependent and old. Those who are deemed to be in this category – the fourth age – exist in a feared category of abjection where pity seems to be the only response and a clear distance is kept by those still able to demonstrate independence. This transformation of ageing presents a number of challenges for thinking about religion and spirituality. This paper argues that not only does the third age accentuate an individualised spirituality based upon choice and a rejection of authority, it also projects the more institutionalised practices of mainstream religion as inflexible and dogmatic.

This position is a consequence of the generational habitus of the baby-boomer cohorts whose members find themselves habitually ill-at-ease with notions of hierarchy and tradition. Instead, the emphasis on choice and agency which is a major component of the culture of the third age leads not only to a distancing from the fourth age but also a rejection of the people seen to be in it. This configuration poses important questions for those interested in the issues of spirituality and religion in later life, not least whether an emphasis on spirituality rather than religious tradition leads to an abandonment of concern for those confronting the dependencies and disabilities of deep old age This chapter does not provide solutions to this dilemma but rather uses it as an illustration of the way that the re-configuration of old age has implications for religion and spirituality in later life.

The Third Age

The idea of the third age in social gerontology was popularised by the Cambridge historian, Peter Laslett, in his book *A Fresh Map of Life*, (Laslett, 1989) as a way of explaining how old age was being transformed at both a social and an individual level. Echoing previous attempts to order the life course into distinct stages and ages, Laslett's work highlighted the distinction between a fit, healthy and productive later life and an old age that was dogged by ill health, incapacity and neediness. This approach challenged the dominance of more unitary approaches to old age such as structured dependency theory (Townsend, 1981) and its variants which saw old age as a product of social and health policy directed at the construction of residual social category. Under this approach old age was constructed by pensions policy and any potential freedom was the product of an earlier accumulation of income or wealth which could be utilised in retirement. Not surprisingly, retirement and old age were not seen as desirable end points. Laslett in his work sought to challenge this view by pointing out that the third age could be much more than a residual category of social policy and instead could represent a 'crown of life' where individuals were freed from the responsibilities of work and family to pursue their own interests. The reception of Laslett's work was relatively lukewarm in the United Kingdom with many writers seeing it as describing the relatively affluent retirement of middle class men (Bury, 1995). In the United States, on the other hand, the idea meshed with more positive ideas of ageing such as productive ageing and wasn't considered so controversial that it couldn't be incorporated into views of various models of 'successful ageing'.

However, the third age as an analytic tool was less successful and although the term became widely used in organisations such as the University of the Third Age (U3A) it lacked a more rooted sociological significance. This significance was provided in a series of works by Gilleard and Higgs (2000, 2005, 2007, 2010) and Higgs and Gilleard

(2014) who sought to view the third age/fourth age distinction through a less individualised lens and instead focused on the social, material and cultural resources that support these distinctions. Drawing upon Bourdieu's cultural sociology and Karl Mannheim's sociology of generations, they argued that the third age is primarily a generational cultural field, with varying levels of participation by individuals in later life (who may be loosely characterised as aged over fifty). This field is 'bounded' on the one side by the secular progression into later life of a particular consumer oriented post-Second World War generation, and on the other by the intensification and elaboration of the 'social imaginary' of a deep old age, a fourth age, with its projection of decline, dependency and decrepitude.

The logic that operates within the cultural field of the third age, these authors argue, derives from the role of consumption and the widening access to consumer products that took place during the latter half of the twentieth century. The rise of post-war youth culture, the widespread rejection of what was 'old' in favour of what was 'new' and the growth and diversification of youth subcultures and their associated counter-culture helped solidify what they describe as a persisting generational schism (Gilleard and Higgs, 2005: 62–100). It is this schism that has been so strongly embodied in the lives of a distinct generation and which has provided the foundations for the emergence of the third age.

The ageing of this iconic cohort has shaped a distinctive cultural field, whose parameters of personal choice and individualised lifestyle have sustained the pursuit of 'distinction' into later life (Gilleard and Higgs, 2007). For this generation there is a need for those entering retirement to continue to make purposeful choices about how they wish to live their third age and what they think the choices should be. Consumption has come to symbolise the virtues of choice, self-expression, autonomy and pleasure that were emblematic for a generation who grew up during the 'long sixties' (Marwick, 1998). In the process, the emerging later life-styles of this generation are a continuation of the undermining of the old institutionalised structures of the life course that occurred all through their individual lives (Higgs et al., 2009).

One area where this undermining was most evident was in the world of work and family. From the 1960s onwards youth rebellion was not just aimed against the institutions of the state but also extended to the institutions of employment and marriage. The notions of the ascribed class identities of work were challenged because they were seen to be constricting and hierarchical. For the more middle class employees these relations were also viewed as oppressive given their focus on career and seniority. The generation of the sixties wanted to end this focus on stability and advancement and replace it with more flexible visions of work and decision making; ones that became more familiar in the era of the 'flat' management structure of the current day.

Similarly the 'hetero-normative' assumptions that were built into welfare and social policy were perceived to not only reflect a world of gender oppression but to be actively implicated in a culture of gender roles which centred on marriage and family life. The full effect of these challenges only became apparent towards the end of the twentieth century when the household structures of Europe and North America reflected many more different forms than had been present in the immediate post-war period. So profound have been these changes that Ulrich Beck describes them as constituting a 'revolution by side effects' and Esping-Andersen (2009: 25) suggests we are witnessing a 'new logic of family formation'.

As work has become less secure, more flexible and a less homogenising experience, work-based identities no longer seem to exercise such a dominating influence on lifestyles. It can also be argued that there has been a decline in the influence of work, family and indeed community on individual lifestyle (Jones et al., 2008). Instead the dominant form of cultural and symbolic capital deployed is based upon lifestyle choice rather than on ascribed identity. In a similar fashion the dominant form of social capital is derived as much from extended horizontal networks as it is from vertically aligned kinship. The linkages established between lifetime friends and lifetime 'partners' overshadows previously privileged vertical forms of social capital based upon 'family' and the spatially secured bonds of intergenerational solidarity. This does not mean there is no interchange between the generations; there is, of course, but it has become a less salient source of cultural capital.

The major consequence of this generational field is that it has created a generational habitus which has transformed society as the people who participate in it grow older. Gilleard and Higgs (2005) have argued that one result is that the arenas of choice have expanded beyond the traditional boundaries of the market, incorporating aspects of the life world previously held to be the preserve of the family, the professions or the state. Within this post-sixties culture, it is not youth *per se* that is bought and sold so much as the ideologies of youthfulness and opportunity, symbolised by the consumerist quartet of virtues – choice, autonomy, pleasure and self-expression. It is therefore not too much of an extension to include the world of religion and spirituality in this remade social world.

If rejection of the past made up one of the aspects of the generational schism of the 1960s in the Western world then it is not too hard to see that religion as expressed in terms of institutional Christianity was seen to be one of the representations of the old world that had to be rejected. It was seen as intractable, dogmatic and unbending and ultimately did not allow for the expression of choice or individualism. Ulrich Beck (2010) argues that under the contemporary conditions of individualisation it is no longer possible to accept such institutional un-reflexivity and that rather we have to accept the emergence of what he terms 'a God of one's own'. More prosaically it means the acceptance that not only is there a pluralistic choice of religious beliefs in contemporary society but also that the content of these choices can vary in terms of practices, intensity and indeed the compatibility of different approaches. As we shall see in the next section, the generational habitus that is forming the culture of the third age regards spiritual belief as an issue of choice rather than of religious affiliation.

If the third age has been constituted by Gilleard and Higgs as an expanding cultural project capable of taking in and reconstituting much of society, then the understanding of the fourth age returns their gaze to a point familiar to Laslett's conception of an old age that was dogged by ill health, incapacity and neediness. In his original conception the fourth age compresses all the disabilities and dependencies of old age into a 'compression of morbidity' which ends in death. Unlike the third age, Gilleard and Higgs argue, the fourth age is not a cultural field but rather a social imaginary, realised less in lifestyle and lived experience than in and through the gaze of others, whether mediated by the discourse and practices of social policy or through the cultural representations of the lives of others.

The 'social imaginary' of the fourth age represents not so much the circumstances of people from a particular cohort or at a certain stage of life but a terminal destination, a location stripped of the social and cultural capital which allows others to articulate choice, autonomy, self expression and pleasure in later life. Gilleard and Higgs liken it to a cosmological 'black hole', whose location in social space is determined by such factors as the progressive densification of death within the life cycle, institutional responses to perceptions of frailty in later life and subjective reactions to the abjection embodied by the loss of agency and the preservation of human dignity (Gilleard and Higgs, 2011). Consequently, one of the dilemmas for older people is negotiating what Gilleard and Higgs (2010) term the 'event horizon' between being able to participate in the culture of the third age as an agentic individual and being deemed too 'frail' to manage this successfully and becoming subject to the health and social care discourses of the fourth age.

For some writers this situation is much truer to the 'real' nature of old age and should be seen as something that is both natural and not to be resisted (Vincent, 2003). It is certainly true that the conditions that make up the core of the social imaginary of the fourth age are ones that can be better explained by the 'valued symbolic meanings' of religion than by the technological imperatives of the painless 'good death'. This is explained by John Vincent:

> In the fourth age older people lose control of their bodies to the medical professionals. Life at this stage is circumscribed by the postponement of death. However, medical knowledge is structured around the preservation of life and the avoidance of death, and involves a sense of failure (and the possibility of accusations of negligence) if life is not preserved ... The good death is thought of in bodily terms, not human terms. It is constructed in the right dosage of medication; it is not constructed out of human relationships and symbols that transcend individuals and their bodies. (Vincent, 2003: 159)

For Vincent the culture of the third age with its emphasis on maintaining health and independence leads to a culture of 'medical immortality' which robs old age of its dignity and its proper place in society. Again, as we shall see the third age therefore raises profound issues relating to spirituality and religion as the cohorts that propel it move through the life course.

Religion and Spirituality in Later Life

The long term rise of secularisation was one of the tropes of sociologists of modernity from the nineteenth century onwards and Max Weber's notion of the progressive 'disenchantment' of the modern world is probably the most well known as well as being the most influential (Turner, 2011). Classical social thinking took it for granted that with the rise of industrialisation, urbanisation and the nation state, religion, religious belief and religious practice would gradually fade out. While maybe never disappearing, the role of religion in mediating life would consequently become considerably less influential in society. It would move from the public to the private sphere.

This template seems on first sight to have considerable descriptive power as far as the mainstream Christian denominations in Europe and North America are concerned. In Europe, the further north one goes, both membership of Christian churches and adherence to their core beliefs seem to be declining (Greeley, 2007). Even in the United States, which on the surface seems to maintain an image of high levels of religiosity, the patterns of attendance appear to reflect a much more volatile 'faith' market with a corresponding high level of 'churn' as individuals and families move from one church or denomination to another. These facts give rise to the idea that within Europe and North America at least the process of secularisation is quite advanced and that it is irreversible. Within this framework religious belief and practice is seen to be increasingly confined to older cohorts whose socialisation into religious practice still organises personal life.

As any astute observer of the sociology of religion will be aware this is far from the complete story even in Europe and North America and even in relation to just Christianity. While it may be going too far to argue as some have that we live in a 'post-secular' world (Habermas, 2010) and that instead of diminishing, religious affiliation and practice are becoming globally more prominent, what is clear is that the disenchantment of the world that Weber inferred would be a consequence of modernity has found itself subjected to a 're-enchantment'. Zygmunt Bauman (1992) is just one thinker to have pointed out that the idea of the post-modern is based in part on the dissatisfaction with the answers that classical modernity has provided in response to the problems created by the modern world. At its most extreme it is the rationality that lay at the heart of the Holocaust (Bauman, 1989) but at more mundane levels it can lie in the solutions of modern consumption (Ritzer, 1999).

This re-enchantment takes many forms but we can already see some of the connections with the account of the emergence of the third age presented above. The structures of the modern world that gave rise to the institutionalisation of the modern life course also gave rise to the structures of modern secular rationality. It is therefore not surprising that part of the generational ferment of the 1960s was also about the possibility of multiple forms of what came to be termed spirituality; forms that often accentuated a freedom of belief from doctrine and a focus on sensual experience.

Such a distinction between religion and spirituality may be glib but it is certainly one that has come to dominate many discussions. Ellor and McFadden (2011) point out that while there has been a long tradition of studying religion, religious institutions and religious practices the use of the term spirituality is used to refer to something more personal and private. They also endorse a view of spirituality as representing a new kind of hermeneutic that lies 'beyond the traditional differentiation of religions according to their specific beliefs and practices, particularly in terms of how they approach the intersection of the human and the divine' (Ellor and McFadden, 2011: 52). However, this may not just be a way of being more expansive but could be seen, as one commentator put it, as the 'secularisation of spirituality' in that the definition is set against that of religion (Matthews, 2010).

She argues that this is made explicit in a UK Royal College of Psychiatry document where spirituality is identified with 'a deep seated sense of meaning and purpose in life, together with a sense of belonging. It is about acceptance, integration and wholeness ... It applies to everyone, including those who do not believe in God or a higher being. The universality of spirituality extends across creed and culture; at the same time spirituality is felt as unique to each and every person'. The RCP document distinguishes spirituality from religion which, it claims, offers 'community-based worship, each faith having its own set of beliefs and sacred traditions. However, when there is a lack of respect for differences of belief, religion has been used as a social and political tool leading to intolerance and divisiveness' (RCP 2006, cited in Matthews, 2010: 289–290). While this distinction can be given too much prominence, it could also be the case that it represents one of the fault lines of the contemporary culture that was amplified by the baby-boomer cohorts as they sought to rework the cultural parameters of the society in which they existed. Some sociologists of religion such as Grace Davie have used terms such as 'believing not belonging' (Davie, 1994) and 'vicarious religion' (Davie, 2010) to explain some of these changes that have been occurring in societies such as Britain and elsewhere. Challenging the generalising nature of the notion of secularisation, both concepts point to religion becoming a minority activity carried out 'on behalf' of the majority in order that this latter group has access to heritage and cultur-ally appropriate settings for events such as marriage and funerals.

While there have been a number of commentators who have noted the drift from religiosity to notions of spirituality in the ferment created by the 'new atheism' (see Bentley-Hart, 2009), others have located the problem in both secular change and in generational dispositions. Robert Bellah and his colleagues in *Habits of the heart* (1996) noted the role of individualism in undermining the social stability that was a product of the religious belief prevalent in the United States and its replacement by a more materialistic individualism. Aldridge summarises this point when he writes:

A cultural shift away from a conception of religion as a mandatory set of beliefs and practices incumbent on all the faithful, towards the conviction that individuals have to choose for themselves their particular path to salvation, has taken place not simply on the periphery (in 'the cults') but in the mainstream of Western cultures. The transmission of religion from generation to generation is becoming more fluid and less certain. (Aldridge, 2007: 192)

The role of generation in producing what Bryan Turner describes as a 'low intensity religion' (Turner, 2009) where religiosity is low on com-mitment, is individualistic, highly subjective and post-institutional, is an interesting question. Until relatively recently, however the role of the baby boomers in transforming these issues has received relatively little attention within the field of social gerontology. Judith Marston (2010) from an Australian context comments that the baby-boomer cohorts have often been seen as the 'me' generation and she points out that spirituality rather than religion seems to be a better term to describe their range of beliefs which centre on a sense of 'connectedness' with others and nature as well as with God. MacKinlay (2014) in a special themed section of the *Journal of Religion, Spirituality and Aging* does directly address the issue of generational change and the baby-boomer cohorts in particular. She acknowledges that this group has a strong focus on autonomy, control and material benefits but once again sees the issues thrown up as being ones centred around what she describes as the spiritual tasks of ageing which she sees as a necessary answer to some of the dilemmas created by the third age's promotion of 'successful ageing'. Again these tasks focus on the self and personal transcendence rather than on organised religion, and this distance is in fact encouraged in order to reach the largest number of baby-boomers. As she writes 'in the twenty-first century, spiritual care is too often seen only as religious care, not in the broader context of spiritual care; that is a real need of people who do not have a religious faith' (MacKinlay, 2014: 116).

However, outside of these specific reflections on generations, the tension between religion and spirituality is often placed in the context of social change rather than being connected to the third age or generational habitus. Paley (2007) uses a stretch metaphor for spirituality in order to connect religious belief to more esoteric practices such as amulet or charm wearing. He acknowledges that some within the field think that this is going too far but what is remarkable is the ready acceptance that the term can be stretched and that it can be connected to the market of religious and spiritual choice; a market that as Bryan Turner (2009) has pointed out, now has many different vendors and lifestyle options. This does not mean that spirituality so defined has no special status within the contemporary world. When necessary, Paley argues, spirituality uses the special status afforded to religion in the past to 'fireproof' itself against challenges that see it purely as a lifestyle choice. In the case of complementary health provision, for example, assertions that such procedures have no evidence base can be countered by re-drawing them as providing spiritual benefit. In this way the stretched concept of spirituality overwhelms and incorporates religion into a much more pliable notion.

If this argument is accepted it suggests that the generational habitus of the baby boomers, which put a high premium on choice and challenging authority, has had a powerful impact on the status of organised religion and the promotion of a much more diffused spirituality. If we then extend this argument to the cultural field of the third age, not only can we see a decline in religious activity and belief but also a corresponding increase in personal choices about spiritual issues whether this is in terms of religious belonging or views about belief. Consequently, debates about the role of religious or spiritual factors in later life need to take these changes into consideration. Outside of the way that these changes may impact on the numbers acknowledging membership of churches and other religious institutions, one area where this has become a controversial topic, at least in the United Kingdom, has been in hospitals and other health care settings. In England where the Church of England is the established church and where the majority of the population is formally identified as Anglican, it is commonplace for hospitals to have chaplains drawn from that denomination, and these are often paid for by the health care provider. The contested issue is the nature of the work that they do. Is it religious or is it spiritual? Given the pressures outlined above it is unsurprising that it is often presented as the latter, with many chaplains promoting their activities as being part of a particular skill set known as 'spiritual care' (Swift, 2009). While the debate on this issue is sure to continue, as bodies such as the National Secular Society continue to seek to remove all funded religious posts from the public sector (National Secular Society, 2009), what is of more interest is that religiously ordained chaplains have sought to redefine their roles as ones contained by the idea of the spiritual rather than by the religious. There may be all sorts of pragmatic reasons for this but it would seem to reflect in part the power of the cultural changes brought about by the generational habitus of the baby-boomers and their progression through the life course.

Up to this point I have not addressed the issue of the fourth age. In part this is because, as pointed out earlier it functions as the feared binary opposite of the third age. For a generation who hoped they 'would die before they got old', the potential abjection of a dependent old age is something that cannot be contemplated. It is not surprising therefore that in the era of the third age we have continual calls for the legalisation of euthanasia and assisted suicide. MacKinlay (2014) in her article addresses the topic of the dependency inherent in the fourth age and sees the spiritual tasks of ageing and the meaning and self-transcendence created out of them as providing a way out of dealing with the vicissitudes of old age. However, one difficulty with the argument is that it doesn't deal with the issues more commonly associated with the fourth age such as profound physical and cognitive dependency which are for Higgs and Gilleard (2014) the crucial categories of the abjection connected with its projected 'social imaginary'. Equally the notions of transcendence, meaning, forgiveness and gratitude might be appropriate in certain forms of end-of-life care but do not easily extend to life with severe dementia.

Malcolm Johnson (2013a, b) is aware that the nature of living to a very old age poses a number of challenges to ideas of spirituality and has developed the idea of Biographical Pain. Biographical Pain for him is 'characterised by the surfacing of deeply buried fractures in the life biographies of individuals who always intended to "put things right" but have now run out of capability to bring about that resolution. They will no longer be able to apologise, seek or give forgiveness, deliver restitution, or deliver a good to balance out the bad for an evil act. The opportunity to redress wrongs has passed by, and the individual is left with an overwhelming sense of guilt' (Johnson, 2013a: 185). He points out that older people need new forms of spiritual care that embrace such pain often outside formal religion if 'new social rituals' are to be created for 'putting things right'. However this plan for 'a good fourth age' (Johnson, 2013b) is still problematic if it is founded on the capacity to reflect on the life lived with a sense of satisfaction and worthiness. Johnson also observes that the long history of religious practice has had time to build up such rituals which can help negotiate this existential challenge. It seems unlikely that spirituality *qua* spirituality is likely to have the same resources or time available to it.

In a similar fashion, it could also be argued that if choice and agency are paramount values to the baby-boomer cohort and to the culture of the third age, then it is not unexpected that these generational dispositions are extended into the realm of the ending of life itself. Connecting this to the debate regarding the differing statuses of religion and spirituality, it is interesting to note that most religions have strictures against euthanasia and suicide while the individualised nature of spiritual belief can be presented as a great deal more flexible on the subject.

Following John Vincent (2003), we can see that institutionalised religion has more resources available to explore the nature of frailty and dependency that makes up key elements of the fourth age. Not only does it often have centuries of experience regarding the end of people's lives, it also has explanations for what is occurring to older people's bodies. Again individual spiritual beliefs can draw on these resources but the absence of the nature and ritual of collective belief limits the power of these materials. In the fourth age the pastoral role of religion may be one of its greatest strengths as it provides succour for its adherents. It is therefore interesting that, as Matthews (2010) notes, religion and religious practice is often seen to offer less to patient health when compared to the development of inner resources.

Even in the fourth age, therefore, the agentic assumptions of the third age are often promoted in the advocacy of an unproblematic spirituality. Even with regard to one of the core elements of the fourth age, that of dementia, it can also be postulated that religious belief *qua* religious belief as a form of engagement with organised religion can be helpful for those with the condition as well as those caring for those with the condition (Sullivan and Beard, 2014). This might in turn might be related to what Hughes (2011) sees as the different views of bodily transcendence and personhood permitted within a theological approach that acknowledge the response to rituals and familiar prayers of individuals severely affected by dementia. As a result, it might be argued that there is an important continuing role for religion in situating responses to the problems of the fourth age. It may be that we have to revisit ideas of moral worth, compassion and the idea of pity if we are not to despair at the 'Black Hole' of the social imaginary of the fourth age (Higgs and Gilleard, 2015).

Conclusion

In this chapter I have tried to provide an account of how an understanding of the third age as an expression of the generational habitus of post-war cohorts has had an impact on our understanding of themes of spirituality and religion in later life. Overall I have presented an argument that suggests that there has been a profound change in the nature of the role of religion and spirituality in people's lives and that this echoes some of the dispositions that this generation have developed across their lives through their focus on the key themes of choice and autonomy. That these dispositions are not incidental to the profound social changes that are also occurring, but are part and parcel of them, is also part of this argument. The specific argument that I am also making is that the shift from institutionalised religion to a more pluralistic spirituality is something that will continue into later life. As I have pointed out, this is not a simple echo of an unproblematic secularisation thesis but is bound up in the transformations that are part of Beck's notion of a second modernity. As he points out, it is 'reflexive modernisation' itself that gives rise to a resurgence of spiritual belief because it emphasises the sovereignty of the individual in the form of 'a God of one's own'. Such individualisation is both a great boon to self-identity and a source of instability in the modern world. As Charles Taylor (2002) has noted such transformations reflect the importance of choice but do not necessarily provide security for both individuals and societies. It is in this context that issues of religion and spirituality continue to have prominence in the modern world because they reflect the issues of contingency that abound everywhere, even in the reaches of later life which previously was seen to be beyond such concerns. Viewing religion and spirituality through the lens of the third and fourth age provides, I would argue, a valuable additional insight into the changing nature of later life.

References

Aldridge A. (2007) *Religion in the contemporary world*. Cambridge: Polity Press.

Bauman Z. (1989) *Modernity and the holocaust*. Cambridge: Polity Press.

Bauman Z. (1992). *Mortality, immortality and other life strategies*. Stanford: Stanford University Press.

Beck U. (2010) *A God of one's own polity*. Cambridge: Polity Press.

Bentley-Hart D. (2009) *Atheist delusions*. New Haven: Yale University Press.

Bury M.(1995) Ageing, gender and sociological theory. In S. Arber and J. Ginn (eds.), *Connecting gender & ageing: A sociological approach*. Buckingham: Open University Press, pp. 15–29.

Davie G. (1994) *Religion in Britain since 1945: Believing without belonging*. Blackwell: Oxford

Davie G. (2010) Vicarious religion: A response. *Journal of Contemporary Religion* 25(2): 261–266.

Ellor J. and McFadden S. (2011) Perceptions of the roles of religion and spirituality in the work and lives of professionals in gerontology: Views of the present and expectations about the future. *Journal of Religion, Spirituality and Ageing* 23: 50–61.

Esping-Andersen G. (2009) *The unfinished revolution*. Cambridge: Cambridge University Press.

Gilleard C. and Higgs P. (2000) *Cultures of ageing: Self, citizen and the body*. Harlow: Prentice Hall.

Gilleard C. and Higgs P. (2005) *Contexts of ageing: Class, cohort and community*. Cambridge: Polity Press.

Gilleard C. and Higgs P. (2007) The third age and the baby boomers: Two approaches to the social structuring of later life. *International Journal of Aging and Later Life* 2: 13–30.

Gilleard C. and Higgs P. (2010) Aging without agency: Theorizing the fourth age. *Aging & Mental Health* 14: 121–128.

Gilleard, C., and Higgs, P. (2011). Frailty, disability and old age: a re-appraisal. *Health (London)*, 15 (5), 475–490.

Greeley A. (2007) *Religion in Europe at the end of the second millennium: A sociological profile*. New Jersey: Transaction Publishers.

Habermas J. (2010) An awareness of what is missing. In J. Habermas (ed.), *An awareness of what is missing: Faith and reason in a post-secular age*. Cambridge: Polity Press.

Higgs P. and Gilleard C. (2014) Frailty, abjection and the 'othering' of the fourth age. *Health Sociology Review* 23(1): 10–19.

Higgs P. and Gilleard C. (2015) *Rethinking old age: Theorising the fourth age*. Basingstoke: Palgrave Macmillan.

Higgs P., Hyde M., Gilleard C., Victor C., Wiggins R. and Jones I. R. (2009) From passive to active consumers? Later life consumption in the UK from 1968–2005. *Sociological Review* 57: 102–124.

Hughes J. (2011) A situated embodied view of the person with dementia: Where does the spiritual come in? In A. Jewell (ed.), *Spirituality and Personhood in Dementia*. London: Jessica Kingsley Publishers.

Johnson M. (2013a) Biography and generation: Spirituality and Biographical Pain at the end of life in old age. In M. Silverstein and R. Giarrusso (eds.), *Kinship and cohort in an aging society: From generation to generation.* Baltimore, MD: Johns Hopkins University Press, pp. 176–189.

Johnson M. (2013b) The changing face of ageing and old age in 21st century Britain. In K. Albans and M. Johnson (eds.), *God, me and being very old.* London: SCM Press.

Jones, I.R., Hyde, M., Victor, C.R., Wiggins, R.D., Gilleard, C., and Higgs, P. (2008). *Ageing in a consumer society: From passive to active consumption in Britain.* Bristol: Policy Press.

Laslett, P. (1989) *A Fresh Map of Life.* London: Weidenfeld and Nicolson.

MacKinlay E. (2014). Baby boomers ageing well? Challenges in the search for meaning in later life. *Journal of Religion, Spirituality & Aging* 26(2–3): 109–121.

Marston J. (2010) Meaning in life: A spiritual matter – projected changes post-retirement for baby-boomers. *Journal of Religion, Spirituality and Ageing* 22: 329–342.

Marwick A. (1998) *The sixties: Cultural revolution in Britain, France, Italy, and the United States, c. 1958-c. 1974.* London: Bloomsbury Publishing.

Matthews P. (2010) Religion and the secularisation of spirituality: A Catholic perspective on spirituality in the care of the elderly. *Journal of Religion, Spirituality and Ageing* 22: 283–290.

National Secular Society. (2009) Chaplaincy costs survey, England. Available at: www.secularism.org.uk/uploads/chaplaincy-costs pdf, 2009. Accessed 28 June 2012.

Paley J. (2007) Spirituality and secularisation: Nursing and the sociology of religion. *Journal of Clinical Nursing* 16: 175–186.

Ritzer G. (1999) *Enchanting a disenchanted world.* Thousand Oaks: Pine Forge.

Sullivan S. C. and Beard R. L. (2014) Faith and forgetfulness: The role of spiritual identity in preservation of self with Alzheimer's. *Journal of Religion, Spirituality & Aging* 26(1): 65–91.

Swift C. (2009) *Hospital chaplaincy in the twenty-first century: The crisis of spiritual care on the NHS.* Basingstoke: Ashgate.

Taylor, C. (2002) *Varieties of religion today.* Cambridge, MA: Harvard University Press.

Townsend P. (1981) The structured dependency of the elderly: A creation of social policy in the twentieth century. *Ageing and Society* 1(1): 5–28.

Turner B. (2009) Goods not gods, new spiritualities, consumerism and religious markets. In I. R. Jones, P. Higgs and D. Ekerdt (eds.), *Consumption and generational change: The rise of consumer lifestyles and the transformation of later life.* New Jersey: Transactions Press, pp. 37–62.

Turner B. (2011) *Religion and modern society: Citizenship, secularisation and the state.* Cambridge: Cambridge University Press.

Vincent J. (2003) *Old Age.* London: Routledge.

Part III

Searching for Meaning in Later Life

10   Religion, Faith, Belief and Disbelief in Old Age
"A full-hearted evensong"

Susan A. Eisenhandler

Introduction

In the process of socialization, individuals are introduced to manifold ideas and beliefs about the purpose of life and the ways in which group members are expected to act as they move through life. Our lives are simultaneously personal and social; that is to say our identity is intertwined within these strands though how tightly or loosely varies. Religion is a system of beliefs and behaviors connected to the sacred (Durkheim, 1965) howsoever the sacred is defined within a society or culture. Indeed, there are likely to be several religious social worlds in any society with differing perspectives on the sacred and unique emphases on the divine with attendant observance or practice differing.

Some religions have complex beliefs and social roles, others offer a blend of ideas and behavioral desiderata consonant with meanings and understandings that are clearly and simply arrayed. Communal gathering to act on religious beliefs similarly exhibits a range from solitary worship and communal meeting for social purposes to communal practice with little emphasis on personal or private practice outside of communal worship. Sociologically speaking, religions are the same and yet different from other social institutions or social worlds that orient group members to a larger social reality or culture. In other words, religions shape social identity in linking individuals to others. The focus of religious beliefs and behaviors is unique with regard to transcendence and is responsive to human needs. Other social institutions meet different human needs and they too shape identity. A single way of connecting to others vitiates the tie between person and group and redounds unfavorably for each. Likewise the content and focus of beliefs and behaviors coalesces around some shared ideas and behaviors in order to foster a commonality or social solidarity that unifies members apart from their membership in unique social worlds. Analytically, some social worlds articulate ways of moving through time and place in order to reproduce themselves and to move their members into another "better" or other-worldly direction.

For more than ninety years, beginning in 1922 for American social gerontologists with publication of *Senescence* by G. Stanley Hall, the aging experience has been tethered to historical, generational, and social contexts as much as it is understood to be a personal or individual experience. Life course is built by the individual and surrounding social structure. Social change emerges in part from the succession of time, constructed as history with the passage of cohorts and generations that expire and are then absorbed into the repository of memory and what we call the past. The dilemma of living to a great old age or an ordinary old age (i.e., meeting the life expectancy of our age peers), no matter how we are specifically tied to cohort and generation or social structure, is found in the inevitable encounter with death and the wintry landscape preceding it or surrounding it. (It is only the category of "untimely" death that perhaps spares a person from this confrontation.) This face-off is captured vividly and unforgettably in Hardy's poem, *The darkling thrush*.

Observers of the singularly cold landscape of old age, like the observer in Hardy's poem who is unable to fathom the "joy illimited" of a full-hearted evensong in the midst of a bleak winter's twilight, are outsiders experientially and imaginatively and are unaware of the true dimensions of the world inhabited by the darkling thrush. Hardy's observer and we who are academic observers of people in old age are almost always convinced that a harsh, external reality dictates the quality of life, the meaning of life, and even determines the value of life for those we observe. However, the deficit of awareness and imagination lies with the observer not with the darkling thrush or the old. Likewise, I, standing in good company with some social gerontologists, suggest that contemporary observers of the old still concentrate almost exclusively on harsh, observable features of old age whereas we cannot see or hear the possibilities and realities of hope found therein.

The chapter I contribute to this collaborative edition is best characterized as an evocative essay that seeks to depict a specific social world – a small retirement community – and the ways in which gardening by the residents helped them in offering a full-hearted evensong about life while standing squarely in front of the prospect of death. I wish I were as eloquent as Hardy or as refined in order to create a delicate but compelling image of the songs possible in the social worlds of later life. My sociological analysis culled from past and current qualitative research will have to suffice.

The chapter title appropriately identifies four nonmaterial and material dimensions – religion,[1] faith,[2] belief,[3] and disbelief[4] – other-worldly and ideologically grounded domains of meaning that are important in the social worlds of the old. Though each dimension is analytically distinct,

---

[1] Religion: From a sociological perspective religion is a mix of belief and behavior oriented to the other-worldly. Whether we call the other-worldly god, gods, supernatural power, or the divine, all of these categories invoke the transcendent as well as the characteristic of regular interaction among adherents in activity directed toward the other-worldly. Because the group figures prominently in this approach it is logical for sociological study of religion to explore intragroup and intergroup social interaction as well as the ideological or nonmaterial domain of beliefs. There is on the part of sociological theory an implicit acknowledgment of amorphous differentiation within collective worship between clergy and congregants in order to distinguish the boundary of social roles based on knowledge of the other worldly and the legitimate authority to organize activity around that among some members (clergy) as contrasted to all members (participants/laity). With economic and cultural change in societies as well as population growth, these relatively amorphous roles become institutionalized; that is to say they acquire structure and their occupants wield different levels of power. In terms of social inequality it is this initial distinction of a preferred connection to the divine that shapes one dimension of what later emerges as social stratification. The succession of generations and socialization of new members across generations and eventually the recruitment of nongroup adherents (coerced or voluntary) builds the strength of religions and involves a range of other social actors in the process of spreading faith.

[2] Faith: The capacity for belief in the other-worldly without the support of material evidence, past experience, or consistent interaction with others. In secular settings, we often speak of having faith in the future: things will be better in the days that lie ahead in the time that will come. This idea is literally faith in progress and a faith in evolutionary progress. It is a way to orient ourselves to time and to understand and interpret human existence. Religious faith is the belief in the unseen, the supernatural and a trust in the unfolding of time. Scientific faith is a belief in the unseen (prediction) as well as the belief in a system of proof that is based on falsification of hypotheses and the procedures of scientific method. Both religion and science are systems of rationality at least in a Weberian sense and each is thought to be an improvement on irrational or esoteric ways of knowing and interpreting human existence.

[3] Belief: Ideas and thoughts important to individuals and groups. Beliefs are legion and may be specific or generic with variation in salience for the individual. Helpful to consider beliefs as hooks, that is to say, points of attachment for behaviors. Difficult to put beliefs into reality without interaction in groups. Groups may be small – Simmel's dyads or triads – nevertheless it is interaction which sustains beliefs. Postmodernism has multiplied the menu of belief and cybertechnology has multiplied the contact points for communication without necessarily increasing forms or occasions of interaction. Emergent meaning, definitions of situations, and salience of meaning and situation are derived from interaction in groups not from communication across numerous contact points.

[4] Disbelief/unbelief or the profane/secular: Something more than healthy skepticism or ambivalence about the divine. A *forensic* approach to ideas where areligious or nonreligious debate and argument are thought to be sufficient for understanding human behavior. I suppose this is what I have in mind. Atheism is disbelief about the divine or the sacred though atheists often believe strongly or passionately in secular and scientific ideas and may be religious and zealous about defending them, or, indeed, about provoking others into debate and argument. Atheism is not a separate continuum of rationality or dimension of neutrality though it may pose as that.

in the real world of social experience these domains overlap, or, in the words of one older woman, they are *intertwined*. Apart from the fact that this word was used by an older woman in a research study, the imagery of interweaving is apt as a theoretical concept and an empirical reality. Indeed, believers and nonbelievers I have interviewed and observed have all identified central ideas or principles as significant to them and most of those have been related to the transcendent, i.e., the divine or supernatural. This is as true for avowed atheists (a small number in my research studies but represented and found among the old) as it is for those with a deeply felt, longstanding attachment to religion or faith.

Over the years and in various groups I have studied, the fragmentation of sacred meaning has been paramount. The social structural element that establishes such robust meaning across dimensions is generational and also associated with cohort experience of older Americans. As I argued in *Keeping the faith* (Eisenhandler, 2003), a qualitative study of Connecticut, the relevant tipping point or generational and cohort divide falls in the year 1939. Generations and cohorts born after 1939 reflect different, "modern," structures and social worlds that by the mid 1970s, post-Vietnam for the sake of argument, begin to change dramatically at a pace which accelerates (circa the mid-1980s) with advances in cyber-technology. My sense is that present cohorts of older Americans have strong bedrock socialization in terms of religion, faith, and belief; however, the bedrock becomes porous or is not found as uniformly among the "boomer" generation (1946–1964) especially among the youngest cohort of boomers (post-Sputnik, 1958–1964).

Religion and Faith

Some years ago as part of the study described in *Keeping the faith* (Eisenhandler, 2003) I met Andrew and Lydia (all names are pseudonyms). As individuals and as a couple, married sixty-four years at the time of the interview, Andrew and Lydia were strongly centered in religious beliefs and the practice of their faith. Andrew noted that "Personally, I thank the Lord every day for the blessings that we have – every day we continue to enjoy our blessings. And church just magnifies that, as well as assuring us that as days go along ... I feel assured that every day is going to be a good day." Lydia added: "We live by faith. Without faith, it's impossible to please God. Because we have to have faith to even believe he exists. And if we believe he exists, then he makes himself known many times to us that it is not in a literal way, but spiritually he reveals himself to us so that we know he's there." Their faith confidently oriented them to the past, present, and future. They are hopeful and derive a sense of confidence about their well-being as nonagenarians.

The kind of hope described by the couple is close to that envisioned by Kierkegaard when he said, "certainly the eternal has range enough for the whole of life; therefore there is and shall be hope until the end. Therefore no particular age is the age of hope, but the whole of a man's life shall be the time of hope!" In *Works of love*, Kierkegaard expressly links hope to the "possibility of the good," and goes on to say that "everyone who lives without possibility is in despair; he breaks with the eternal; he arbitrarily closes off possibility, and without the assent of eternity makes an end where the end is not" (Kierkegaard, 1962, p. 236). Regardless of the religious tradition or practice, faith affords hope and the "possibility of the good." Faith evokes the eternal and the possibility of transformation of the ordinary into the good and beautiful. Gardening also directly involves people in the continuous action that opens its planters and weeders, harvesters and cooks to the "assent of eternity."

Andrew indicated this aspect of openness and timelessness by noting the connection between nature and God in a creative activity he enjoyed – wood-working. He showed me several pieces of wood – beautiful grained, half-formed pieces – some that would eventually be turned into finished objects. "We have two round pieces. But to put a piece of ordinary wood and start turning, as we call it – to watch that rough piece of wood turn out to something that comes to be a thing like that [a finished, turned table leg], is what I get the biggest charge out of . . . It's a faith. Yes. It's a faith." This is the possibility and orientation to the good that religious and creative activity share. Practicing faith confers benefits upon the wood-worker; a benefit larger than the material object that emerges from working the wood.

Another striking example of how people defined faith comes from Maxine. Key features are a "thoughtful" trust in the future which provides scope to the person's life and reassurance about the purpose of life. For Maxine, "Faith comes in a lot of forms, I think. And it has developed because of living thoughtfully all these many years." When asked if faith gave her strength she says "Oh, absolutely. It's more than that. I think I'd rather call it support because we know on whom to lean. Yes. Support. I prefer that word." She linked faith to love "or the beauty of nature – whether it be a snowstorm or a clear, blue sky. And faith must have a simpler explanation than long, verbose description. It lessens it, I think, when we try to explain it. It is something that is there like love."

The Dynamic of Reflection and Action: Belief and Disbelief

Among the aged I have studied some have doubts and questions or musings about the tension between belief and disbelief. There is a sense among most older people that their questions will remain unresolved that definitive answers may not be found. For instance, a long-time, former member of a synagogue differentiates a core set of beliefs from other human constructions of faith and practice. "I believe – you see, the important thing, for me, is to believe in our creator, and believe in the Ten Commandments ... But what was written after – I don't believe in that." ;

Others had evolved their own understandings as well. Walter, for example, did not believe in Hell, God, yes, but "I don't believe in Hell. I don't believe in Hell at all. I believe we make our Hell on earth, and that we all go to the same place [after death]." Another put it this way, "I doubt hell a little bit ... Well, God is good. We believe that God is good. He's great. He's merciful. He's forgiving. He's this; he's that. Why would he torture people after they're dead? To hell? To burn in hell – which is scary. Why would he do that to someone unless they were, I really don't know what you'd have to do in order to go to hell, really. You know, you take a guy like Hitler. But if he said before he committed suicide, "I'm sorry, Lord," he probably didn't go to hell. Who knows? ... So I don't know, I've got a feeling that we're all going to the Promised Land of some sort." The fact that this stance was not part of institutional theology or denominational doctrine did not prevent Walter and a second elder from reflecting about hell and from drawing their own conclusions.

Wanda's musings about life after death brought her close to discarding central religious beliefs. "Well, I, I don't know ... As we get older, you think more about death because you know you're not going to be around too many years. And you think about that a lot. And I do. I do ... I think there's a God but I don't know as I believe everything. That's awful to say."

Disbelief or Atheism

Of special interest here are those who used the word atheist to describe their religious beliefs and faith. Many of the small subset of atheists were active members of their respective congregations. Though his recognition of unbelief came as something of a surprise to Larry, a man with extensive and ongoing religious socialization, he stated matter of fact that he did not believe the Bible or even in Jesus. "I guess in some respects I may be an atheist. It's an interesting story [the Bible], but it hasn't made a believer out of me." His beliefs are found in the values and models of "a Christian way of life," but for Larry a Christian way of life did not require a belief in God as a tenet of faith. Larry had served in a host of responsible congregational roles during his life. Another, Peter, described his experience with religion as "being raised on fear and guilt." Asked if other beliefs had replaced the Roman Catholic ones that had been inculcated, he said no. With various health problems that had recently intensified, he does not often attend mass these days. However, he remains a member of a parish. His epigraph on living and old age, "Any day above ground is a good day," was not offered in a humorous or sardonic tone. He did not believe in God and described himself as putting little effort into following religious practices that were once important to him.

Libby had this to say. "Do I believe in God? I don't know. I'm open thinking about it. Maybe, maybe not. Do I believe in a personal God? Absolutely not. Absolutely not. Everything tells me there cannot be a personal God. What personal God would let a Holocaust happen? I mean, there may be a force. I suspect that the Oriental religions have the right idea. A whole universe that's one. Everything is an integral part of everything else. The microbes are part of us, and we're part of, 'we don't know what.' You know, I can see it that way. But a personal God, no."

Alex shares these views about religion, "It doesn't mean anything to me. I don't believe in God. I don't believe it." When a tenth person is needed for worship, the synagogue calls him, and he conscientiously attends the service as the tenth man. Alex adds, "If they need the tenth person – if they would call me, I would go. I would go because I feel needed, so I would go. But from a religious point of view – no, no, no. I don't know when I lost complete need for religion, but I lost it somewhere along the lines. I suppose we try to talk to our parents, you know?" He does not believe in God and with respect to prayer even during formal services he says, "No, I don't. No, I wouldn't say I pray, but I read the books. Every word has a meaning to me. It isn't that I read and it doesn't have any sense to me . . . but to me, you know, I read and I say, 'What am I saying? To whom am I praying? What am I praying to? Who am I praying?'" He tries to solve this dilemma by returning to the question of when this change occurred. "I don't know exactly when did it happen? There's no need for religion at all – no need, no need . . . But some things we support maybe because we are needed or because it's necessary. . . Necessary for other people."

"So, in between I believe in God"

I have interviewed others, similar to the atheists described above, yet distinct from them. The betwixt and between group has faith and religious observance but the most prominent feature is that older people are ambivalent about them. For example, Phil says that he tries to live a good life "and if I see people not living a good life it annoys me." As to the value of religion, "It's probably more important than I would acknowledge at first ... without religion think what we would be. So, I mean, the impact of religion is very important. I am happy to acknowledge that."

Stephen says that religion was important to him when he was growing up. "But in recent years, I've become interested in the space program... it's shaking my faith. How could, when you look at the entire sphere of things, the earth is so tiny and so ... I've read the history of this planet ... and how the oceans were formed and how life began and how plants began, and now we're talking about a man who created it in six days and rested on the seventh. So I'm not doing well at all in that department. I know there's some energy out there somewhere, but where and how and what, I don't know." He sums up "sometimes I've been tempted to believe that what we see is what it is." Stephen is also concerned about doing what is good. As a young man, he created his own daily prayer. He was often on the road developing a construction business which eventually became a leader in its specialty and he wanted to start the morning off right. "When I was working as a young man, my prayer everyday was, ... 'May I this day do what's right, say what's right, and think what's right.' That was my start of every workday ... They were words that I believed in. I didn't get that from anyone. That was what – I came from the old-type home where integrity was important, honesty was important and dependability was important. It was a home that was founded on those things, and you know those things, and you know they exist in spite of what's happening." In his home Stephen still keeps a copy of the "first New Testament that was given to me in Sunday school." Alongside it is his first dictionary. The imagery of these texts as neighbors after more than three quarters of a century offers a compelling picture of the complex overlap between ideas based in religion and ideas based on morality.

Wanda is included in this group of people who fluctuate between accepting religious tenets and questioning them. She is clear on the core belief in God, "I believe there's a God, yes. I believe there's a God but I think what we have is a lot of our hell is here on earth, [chuckles], you know." Wanda's observations are echoed by Joan. "I don't understand too much, to tell you the truth, you know. But I believe in God. [laughs] Oh, yes. I believe in God. And that's why it makes me the way I am ... I figure all the people that believe in God, they're all the same. It's a funny thing. Nobody came back from over there [heaven], you know, and tell us how it is and what's gotten them in. The only thing I don't understand is that God—why He allowed to have so many Jewish people murdered. Kids. Little kids. Suffering. They used to come around and grab the small kids out of your hands. And they used to cut their throat and stuff like that. Why does God allow things like that, if there is a God? So, in between, I believe in God, but I want to know where He is, and why He would do something like that."

Jean understood religion as "an inner thing" and something evident in daily life where it "shows up" in people "doing their everyday work." Jean used Mother Theresa as an example of a person who was religious. Many people were reluctant to define or think of themselves as religious people. They equivocated or even rejected the term as valid for themselves. Mostly they demurred by saying, "I guess so." Or, Alice's "Oh, I think so. I think so." Edward noted an aspect of the distinction between a religious person and others, " You don't have to belong to a religion to be a religious person. . .some people probably need that group to keep their religion alive. If it wasn't for the group they probably wouldn't have any [religion]. . .there's no difference between a religious person and a good one except he don't have the religion." Edward said that religion made him "more caring." Practicing religion and keeping his faith sensitized him to others in and out of his community.

Julia takes a slightly different tack in thinking about this, "I think a truly religious person doesn't have to go to church every Sunday. And doesn't have to get all dressed up." For her, empathy, and being non-judgmental about people who have troubles and difficulties gets to the heart of characterizing both a religious and spiritual person. As she considers the distinction between them, she says that they are "inter-twined. I think they intertwine, all these things we are talking about today, they all intertwine."

Grace has lived for a half dozen years in a large publicly funded high rise housing project in Connecticut's capital. The recent repossession of her car spurred her to move into the project. She thinks of herself as religious "because I go to church and I feel a good spirit." Yet she admits that "well, we can have religion any way. Its [goodness] got to be within yourself . . . like some folks who don't even go to church." More import-ant, she says that "religion gives me hope. Yes, you've got to have hope and justice." She was one of the few people in the study who explicitly linked religion with justice. As a black woman from a childhood that featured education and practice in both Baptist and Roman Catholic traditions, it was not surprising to hear the theme of justice articulated. The surprise is that justice was not a larger theme in the open-ended interviews I have completed throughout the years. Younger age cohorts may resonate more strongly with the chords of justice in religious beliefs and behaviors.

For Beth, worship is a central feature of religion. "Well, I imagine there are a lot of good people who aren't going to church, but I think church reminds you – it makes you think more about other people, and their needs and just brings it home to you. Things we need to be reminded of … I think church is necessary. I suppose people can be good. But I think they miss a lot [without attending]." This idea arises again as she defines a religious person as someone who has "kindness and compassion for other people … It's probably harder to be a good person if you don't have the feeling that God knows how you—what you do and how you behave [matters]… And if you don't believe in a higher power, God, whoever, it must be hard to be good. I don't know if people are born good, but it must be easier to stray if you're not religious, I should think."

Nora describes herself in terms of religion as "Average, average religion. Not a religious fanatic, you know what I'm saying?" When asked about what characterizes a "religious person" she says, dedication, "I would say she's almost saintly, and that religion seems to be on her mind at all times, whereas mine wouldn't be at all times." Religion gives her, "Well, in my case it would be the strength to go on. To keep going. And to hope for the best… I think that's peace of mind. I would hate to think that – if I had no religion, I'd hate to think – it would be a very vacant life for me. But that's me. I'd have an awful void – an empty feeling."

Robert said that attendance is central to his sense of faith. He attends church weekly without fail, "I don't believe in this two or three Sundays a year. Every Sunday I'm there. As a matter of fact, our service starts at ten. I'm at church at nine-thirty." His attitude and behavior was shared by eighty-seven-year old Pauline who has only missed church twice in twenty-seven years. "Well, I feel as though if I miss church, my week don't go good. I mean, things just—everything is just so wonderful when I go to church. I have that wonderful feeling and I can't really explain how."

When asked about what she derives from religion, Lucy said: "I feel that it's a steadying force." Maxine offers this response to distinguishing between religious and good: "Let's put it this way. A person can be good without faith, but he or she can be more joyous and more secure if he or she does have faith. And I mean sincere faith. Not just fly-by-night kind of thing." She does not want to label herself as religious or spiritual: "Better to say, if possible, that I'm living as I think the Lord would want me to live. I do not dread the Big Tomorrow (her phrase for death)."

In my research with older people across the past quarter of a century, most did not and could not distinguish religion from spirituality, but Jack is one of the few people who did. He characterizes the difference this way: "Religion is, as I know it, as I was taught and grew up in. Spirituality, I can connect to the entire, to the whole universe. I think there's a connection there. Religion is [more institutional]. Spirituality, I have a feeling that in the general workings of the universe, it might be there. Yes, I'm looking for an energy from the universe." As Maxine phrased it, "Religion is a part of living. It's a little like breathing. It's a natural thing."

Interiority and Development of "Inner Resources" in Later Life

Bernice Neugarten understood interiority to be related to ego and cognitive functions of personality. The idea is that as one grows old smaller amounts of energy are available to be harnessed for living. Consequently there is a shift in the locus of self-organization processes and in the engagement of the older person. Older people move away from previous levels of participation in social life and activities. Neugarten coupled this reduction in engagement to a corresponding decrease in impulse control among older adults. She concluded from community research that these linked shifts were conducive to the emergence of interiority, a turning inward, that was not "directly reflected ... until the mid-sixties." She also noted that data from contemporaneous studies suggested that such a change in personality could be found as early as the forties (Neugarten, 1963, p. 332). The finding of "increasing interiority" among older adults was first embraced, then subjected to critical review.

Though general social gerontological discourse has moved some distance from the concept, I return to it now because some people have spoken about the kind of shift in their religious attachment that is consonant with "increasing interiority." Thus, the concept may have a useful, heuristic value for this discussion and for thinking about faith in later life. Remarks about social activities, including religious participation, as well as accounts and stories about changes in the level of engagement with others, all point to substantive and real shifts away from broader social ties to a more inward looking and more internally focused sense of self and identity. Such expressions about lower levels of social and religious engagement reflected a marked difference from earlier stages and ages of their lives – in a direction and consistent with Neugarten's original formulation of interiority. These changes in orientation occurred among those who had high levels of engagement previously and among those who had lower levels of engagement during earlier years.

The shifts are consistent with looking inward, yet they are in some measure qualitatively and analytically distinct from other reflective processes such as life review (Butler, 1963) or reminiscence (Birren and Deutchman, 1991).

Ellen's life highlights features of "increased interiority." Ninety-years old, single, well educated, with a long career in the private sector in a position that marked her as a pioneer, she had recently moved into a nursing home. Many of the details about Ellen's faith and life suggest that for some time she had been drifting away from active engagement and was instead looking inward for the sources of faith and the beliefs that would help her move through this acute health crisis. She had been raised in Christian Science and still found those teachings and principles to be mainstays of her current life although she had been a member of a congregation many years ago that was not Christian Science. Since leaving that congregation, she had not maintained a formal membership with any other. She told me that she found great insight and comfort in the books she now kept in her small bedside table, but the communal activity and formal membership had faded as she grew older and now were nonexistent. The intellectual aspects of Christian Science principles were, however, important to her. Her subscription list was extensive and she managed to keep the current, social world before her, at a distance to be sure, but there. Unsurprisingly, and reinforcing Neugarten's original linkage of health and interiority, Ellen's acute health problems were gently pushing her orientation further inward.

It strikes me that as a greater percentage of first-world elderly live into eight and nine decades, the concept of interiority has much to offer our understanding of well-being. Depression has been a concept wielding great influence in discussions of growing old. Clinical depression invariably leads to withdrawal from social interaction and even greater social isolation. Increased interiority should not be confused with depression. Interiority is characterized by what Helen Black has described as the "miniaturization of life" that has salutatory effects for the individual prepared to reflect on life and in terms of laying the ground for developing and sustaining "inner resources."

Gerotranscendence

In the opposite vein, a key feature for an equally small number of older adults is the experience of gerotranscendence. This concept originates in the writing of Joan Erikson. She proposed a fourth adult developmental stage or a ninth and final stage to her husband's model of developmental sequences across the life course of an individual (Achenbaum and

Modell, 1999). Gerotranscendence was a stage of "final maturity" that emerged from "withdrawal not wisdom" (Achenbaum and Modell, 1999, p. 25). In this regard, Erikson and Neugarten link their differing orientations to self and others to the same precipitating factor, diminishing biological and physical resources and the lack of energy characteristic of later life. With the decline in energy and increased interiority, Erikson posits a possible outcome of gerotranscendence. She contends that gerotranscendence is a culminating stage of development, a point, "surpassing of all human knowledge and experience," a period of possibility for an awareness of oneness with others and life itself. This quality of cosmic awareness and an appreciation for the mutable boundaries of human life – going beyond or transcendence of conventional boundaries – has sparked recent research into the concept by sociologists Lars Tornstam (2005) and Robert Atchley (2009) and others. Specifically each has probed the concept with an eye toward offering ideas about measuring or operationalizing it and searching for evidence of its existence among older adults.

In the qualitative studies I have conducted interiority and gerotranscendence are not broadly found as themes or orientations in people's lives. However, interiority and gerotranscendence are what I call boundary markers of the intertwined domains of religion, faith, belief, and disbelief. They stake out divergent frontiers which are open to those in later life but not yet regularly crossed.

Two examples of gerotranscendence are evident in the accounts and experiences described by Anne and Jack. Anne was a religious searcher, ahead of her time. Her religious experiences map out the kind of personal searching detailed in *The five stages of the soul* (Moody and Carroll, 1997) and in the spiritual search by baby-boomers described by sociologist, Clark Roof (1993, 1999). Her present religiosity is centered around a heightened awareness of a *transpersonal bond* with others. Anne spoke at length of the spiritual journey that had threaded through her life, from her days in high school through cross-country moves, a divorce, and the uncertainties of raising children on her own at a time when one held a pariah status for doing so. Anne had reached a level of oneness with others some years ago when she actively sought out different religions and different traditions in order to move to a faith that understood that the dilemmas of divorce – one that did not cast the divorced person's spirituality into a void. Her extensive contact with other traditions as well as the education she obtained brought her almost full circle in terms of her religious identification today. But as she stated emphatically, it was not the "religion itself that was important, it was the realization that after all, we were one." It is this higher level of spiritual understanding that defines her life as meaningful even though she now resides in a nursing home with ties to the faith that had excluded her many years ago.

Jack talked extensively about being drawn to a different level of understanding about the meaning of life and man's relationship to God. He commented on the findings from physics and astronomy – findings about the universe that shed new light on our purpose here as human beings. This was not the kind of talk that would endear him to the majority of his local congregation, nor is it the kind of talk he would think of expressing to them. He noted how his growing awareness of the limitations inherent in conventional understandings of faith and the very definition of God had sparked new ways of thinking about spirituality and consciousness.

Thoughts about Nature, Gardening, and Faith

The physical environment that surrounds us influences our understanding of aging and daily life both sacred and profane. The imagery evoked in Hardy's poem, of "an aged thrush ... in blast beruffled plume," amidst "Winter's dregs made desolate," singing joyfully captures the experience of many older adults – gardeners in particular. The inherent and primary integration we have with nature threads its way into many conversations about religion and belief in later life. In earlier research projects, participants had identified nature with religious faith and as an important touchstone in their lives. One person described walking in nature as a religious feeling, saying it was like "the hand of God on my shoulder."

Gardening, observing backyard and neighborhood wildlife, hiking or walking in the woods, caring for pets and plants, and simply being attuned to cycles of nature were mentioned frequently as spontaneous sources of religion, faith, and experiencing the divine. Nature is often a parallel track that complements institutional forms of religion and on occasion becomes its own track. As Eugene says, "Sometimes you feel like talking to the Lord, when you're out tending the garden, and no one is around to bother you." Others, like Anne and Julia, convey a reverence for the natural world and described natural settings as places where they have found God. Anne "loved outdoors and nature. It was something that perhaps fairly early on made me pause from activity ... And the beautiful part of it is we're always – no matter how old we are and how far we are removed from our childhood, we're surrounded by it [nature]." Clara spoke of rural, agricultural roots where part of faith and belief in God was reflected in the appreciation for the land and the experience of working the land. "Well, yes. It has to be, don't it? Because when you're farming, you plow up the ground, sow the seed. You have to have faith that it's going to grow, don't you? Or you wouldn't put it in there ... You

put that seed in there, you don't know if it's going to grow or not."
Another example of the symbolic significance of faith and nature is found
in Lucy's home. Prominently displayed in her kitchen is beautiful print, a
circular garden, with an inscription: "A person's good deeds are used by
the one above as seeds for planting trees in the Garden of Eden. Thus,
each of us creates our own paradise."

Based on the association of nature with religion, belief, and faith, I set
out to understand how gardening, what I generally define as intentional
caring for other forms of life (as distinguished from tending forms of life
as part of a livelihood, i.e., farming family or corporate) influences the
social well-being of older people. For the past several years (2005–2012)
I have studied a small retirement community in Connecticut. This
retirement community, given the pseudonym of Kahehtiyo[5] (a Mohawk
word meaning a good field), is located in one of the smallest towns in the
state, Bartram (also a pseudonym honoring the first colonial botanist and
gardener extraordinaire, John Bartram). The research is qualitative con-
sisting for the most part of participant observation with loosely structured
interviews of residents, staff, and people with some connection to the
community or its programs. Visual evidence of community life and
gardening in particular is documented in photographs of the people
and the place; their dooryard gardens and the interaction that sustains
and changes the gardens, the gardeners, and the community as a whole.
A key feature of the culture in this community is the gardening residents
brought into their new homes two decades ago. This factor – establishing
their own gardens – and working them in various ways over the years is
crucial to their well-being. Not everyone who moved into Kahehtiyo was
a gardener but separately and as a result communally they created a
culture that enhanced life for them and for other species as well.

Creative, self-initiated activity such as gardening offers people a real
way to glimpse the ineffable beliefs and ideas they hold close through the
continuing actions they take to achieve as part of the reality surrounding
daily life. Gardening is expressive of the individual at the same time that
its presence offers evidence of the eternal or what McPhee (1980) called
"deep time." My understanding of "deep time" is the sense of immanence of time if not of a divine or supernatural element. Gardening has
moments of prayer, transcendence, and a recognition of immanence: it
connects gardeners to the past, present, and future in each constituent

---

[5] A few details about Kahehtiyo: a total of twenty semidetached units; eighteen at
650 square feet and two at 700 square feet. Well water and septic system part of the
approximately ten acre setting. First residents in 1992. Community building and the town
of Bartram Senior Citizen building are integrated into the residential complex.

step that builds the tasks of a gardener's work across a calendar year and across the years. Intrinsic to the very activity of planting and tending to forms of life, is a heightened appreciation for the "use and delight" plants have for people. Such an appreciation places gardeners into the metaphysical unfolding of generations and a universal history people share yet seldom perceive in the compartmentalized places that shape our awareness. Thus, gardening locates gardeners in a comprehensive social world that touches the eternal.

Without necessarily grasping the vast age or deep time of the universe we inhabit, and how we are dwarfed by its power, we place ourselves within instrumental and expressive work that has been a primary part of our heritage and to the existence of innumerable species. It is not, as many people suggest to me in talks and discussions that gardening is "therapeutic," as it well may be; it is instead that gardening is a part of living and being, an otherwise readily adopted activity that moves its adherents and practitioners beyond the profane and the ordinary for varied periods of time. Therapeutic arguments often neglect to mention that therapy or intervention is needed and required precisely because people have moved into social worlds that are in some way harmful to them. Transcendence in gardening may be transitory or impermanent, as anyone striving to protect blossoms without annihilating insects knows, but when it occurs it is real and intrinsically rewarding which is why despite hardship and uncertainty about tangible outcomes gardeners persevere and in persevering get beyond the confines of self and time. Gardening confers an inexpressible connection to human existence that other creative activities such as music, art, poetry, dance, and religious faith and spirituality offer to their participants. Such joy in living may indeed be partial and ineffable but it is the soul of singing a full-hearted evensong. I will take some moments now to introduce a handful of people from the community and the gardens they created.

Gardeners and Gardens of Kahehtiyo

From the fall of 2005 through December of 2012, I observed, interviewed, and photographed the gardeners and the gardens of Kahehtiyo. The photographs (which sadly could not be reproduced in this volume) provided visual evidence of how gardeners changed the landscape surrounding them and in so doing changed themselves. Before the first "pioneer" residents moved into the complex the area around the dwellings was colorless and barren. But the beauty cultivated by the gardeners and encouraged by nature between 1992 and the summer of 2008 created a dramatic transformation.

Notwithstanding the differences in technology and in weather, it is clear that the culture of gardening created and practiced by the residents (not so much seen in the lawn which was put in by the town of Bartram, but in the trees and plant foliage) resulted in an attractive and pleasant setting for life.

The cultivated spaces had the door-yard scale of the gardens created by the gardeners. Some scholars of gardening have noted that the phrase, door-yard gardens, may be traced to Chaucer, though a fine study of American door-yard gardens (Westmacott, 1992) reinforces its currency today. Such gardens are not synonymous with vast estates and hired labor, or with commercial activity that may be part of estate and truck-farms more generally. Door-yard gardens are small, accessible gardens with a variety of plant life from vegetables and herbs, to flowers and fruit trees, to shrubs and berries. The key feature is their threshold status or their position adjacent to front, back, or side yards of a dwelling. Walking to the garden is a feature of caring for it and appreciating it but walking is not onerous nor does it become an obstacle. Similarly, door-yard gardens may include plants in-ground, in containers, or in raised beds. The scale and contents of the door-yard gardens correspond with elements of miniaturization of life in old age noted earlier in this chapter and original to the scholarship of Helen Black and Robert Rubenstein (2000).

The quality of the gardens, their ability to thrive and to offer pleasure, is the result of the gardener working in concert with nature or the uncontrollable and unpredictable dimension of the larger reality surrounding all of us. This is the lived experience that firmly places old gardeners into the present. In tending their gardens, aged gardeners actively create a future and contribute something of value to the past. Thus, they glimpse the timeless or eternity which is a transcendent aspect of grace either natural or supernatural. They brush up against the glory of the natural world from being grounded in social interaction. Carl and Beth are talking, yes, about the weather and the prospects of rain. Neighborly interest in "keeping up the property" is augmented when residents share thoughts and tips on caring for and providing the best for their plants. Indeed, the friendly competition that emerges from observing and acting toward the physical environment – seeing the first hummingbird, picking the first or largest tomato, making the tastiest blueberry jam – renew and extend the meaning of daily life. The fruits of one's gardening are important and status-enhancing. At county or town fair time, the friendly competition develops keener edge, but in general does not undermine the satisfaction derived from everyone's success in their door-yard garden. Carl's "square-foot" raised bed a few weeks later in the season yielded a crop of cucumbers, jalapeno peppers, and tomatoes amidst the foliage. A reminder as well that the taste of one's own vegetables is far superior to anyone else's fresh produce.

To underscore the sensational dimension of gardening, the stimulation of sight, taste and smell, each incapable of being captured by words or images, imagine the scent from the Stargazer lilies in Kate's garden. The sheer beauty of flowers is one reason that flowers are grown in Kahehtiyo. Fragrance and the shelter given by the blossoms to bees were often mentioned as other reasons to devote space to loveliness where a tomato might be more useful. Kahehtiyo's gardeners were not primarily flower-growers or bouquet makers, instead they appreciated scent and elegance in their door-yards and in the community. A close cousin to the aesthetic appreciation of life forms is seen with the juxtaposition of Emily's bench, a utilitarian object, paired with a bright red geranium for a blast of color. This bench always remained outdoors as part of Emily's front-yard garden. Each season brought forth another pairing even in winter when dried or man-made plants were the best-suited complements and accordingly displayed by the side of the bench.

The opportunity to garden into later life was acknowledged as one of the most important reasons to live in Kahehtiyo. The community has never been without a "wait-list" for prospective occupants, but the gardens individually and collectively put the small, twenty unit complex, at the top of the list for many of the elderly in nearby towns and cities. Its rural placement limits further development as water here is well-water and the waste system is septic. That means that thirteen years later, in 2005 when I began this study, there were many "pioneer" residents who were actively gardening. Pat and her dog, Rosie. Pat and her husband had been among the first cohort of residents, and after his death, Pat remained in Kahehtiyo. She had strong, social ties to the larger community of Bartram, and she always looked forward to her front, back, and side-yard gardening, in later years accompanied by Rosie. The one difficulty that many residents of Kahehtiyo discussed, Pat included, was the fact that their rural setting (a superlative for having close connection to nature and gardening) was, indeed, a limiting factor in terms of access to some services and to alternate transportation when one could no longer drive an automobile. Residents almost always said "winter on the hill was tough," but adding to the temporary isolation was the distance away from and access to stores, health services, and in some cases, formal religious participation. That being said, virtually all of the "pioneers" remained residents and gardeners until the nursing home or an extended hospitalization forced a change in housing. As one resident said, "It's not a rose garden up here, but I wouldn't want to leave."

The extensive, and, indeed, largest back-yard garden of Kahehtiyo was – the garden of Millie and Tim. The flowers, vegetables, trees, and shrubs, always well-tended, created its own cultivated setting that blended harmoniously into the hill-top and field surrounding the community. A place to work and improve each gardening year and at the end of his life a place for Tim to be part of integrally and organically if not as in years past as the active gardener and creator. Millie remains to tend this garden today, although I think Tim might agree with these words written more than a century ago in an autobiographical essay on old age, "Without effort on my part life has handed me these extra hours in which to look around the world and enjoy the beauties of it with peace in my heart, and it seems that for those who look upon age rightly, life becomes a spacious, roomy place" (Deland, 1911, pp. 110–111). I only add that the spacious place of a small garden is a way to touch the eternal.

Conclusion

Across varied social and individual experiences of aging and old age, is there an aged gardener who would substitute something else for the experience of growing butterfly bush, bee balm, or cardinal flower, and subsequently observing hummingbirds, monarchs, and swallowtails nestle into those blossoms on a summer's day? All of the moments of physical effort beforehand, monitoring yet being powerless when confronted by the vagaries of weather, recognizing that your plants do not compete as favorably as those of your neighbors, none of this defeats the dedicated gardener. Gardeners are implicitly oriented to an uncertain and unknowable future with a kaleidoscope of possibilities ever turning and without predictable outcomes except the hope of seeing and tasting the fruits of labor. Gardening is an activity that seeks to materialize or make real the promise and potential of human activity – a bridge spanning past, present, and future. Gardening lifts people out of ordinary time if only for shorter or longer moments. Gardening and other meaningful, freely chosen activities are transcendent in a sociological sense – they move individuals beyond self. It is worth pointing out to those thinking how social agencies might offer gardens to people and gain enthusiastic response: the one failure of gardening in the twenty years of Kahehtiyo's existence was the "community" garden that was started one year and died the same year from neglect by residents with respect to watering and weeding. Gardening is as much about freedom and autonomy as part of the path to the timeless and the good. Much as community gardens are worthwhile and of much interest lately, they are qualitatively different when it comes to gardeners and gardening.

Arguably the greatest challenge of growing old resides in balancing one's place in the departure lane with one's desire to continue along as if the sidetrips and adventures could go on forever (this image is one suggested by a former study participant who continued to drive at age seventy-seven). Some authentic part of being alive is closely connected in later life to finding a way to preserve a sense of self, to grasp the symbolic immortality of living (Lifton and Olson, 1974, p. 60). "We can see the sense of symbolic immortality as reflecting man's relatedness to all that comes before him and all that follows him. This relatedness is expressed in the many kinds of symbolization that enable one to participate in ongoing life without denying the reality of death." One may prefer Erikson, or others, in terms of a theoretical framework for the tasks and resolutions of later life – but a central theme for scholars from the humanities and social sciences is that there is no way around the task of recognizing and taking account of changes in self and identity if one is to age well, that is, if one faces, like the thrush, the bleak dimensions of the landscape yet sees the beauty that may be found. The capacity to adapt is ongoing – perhaps, following Neugarten here – and may not be step-wise. In other words, people may be off-time in understanding time's flow and aging; that is, ahead or behind his or her time and age. Gardening is the kind of activity that permits a larger awareness of life and a glimpse of the eternal. Creative interaction including domains of religion and belief lend dimensionality and texture to our models of on-time/off-time normative transitions in social roles and aging. Today we are as much unaware of the "blessed hope" in the full-hearted evensong as was Hardy's observer, though within the boundaries marked by a coppice-gate such possibilities are realized.

References

Achenbaum, W. A. and Modell, S. M. 1999. 'Joan and Erik Erikson and Abraham and Sarah: Parallel awakenings in the long shadow of wisdom and faith'. In L.E. Thomas & S.A. Eisenhandler (Eds.), *Religion, belief, and spirituality in late life* (pp. 13–32). New York: Springer.

Atchley, R. C. 1999. *Continuity and adaptation in aging: Creating positive experiences*. Baltimore: Johns Hopkins.

Atchley, R. C. 2009. *Spirituality and aging*. Baltimore: The Johns Hopkins University Press.

Birren, J. E. and Deutchman, D. E. 1991. *Guiding autobiography groups for older adults*. Baltimore: Johns Hopkins University Press.

Black, H. K. and Rubenstein, R. 2000. *Old souls: Aged women, poverty, and the experience of God*. Hawthorne, NY: Aldine de Gruyter.

Butler, R. N. 1963. The life review: an interpretation of reminiscence in the aged. *Psychiatry*, 26, 65–76.

Deland, M. 1911. *Autobiography of an elderly woman*. Boston: Houghton Mifflin.

Durkheim, E. 1965. *The elementary forms of the religious life*. New York: The Free Press. [first published 1915 by George Allen and Unwin Ltd.]

Eisenhandler, S. A. 1989. More than counting years: Social aspects of time and the identity of elders. In L. Eugene Thomas (Ed.), *Research on adulthood and aging: The human science approach*. Albany, NY: State University of New York Press.

Eisenhandler, S. A. 1994. A social milieu for spirituality in the lives of older adults. In L. E. Thomas & S. A. Eisenhandler (Eds.), *Aging and the religious dimension* (pp. 133–145). Westport, CT: Auburn.

Eisenhandler, S. A. 1998. Reading between the lines: Aspects of transcendence and spirituality in one group. In L. E. Thomas & S.A. Eisenhandler (Eds.), *Religion, belief, and spirituality in late life*. New York: Springer.

Eisenhandler, S. A. (2003). *Keeping the Faith in Late Life*. New York: Springer.

Eisenhandler, S. A. 2005. Religion is the finding thing: An evolving spirituality in late life. *Journal of Gerontological Social Work*, 45, 85–103.

Eisenhandler, S. A. 2007. All seasons shall be sweet: gardening as a source of transcendent meaning. Paper presented at meetings of the Association for the Sociology of Religion. New York City.

Eisenhandler, S. A. 2013. Blossoms in crevices: Faith in later life. Paper presented at meeting of the Society for the Scientific Study of Religion. Boston, MA, November 9.

Fowler, J. W. 1981. *Stages of faith: The psychology of human development and the quest for meaning*. San Francisco: Harper and Row.

Goldman, C. 2006. *Tending the earth, mending the spirit: The healing gifts of gardening*. Minneapolis: Nordin Press.

Hardy, T. 2001 [1976]. The darkling thrush. In J. Gibson (Ed.), *Thomas Hardy: The complete poems*. New York: Palgrave. Subtitle, "a full-hearted evensong," is a phrase taken from line 19, p. 150. Original poem dated December 31, 1900.

Helphand, K. I. 2006. *Defiant gardens: Making gardens in wartime*. San Antonio, TX: Trinity University Press.

Heschel, A. J. 1981. The older person and the family in the perspective of Jewish tradition. In C. LeFevre & P. LeFevre (Eds.), *Aging and the human spirit: A reader in religion and gerontology* (pp. 35–44). Chicago: Exploration Press.

Idler, E. I. 1994. *Cohesiveness and coherence: Religion and the health of the elderly*. New York: Garland Publishing, Inc.

Kaplan, R. L. and Kaplan, S. 1989. *The experience of nature: A psychological perspective*. New York: Cambridge University Press.

Kaplan, R., Kaplan, S. and Ryan, R. L. 1998. *With people in mind: Design and management of everyday nature*. Washington DC: Island Press.

Kierkegaard, S. 1962. *Works of love* (H. Hong & E. Hong, Trans.). New York: Harper and Row. (Original work published in 1847)

Lifton, R. J. and Olson, E. 1974. *Living and dying*. New York: Bantam.

Luke, H. M. 1987. *Old age: Journey into simplicity*. New York: Bell Tower.

McFadden, S. H. 1999. Surprised by joy and burdened by age: The journal and letters of John Casteel. In L. E. Thomas & S. A. Eisenhandler (Eds.), *Religion, belief, and spirituality in late life* (pp. 137–149). New York: Springer.

McPhee, J. 1980. *Basin and range.* New York: Farrar, Straus, Giroux.

Moody, H. R. and Carroll, D. 1997. *The five stages of the soul.* New York: Anchor.

Myerhoff, B. 1980. *Number our days.* New York: Touchstone.

Neugarten, B. 1963. Personality and the aging process. In R. H. Williams, C. Tibbitts, & W. Donahue (Eds.), *Processes of aging: Social and psychological perspectives* (pp. 321–334). New York: Atherton.

Pogrebin, L. C. 1996. *Getting over getting older.* Boston: Little, Brown.

Rodin, J. and Langer E. J. 1977. Long-term effects of a control-relevant intervention with the institutionalized aged. *Journal of Personality and Social Psychology* 35, 897–902.

Rodin, J. 1978. Erratum to Rodin and Langer. *Journal of Personality and Social Psychology.* 36, 462.

Roof, W. C. 1993. *A generation of seekers: The spiritual journeys of the baby boom generation.* San Francisco: HarperSanFrancisco.

Roof, W. C. 1999. *Spiritual marketplace: Baby-boomers and the remaking of American religion.* New Jersey: Princeton University Press.

Thomas, L. E. and Eisenhandler, S. A. 1994. *Aging and the religious dimension.* Westport, CT: Auburn/Greenwood.

Thomas, L. E. and Eisenhandler, S. A. 1999. *Religion, belief, and spirituality in late life.* New York: Springer.

Tornstam, L. 1999. Late-life transcendence: A new developmental perspective on aging. In L. E. Thomas & S. A. Eisenhandler (Eds.), *Religion, belief, and spirituality in late life* (pp. 178–202). New York: Springer.

Tornstam, L. 2005. *Gerotranscendence: A developmental theory of positive aging.* New York: Springer.

Vaillant, G. E. 2002. *Aging well.* Boston: Little, Brown.

Westmacott, R. 1992. *African-American gardens and yards in the rural south.* Knoxville: The University of Tennessee Press.

Wuthnow, R. 2003. *All in sync: How music and art are revitalizing American religion.* Berkeley, CA: University of California Press.

11 Finding Meaning and Sustaining Purpose in Later Life

Albert Jewell

Introduction

My personal interest in the area of meaning and purpose in life is pastorally inspired and pastorally directed. During the second half of my fifty-year ministry I became increasingly fascinated by the evident resilience of church members, most of them women, in their seventies, eighties and nineties. I began to wonder what might be the source, or more likely the sources, of this resilience. I recognised that personality type could be a determinative factor – some by their very nature would be more vibrant than others. Life experience was also bound to play its part, for many of these impressive elders had worked in West Yorkshire woollen mills and other manual occupations in their earlier days, had lived through two world wars and had struggled to bring up large families in times of considerable adversity. They had fascinating life stories to tell and did so with real humanity and humour.

Most were sustained by a lively faith and by continued participation in the life of their church and community. Above all, they seemed to have retained, or discovered, a resilient sense of purpose. Then, when for seven years prior to my retirement, I served as pastoral director of Methodist Homes for the Aged (now MHA Care Group) I had the opportunity to meet many more such impressive individuals, including a remarkable number of centenarians. This background helps explain why, in my retirement, I chose to pursue a PhD study of well-being in some 500 older Methodists in the Leeds district where I reside, taking purpose in life as my focus or 'dependent variable' (Jewell 2007, 2010).

The sustaining of a sense of purpose in life appears to be one of the most significant factors in ensuring the mental, emotional and spiritual well-being and even, in some extreme circumstances, the physical survival of human beings throughout their lives. Paul Wong (2000, p. 24) regards personal meaning as the hidden dimension of successful ageing because 'having a positive meaning and purpose in life will not only add years to one's life, but also life to one's years'. Wong, together with many other writers, appears to regard 'meaning' and 'purpose' as virtually interchangeable. However, Irvin Yalom (1980) argues that 'meaning' and 'purpose' have different connotations, the former referring to coherence – making sense of one's life thus far – and the latter to intention.

But is this really how most people see things? I have a vivid memory of being asked in the mid-1980s to prepare a bible study course for the joint Anglican-Methodist groups that met in the local parish during Lent. One session was devoted to the somewhat obscure Old Testament book of Ecclesiastes, with its recurrent refrain, 'Futility, futility, everything is futile' (or 'vanity, vanity...' in the King James's Version of the Bible). The group members were asked to discuss what gave meaning to their lives. The almost unanimous response reported to me was that they had never asked themselves this, and they really had no idea what was meant. I realised that had I foreseen this and asked what gave purpose to their lives they might have been rather more forthcoming. I was able to rectify this more recently, when conducting seminars on finding meaning in later life with several groups of older people in which, based upon earlier work with Roman Catholic nuns (Jewell 2004), participants were invited to identify the most significant event or experience in each past decade of their life, to balance the advantages and disadvantages of growing old in their present experience, and to come to some decisions as to their priorities for the future. The view taken in this chapter is that meaning and purpose both belong to the same dimension of what it means to be a human being but that the first is the more basic construct because it incorporates past, present and future: making sense of the whole of life including 'the last lap', whatever that might bring.

In brief, this chapter will:

- Summarise the seminal contribution of Viktor Frankl.
- Underline the specific relevance of 'meaning-finding' for older people.
- Recognise the special case of those with dementia.
- Report the findings of my research.
- Discuss some of the lessons that can be drawn.

The Contribution of Viktor Frankl

The Austrian neurologist and psychologist Viktor Frankl (1964, 1971, 1978) founded a new school of psychotherapy called 'logotherapy' arising out of his experiences in the Second World War German concentration camps, where he reasoned that the only freedom remaining in such totally confining situations was that of adopting an inner attitude that enabled the prisoner to cope. Prisoners might choose to escape into the past. They might find beauty or purpose in the present: Frankl (1964) cites retaining a sense of humour, rejoicing in small mercies and doing something – whatever that something might be. And they might keep firmly in mind some future goal for which to go on living: the hope of eventual release and reunion with loved ones. Frankl observed: 'The prisoner who had lost faith in the future – his future – was doomed. With his loss of belief in the future, he also lost his spiritual hold; he let himself decline and became subject to mental and physical decay' (Frankl 1964, p. 74). In his preface to Frankl's *Man's search for meaning: An introduction to logotherapy*, Gordon Allport (1964, p. xi) notes the author's fondness for quoting Nietzsche's maxim, 'He who has a *why* to live can bear with almost any *how*'. It is this sense of purpose, according to Frankl, that continually 'pulls' a human being (Frankl 1971, p. 43). From this experience Frankl derived four main tenets of logotherapy:

- The irreducible freedom of will, whatever a person's circumstances.
- The will to meaning, innate in every human being and without which they experience a deep *ennui* or existential vacuum.
- The meaning of life, which will vary from person to person and from situation to situation.
- What he terms 'responsibleness', which provides the will to action.

Frankl summarises what he calls 'the values' that give meaning to life as threefold: *creative* (what a person gives to the world), *experiential* (what a person takes from the world and encounters in it), and, perhaps most importantly, *attitudinal* (the stand a person takes to his predicament when he must face a fate which he cannot change). He is strongly of the view that: 'If there is meaning in life at all, then there must be meaning in suffering. Suffering is an ineradicable part of life, even as fate and death. Without suffering and death human life cannot be complete' (Frankl 1964, p. 67). He urges that suffering ceases to be suffering in some way the moment it finds meaning such as 'the meaning of a sacrifice' (Frankl 1971, p. 115) and this can give it moral value. Only by such acceptance can 'a powerful fate ... be transmuted into something meaningful' (Frankl 1971, p. 72) and enable *homo patiens* (the suffering human being) 'to capitalize on the spirit's strength to transform a tragedy into a triumph' (Xu 2010, p. 182).

Although values and meanings were in his view relative, Frankl believed that there may remain an ultimate or cosmic meaning to human life, even if this proves inaccessible, and for his part declares: 'it is my contention that faith in ultimate meaning is preceded by trust in an ultimate being, by trust in God' (Frankl 1971, p. 145).

Relevance for Older People

Frankl's understanding of what it means to be human is obviously inclusive of people whatever their age. Nonetheless it does have particular relevance for older people, although 'meaning-based' research in this age group has admittedly been rather limited. Koenig, Larson and Matthews (1996) argued that, facing physical decline, it was natural that older people needed to find a sense of purpose and hope in their lives. As Harry Moody puts it: 'Human beings contemplate aging and death, and they reach backward and forward in time to pose questions about the meaning of existence' (Moody 1998, p. 437). Melvin Kimble edited a book devoted to *Viktor Frankl's contribution to spirituality and aging* (Kimble and Ellor 2000), in which the various contributors relate logotherapy to pastoral counselling, personhood in dementia, care of the terminally ill, adult major depression, long-term care settings and Christian theology.

Kimble and Ellor (Kimble and Ellor 2000, p. 14), whilst acknowledging that 'the crisis of aging appears to be a crisis of meaning', describe logotherapy as providing 'an understanding of life at all of its diverse stages, including old age, as life lived *sub specie aeternitatis*' (p. 21). Peter Coleman (2006, p. 5), for his part, draws a distinction between different 'horizons' of meanings: 'surface' meanings relating to immediate goals and 'ultimate' meanings which reflect 'values, hopes, concerns for the future'. As people grow older the latter tend to have special resonance.

Elizabeth MacKinlay (2001) grounded her book *The spiritual dimension of ageing* upon qualitative studies of community-dwelling older people and those living in nursing homes in Canberra, Australia. Her approach is explicitly Frankl-based. Older people are mostly retired from their main occupation and some at least of their previous roles in life. As Coleman (1993, p. 9) remarks: 'In old age the issue of meaning often becomes more acute because previously given meanings disappear, contained for example in the tasks that society requires of one in growing up, working, raising a family, and so on.' This can precipitate a crisis of meaning and identity because: 'Meaning in life is very much at the heart of what it is to be human' (MacKinlay 2001, p. 14). The situation of the very old can be even more challenging; writing of those in nursing care MacKinlay declares:

in a sense there is no meaning in life for these frail older people . . . waiting to die, in the back room of a death-denying society . . . There is a need to explore ways of affirmation and acceptance of the person, simply because they are created in the image of God, not because of what they can contribute to society or even to their neighbour. (p. 21)

Such situations will raise deep questions for any thinking person, and the 'frail elderly' themselves need encouragement to find their own answers, to come 'to a deeper understanding of who they are and why they are and have been here on earth' (p. 66), and so to preserve their sense of purpose in life and self-image.

MacKinlay recognises that the search for meaning becomes more important for older people in view of the nearness of death, and that there is a need to re-examine 'provisional meanings' in the light of subsequent experience so that 'final meanings' can be constructed. She maintains that: 'This search for meaning may be for many a search for transcendent relationship, a sense of "otherness" missing from their own lives' (2001, p. 15). MacKinlay conducted in-depth interviews with twenty-four older persons, during the course of which they were asked, 'Who or what gives greatest or deepest meaning to your life?' Eleven spoke of a conscious search for meaning as they grew older and eight spoke in terms of a spiritual journey.

In relation to older people, both Eileen Shamy (2003) and Leo Missenne (2004) examine the main categories of Frankl's 'values' that give meaning to life. *Creativity* remains significant for people of whatever age, declares Missenne (2004, p. 116): 'The point is that a person has to do, to create something, in order to find meaning.' *Experiential values* are realised 'by experiencing the good, the true and the beautiful, or by knowing one single human being in all his or her uniqueness' (p. 116). Here Missenne points to the love of older people for their grand-children and Shamy, for her part, to the affection that some may have for a pet. *Attitudinal values* come into play especially in the face of the suffering and losses many older people will face. Missenne (2004, p. 116) goes so far as to say: 'No one can better exemplify what life is all about than a person who is sick or dying. The best lesson about life and death is given by a sick person.' Shamy (2003, p. 63) argues that: 'Most people would be able to identify someone they know who has been able to rise above undeserved suffering without despair or bitterness; one who is still able, in spite of the cruellest circumstances, to embrace life positively.'

MacKinlay (2001), Missenne (2004) and Shamy (2003) are not alone in pointing to the importance of retaining or discovering a sense of purpose or meaning in life for psychological well-being in old age. Fischer (1998, p. 31), for example, writes: 'The emotional isolation experienced by many old people is a kind of boredom born of indifference. They have nothing worthwhile to do, no goals or plans.' Debats (1996, p. 504) regards 'meaningfulness' as having a direct effect on psychological health, enabling people to cope better after experiencing trauma and losses. Moreover, making a distinction between 'meaning' and 'purpose', he concludes (p. 511): 'the subjective feeling of meaningfulness in life is a more important determinant of psychological well-being, such as self-esteem, than just the presence of life goals or purpose in existence.'

Persons with Dementia

Because of increasing longevity, the incidence of people with Alzheimer's and other forms of dementia is ever growing in the United Kingdom and in many other countries. Indeed, it is reckoned that past the age of sixty as many as a third of people will experience a diagnosable level of dementia before they die, although this by no means always means that they will require residential or nursing care. Since dementia affects memory and other cognitive processes, and can lead to a sense of total incoherence concerning one's life, it is pertinent to ask how far the concepts of meaning and purpose are relevant to them. It is largely as we reflect upon our life-course that we evolve a sense of personal meaning in life, but this becomes difficult for the person with mild or moderate dementia and arguably impossible in its later stages.

Prospective memory (remembering what to do in the future) can also be adversely affected and so it becomes increasingly hard to sustain purpose in life even in relation to quite everyday tasks. However, Phyllis Braudy Harris (2008) in her small-scale study shows how some people with dementia are able to cope with their condition by a positive and planful attitude, which dispels the sense of uselessness. Christine Bryden in her autobiographical account of *Dancing with dementia* (2005) is an outstanding example of this.

Both John Killick and John Swinton, as contributors to *Spirituality and personhood in dementia* (Jewell 2011), emphasise that people with dementia live largely in the present moment and that they can find a real measure of purposeful well-being from the quality of that moment. This can arise from the enjoyment of play and creative activity, as illustrated by Harriet Mowat (2011) and Susan McFadden (2011), from enjoying the natural world (Gilliard and Marshall 2012; see also Chapter 10 in this book), or from the time and loving attention given by those who care about them (Killick 2011; MacKinlay 2011). Craig (Killick and Craig 2012, p. 78) points especially to the significance of working with such abiding materials as stone, wood, metal, and glass 'for some people for whom the idea of leaving a mark, a legacy for future generations has mattered, something to say "I was here"'.

Such fulfilment is more than the discovery of 'surface meaning' (Coleman 2006) both because it can have an enduring effect and, more significantly, because in the Judeo-Christian tradition 'being made in the image of God' would seem to reflect the meaningfulness of human creativity and the capacity to be in relationships. Those with dementia therefore are not to be regarded as excluded from the status of what may be termed *homo fabricans* and *homo amans*.

Indeed, Gilliard and Marshall (2012) present many examples to show how active involvement in gardens and allotments, regular shared walks and helping to care for a whole variety of animals can give purpose and sparkle to the everyday lives of those with dementia and to stimulate good conversation. In addition, for many communing with nature and relating to the rhythms of the seasons seem to bring a renewed sense of meaning to their individual lives within a meaningful and predictable universe, thereby arriving at a sense of peace.

Jewish and Christian believers derive much of their personal sense of meaning and purpose from the great 'meta-narratives' of their faith, the story of God's ongoing relationship with his chosen people and the Jesus story. These are derived primarily from their scriptures, traditions and regular liturgies. Those with memory loss cannot easily continue to access these fertile sources (Davis 1992), or readily recall their own faith journeys. It is therefore incumbent upon their community of faith to remember with and for those with dementia so that they are kept within the nourishing stream that gives purpose, direction and ultimate meaning to human life, arising from a sense of continuity, identity and security.

One of the most revealing studies of recent years is that by David Snowden (2001) of 678 Notre Dame sisters in the United States. To his surprise, the autopsies he was given permission to carry out showed that some nuns whose brains revealed advanced dementia had apparently given no sign of the condition in their lives in community. There seemed to be no genetic, dietary or other obvious 'scientific' explanation for this and he concluded the reason might well lie in their spirituality, in particular the regular pattern of their liturgical day and the strength of their corporate fellowship – areas on which he felt incompetent to comment further. This is what seems to have given an ongoing sense of meaning and purpose to their lives. Although the life of faith communities such as local churches cannot be as intense as that of a religious order, the sense of corporate inclusion is highly important to many of those with dementia. Feeling wanted, valued and loved helps them to retain a sense of meaning at an emotional rather than cognitive level.

My Research

In brief my study encompassed 535 members of the Leeds Methodist District aged between sixty and ninety-four, two-thirds of whom were female, one-third were male. The Methodist Church in the United Kingdom may be regarded in the main as belonging to the Protestant liberal-evangelical tradition and it is not claimed that older members from other traditions (Catholic, Orthodox, charismatic) or other religions would necessarily produce similar data. Almost 80 percent of the sample returned completed questionnaires comprising 241 items. Respondents were also asked if they would be prepared to undertake an interview. In the event thirty-one agreed, of which seventeen completed (the remainder being interviewed after the submission of the dissertation). The open-ended interview questions majored on their sense of purpose in life and also covered their attitude to ageing and death; their faith, including belief in an afterlife; what were the major stressors in their life; and how they coped with these (Jewell 2007, 2010).

Measuring Purpose in Life

Meaning or purpose in life is a difficult concept to measure. Frankl himself, in order to estimate the level of existential vacuum in his patients, used an informal series of thirteen questions, less than half of which were quantifiable. Some instruments that measure psychological well-being or happiness include some specific items concerned with purpose (Argyle, Martin and Crossland 1989; Hills and Argyle 2002; Paloutizian and Ellison 1991); however, the most widely used Frankl-based instrument has been the Purpose in Life Test (PILT) of Crumbaugh and Maholick (1964, 1969; Crumbaugh, 1968). The main identifiable components of the twenty-item test would appear to be: inner excitement/ennui; the presence and achievement of goals (retrospective, present and prospective); despair; attitude to the world; responsibility and locus of control; and death anxiety. McIntosh (1999), in his review of the PILT, notes its complexity and suggests that there is a lack of conceptual coherence in the measure. He also questions the degree to which it may be contaminated by social desirability and American-based cultural bias. The following are representative items of the PILT (employing a Likert-style scale marking seven degrees):

> *I am usually: Completely bored ... Exuberant, enthusiastic;*
> *Every day is: Constantly new, different ... Exactly the same;*
> *I am a: Very irresponsible person ... Very responsible person.*

Kenneth Pargament points to a further possible conceptual weakness arising from his view that Frankl's logotherapy is, at basis, implicitly religious. Although there is no explicit mention of God in the PILT Pargament comments: 'Underlying the search for religious purpose is the belief that life has an ultimate goal. What gives the search its *religious* quality is the belief that purpose is transcendental in nature, going beyond whatever the individual may make of it on his own or her own' (Pargament 1997, p. 237).

Because of these reservations, I chose in my study (Jewell 2007, 2010) to employ the twelve-item Likert-style Purpose in Life Scale (PILS) of Robbins and Francis (2000). Examples of the items are:

> My life seems most worthwhile
> There are things I still want to achieve in my life
> My personal existence is full of direction
> There is no meaning to my life
> My life has clear goals and aims.

The reliability of the PILS used in the study was demonstrably high. The favourable percentages amongst the sample ranged between 68 percent and 87 percent for ten out of the twelve items, reflecting a robust though not unrealistic outlook on the part of the great majority of participants in the study. It was particularly pleasing in an aged sample to find that 78 percent of respondents said that they had things they still wanted to achieve in life. Overall, respondents seemed largely to have distinguished between 'meaning', 'purpose' and 'direction', the first tending to produce the highest scores. This is consonant with a view of ageing that becomes more concerned with understanding than achievement.

The Interviews

Two of the open-ended questions used in the interviews related to continuing purpose in life, one specific and the other couched in terms of what the interviewees looked forward to in life. As might be expected, virtually all those in the sixty to sixty-nine age group were already fully engaged in purposeful activities, which they hoped to continue and extend in the future. Interviewees variously mentioned wanting to undertake a writer's course, studying herbal medicine, travel, the University of the Third Age and pursuing the Duke of Edinburgh's discovery award. Several specified maintaining contact with and caring for their families whilst not wishing to appear too demanding. However, one woman forthrightly declared: 'My family are still there but they are not my purpose. My purpose is to continue unfolding the gifts I've been given – and that will continue as long as I live.' Several of those interviewed, however, openly recognised that what they could realistically look forward to would largely depend upon their future circumstances and health.

In the case of the interviewees who were in their early seventies, there was a more marked sense of actual or impending redundancy in relation to those active leadership roles in church and community that had previously helped give them purpose in life. The two persons in their later seventies showed some degree of contrast in their responses to the purpose questions. One who had spent many years as a voluntary worker with overseas students looked forward to continuing her links all over the world in future largely by correspondence. The other interviewee showed a more marked recognition of her mortality: 'You realise eventually that you are going to have to die, which you hadn't given thought to before. Then you think, what should I be doing? Should I be preparing myself? What do I want to do before I die – is there anything I've always wanted to do?' Thus, 'you hope that you are preparing yourself in a spiritual way'. Meanwhile she contented herself with simple things in the near future, such as going out for a meal with a friend or attending a concert.

Those in their eighties who were interviewed comprised two men who had enjoyed distinguished careers, in education and the civil service respectively, and two widows in their late eighties. Both the men retained a great zest for life. One commented that living in the countryside he found very uplifting and he continued to enjoy gardening in particular. The educationist continued to give private tuition to pupils in his home. Both found enormous personal fulfilment in their families though one was finding it very difficult to adjust to the recent death of his wife to whom he was devoted, doing the household chores being a particular challenge. However, he had no hesitation in specifying that 'meeting people' gave him purpose in life. The same was true for the two women, both of whom had mobility problems and always looked forward to receiving visitors.

Both the male nonagenarians interviewed displayed remarkable resilience despite acknowledged health problems. The more active of the two continued to produce works of art and to mend clocks and watches as a hobby, and had been the prime organiser of a recent gala bowling competition for the over-nineties in his community. His family remained important to him, although he was always glad to get back home after staying with them, and he found that helping others in his locality gave him most sense of purpose. Although the other man had laid down a number of church offices and could no longer take services as a local (lay) preacher, he continued to visit people pastorally when he could get the requisite transport. He appeared to be accepting of the imminent prospect of moving into residential care near to his son and remarked that the recent death of a much-loved friend had caused him to think much more deeply about what the future might hold.

Relevant Correlations

Crumbaugh and Maholick (1969) reported significant relationships between PILT scores and other variables, especially, as might be expected, scales of anomie/depression and also personality traits, though none with either sex or age. However, in common with many studies, using the PILS I found that purpose declined with advancing years in my sample. It was also significantly lower in women, perhaps reflecting the so-called empty-nest syndrome. After reviewing the results obtained in a number of studies using the PILT, Yalom (1980) concluded that, for all age groups, the less sense of meaning in life, the greater the severity of psychopathology in the subject. Conversely, a positive sense of meaning in life was associated with deeply held religious beliefs, self-transcendent values and adoption of clear life goals, as well as with membership of human groups and dedication to causes. Yalom fully recognised that types of meaning and values are likely to change over the course of an individual's life.

Missenne, employing the PILT with a sample of people aged 60 and over in Nebraska, found that 63 percent of the respondents felt that their life had definite purpose and meaning. Contrary to my findings and those of Crumbaugh and Maholick, however, those aged between seventy-three and ninety-five years scored significantly higher than those aged sixty to seventy-two years. Missenne (2004, p. 121) suggests two possible reasons for this: it may be that the older persons had already adjusted to retirement and discovered new ways of finding fulfilment; in addition, 'those older adults who have meaningful lives [may] simply live longer than those who have nothing to live for'. Reker, Peacock and Wong (1987), in their study of 300 men and women with an age spread from sixteen to seventy-five years and above, using a forty-six-item Frankl-based Life Attitude Profile (Reker and Peacock 1981) together with a Perceived Well-Being Scale (Reker and Wong 1984) similarly found that life purpose and death acceptance increased with age, especially amongst the old–old, although goal seeking and future meaning decreased.

My own study sought to investigate the relationship between wellbeing as expressed in purpose in life and a number of other variables. In regard to personality, purpose in life was higher in extraverts, as measured both by the Eysenck instrument (EPQR-A, Francis, Brown and Philipchalk 1992) and the Francis Personality Type Scales (FPTS, Francis 2005), in those with lower scores on Eysenck's neuroticism scale, and in those who were more intuitive as against those preferring sensing according to the FPTS. My study used a gerotranscendence scale (Brown and Lowis 2003) which measures Tornstam's contention (Tornstam 1989, 1992, 1996, 2005; Erikson and Erikson 1997) that advanced old age could be marked by significant changes at three levels – cosmic, self and social – including (as examples) decreased fear of death, increased altruism and greater need for solitude. The data from my sample showed that gerotranscendence correlated positively and significantly with purpose in life. However, unlike purpose in life, gerotranscendence increased with age, which would appear to show that it measures something different from the former (Francis, Jewell and Robbins 2010). It is noteworthy that Brown and Lowis (2003) also found that in their sample of seventy older women, those in their eighties and nineties scored significantly higher on gerotranscendence than those in their sixties. Using the Death Attitude Profile (Gesser, Wong and Reker 1987–1988) in my study the approach-oriented attitude to death (linked with belief in an afterlife) was the only attitude manifesting a (significant) positive correlation with PIL, whereas fear of death/dying and escape-oriented attitudes correlated negatively with PIL.

Since mine was a churchgoing sample, a number of specifically religious measures were used in the study, amongst which three revealed significant correlations with purpose in life. Religious orientation (NIRO, Francis 2007) posits three basic orientations: extrinsic, which does not give religion top priority in life and uses it for social and personal support; intrinsic, which is committed religion for God's sake rather than one's own; and quest, which expresses a searching/struggling/wondering religiosity. The intrinsic orientation was the only one to show a significant positive correlation with purpose in life (although some 60 percent of respondents were also 'questers' who demonstrated openness to change in their religious beliefs). This finding, taken along with the 77 percent of the sample who said that they prayed daily, is consistent with the view that personal prayer may function as an indicator of intrinsic religiosity and a higher sense of purpose in life, as demonstrated by Francis and colleagues in relation to younger people (Francis and Burton 1994; Francis and Evans 1996).

Also used in my study was the Spiritual Transcendence Index (Seidlitz et al. 2002) which comprises two sub-scales measuring general and more specifically 'God-related' spiritual experience, the former revealing a significant positive relationship with purpose in life in my study. The findings from my study would appear to conform with the longitudinal study of older people by Wink, Dillon and Larsen (2005) which found that, regardless of health status, those rated higher in religiousness appeared to be buffered against depression, which can of course be associated with lack or loss of purpose.

Thirdly, in my study Pargament's eighteen-item shorter Religious Problem-Solving Scale was also used (Pargament 1997, Pargament et al. 1988). This posits three styles of coping reflecting different levels of responsibility attributed to the individual and to God in the face of various life stressors: self-directing, deferring (to God) and collaborative (expressing a partnership). In my sample, the self-directing style was significantly and negatively correlated with PIL, whereas the collaborative style revealed a significant and positive correlation. Personal 'responsibleness' alongside seeking support from God would appear to enhance purpose in life in my sample.

Discussion

As people grow older, it is important for their physical and psychological well-being that they maintain a sense of purpose in their lives and thus sustain their resilience. Retirement brings an end to major roles that have to a large extent directed individuals' lives. It also frees them to continue or revive other interests and pursue new ones. This may require a process of 'selection and optimisation' (Baker and Wheelwright 1983; Baltes and Baltes 1990), not attempting to go on doing everything they have previously done but concentrating on fulfilling activities or interests which give meaning to their lives and promote their continued personal growth in advancing years. Those interviewed in my study from their sixties into their nineties manifested this adaptation process.

Most older people are aware of the wisdom, indeed necessity, of this but may be slow to put it into practice because of an aversion to change or a reluctance to let others down. However, it would appear better for individuals to begin to make the desired choices before these are forced upon them by ill health or changed circumstances. Some older people choose to focus upon devoting more time to families and friends, for it is through such relationships that they feel wanted and affirmed, but many are reluctant to become a burden. Churches and local voluntary organisations mostly welcome the active input of their older members, indeed could hardly survive without them, but again the persons themselves will need to select and optimise as the years pass. Less physically active but nonetheless valuable roles can be fulfilled by older people in such organisations if due sensitivity is shown towards them. A prime example is the prayer ministry exercised by many older people in churches, the affirmation of which can increase their sense of purpose in life, especially perhaps in those who are introvert in personality.

Older people face the challenge of finding meaning in their existence as they reflect upon their lives in the light of the diminishments of older age and the nearer proximity of death. It is indeed true that in later life understanding tends to become more important than achievement. Such reflection, which can more effectively be done unencumbered by the busyness of earlier life stages, is to be seen much more in terms of an interpretation or apologia rather than just a factual account. It is by such reflection that individuals resolve Erikson's (1982) projected eighth life crisis of *integrity* (making sense of the whole) versus *despair* at the losses and diminishments that can characterise old age and at the state of the world. As Frankl asserts, it is the individual's attitude towards suffering that can potentially transform it. There is evidence from a number of studies to support Tornstam's repeated contention (1989, 1992, 1993, 2005) that some people in advanced old age do experience a significant shift in meta-perspective that enables them to rise above the limitations of advancing years (Hyse and Tornstam 2009; Raes and Marcoen 2001; Wadensten 2005), although other scholars question the universality of Tornstam's theory of gerotranscendence and feel that it is too culturally determined (Kastenbaum 1999, Bruyneel, Marcoen and Soenens 2005; Thorsen 1998). My own study showed a strong positive correlation between increasing age and gerotranscendence, as measured by the Brown and Lowis scale (2003). Particularly impressive were the 52 percent of respondents who felt that 'meaning in life is more clear now' and the 71 percent who declared purposefully that they believed they had 'new positive spiritual gifts to explore'. This is something worthy of celebration within the wider community in contrast to the negativity characterising the ageism which tends to pervade western society.

It is in the discovery of meaning in life that a person's spirituality and religion can have a major part to play. Reflecting on one's life *sub specie aeternitatis* for many people requires some concept of God, as Frankl acknowledged. MacKinlay (2001) found this to be the case with most of the subjects she interviewed in the course of her research, as did I. Quantitative studies can certainly be helpful in this regard but time spent in conversation with older people may be even more so, thereby allowing the interviewees space and hence a sense of being affirmed. In such one-to-one situations (as I found in the interviews in my study and in my pastoral work) older people seem more ready than those who are younger to talk about such matters as their spiritual experience, how they cope in life and their attitude to death, as well as their questions and doubts. Indeed, they can be relieved to be afforded such an opportunity, perhaps especially within churches and faith groups which may often give the impression of taking their older members for granted rather than affirming them and accompanying them through the final stages of life. It is sad that all too often the lives of older churchgoers are not celebrated until their funerals, and that there do not seem to be appropriate rituals or liturgies for this to happen whilst they are still alive.

Amongst the churches there does seem to be a lack of both any theology of ageing and a positive attitude towards what is regarded as 'the fourth age', in which many older Christians are more concerned with reflection and contemplation than with continued agency, with learning to be rather than to go on doing, and ultimately with letting go at the end of life into the hands of God. Graham Hawley, who has for some time led small groups of older pilgrims facilitating reflection on the last part of their journey, gives valuable advice about creating a safe space for this to happen (Hawley and Jewell 2009). Ann Morisy in her chapter in this volume has written about the workshops for older people run by the London-based PSALM organisation. It is to be hoped that this book will encourage faith groups to keep ageing very much on their agendas so that their elders may find strength to complete the 'last lap' meaningfully and to die well.

If well-being is seen to be expressed in continuing meaning and purpose in life, then some of the findings from my study of churchgoing older people (Jewell 2007, 2010) should be helpful. Greater purpose in life in my sample is linked with intrinsic or committed religiosity, to be found, for example, in personal prayer, an approach to coping that is based upon recognising a partnership with God, and belief in an afterlife. Such spiritual considerations tend, understandably, not to be at the forefront for the providers and practitioners of social care but they would do well to note their significance for many older people – as of course should churches and other faith communities.

Jianbin Xu, in his article 'Logotherapy: A balm of Gilead for aging' (2010), suggests that 'we need a model of successful aging that incorporates meaning and spirituality and that can (1) help older adults integrate their lived experience; (2) help older adults transcend their lived experience; and (3) be universally applicable. Based on logotherapy, a meaning-based model of successful aging, which defines successful aging as having a sense of meaningfulness of life, can be such a model'. (p. 187)

References

Allport, G.W. (1964). 'Preface', in Frankl, pp. 9–13.

Argyle, M., Martin, M. and Crossland, J. (1989). 'Happiness as a function of personality and social encounters', in Forgas, J.P. and Innes, J.M. (eds.). *Recent advances in social psychology: an international perspective*, pp. 189–203. North Holland: Elsevier Science.

Baker, B. and Wheelwright, J. (1983). 'Analysis with the aged', in Stein M. (ed.) *Jungian analysis*, pp. 257–258. La Salle, Illinois: Open Court.

Baltes, P.B. and Baltes, M.M. (1990). *Successful aging: Perspectives from behavioural science*. New York: Cambridge University Press.

Brown, C. and Lewis, M.J. (2003). 'Psychosocial development in the elderly: an investigation into Erikson's ninth stage', *Journal of Aging Studies* 17(4): 415–426.

Bruyneel, S., Marcoen, A. and Soenens, B. (2005). 'Gerotranscendence: components and spiritual roots in the second half of life'. Accessed at www.soc.uu.se/research/gerontology/gerotrans.html on March 19, 2009.

Bryden, C. (2005). *Dancing with dementia*. London: Jessica Kingsley Publishers.

Coleman, P.G. (1993). 'Adjustment in later life', in Bond, J., Coleman, P. and Peace, S. (eds.) *Ageing in society*, pp. 97–132. London: Sage Publications.

Coleman, P.G. (2006). *Last scene of all*. Southampton: University of Southampton.

Craig, C. (2012). 'Working with the hard stuff', in Killick and Craig, pp. 78–83.

Crumbaugh, J.C. (1968). 'Cross-validation of purpose in life test based on Frankl's concepts', *Journal of Individual Psychology* 24(1): 74–81.

Crumbaugh, J.C. and Maholick, L.T. (1964). 'An experimental study in existentialism: The psychometric approach to Frankl's noogenic neurosis', *Journal of Clinical Psychology* 20(2): 200–207.

Crumbaugh, J.C. and Maholick, L.T. (1969/1981). *Manual of instructions for the purpose in life test*. Abilene, TX: Viktor Frankl Institute of Logotherapy.

Davis, R. (1992). *My journey into Alzheimer's disease*. London: Tyndale.

Debats, D.L. (1996). 'Meaning in life: Clinical relevance and predictive power', *British Journal of Clinical Psychology* 35(4): 503–516.

Erikson, E.H. (1982). *The life cycle completed*. New York: W.W. Norton.

Erikson, E.H. and Erikson, J.M. (1997). *The life cycle completed* (extended version). New York: W.W. Norton.

Fischer, K. (1998). *Winter grace: Spirituality in aging*. Nashville, TN: Upper Room Books.

Francis, L.J. (2005). *Faith and psychology: Religion and the individual*. London: Darton, Longman and Todd.

Francis, L.J. (2007). 'Introducing the new indices of religious orientation: Conceptualization and measurement', *Mental Health, Religion and Culture* 10(6): 585–602.

Francis, L.J., Brown. L.B. and Philipchalk, R. (1992). 'The development of an abbreviated form of the Revised Eysenck Personality Questionnaire (EPQR-A): Its use among students in England, Canada, the USA, and Australia', *Personality and Individual Differences* 13(4): 443–449.

Francis, L.J. and Burton, L. (1994). 'The influence of personal prayer on purpose in life among Catholic adolescents', *Journal of Beliefs and Values* 15(2): 6–9.

Francis, L.J. and Evans, T.E. (1996). 'The relationship between personal prayer and purpose in life among churchgoing and non-churchgoing 12–15 year olds in the UK', *Religious Education* 91(1): 9–21.

Francis, L.J., Jewell, A. and Robbins, M. (2010). 'The relationship between religious orientation, personality, and purpose in life among an older Methodist sample', *Mental Health, Religion and Culture* 13(7–8): 777–791.

Frankl, V.E. (1964). *Man's search for meaning: An introduction to logotherapy.* London: Hodder and Stoughton.

Frankl, V.E. (1971). *The will to meaning: Foundations and applications of logotherapy.* London: Souvenir Press.

Frankl, V.E. (1978). *The unheard cry for meaning: Psychotherapy and humanism.* New York: Simon and Schuster.

Gesser, G., Wong, T.P. and Reker, G.T. (1987–1988). 'Death attitudes across the life-span: the development and validation of the Death Attitude Profile (DAP)', *Omega* 18(2): 113–128.

Gilliard, J. and Marshall, M. (2012). *Transforming the quality of life for people with dementia through contact with the natural world.* London: Jessica Kingsley Publishers.

Harris, P.B. (2008). 'Another wrinkle in the debate about successful aging: the undervalued concept of resilience and the lived experience of dementia', *Aging and Human Development* 67(1): 43–61.

Hawley, G. and Jewell, A. (2009). *Crying in the wilderness: giving voice to older people in the church.* Derby: MHA Care Group.

Hills, P. and Argyle, M. (2002). 'The Oxford Happiness Questionnaire: a compact scale for the measurement of psychological well-being', *Personality and Individual Differences* 33: 1073–1082.

Hyse, K. and Tornstam, L. (2009). 'Recognising aspects of oneself in the theory of gerotranscendence'. Accessed online at www.soc.uu.se/research/gerontology/gerotrans.html on December 9, 2011.

Jewell, A. (2004). *Report on sisters work.* London: Conference of Religious in England and Wales.

Jewell, A. (2007). *Well-being in older Methodists: an empirical study.* Unpublished PhD dissertation, University of Wales, Bangor.

Jewell, A. (2010). 'The importance of purpose in life in an older British Methodist sample: pastoral implications', *Journal of Religion, Spirituality and Aging* 22(3): 138–161.

Jewell, A. (ed.)(2011). *Spirituality and personhood in dementia.* London: Jessica Kingsley Publishers.

Kastenbaum, R. (1999). 'Endpiece', in Thomas L.E. and Eisenhandler S.A. (eds.) *Aging and the religious dimension.* Westport, CT: Greenwood Publishing Group.

Killick, J. (2011). 'Becoming a friend of time', in Jewell, A. (ed.) *Personhood and spirituality in dementia*, pp. 52–63. London: Jessica Kingsley Publishers.

Killick, J. and Craig, C. (2012). *Creativity and communication in persons with dementia.* London: Jessica Kingsley Publishers.

Kimble, M.A. (ed.) (2000). *Viktor Frankl's contribution to spirituality and aging*. Binghamton, NY: The Haworth Pastoral Press.

Kimble, M.A. and Ellor, J.W. (2000). 'Logotherapy: an overview', in Kimble (ed.), pp. 9–24.

Koenig, H.G., Larson, D.B. and Matthews, D.A. (1996). 'Religion and psychotherapy with older adults', *Journal of Geriatric Psychiatry* 29(2): 155–184.

MacKinlay, E. (2001). *The spiritual dimension of ageing*. London: Jessica Kingsley Publishers.

McFadden, S. (2011). 'Gathering and growing gifts through creative expression and playfulness', in Jewell, A. (ed.) *Personhood and spirituality in dementia*, pp. 100–110. London: Jessica Kingsley Publishers.

McIntosh, D.N. (1999). 'Scales of related constructs 17.4. Purpose in Life Test (Crumbaugh and Maholick 1964)', in Hill, P.C. and Hood, R.W. Jr. (eds.) *Measures of religiosity*, pp. 503–508. Birmingham, AL: Religious Education Press.

Missenne, L. (2004). 'The search for meaning in life in older age', in Jewell, A. (ed.) *Ageing, spirituality and well-being*, pp. 113–123. London: Jessica Kingsley Publishers.

Moody, H.R. (1998). *Aging: concepts and controversies*, 2nd edition. Thousand Oaks, CA: Pine Forge Press.

Mowat, H. (2011). 'Working with people with dementia', in Jewell, A. (ed.) *Personhood and spirituality in Dementia*, pp. 74–86. London: Jessica Kingsley Publishers.

Paloutzian, R.F. and Ellison, C.W. (1991). *A manual for the spiritual well-being scale*. Nyack, NY: Life Advance Inc.

Pargament, K.I. (1997). *The psychology of religion and coping: Theory, research and practice*. New York: Guilford Press.

Pargament, K.I., Kennell, J., Hathaway, W., Grevengoed, N., Newman, J. and Jones, W. (1988). 'Religion and the problem-solving process: Three styles of coping', *Journal for the Scientific Study of Religion* 27(1): 90–104.

Raes, F. and Marcoen, A. (2001). 'Gerotranscendence in the second half of life: first empirical investigation in Flanders.' Accessed at www.soc.uu.se/research/gerontology/gerotrans.html on December 11, 2011.

Reker, G.T. and Peacock, E.J. (1981). 'The Life Attitude Profile (LAP): a multidimensional instrument for assessing attitudes toward life', *Canadian Journal of Behavioural Science* 13(3): 264–273.

Reker, G.T., Peacock, E.J. and Wong, P.T.P. (1987). 'Meaning and purpose in life and well-being: A life span perspective', *Journal of Gerontology* 42(1): 44–49.

Reker, G.T. and Wong, P.T.P. (1984). 'Psychological and physical well-being in the elderly: the Perceived Well-Being Scale (PWB)', *Canadian Journal on Aging* 3(1): 23–32.

Robbins, M. and Francis, L.J. (2000). 'Religion, personality, and well-being: the relationship between church attendance and purpose in life among undergraduates attending an Anglican college in Wales', *Journal of Research in Christian Education* 9(2): 223–238.

Seidlitz, L., Abernethy, A.D., Duberstein, P.R., Evinger, J.S., Chang, T.H. and Lewis, B. (2002). 'Development of the spiritual transcendence index', *Journal for the Scientific Study of Religion* 41(3): 439–453.

Shamy, E. (2003). *A guide to the spiritual dimension of care for people with Alzheimer's disease and related dementias*. London: Jessica Kingsley Publishers.

Snowden, D. (2001). *Aging with grace*. London: Fourth Estate.

Swinton, J. (2011). 'Being in the moment', in Jewell, A. (ed.) *Personhood and spirituality in dementia*, pp. 175–185. London: Jessica Kingsley Publishers.

Thorsen, K. 1998. 'The paradoxes of gerotranscendence: The theory of gerotranscendence in a culturally gerontological and post-modernist perspective', *Norwegian Journal of Epidemiology* 8(2): 165–176.

Tornstam, L. (1989). 'Gero-transcendence: a reformulation of the disengagement theory', *Aging*, 1(1): 55–63.

Tornstam, L. (1992). 'The quo vadis of gerontology: on the scientific paradigm of gerontology', *The Gerontologist* 32(3): 318–326.

Tornstam, L. (1993). 'Gerotranscendence: A theoretical and empirical exploration', in Thomas, L.E. and Eisenhandler, S.A. (eds.) *Aging and the religious dimension*, pp. 203–225. Westport, CT: Greenwood Publishing Group.

Tornstam, L. (1996). 'Caring for the elderly: introducing the theory of gerotranscendence as a supplementary frame of reference for caring for the elderly', *Scandinavian Journal of Caring Science* 10(3): 144–150.

Tornstam, L. (2005). *Gerotranscendence: Aa developmental theory of positive aging*. New York: Springer Publishing Company.

Wadensten, B. (2005). 'Introducing older people to the theory of gerotranscendence', *Journal of Advanced Nursing* 2(4): 381–388.

Wink, P., Dillon, M. and Larsen, B. (2005). 'Spiritual development across the adult life course: Findings from a longitudinal study', *Research on Aging* 27 (2): 197–220.

Wong, P.T.P. (2000). 'Meaning of life and meaning of death in successful aging', in Tomer, A. (ed.) *Death attitudes and the older adult: Theories, concepts, and applications*. Philadelphia, PA: Brunner-Routledge.

Xu, J. (2010). 'Logotherapy: A balm of Gilead for aging?' *Journal of Religion, Spirituality and Aging* 22(3): 180–195.

Yalom, I.D. (1980). *Existential psychotherapy*. New York: Basic Books.

12   Spirituality, Biographical Review and Biographical Pain at the End of Life in Old Age

Malcolm Johnson

The human spirit is capable of responding to the whole range of emotions and experiences that form the lifespan of an individual. It is the agency that registers emotions across the whole spectrum; from the elation of joy at wondrous experiences, events, achievements and relationships, to the despair and degradation of profound pain and loss. Whilst most of us are treated to great pleasures and exquisitely lofty emotional highs on occasions, some live lives of endless oppression and cruel misuse. So reflecting on our past lives, as we all do, may be affirming and pleasurable. It may be harrowing, painful, full of guilt and anger. Or it may be a mixture of these two extremes, with the mix changing at different times and in different circumstances. As we get closer to the end of life this life review and self-evaluation becomes more frequent and more problematic.

In his prize winning novel, *The sense of an ending* (2011) Julian Barnes plots the lives of four bright eighteen-year-old young men as they prepare themselves for university. They are bonded friends who are being taught history and philosophy by an exceptional teacher. So they compete to be reflexively clever. Their tangled student lives and an unexplained suicide receive detailed attention. But their adulthood, the middle part of their lives, is passed over with only the merest of narratives. The heart of the book focuses on Tony, who says of himself in old age:

What did I know of life, who had lived so carefully? Who had neither won nor lost, but just let life happen to him? Who had the usual ambitions, and settled all too quickly for them not being realised? Who avoided being hurt and called it a capacity for survival? Who paid his bills, stayed on good terms with everyone as far as possible.

Tony concludes: 'You get to the end of your life – no, not life itself, but something else: the end of any likelihood of change in that life. You are allowed a long moment of pause, time enough to ask the question: what else have I done wrong? ... (p. 142) There is accumulation. There is responsibility. And beyond these, there is unrest, There is great unrest ...' (pp. 149–150).

It is within this inescapable ordinariness of a spiritual void which grows out of the experience of so many (how many, in empirical terms, we cannot yet know) that my preoccupation lies. The case for taking it so seriously is magnified by the doubling of the lifespan over the past 150 years, the welcome facility of retirement and the often daunting experiences of the fourth age. Living to be old is still considered to be a great benefit. But dying slowly and painfully, with too much time to reflect and with little or no prospect of redressing the harms, the deficits, the deceits and the emotional pain, has few redeeming features.

It is well recognised that as individuals move into the later stages of life, they are less occupied by the driving force of paid employment and spend more time in reflection about the life lived. In part this is due to the onset of infirmities, as chronic diseases take their toll on mobility and autonomy. Unchosen solitude and the frustration of a failing body both prompt recollections of more engaged times and draw attention to the deficits of old age.

Gerontologists have committed a vast amount of research resource to mapping the physical, social and psychological deficits and maladies associated with later life. Yet remarkably little to observing and comprehending the inner lives of the old. Other discourses refer to this dimension as the soul (as Rick Moody reminds us here); some to the existential self, others to spirituality. Whilst I will use the term spirituality, our field of interest is still grasping at a vocabulary that embraces the religious and the secular. What is not in doubt is the epidemiology of the fourth age to which attention is drawn here.

Experiencing the Fourth Age

Living longer is a remarkable bonus for many who live in the richest countries of the world, where the fastest growing sector is those over eighty-five years. As the whole world experiences greater life expectancy, we shall see global ageing on a massive scale. The United Nations (UNDSA, 2011) predict that by mid twenty-first century one in five of the world's population will be over sixty. Inevitably developing nations will soon need to recognise the particular contributions and needs of older people. In what follows about living in the fourth age of dependency, we will examine data from the United Kingdom and United States; but they represent the current position in many advanced nations and the rising prospects in the wider international community.

Gerontologists increasingly use a delineation of the post retirement phase of life in two parts – the Third Age (3rd Age) and the Fourth Age

(4th Age). These age-related but not age-span categories were promulgated by Peter Laslett in his book *The fresh map of life* (1989) where he identifies a new period of active and predominantly healthy life, following retirement from mainstream employment: the 3rd Age. During this phase the 'young old' have the opportunity to develop themselves and take an engaged part in the life of families and communities. What may follow for many is the final phase of life characterised by illnesses, disablement, declining cognitive functioning and loss of the capacity for independent living – the 4th Age.

The term and the concept has inevitably attracted critical attention. Most prominent amongst the detractors are Gilleard and Higgs (2009). In this volume (Chapter 6) Paul Higgs puts their case as follows: 'Unlike the third age, Gilleard and Higgs argue, the fourth age is not a cultural field but rather a social imaginary, realised less in lifestyle and lived experience than in and through the gaze of others, whether mediated by the discourse and practices of social policy or through the cultural representations of the lives of others.'

This sociological interpretation seeks to infuse the label – used to enable attention to be focussed on the final stage of life which is characterised by restricting ill health and severely reduced agency – with a more nuanced set of understandings. Their critique sets the 4th Age in a frame shaped by a culture of consumption and restricted access to the inherent values of choice, autonomy and pleasure. In recognising the value of the ensuing discourse, I nonetheless wish to draw attention to the two key features of being on the last lap of life, in order to highlight the manifest and well-evident losses: multiple chronic illnesses and the ways these confine personal living and connections with personal networks and wider society. The purpose of doing so, is to consider the impact on identity, self esteem, life review and spiritual evaluations.

In England around 470,000 people die each year. Eighty percent of all deaths are people over 65. Two-thirds of deaths are people over 75; one third are 85+. In simple terms this means that at any one time there is an annual cohort of approaching 315,000 people over 75, plus another group of 65,000 people approching 65–75s who are 'on the final lap' of life. These 380,000+ are destined to die, each year, from degenerative diseases that make their health frail for a long period before death. Heart disease, cancers, organ system failures (liver, kidney, heart, respiration) along with strokes and dementia account for the overwhelming majority – around 90 percent.

What we know about the living circumstances of these increasingly frail older people is that two-thirds of those over 75 are women (more in the higher age groups) and that two-thirds of this group of women live alone, widowed or never married. As an overlay to the cluster of chronic illnesses that will bring their lives to an end they will typically suffer severe visual impairment. Of the one million 'blind' people in the United Kingdom, 90 percent are late onset sufferers, principally of the unremediable condition macular degeneration. Similar proportions are severely hard of hearing. Dementia is essentially a condition of old age, the incidence of which rises steeply with age and affects women more than men. Among the over eighties around 30 percent (Peters, 2001 in Stephan & Brayne; Downs & Bowers, 2008) suffer from dementia. Depression is the most extensive condition of old age. The prevalence of incontinence is less well documented but studies show (Chrome et al., 2001) levels of over one-third of older people in the later stages of life.

The most comprehensive analysis of the macro data about health status in the 4th Age was produced by Lyn and Adamson (2003) in a benchmark publication from the Rand Corporation. They delineated three clearly identifiable end of life trajectories.

Trajectory One: Is described as a short period of evident decline – typical of cancer. Most patients with malignancies maintain comfort and functioning for a substantial period. However, once the illness becomes overwhelming, the patient's status usually declines quite rapidly in the final weeks and days preceding death. A palliative care approach is recommended: 'pain relief and personal support.'

Trajectory Two: Is presented as long-term limitations with intermittent exacerbations and sudden dying – typical of organ system failure. Patients in this category often live for a relatively long time and may have only minor limitations in everyday life. From time to time, some physiological stress overwhelms the body's reserves and leads to a worsening of serious symptoms. Patients survive a few such episodes but then die from a complication or exacerbation, often rather suddenly. The recommended treatment is ongoing disease management, advance care planning, and mobilizing services to the home.

Trajectory Three: Is given the inelegant but highly descriptive label: Prolonged dwindling – typical of dementia, disabling stroke and frailty. Those who escape cancer and organ system failure are likely to die at older ages of either neurological failure (such as Alzheimer's or other dementia) or generalised frailty of multiple body systems. Here Lynn and Adamson prescribe supportive services at home, followed by institutional long-term care facilities.

Analyses of Medicare claims show that about one-fifth of those who die have a course consistent with the first group (mostly cancer patients); another fifth share the course of the second group (mostly organ system failure patients) and two-fifths follow the third course (frailty/dementia). The last one-fifth of those who die are largely those whose deaths are sudden.

What will be apparent from these descriptions of the 4th Age is how it is so frequently characterised by greatly restricted social interaction, being largely or wholly housebound and being alone for long stretches of most days. During the earlier periods of life, having too much to do and the multiple demands of others leave too little time for thinking and reflection. The 4th Age is one of an overabundance of time to think. With too little stimulation, older people turn to thinking about what they know best; their own lives and times. This is one of the principal causes of depression (the epidemic condition of old age) and mental illness in older people in late life.

Does Psychological Functioning Predict Mortality?

The psychological literature has explored the proposition (first made by Robert Kleemeier in 1962) that lower levels of psychological functioning, and especially cognitive functioning, are associated with imminent death (Maier & Smith, 1992). A more recent major Swedish study by Laura Fratiglioni and colleagues counsels caution on making a direct correlation between cognitive deficits and time to death (Small, Fratiglioni & Backman, 2003). This analysis from a very large study makes it clear that cognitive decline is as complex as physical decline. It is reasonable to suggest that the different pathways related to groups of chronic illnesses (which we saw earlier) are also likely in psychological functioning. Indeed the same Karolinska team has provided some of the markers, by attempting to articulate the patterns of co-morbidity and multimorbidity. Two central features of the last phase of life are *depression and cognitive decline*. With or without a diagnosis of dementia, the Berlin Ageing Study showed, there is a high probability that intelligence and cognitive functioning show decline during old age (Baltes, Staudinger & Lindberger, 1999).

As Margaret Baltes put it 'even though the onset time and regulation of decline may differ across psychological domains, all domains will eventually exhibit some type of dysfunctionality and this may take the form of a cascade of decline. The Fourth Age would thus be characterised by a functional breakdown of the psychological system and less desirable psychological profiles (eg loss of positive wellbeing, psychological dependence on others, poor memory and impaired *reasoning*)' (Baltes, 1998).

The first group who are dying from cancers are likely to receive well-developed services, designed to provide information, treatment and support. Their time of intense symptom distress will most probably be short. But the second and third groups are likely to face an extended period of dependency on others, linked with greatly restricted mobility and deterioration of key multiple cognitive capacities.

Lyn and Adamson use the chilling clinical descriptor Prolonged Dwindling for group three. It is also appropriate for many in group two, for whom the active living phase of life has terminated. This sub set of older people, living out the last distressing remnants of their lives, make up roughly half of the over 65s who die each year.

Death in the Province of Old Age

We have already noted that the systematic reductions in premature death, which took place across the developed world during the twentieth century, have made death in childhood, youth or adulthood prior to retirement a comparative rarity. When such deaths occur they create a sense of shock. Where the person is under 50, the reactions tend to focus on the unfairness of a life tragically ended long before time. Child deaths arouse the strongest emotions. The culturally accepted stretched lifespan has incorporated the marked extension of life expectancy. So there is a new norm for death, which is embedded in the collective psyche; though the normative framework has yet to permeate into any socially recognisable patterns that signify the importance and meaning of dying in later life.

A range of social scripts exists for premature deaths. 'His life has been cut off in its prime'. 'She still had so much to give'. 'How tragic he has left a growing family – how will they manage?' 'Her whole life was ahead of her and now it will never happen'. Underpinning these ready responses is an implicit theory of the lifespan. It is based on a demographic assumption that our cohort can expect to live beyond pensionable age and well into retirement. Even deaths of individuals in their late sixties, produce indications of a too early demise. 'He was still quite young – could have lived for years yet'.

By contrast the reactions to a 4th Age death are more typically ones which speak about 'having had a good innings' and 'it must be a relief'. The embedded disengagement concept sees death in old age as a death certificate stamped 'Time Expired'. Only the few are accorded the privilege of fuller recognition of their contribution to the lives of others. As those facing death worry about how they will be remembered and what their legacy will be, they also know that their passing will do little to disturb the busy world they leave behind.

Remembering in Pain

Everyday experience of living or working with older people, particularly those who have lost their independence, reveals that the ones who maintain a positive hold on life are far outnumbered by the depressed and the disappointed. For a subset of this unhappy group, the sequence of losses they have experienced leads to a state of anguish which steals from them many if not all of the former pleasures of living.

In my own work (over more than thirty years) I have interviewed many older people who have come under this unlifting shadow. These experiences have occurred throughout my professional life, but have recently reappeared through interviews with older people with severe visual impairment. Here the most prominent finding was of almost unrelieved isolation combined with a grieving for the losses which come with blindness and infirmity. In a group which numbers almost 1 million across the United Kingdom (one in ten of the retired population) there is a disturbing paucity of services.

Inevitably, many of the most frail and dejected are to be found in residential (assisted living) and nursing homes. Entering reluctantly and distressed by the deprivation of their life's acquisitions and freedoms, such people are deeply unhappy despite the best possible care. Entry to a care home requires the individual to leave the independent dwelling they regard as home and transfer to a form of collective living, where much of each day is spent with unchosen strangers, both fellow residents and staff. Accompanying the multiple losses of personal space, familiar locality, personal domain and personal/family history, is the stark recognition that you have entered the 'last lap' of life.

Religion and the support of faith communities can ease the path; especially for the current cohorts of elders, for whom religious values, beliefs and practices were instilled early and transmitted across the generations. Research conducted by Coleman and his colleagues (Coleman, 2004, 2011; Coleman et al., 2007) at Southampton, on the spiritual beliefs of older people showed that those who had strong religious convictions were less likely to be depressed and more likely to be at ease with their personal past and the prospect of death. Moderate believers and those with little or no religious faith revealed lower estimates of personal worth and a proneness to depression. These results, added to the research-based estimates of declining levels of belief in later life, indicate two broad observations. Firstly that religious belief and spiritual capability are positive attributes in dealing with the decrements of old-age. Secondly, there are indications of low levels of spirituality – even though today's old people have had much greater exposure to religious and spiritual experiences.

In seeking a solid platform for a proposition to capture the all too common anguish found in life histories, I have turned again to the analysis of personal biographies. The distilled, refined, polished but often flawed and jagged story we fabricate from the recollections of life lived has been one of the tools I have used in attempting to explain the processes of ageing for over thirty years. (It was in 1976 that my paper 'That Was Your Life: a Biographical Approach to Later Life' was first published.) Discovering, as did Kierkegaard, that life can best be understood backwards, though it must be lived forwards.

Biographical perspectives help to explain the new estimates of low late life epidemiology of spirituality, even in contemporary societies which host obsessions with 'discovering one's inner self' and searching for holism in nature, alternative medicine, the 'talking therapies' and the rise of evangelical sects – let alone the largely spurious search yourself revelation through drugs.

As human beings we are the accumulation of our life experience. What we have lived, observed, thought, felt and done are the essence of our personhood. Our journey along the lifepath is unique, even if it has been shared with others who have lived in the same places, lived in the same houses, been to the same schools, experienced the same world and local events, gone through the stages from childhood to now; loved some people and disliked and been hurt by others, been sometimes lucky and also suffered hurtful losses. The distinctive nature of our journey is our personal biography. The story of our lives is a detailed narrative that we have constructed from millions of recollections to form an account of who we are. As we have gone through life we have been mentally writing this story; adding to it new features and editing others out.

Curiously, we very rarely get the opportunity to tell the whole life story. Many individuals will have heard fragments, episodes and stories of special note. Some family members and close friends may have heard these noteworthy tales more times than they would have liked. But unless we have been in extended therapy, it is likely that even our closet kin have never heard the whole. There are two sides to this – lack of opportunity and an inbuilt restraint, which makes us reluctant to expose the totality of ourselves to another person. We will come to the reluctance later. As for the opportunities, in a world of busyness and schedules, there are few people with whom we would feel comfortable enough to relate our story to, who would have the several hours it would take even to make a good start.

Being listened to, without constant interruption, by a nonjudgmental listener is a rare and special opportunity. Having your life recollections heard with engaged interest and your interpretations of what they mean to you taken seriously is a particular privilege. As a researcher, I have enumerable times, listened to an older person's lifestory, mindful of the trust invested in me and surprised at the extent of intimate revelation. Often times it emerges that the account of extramarital relations, even babies aborted or given up for adoption whilst husbands fought in a war, revelations by women of sexual and physical abuse and dishonest practices have been told for the first time. They are told to, what I describe to students, as 'a safe, interested stranger'. All too often it becomes apparent that these are stories of deep guilt, protected over decades and made wholly unavailable to even the closest kin.

The converse of the rationing of significant biographical information is the frequent unwillingness of children to listen to the wishes of their elderly parents. 'I want to talk to you about my funeral'. 'No, you don't want to talk that way, you will live for years yet'. Children are frequently unable or unwilling to talk with their parents about issues of mortality and spiritual concern. So where do older people at the far end of life turn for a listener?

Life review, reminiscence or simply recalling a fragment of the past prompted by a random cue is the daily universal experience. But the nature of the experience is undoubtedly age related. The older you are, the more you have to remember. The older you are the closer you are to the end of your life – the less opportunity to fulfil your dreams and deal with the failings, fissures and hurts of the past. At the same time the long lived are more alone. Aloneness in itself is not necessarily undesirable. But it does present unaccustomed unoccupied space for biographical reflection. This may provide pleasurable recall of the good times in every life. It may also be the sponsor of depression (endemic among the very old, for clearly observable reasons), distress and profound pain.

Biographical Pain

The starting point for me was the now received wisdom, created by leading figures in the hospice movement, that palliative medicine could deal with all kinds of physical pain, but there was also a neglected dimension of pain, which it would label spiritual pain. It grew up as a concept fully grown from the mixture of motivations and convictions of the pioneers of the modern hospice movement, notably Cicely Saunders. The hospice idea predates St Christopher's Hospice by many centuries; but Dame Cicely's creation of this establishment marks the acknowledged commencement of the modern hospice movement and the serious beginnings of the medical specialty of Palliative Medicine (Du Boulay, 1984). Soon spiritual pain became a portmanteau term to deal with pain which was not physical or demonstrably psychiatric. In recognition that many people have little or no spiritual vocabulary, let alone experience of practice, I felt there was need for another category and another descriptor. Aware that the pain I have observed appears to grow in intensity as individuals get closer to death – either because of terminal illness or advanced old age – I created the term Biographical Pain; which is defined as:

> *The irremediable anguish which results from profoundly painful recollection of experienced wrongs which can now never be righted. When finitude or impairment terminates the possibility of cherished self promises to redress deeply regretted actions.*

The presence of serious Biographical Pain is characterised by the surfacing of deeply buried fractures in the life biographies of individuals who always intended to 'put things right', but have now run out of capability to bring about that resolution. They will no longer be able to apologise, seek or give forgiveness, deliver restitution, deliver a good to balance out the bad for an evil act. The opportunity to redress wrongs has passed by and the individual is left with an overwhelming sense of guilt.

It is the very slowness of late life which provides the opportunity for such life reviews to surface. During the busyness of independent living, we're able to submerge our worst worries and fears deep into our inner selves. Sometimes the repository becomes covered over; then the resurfacing of wiped out recollections is all the more painful (the giving away of a child born out of wedlock, the cheating of a relative or friend out of their business, the break-up of a trusting relationship).

Biographical Pain is something we all experience in some degree. Sometimes we can 're-frame' the events and see them in a better light, or provide a personal accounting which balances them out. Those who have religious faith may seek forgiveness through a priest, by prayer or via redemptive good works. But for the many who are spiritually unlearned, the options are less available.

In the case of old people there is a need for a spiritual care which embraces Biographical Pain without claiming it as a religious entity. We need to create new social rituals for this 'putting right'. When the churches and Christian communities in pre-industrial times provided asylum to those in desperate need they offered more than food and shelter. Their Christian task was to help mend the broken spirit, through love and service and prayer. In our day this task is still needed and the best old people's homes provide something approximating to it.

Secular society in Western Europe will not welcome a wholly religious formulation for addressing the spiritual needs and the biographical anguish of people coming to the close of their lives. But as we rethink the care of those who must live in grouped settings – ways of supporting residents with biographical disturbances (for which there are no drugs or potions) should be high on the agenda.

Late Life Spirituality

The lack of a clear definition of the term spirituality is considered by most of the authors in this volume and indeed in the wider literature. A full rehearsal of the debates and alternative formulations is not proposed here. But a recognised starting point, when looking for an anchor, is the work of Viktor Frankl, an Austrian psychiatrist, who created the definition 'the search for meaning'. As Walter (2002) points out, Frankl himself termed this as an existential, rather than a spiritual search. 'It is primarily the English who have replaced the term "existential" with "spiritual"' (p. 133). Nonetheless, the many new and refurbished secular spiritualities, are ready to shelter under this canopy definition, even if their practices, rituals and orthodoxies are distinct.

Contemporary commentators appear to agree that amongst the leading proponents of the search for meaning approach are to be found in the health professions, particularly nurses. In their paper on the links between spirituality and successful ageing, Sadler and Biggs (2006), draw on reviews of the nursing literature by Oritz and Langer (2002) and Tanyi (2002) and report five elements in the nursing spiritual repertoire: transcendent belief in a higher power, experiencing a sense of connection; and drawing on inner resources, such as strength and peace.

Other features such as 'meaning making' and 'manifest expressions' are to be found in the literature. Extensive debates about the descriptive and heuristic value of these statements can be found in the heath professional press and most notable in writings within and about palliative care (see below). Rumbold (2000) provides some clarification by treating spirituality as a worldview, a way of looking at the meaning and purpose of life. A more comprehensive taxonomy of meanings within healthcare is provided by Kellehear (2000) who classifies the key 'needs' domains in which spirituality operates or is perceived to be present in the lives of people experiencing serious or life-threatening illness. He identifies situational, moral and biographical needs, and religious needs, and suggests that practitioners seeking to assess spiritual needs should first clarify which category is being explored.

Within the study of ageing there is ample evidence that as people age and get closer to the expected end of their lives, the spiritual dimension gains in prominence. In recent years there have been more systematic studies which attempt to make the measurement of spirituality more possible. MacKinlay (2001) set out to map the spiritual dimension of a number of independently living adults, and to design a tool for measuring the spiritual needs of older people. She was truly honest in recognising that she was more successful with the former than the latter. Nonetheless her well-documented journey has provided valuable advances in measurement potential.

In a more macro piece of theorising, Tornstam (2005) produced his theory of *Gerotranscendence*. As a mainstream gerontologist, his explorations of this explanatory framework for positive ageing have appeared in the literature since the term was first brought to prominence in 1990 (Tornstam, 1989), as a reformulation of disengagement theory. His purposes have been to shift gerontological thinking from the despairing old age of Erikson and Cumming and Henry, into a paradigm that sponsors old age as a period of living worth achieving because of its own true benefits. He questions the underlying assumptions of the 'successful ageing' concept 'with the typical emphasis on activity, productivity, independence, efficiency, wealth, health and sociability'(p. 3). Having observed the normative expectation that good ageing is the continuation of the midlife patterns indefinitely, Tornstam asserts that there is continuous development into old age. A complex set of empirical analyses, which indicate the characteristics of gerotranscendence.

In the world of care for these very same individuals at the far end of life is another kind of discourse, which has its own powerful orthodoxies incorporating entrenched presumptions about who should be the societal managers of dying, death and bereavement. Palliative care and its sponsor, the hospice movement, has articulated its own rules about the appropriate ways to die and how pain should be palliated through a religio/medical model. Here concepts of spirituality and finitude are formulated in very specific ways and in line with the lifespan theorists and the 'successful ageing' proponents; focus on 'living to the end' whilst avoiding the distasteful reality of death and its aftermath.

Life Hurts: Beyond Successful Ageing

Whilst acknowledging the value of Tornstam's critique of gerontological lifespan perspectives and his life-affirming alternatives, I part company with him on empirical grounds. We do need to get beyond the successful ageing paradigm, to see the realities of life in the 4th Age. The loss of joy and the depression of recollection is promoted by 'too much time to think' and the looming of finitude. To do so is not to fall into fatalistic despair, but to reach a more honest evaluation of the realities of the dwindling trajectory to death. Only when we can see behind the eyes and into the biographical archives, will it be possible to truly help those for whom there are no clergy or gurus and who have no access to redemptive rituals or confessional forgiveness.

Within the covers of this volume, the reports of empirical studies of how older people cope with shifting views on religion, faith, beliefs, beliefs and self esteem are on balance pretty positive. Both Ellen Idler (Chapter 8) and Susan Eisenhandler (Chapter 10) present accounts from interviews with elders that are mature, reflective and relatively at ease with themselves and what they believe. Their authentic personal revelations add weight to the contemporary view that old age brings with it a capacity for resilience. Similarly Bengtson's (2013) large-scale Longitudinal Study of the Generations in its examination of transmission of religion across the generations finds clear evidence of the sustained impact of religious values across generations. It leads to the proposal of a new concept: Intergenerational Religious Momentum (p. 192). In Chapter 6 of this book we see a refinement, which highlights the way older generations differentiate their beliefs from teachings of earlier times and that this trend of re-interpretation is more marked in each succeeding generation.

Elizabeth Mackinlay also finds both emotional and spiritual resilience, not only in her home nation Australia but also in societies that have yet to produce indigenous studies. Albert Jewell observes in his studies of churchgoing elders an awareness of the need to be wise about faith and its meanings as death approaches, and not surprisingly, he found in his survey a variable level of enduring certainty. He does not expand on the concept of resilience, whilst seeing its presence among older Methodists in Leeds.

In a professional lifetime of researching the experiences of ageing, beliefs, social change and life meanings, Peter Coleman has produced powerful and nuanced accounts of how individuals cope with the eventualities as well as the pleasures of living. His latest book *Self and meaning in the lives of older people* (2015) is a detailed analysis of case studies of very old people, now in their nineties, whose lives he has monitored and investigated over nearly four decades. In general, this group of survivors demonstrate remarkable capacity for overcoming adversity and many of them firmly attribute their positive approach to strong beliefs and the sustaining presence of the church community and its rituals. Yet here too (as revealed in Chapter 7) there are those who have struggled both with life and faith.

As Nygren et al. (2005) observe from a substantial study employing resilience scales on a Swedish sample: 'The conclusions are that, the correlation between scores on the different scales suggests that the scales measure some dimension of inner strength and that the oldest old have this strength at least in the same extent as younger adults. Another conclusion is that the dimensions that constitute mental health differ between women and men.' Women score more highly on these measures. Such views have become a staple amongst gerontologists. Yet there is reason to be concerned that the methods of enquiry and sometimes the nature of the study populations leave room for doubt about the character of this coping.

Researchers on ageing will not be surprised to read of positive attitudes and determination of older people to maintain themselves, their loved ones and even the continuing bonds with deceased family members (Valentine, 2008). But it is necessary to take the evidence of resilience along with observations of older people in the 4th Age; barely sustaining existence in 'institutions of one', continuing alone in their own homes in neglect and despair (Cann and Dean, 2009).

This volume includes contributions from the leading scholars in our emerging field and their studies tell us both of the life skills that develop over the lifecourse and the agonies of loss. As yet we know too little about the anger and guilt, the burning resentments and the unresolved wounds of earlier life and how those near to the end smoulder with injustice at what was done to them – or with self-loathing at what they did to others.

The Spiritual and the Biographical

In the wider literature that addresses the diversity of human life, we are familiar with the great themes of living. Literature, drama, philosophy, theology and art have been and are preoccupied by them (the chapters from Andrew Achenbaum, Rick Moody and Ron Manheimer remind us). History is dominated by accounts of conflict and its consequences. These are the portals through which we see the ways individuals deal with maladies, broken relationships, collapsed aspirations, psychological and physical abuse, broken dreams, death of loved ones and the ultimate decline of physical capacity.

A central theme of the human story is survival and the resilience of the human spirit. Yet there is also the collateral damage of social and personal change. Not all biographical journeys are triumphs of attainment. Nor are all journeys of faith, belief and the inner life linear, sure and untroubled. Unless it manifests itself in physical or mental illness, we rarely observe what here is called Biographical Pain. Being able to contain and hide profound anguish at the recollection of the life lived, may well be a component of resilience. But if it were a cancer or a condition like AIDS, we would mobilise to diagnose and treat it.

Life hurts. Yet there are and there will be ways that greater understanding and recognition of the accumulation of these hurts in old age can be addressed and relieved. This is a spiritual venture.

As Julian Barnes says through his character: 'You get to the end of your life – no, not life itself, but something else: the end of any likelihood of change in that life. You are allowed a long moment of pause, time enough to ask the question: what else have I done wrong? ... (p. 142) There is accumulation. There is responsibility. And beyond these, there is unrest, There is great unrest', (pp. 149–150). I call the 'great unrest' Biographical Pain. It doesn't go away on its own. The more you visit it the worse it gets.

There is a challenge to discover, perhaps by nonjudgemental biographical listening, where the listener is trustworthy and the teller is in charge of the process and whatever might follow, a new spiritual release might emerge. Being old and sick does not have to be frightening nor does the future journey have to be an existential nightmare. But for too many it still is.

References

Achenbaum, A. (2005) *Older Americans, vital communities: A bold vision for societal aging.* Baltimore: Johns Hopkins University Press.

Baltes, M.M. (1998) The psychiatry of the oldest-old: the fourth age. *Current Opinion in Psychiatry,* 11: 411–415.

Baltes, P., Staudinger, U.M. & Lindberger U.(1999) Lifespan psychology: theory and application to intellectual functioning. *Annual Review of Psychology,* 50: 471–507.

Barnes, J. (2011) *The sense of an ending.* London: Jonathan Cape.

Bengtson, V.L. (1973) *The social psychology of aging.* Indianapolis: Bobbs-Merrill.

Bengtson, V.L. (2013) *Families and faith: How religion is passed down across generations.* New York: Oxford University Press.

Bengtson, V.L., Elder, G.H. Jr & Putney, N.M. (2005) The lifecourse perspective on aging. In Johnson, M.L., Bengtson, V.L., Coleman, P.G. & Kirkwood, T.B.L. (Eds) *The Cambridge handbook of age and ageing.* Cambridge: Cambridge University Press.

Bengtson, V.L., Putney, N.M. & Johnson, M.L.(2005) Are theories of aging necessary? In Johnson, M.L., Bengtson, V.L., Colemann P.G. & Kirkwood

T. (Eds) *The Cambridge handbook of age and ageing.* Cambridge: Cambridge University Press, pp. 2–20.

Cann, P. & Dean, M. (Eds) (2009) *Unequal ageing: The untold story of exclusion in old age.* Bristol: Policy Press.

Carrette, J. & King, R. (2005) *Selling spirituality: The silent takeover of religion.* London: Routledge.

Coleman, P.G. (2004) Is religion the friend of ageing? *Generations Review,* 14(4): 4–8.

Coleman, P.G., McKeirnan, F., Mills, M. & Speck, P. (2007) In sure and uncertain faith: belief and coping with loss of spouse in later life. *Ageing and Society* 27(6): 869–889.

Coleman, P. (2011) *Belief and ageing: Spiritual pathways in later life.* Bristol: Policy Press.

Coleman, P., Ivani-Chalian, C. & Robinson, M. (2015) *Self and meaning in the lives of older people: Case studies over twenty years.* Cambridge: Cambridge University Press.

Crome, P., Smith, A.E., Withnall, A. & Lyons, R.A., (2001) Urinary and faecal incontinence: prevalence and status. *Reviews in Clinical Gerontology,* 11(2): 109–113.

Du Boulay, S. (1984) *Cicely Saunders: The founder of the modern hospice movement.* London: Hodder & Stoughton.

Downs, M. & Bowers, B. (2008) Caring for people with dementia. *British Medical Journal,* 336(7638): 225–226.

Dannefer, D. & Ullenberg, P. (1999) Paths of the lifecourse: A typology. In Bengtson, V.L., & Schaie, W.K. (Eds) *Handbook of theories of aging.* New York: Springer Publishing Co., pp. 306–326.

Frankl, V. (1987) *Man's search for meaning.* London: Hodder and Stoughton.

Gilleard, C. & Higgs, P. (2009) The power of silver: Age and identity politics in the 21st century. *Journal of Aging Studies,* 21(3): 277–295.

Gilleard C. & Higgs P. (2010) Ageing without agency: Theorizing the fourth age. *Aging & Mental Health,* 14: 121–128.

Johnson, M.L. (1976) That was your life: a biographical approach to later life. In Munnichs, M.A. & van den Heuvel, W. (Eds) *Dependency or interdependency in old age.* The Hague: Martinus Nijhoff, pp. 147–173.

Johnson, M.L. (2002) *Committed to the asylum: The long term care of older people.* Leveson Paper Number 3. Temple Balsall, UK: Leveson Centre for Ageing and Spirituality.

Johnson, M.L. (2009) Spirituality, finitude and theories of the lifespan. In Bengtson, V.L., Gans, D., Putney, N.M. & Silverstein, Merril (Eds) *Handbook of theories of aging,* 2nd edition. New York: Springer, pp. 659–674.

Kellehear, A. (2000) Spirituality and palliative care: a model of needs. *Palliative Medicine* 14(2): 149–155.

Kleemeier, R. (1962) Time, activity and leisure. In Kleemeier, R.W. (Ed) *Aging and leisure.* New York: Oxford University Press.

Laslett, P. (1989) *A fresh map of life.* London: Weidenfeld & Nicolson.

Lynn, J. & Adamson, D.M. (2003) *Living well at the end of life: Adapting health care to serious chronic illness in old age.* Santa Monica, CA: RAND Corporation.

Lynn, J., Schuster, J.L., Wilkinson, A. & Noyes Simon, L. (2000) *Improving care for the end of life*, 2nd edition. Oxford: Oxford University Press.

Macfarlane, J. (1971) Perspectives on personality, consistency and change, from The Guidance Study. In Jones, M.C., Bayley, N., Macfarlane, J.W. & Honzik, M.P. (Eds) *The course of human development: Selected papers from the longitudinal studies, Institute of Human Development, The University of California, Berkeley*. Waltham, MA: Xerox College Publishing, pp. 410–415.

MacKinlay, E. (2001) *The spiritual dimension of ageing*. London: Jessica Kingsley.

Maier, H. & Smith, J. (1992) The psychological predictors of mortality. *Journals of Gerontology: Psychological Sciences* 54b(1): 44–54.

Miller, A. (1949) *Death of a salesman*. New York: Viking Press.

Nygren, B., Aléx, L., Jonsén, A., Gustafson, Y., Norberg, A. & Lundman, L. (2005) Resilience, sense of coherence, purpose in life and self-transcendence in relation to perceived physical and mental health among the oldest old. *Ageing and Mental Health*, 9(4): 354–362.

Ortiz, L.P. & Langer, N. (2002) Assessment of spirituality and religion in later life. *Journal of Gerontological Social Work*, 37(2): 5–21.

Peters, R. (2001) The prevention of dementia. *Journal of Cardiovascular Risk* 8: 253–256, quoted in Stephan, B. and Brayne, C., 2008, Prevalence and projections of dementia. In Downs, M. and Bowers, B. (Eds), 2008, *Excellence in dementia care: Research into practice*, New York: McGraw-Hill, pp. 9–34.

Rumbold, B. (Ed) (2000) *Spirituality and palliative care*. Melbourne: Oxford University Press.

Rutter, M. (1985) Resilience in the face of adversity: protective factors and resistance to psychological disorder. *British Journal of Psychiatry* 147: 598–611.

Small, B.J., Fratiglioni, L., von Struass, E. & Backman, L. (2003) Terminal decline and cognitive performance in very old age. Does cause of death matter?, *Psychology and Aging* 18(2): 193–202.

Sadler, E. & Biggs, S. (2006) Exploring the links between spirituality and 'successful ageing'. *Journal of Social Work Practice*, 20(3): 267–280.

Tanyi, R.A. (2002) Towards clarification of the meaning of spirituality. *Journal of Advanced Nursing* 39(5): 500–509.

Tornstam, L. (1989) Gero-transcendence: a reformulation of the disengagement theory. *Aging* 1(1): 55–63.

Tornstam, L. (2005) *Gerotranscendence: A developmental theory of positive aging*. New York: Springer Publishing.

Valentine, C. (2008) *Bereavement narratives: Continuing bonds in the twenty-first century*. London: Routledge.

Walter, T. (2002) Spirituality in palliative care: opportunity or burden? *Palliative Medicine* 16(2): 133–139.

UNDESA Population Division (2011) *World population prospects: The 2010 revision*. New York: UN.

13 Embracing Contraries
The Spiritual Quest as a Lifelong Process

Ronald J. Manheimer

The first steps down the path of the spiritual quest may have been taken in a mind befogged by hallucinogenic stupor or an auditory epiphany in the midst of a performance of Bach's St. Matthew Passion. However that initiatory moment arrived, it likely occurred in one's teens or young adulthood. Smitten by the awakening call to that which out leaps the self, the spiritual quest is a lifelong adventure that can take us to ecstatic moments of inner realization but also to the dead ends of failed gurus or self-destructive cults. In the chapter that follows, a multigenerational story of the spiritual search draws on contributions from the fields of life course development, gerontology, neurobiology, and philosophy. The tale has its origins in mid-twentieth century, suburban, and Jewish America. But its implications touch other lives in other places.

"A Serious Man," the Coen Brothers' 2009 dark film comedy about a Biblical Job-like college physics professor, Larry Gopnick, is a biting satire on one man's effort to understand the soul-testing God of the Hebrews. In the movie, Larry's seemingly idyllic, mid-1960s middle-class, suburban life is beginning to crumble. Looking for answers to conflicts at home (his marriage is on the rocks), and at the office (he's up for tenure but hasn't published anything in years), Larry seeks spiritual guidance from rabbis. They preach patience and acceptance, glibly citing the impenetrable ways of HaShem (a substitute for the unutterable name of God). Adding to this woeful tale, Larry's son Danny, ensconced in his room supposedly preparing for his Bar Mitzvah, finds spiritual illumination in the glowing tip of a reefer. Meanwhile, down the hall, older sister, Sarah, is badgering her parents for a life changing rhinoplasty as she heads to the bathroom for another ritual immersion in shampoo and cream rinse.

In hindsight, it is precisely young people like Danny and Sarah who turn out to be among the Jews of the Baby Boom generation destined to venture in search of alternative and New Age spirituality in their adult years. They will join the thousands of Jews, and millions of non-Jews, who set forth on a journey in search of a spiritual home. Their sojourn

215

reminds us that those who pursue spirituality in middle or later life most likely embarked on their quest when they were younger. Our Dannys and Sarahs would be swept up in the civil rights and anti-war movement, the drug culture, women's liberation and the sexual revolutions that reshaped post-war America, the United Kingdom, and Europe. Though the fragrance of weed and hair product may still cling to them, the Gopnick kids have come a long way. Their stories could bring fresh insight to the relationship of spirituality and aging, providing us a multi-generational perspective.

Suppose the Coen Brothers decided to make an updated sequel to "A Serious Man," bringing the Gopnik family into a contemporary perspective. They would benefit by getting hold of Wade Clark Roof's *A Generation of Seekers: the Spiritual Journeys of the Baby Boom Generation* (1993).

Roof illuminates the coming of age of young people of the 1960s. He assigns the label "loyalists" to generational peers who remained steadfast in their religious views and affiliations, despite the political upheavals and social revolutions of the 1960s, 1970s, and 1980s. While "loyalists" make up about a third of his surveyed subjects, another quarter he terms "returnees." These are individuals who dropped out of churches and synagogues only to return as they began to raise families. The remaining 42 percent are the "dropouts" who, at least as of the time of the study, remained standing outside the portals of church or synagogue. Perhaps surprisingly, according to Roof, most of these "dropouts" (90 percent) reported having some religious training or association with a religious organization while growing up. As we will see, Danny and Sarah belong to this latter group of searchers.

Reflecting the larger cohort, the Jewish baby boomers were "home-less," argues Rabbi Richard Schwarz in *Finding A Spiritual Home* (1990). In his generational study, he argues that the American syna-gogue of the post-WW II era failed to meet the needs of a new breed of spiritually alienated young people. Following their Bar and Bat Mitzvah or Confirmation rites of passage, thousands of young Jews wandered away from what seemed to them archaic and irrelevant forms of Jewish practice such as abstaining from eating shellfish or driving on the Sabbath. Yet, asserts Schwarz, despite this groups' aversion to organ-ized religion, over the years its members "have devoted a great deal of time and resources to explore a variety of spiritual groups and discip-lines" (Schwarz, 2000, p. 17). They are the people who have fueled the explosive growth of New Age communes; healing, yoga, and meditation centers; and various mainstream and esoteric Eastern religions. So prominent did Jewish devotees of Buddhism become that the term

"Jewbus" (pronounced Jewboos) was coined (Kamenetz, 1995). Out of this cultural context Schwarz discovered what he calls "the New American Jew." As they grew older, they would swell the ranks of a burgeoning spirituality and aging movement.

Schwarz describes his own and his peers' search for something more than what he calls the post–World War II "synagogue center," which he typifies as a large, suburban edifice where parents dropped off kids for Hebrew school but rarely attended services in the cathedral-like sanctuary. Schwarz claims his peers sought an intimate place of true communion among members vitally involved in helping to lead, reshape, and carry out all aspects of synagogue life from Torah chanting to teaching in the religious school, from committing time to the work of the social action committee to organizing home-based, neighborhood Shabbat dinners. In short, what he characterizes as the "synagogue community."

Schwarz profiles four synagogues, ranging from Reform to Orthodox that, in his estimation, succeeded in transforming themselves into spiritual homes. He identifies critically important qualities such as inclusiveness (of age, mindset, ethnicity), empowerment (encouraging lay-led services), innovation (experimentation with the prayer experience), a social action agenda that is outward looking toward the larger community's needs (dealing with hunger, homelessness, spousal abuse), and a system of personal support for crises (such as illness, divorce, and deaths in the family).

Projecting forward the two Gopnik children from their 1960s Minneapolis suburb to today, we find that Danny, a fifty-eight-year-old medical neuroscientist, is mapping wisdom onto the aging brain, while Sarah, a sixty-two-year-old professor of social work, is doing public policy advocacy on the ethics of care in institutional settings. The adult children have also found their way to new spiritual homes such as Schwarz profiles. Their journeys and their professional contributions to the field of aging brought them to an invitational symposium on spirituality and aging convened at the Cumberland Lodge in Windsor Great Park, England. We join them for this symposium within a symposium, as they exchange views with fellow participant, Ron Manheimer.

(Picture 20 studious looking men and women clad in tweed, plaid, and camel hair jackets surrounding an oval oak conference table with piles of books, note pads, tablet computers, and spectacles spread out before them.)

RON: Danny and Sarah, our symposium organizers summoned us to this
        manorial setting to take up a challenge: to respond to "the pressing
        need to bring to the fore ideas and evidence about the spiritual
        dimension of human lives and in particular as they move into later
        life." (Glances at the participants.) Looks like most of us have made

that move. So I wonder. When we talk about our research subjects and clients, should we include ourselves?

SARAH: (Gesturing with a raised finger.) Danny, if you don't mind, I'd like to jump in here. (Danny nods.) Ron, you know social work professionals are trained to pay close attention to our subjective reactions in working with clients. We practice what Pierre Bourdieu calls "reflexive sociology." As researchers and scholarly interpreters, certain aspects of our personal narratives inevitably come into play, which is fine as long as we are cautious about generalizing from personal experience.

RON: Thank you. That caveat in mind, let's go forward. How should we understand the term spirituality?

SARAH: (Sarah nods, running her hand through her close-cropped gray hair.) I paint spirituality with a broad brush as referring to what "gives meaning and purpose to life" (Puchalski and Ferrell, 2010, p. 4). Research like Harold Koenig's have shown us that spirituality and religious beliefs have a huge impact on how people cope with serious illness and life's stresses and strains (Koenig et al., 2001). But, as social workers, our approach to religious and spiritual orientations in the face of these existential challenges hasn't always been so receptive.

RON: (Cocking his head.) How is that?

SARAH: Well, take the related subject of reminiscence. I remember when our textbooks advised students that reminiscing in old age should be discouraged since it was evidence of pathological withdrawal from the realities of everyday life. We rejected the late 1950s "disengagement theory" of old aging and sang the praises of "activity theory." Consequently, social workers and other practitioners encouraged older clients to stay socially engaged and focused in the present moment.

DANNY: No drifting off into reveries, eh?

SARAH: Right, taboo. But thanks to the work of people like Robert Butler (1963) and McMahon and Rhudick (1964), we discovered that the life review process is a natural and beneficial part of growing old. We never stop searching for meaning. That search is the foundation of the spiritual life. So we changed course. We encouraged our students to help clients engage in purposeful reminiscence. (Sarah pauses, looks around at the group.) Of course, not all forms of reminiscence or life reviewing are beneficial for coping and morale. We can thank Peter (nods to participant Peter Coleman) for pointing out that sometimes preoccupation with events of the past can trigger depression in older people (Coleman, 1986, p. 35).

RON: Peter may have more to say about that as it pertains to spirituality. Please continue. You're saying that the shift to a more positive view of reminiscing in later life also opened the way to greater appreciation of the role of spirituality. Isn't this what our Swedish colleague, Lars Tornstam's work is all about?

SARAH: Yes, and I'm so disappointed he couldn't join us. Lars helped us realize that when we rejected the disengagement theory's assertion that social withdrawal was a normal sign of aging, we may have, as they say, thrown the baby out with the bath water. There's important inner work that many older people need to do as they come to terms with frailty, disability, and the proximity of death. Some degree of withdrawal from social activities may be a good thing. You can't do the work of reconciling yourself to your past if social workers and activity directors keep prodding you to go, go, go. You need time for quiet reflection or maybe to write your life story or a family history. Lars charted these subtle shifts in one's outlook in later life, achieving what he calls Gerotranscendence. He added to our understanding of how many older people become less judgmental, more tolerant of life's paradoxes and contradictions and, do I dare say it among fellow scientists, more "inward" as they, and we, grow older (Tornstam, 2005).

DANNY: I love it. Scandinavian Lutherans turn Zen Buddhists.

SARAH: Danny! Shush.

RON: So you're saying that meaning, purpose, coming to terms with one's past and one's mortality, are all important components of the spiritual in later life?

SARAH: Exactly. Oh, and I'd want to add creativity. Marc Kaminsky showed us there are wonderful opportunities to tap into the personal past for self-expression (Kaminsky, 1984). I think we have to keep art in the picture.

RON: Thanks, Sarah. That helps us get focused. Danny, would you concur with your sister on this?

DANNY: Older sister Sarah? (Chuckles. Strokes his bearded chin.) But seriously, since you have indicated our personal lives are fair game, let's look at our own family history. The Coen Brothers' movie ended with that ominous scene of a tornado looming over the school playground. Fortunately, we survived. Three decades later, I see our family in a new way. Maybe it was a midlife crisis when our parents almost split up and Dad nearly got turned down for tenure. Dad hadn't reconciled his scientific training as a physicist with his uncritical religious beliefs. He started to knock on various rabbis' doors to get help straightening out his life. They counseled patience. He was patient. They said everything was in the hands of HaShem. He waited. Taking a page from the Book of Job, they hinted that maybe Dad was being punished for some transgressions. (Whispering into the microphone.) He was an infrequent synagogue-goer. And worse, he told his college students he believed more highly developed forms of human intelligence existed on other planets. (Returns to normal voice.) Those rabbinic innuendos upset him. Later, when I was in college, he told me that, under the stress of this crisis, the God of his youth, as he put it, "went kaput." Mom continued her involvement with Hadassah but Dad became a synagogue dropout until, a few years later he was smitten with Jewish mysticism.

SARAH: (Drumming her pencil on the table.) Smitten! Yes, but not only with mysticism. Wasn't he sneaking next door to smoke marijuana with that sexpot, Mrs. Samsky?

DANNY: Mrs. Samsky! (Glances at Sarah.) I hadn't planned to go into that. But, yes, it's true she was something of a recreational user. A bit ahead of the times – for the Jewish suburbs, I mean. Still, Mrs. S. played the role of messenger. She told Dad about Reb Zalman. Read about him in her synagogue bulletin. This mystical Jewish rabbi was coming to Beth Israel to do a workshop on the Jewish Renewal Movement. Maybe, if he attended, he could renew his – what did Dad say she called it? Oh, right, his "zest for life."

SARAH: Reb Zalman fits right in to our topic because as he got older, he took on the mantel – or should I say, prayer shawl – of the wise spiritual elder (Schacter-Shalomi, 1995). But back in the 1970s when he was in his 50s, Zalman was a wild and crazy guy who went around turning mild-mannered Jews into enraptured Hasidim. Singing, chanting, dancing. Even meditating. And in synagogue. Imagine. He taught Kabbalah in a way that Dad could integrate with what he knew about physics. Remember him lecturing us about how the Big Bang theory and quantum physics were completely harmonious with the Kabbalah? He loved the idea that in order to create the universe, God, whose presence supposedly filled every inch of the cosmos, had to contract himself to make room to birth a universe. This act of contraction into a tiny ball of energy that then explodes out in all directions is called *Tzimtzum*.

DANNY: Yes, God is energy and we're stardust and everything's connected. (Laughs.) Who'd have expected anything like this coming from Dad? But it helped to pull him out of his slump and, incidentally, I think it made him a better teacher. One of his former students told me that Dad stopped lecturing AT and started talking WITH them about the beauty of mathematical physics. He got them into conversation and they actually started asking questions instead of just sitting there like zombies.

RON: Danny and Sarah, I'm going to have to interrupt here to make sure we stay on track. What I'm hearing you say is that people like Zalman Schachter-Shalomi, as we know him from his various books, inspired your father to discover a more sophisticated and nuanced form of spiritual life than he had previously held. It did not draw him away from his faith tradition but more deeply into it. How do you think that helps us understand the bigger picture about spirituality and aging?

SARAH: (Smiles.) It shows that spirituality is part of both individual development and social change. Our parents were forerunners of the whole spirituality and aging movement before (curling her fingers into quotation marks) "conscious aging" conferences and new academic journals on religion and spirituality cropped up. Dad didn't know that spirituality was supposed to improve his physical and mental health and his prospects for longevity. But connecting to Jewish mysticism helped him pull his life together. Not only in the sense of integrating what were separate and sometimes conflicting pieces, like his rational science mind and his emotional spiritual mind. He was finding his way to becoming (at the risk of sounding trite) a whole person. As he did so, he became a better husband to Mom and definitely a more involved and supportive parent. Wouldn't you agree, Danny?

DANNY: Yes. But I feel the need to interject a note of caution. We have a tendency to push spirituality in a normative way, like if you fail at spirituality you're a loser. What happened to our father, I think, can happen to other people. As he got more and more into Jewish mysticism and studying Torah and making all these connections to physics, he hit a roadblock.

SARAH: Roadblock? More like quicksand.

RON: You mean your father had a breakdown of some sort?

DANNY: (Nodding.) I would categorize it as situational depression. We didn't know this until we were older, but Dad had grown up with a pretty abusive father. We never knew our paternal grandfather, who died of pneumonia before we were born. Turns out that Dad had a rough time as a kid. His father drank and had a temper. His enthusiasm, and even his periodic states of spiritual ecstasy, with or without the aid of marijuana, weakened the shell of repressed memories. It's like he was being pulled upward and downward at the same time.

SARAH: Yes. And this is something else the Coen Brothers completely missed. The year portrayed in the film was the same year as the Six Day War in the Middle East, an event that completely transformed American Jewry. He hadn't been an outspoken Zionist but this was a turning point for Dad. I think spirituality is almost always tinged by politics. The following year, our parents went to Israel and as part of the group tour they visited the Holocaust Memorial, Yad Vashem. Danny, I don't think I can talk about this. You explain.

DANNY: Dad was in the Army during World War II and his unit stumbled onto one of the forced labor camps. His group had to load bodies into trucks and take documentary pictures of the crematoriums and the warehouses filled with piles of human hair and teeth from which the gold had been yanked. We heard this from his younger brother, our Uncle Arthur, who wasn't supposed to tell. Uncle revealed that Dad couldn't understand how God could let down his chosen people, the ones with whom he supposedly had a protective covenant. Like a lot of other vets, Dad put the war and what he had seen and done behind him. But this trip to Israel brought back repressed memories.

SARAH: You might say that in addition to the marriage and tenure upheavals that made him a religious doubter, he had this second theological crisis.

DANNY: Yes, the episode with the concentration camp functioned as a kind of delayed reaction. As teenagers, we had some vague ideas about the

Holocaust but, you know, it was history and it was far away. I guess our parents wanted to protect us. They always whispered when the subject came up.

SARAH: In retrospect, I think that our father's difficulties reflect the kind of struggles that Erik Erikson talks about in his theory of life stages (Erikson, 1968). In his late forties and early fifties, our dad's life is like a documentary of Erikson's stage seven in which people seek to be, as Erikson calls it, "generative." In midlife they hope to pass on their heritage and values to the next generation and, for some, their knowledge and passion for their professional field to their students. Yet they may simultaneously feel used up, disappointed with their careers, bogged down with regrets and setbacks. What Erikson calls (making quotation marks) "stagnation" or "self-absorption."

We could see that in our father's case. Here was this brilliant man who hadn't published a single article since his dissertation and who, while he loved physics, could be a pretty uninspiring teacher and indifferent academic advisor. He wanted to care – which is what Erikson thought should be the outcome of this struggle between generativity and stagnation – but he didn't always care. And then in the next part of his life, after dancing around with Zalman and hanging out with Mrs. Samsky, he had this struggle to unify the different, maybe even divergent, parts of his life. (Counting on her fingers.) One, his repressed childhood anger toward his father. Two, remorse over his less than stellar career. And, three, the war memories. Dad's search for wisdom took him through the stormy period of "integrity versus despair," as Erikson captions his famous eighth stage, the one that's supposed to manifest a quality of wisdom.

RON: (Rubbing his forehead.) Are you and Danny suggesting that pursuing wisdom or the spiritual life necessarily involves conflict?

DANNY: If I may put on my neurological hat. I think what Sarah is alluding to is that, even from an earlier age, our development is shaped by the interplay of counter or even polar opposite forces. Decades ago, Erikson framed this dialectical view based on his clinical work with patients. Today, thanks to neuroimaging, we can actually see this in the brain. My colleagues, Dilip Jeste and James Harris and I have been studying wisdom in later life. Our research may throw some light on spirituality. We've identified two brain regions that are common to different domains of wisdom – the prefrontal cortex and the limbic striatum, phylogenetically the newest and oldest parts of the brain. The brain has to match and integrate the activities of these two areas for us to achieve wisdom. What do I mean? Well, one part involves rational, disciplined, and calculated actions that are necessary for self-preservation. The other involves caring, socially supportive and emotional behavior that we need for species survival. Wisdom involves mediating these opposite concerns – self-preservation through rational calculation and care for others through empathy, which help insure the survival of the group (Dilip and Harris, 2010).

RON: Duality in the make up of human nature is an age-old theme among philosophers. Kierkegaard, for example, argues that to be human is to encompass finitude and infinitude, freedom and necessity, the temporal and the eternal. The very idea of being a self, for Kierkegaard, is a process of seeking to integrate these dualities. Relevant to our purposes, he defines the self as Spirit, which he describes as a self-relating process of reconciling our quest for the timeless with the human condition as mortals of the time bound. Spirituality, for Kierkegaard, is grounded in a person's awareness that his or her ability to engage in this self-relational process, this empowering awareness, is not a given but rather a gift. We discover but we don't invent it. Kierkegaard says the gift comes for what he abstractly calls the Power. This power is what enable us to "choose ourselves" in getting on the path to becoming a fully realized person.

DANNY: Awareness of the gift of the Power. (Scratches his head.) Interesting. I will have to get my fellow neuroimagers busy to see if we can find its location in the brain.

RON: (Laughs.) Good luck. Meanwhile, notice Kierkegaard's phenomenological formulation. We have the experience of dependency on the Power and transcendence through the Power. You've probably guessed that for the Danish Protestant, Kierkegaard, the source of this Power is God and the paradigm or mirror to this human duality of self is the God-man, Jesus. To see your own life as participation in this paradoxical journey is to gain in wisdom. But I wonder. Are they one and the same or is one dependent on the other?

SARAH: They're related but, to my mind, quite different. The version of wisdom we psychologists study comes from people like Paul Baltes (Baltes and Smith, 1990). Very much a matter of advanced cognitive processing involving refined skills of judgment based on lots of experience. Emphasis is put on intelligence. Ironically, Danny's group of white-coated neuroscientists added a whole social and emotional piece. They argue that characteristics of wisdom include empathy, compassion, and altruism. Now even some very intelligent if not brilliant people may lack any or all of these three qualities. Still, spirituality is different. As I see it, when you commit yourself to – or maybe even can't stop yourself from – pursuing a spiritual path, you're taking a leap into the unknown and the uncertain. You don't know what's going to happen or how things will turn out. Like with our dad, it's risky. Who knows what monsters lurk in the depth of the unconscious or, for that matter, what guardian spirits? As I see it, spirituality could be for the good or the bad. Look at the Jonestown Massacre.

Hundreds of people following Jim Jones, their spiritual guru – right up to gulping down the lethal Kool-Aid. Then you've got these amazing French Protestant Huguenots of Le Chambon-Sur-Lignon who during World War II, selflessly risked their lives to hide thousands of Jewish children.

DANNY: I think Sarah's right about this. In our neurological research, we hypothesize that wisdom is good for you in old age because it gives you an adaptive advantage to better plan your survival strategy in the face of the health and socioeconomic challenges of your later years. Practical types, we've got to have some positive results and what could be more practical than individual and species survival? Whereas the people Sarah is describing were not putting much emphasis on self-preservation, either the Jim Jones followers or the good people of Le Chambon.

RON: So wisdom in old age is biologically adaptive but spirituality may not be. We'll let our other symposium participants chime in this topic when it's their turn. For now, I'd like you to reflect a bit more about your family. We've heard a lot about your Dad but not much about your mother. In the movie she is presented as a slightly befuddled, middle-class homemaker.

SARAH: The Coen Brothers showed a lack of empathy.

RON: Uh, huh. So we're missing something here?

SARAH: Oh, incredibly so. And this brings me back to what I mentioned earlier about the role of art in one's spiritual development. You see, after her frivolous love affair with Sy Ableman – yes, that oaf that had managed to crash his Cadillac into a brick wall – she and Dad made up. Miraculously, my brother managed to sleepwalk his way through his Bar Mitzvah (winks at Danny). After these events, she really blossomed. I think the counterpart to Dad's turning mystic Jew was Mom's joining a women's consciousness raising group. For women, you can't separate mid and later life spirituality from what happened in the 1970s. That whole Hadassah bunch got empowered along with millions of other American and European women. I remember seeing Mom sneak a copy of Betty Friedan's *Feminine Mystique* into her handbag to take to one of what she told us was a temple social committee meeting. After all, how can you pursue a spiritual path if you don't feel you have the freedom to shape your own life? Not that Dad was such an ogre. He was really very supportive of Mom though it seemed, at first, he didn't have a clue as to why she needed to "find herself." After all, he'd "found her" and loved her. So that should have been enough. Of course, it wasn't. Not for her or for millions of other women who wanted to be socially productive and creative. The outcome of these group meetings is that she was motivated to go back to school. She wanted to finish the degree she had left incomplete when she opted to marry Dad and they had to move so he could take the teaching job in Minnesota. Like a lot of bright young women of her generation for whom secretarial work,

teaching, nursing, librarianship or, ahem, social work were the
acceptable professions, she had started out majoring in education. But
going back to school in the early 1970s, she chose to major in art. And
it wasn't art education, either. We were shocked. Our mom? An artist?

DANNY: You were already away at school so you didn't see the transformation
of the basement into an art studio. Dad helped her. He was supportive
if puzzled. This was not a side of the woman he'd thought he knew.

SARAH: Right. Apparently, we didn't know her either. She was taking a painting
class at the college. She started out doing conventional landscapes. But
after a few trips to the Walker Art Museum and to downtown galleries,
that all changed. I can only describe what she did as something like the
work of Mark Rothko – the Walker had several of his paintings. She
began working on larger and larger canvases. Now picture this quite
diminutive woman jumping up on a kitchen step stool to make these
huge cloud-shaped fields of color that seemed to hover one above the
other. It was awesome. She did these, Dad said, in an almost trance-like
state, often listening to music.

DANNY: Yikes. That music. I'd come home from high school and hear these eerie
sounds wafting up through the heating vents. What's his name? The
Hungarian composer?

SARAH: Bartok. She had Bartok string quartets cranked up on that old Victrola of
ours.

DANNY: I couldn't understand how she could stand that music. It seemed so
edgy and frenetic. Dad said he would come down the stairs from time
to time and peek to make sure she was okay. He said she would be
hopping on and off the step stool as she waved these big brushes and
dancing around. Our parents. (Shakes his head.).

SARAH: They had started out in young adulthood as Apollonians and in midlife
were transforming themselves into Dionysians.

RON: You're referring to Nietzsche's distinction in *The Birth of Tragedy*,
I presume? I wouldn't think this is part of a social work curriculum.

SARAH: (Laughing.) I was a philosophy major before I decided to do something
more applied. Went to grad school in social work. And, yes, it is from
Nietzsche. His claim that we're pulled between these two divergent
forces of rationality and intoxicated ecstasy, between what makes us
separate and distinct human beings capable of greater and greater
individuation and then what shatters our sense of separateness and
allows us to tap into this raw pagan energy. Carl Jung seized on this in
his psychological theory. Remember Jung's famous statement: "Too
much of the animal distorts the civilized man, too much civilization
makes sick animals" (Jung, 1912).

RON: So there we are, back to our theme about how human nature is driven
by opposites or contraries. Maybe that's what makes life so messy.

SARAH: Yes, messy. That's what was so interesting about Mom's paintings. She
had this incredible energy going and sometimes her paintings turned
out to be quite a muddy mess. She would look at them and laugh,
saying: "Judith, you've done something very, very naughty."

(Sarah laughs, shakes her head.) But when she was good and got a little more control over the piece, she could pull off the kind of effects that brought Rothko his fame. Glowing, hovering shapes that seemed to move up and down, forward and backward. Mom said her paintings were about chaos and order in creative tension. Dad said that when Mom felt she'd gotten it right, she would just stand there looking at the painting. Clad in what had been house painter's white overalls, but now were anything but white, she'd muse: "Oh, my." She was so pleased with herself. "Oh, my."

DANNY: The house was filled with these paintings. We'd say, 'Mom, why don't you exhibit them? You could probably sell some of them and make a fortune.

SARAH: That wasn't her goal. Besides, the truth of the matter is that she didn't want to let any of them go. The painting, the music, this was her spiritual practice.

DANNY: This whole episode in our parents' life was strange. We were supposed to be the new radicals not trusting anyone under 30, protesting the war in Vietnam, going to sit-ins, and marching with Dr. King. Meanwhile, back at the ranch, our parents are acting like college kids with their mysticism and abstract expressionism. Doing all this experimenting that's supposed to be the province of the young.

RON: Weren't they an inspiration? Or did you feel that since they were being the wild and crazy ones that you had to follow the straight and narrow?

DANNY: It's true that they were taking up some of our generational space. They had usurped our destiny. Maybe even eclipsed us. But I think we kind of made up for it. (Laughs.)

RON: Uh, huh. How is that?

DANNY: Well, as we said, Dad was a little into marijuana but that's about all in the way of drugs he tried. Mom didn't seem to need any external stimulants. She had energy to burn. For me, my sophomore year, I dropped acid for the first time. Got some tabs from my high school friend, Benjy Portnoe. We were home on spring break from college and went to the arboretum to walk around. Come to think of it now, it was a Saturday. Now there's a way to celebrate the Sabbath!

RON: Uh, Danny? Reminiscing about drug experiences? Do you think this is a relevant aspect of looking at spirituality and aging?

DANNY: If you want to follow my post – Bar Mitzvah spiritual path, you need to know about psychedelic drugs like LSD, psilocybin, mescaline, hallucinogenic mushrooms, and all the rest of the psychotropic cornucopia members of my generation ingested during the heyday of the quest for higher consciousness (Wolfe, 1968). I agree. We don't want to be bragging about the great profundities we believe we discovered. Amphetamines that were used to mix with pure LSD influenced a lot of that. They trigger the brain's reward system. Tied in with acid's visionary states, the "speed" tends to exaggerate the pleasure you experience, putting a rosy glow around everything and making it all seem very profound. You can't be analytically detached when you're taking LSD. You're swinging way over on the Dionysian side of the spectrum that Sarah spoke about earlier.

RON: (Gives a little cough.)

DANNY: I'll keep this brief. Taking this drug, I had a number of epiphanies. For one, when Benjy and I were walking on this pathway through the arboretum, I remember we were talking about how fantastic everything smelled – even the skunk cabbage in the wetland part of the landscape smelled delicious. Some fleeting impression pulled me up short and I turned around to look at where we had come from. The dirt path – now this was a hallucination – the path turned into multiple paths like multiple conduits in the cross-section of a braided cable. And I saw us passing through a kind of simultaneous history. We were inside one of those conduits but there were people from other times moving simultaneously beside and all around us as if all of history were suddenly not chronological but simultaneous. What had seemed remote – people from another time, previous generations who had been walking through this same landscape, were now walking beside us. They're part of us and we're part of them. (Laughs.) I tried to explain what I was seeing to Benjy. True to form, he just gave me his big toothy smile, nodded, 'Yeah, man, whatever,' and pretended to understand.

RON: Did this experience make you want to major in history? Was that the outcome of this epiphany?

DANNY: (Shakes his head.) More like, the structure of consciousness and the possibility of multiple realities. You have to understand that this was just a beginning, an initiation rite. What followed was a series of investigatory experiences. I didn't give them that dignified label at the time. What is it that Kierkegaard said: "We live life forward but only understand it backward"?

SARAH: Even better, if I might interrupt, is T.S. Eliot's "we had the experience but missed the meaning."

DANNY: Yes, the meaning took a long time in coming. A whole lifetime, it seems. But at that moment, I just wanted to keep having these powerfully educational visions. I thought I was discovering the unseen made visible. Turned out I was gazing into the workings of my own mind. Eventually this accelerated curriculum in mind expansion came to a screeching halt. One night I was tripping with some friends and we were talking about how we could mentally stop time and experience what William James called the "expansive moment." Speed, you know, brings on the "munchies." Someone had brought in a bag of French fries and I was simultaneously jabbering away and stuffing my mouth. Suddenly I started to choke. I couldn't get the French fry bole unstuck from my trachea. This was before we learned the Heimlich maneuver. So here I am. My life is flashing before me, and I'm thinking: What an absurd death. Aspirating on French fries. Fortunately, I managed to dislodge the stuff. Coughed it up. I vowed that this was the end of my tripping. Unlike some of our friends who went off the deep end, some having psychotic episodes that required short-term institutionalization, I managed to get myself under control. I realized that I was trying to do a lifetime's worth of work in a few months. I had to slow this down. That's when I started to read about Zen Buddhism, and also when I got involved for a (fortunately) short time with "est," and "MindSpring." I also borrowed a couple of books from Dad on Jewish mysticism.

In short, my experiments with LSD helped me to realize that I needed to find my spiritual home, which, in certain ways, turned out to be a scientific one. A premed student at the time, I signed up for that major because I had a better than average memory ability, wanted the perks a doctor's life had to offer, and thought I'd do a little good for others. But what I started to learn about my mind made me curious about how and why the brain worked. So that led me to take some psych courses, especially experimental psych, which led me to the neurosciences, a promising field for research just coming into its own. Not to flatter myself, but I'm with Einstein. For me, to be in awe of nature is to find transcendence in scientific theories. I guess I'm something of a rational mystic. Brain science and traversing the spiritual way often seem like two radically different narratives. To me, they're simultaneous realities.

RON: Hmm, sounds like you're still on your trip through the braided cable. Sarah, is Danny's formulation of his spiritual search and where he's coming from, does that fit your take on things?

SARAH: I love hearing Danny talk about what he's discovered. In some ways, we are quite similar but in other ways, quite different. Danny's is a universal type of spirituality. He's essentially a humanistic Jew though he belongs to Adat Shalom, the Reconstructionist congregation not far from where he works at the National Institutes for Health in Bethesda. I don't hold to this view because in seeking to universalize Judaism and remove it from its particularity as a unique heritage and distinct destiny forged between Hashem (there I will also use that funny word) and the Jewish people, the authority of the law gets blurred. Maybe I need more certainty in my life and the presence of a more personal God than Danny's Spinozist version. For Danny, Nature substitutes for Kierkegaard's "the Power." His God is impersonal and mathematical. I'm what they call "frum," or observant. I try to keep Kosher and I attend synagogue on a regular basis. I made regular use of the mikveh, the ritual bath, until I went through menopause. As I've gotten older, I find that my practice of Judaism has a calming effect on me and continuously reminds me that I am part of something greater than myself. By practicing Judaism in this way – as a way of life, not just loyalty to a set of abstract tenets, my outward behavior creates an inner experience, rather than the other way around.

RON: So how does this impact your professional work?

SARAH: To me the sacred isn't restricted to a sanctuary but can occur in the clinical examining room between doctor and patient. This is especially important for midlife and older patients who are more likely to be receiving disturbing information about their health than those younger. In my work on the ethics of care (Noddings, 1984), which is a relational approach to bioethics, I have applied Martin Buber's theory of the "I and Thou." So much more healing can be done in the interaction between doctor and patient when the physician stops hiding behind the doctor persona and becomes a real person who is truly present to the patient. That's my idea of applied spiritual practice.

DANNY: (Clears his throat, sees Sarah glance at him.)

SARAH: I wasn't going to go into this but Danny's giving me the sign and I guess it's relevant to our gathering. You see, I am a lesbian. It hasn't been easy for us liberated Jewish women to find an acceptable place in modern Orthodoxy because we still are not allowed to be called to the bimah, the reader's platform, to recite from the Torah though we can now sit in sections of the main sanctuary along side the men and not, like in the old days, be totally screened off in a rear balcony. Being gay adds another set of challenges because modern Orthodoxy is not particularly gay friendly, unlike Reform and Conservative synagogues.

DANNY: Come on, Sarah, you know that even the so-called "modern" Orthodox congregations are intolerant of homosexuality. They've learned to be nice, even compassionate, and they tolerate you in the synagogue as long as you maintain the appearance of being in a Platonic relationship. But put an arm around Stephanie, in *shul* and see what would happen.

SARAH: (Smiles.) Okay, so I live a life of contradiction. In years past, I probably would have rejected Orthodoxy and taken the easier way – to go where I was accepted for who I am. But as I've gotten older, I've learned to make some compromises. As one of our friends put it, we "dwell in paradox."

RON: (Looking at his watch.) We appreciate your candor about these complicating matters of gender and spirituality. This is a good place to end our conversation. Before we turn the floor over to our next presenter, let's sum up what we've learned about spirituality as a lifelong process.

SARAH: Ever the taskmaster. Okay, Ron, we've highlighted the fact spirituality doesn't take shape when you get old but is something that, for most of us, is part of a lengthy developmental process and a generational cohort one as well. Politics are involved, too. The life course seems to be driven by a play of contrary or oppositional forces, as Erikson pointed out. Part of that development includes a growing awareness of the life cycle itself. And like the earlier stages, the later ones also have this tension or polarity. Spirituality seems an admirable human quality yet it too reveals to us this perpetual struggle to accept and accommodate contrary or polarizing tendencies. Some people imagine that to be a spiritual person means you go around blissful all the time. But that's not my observation. The way I see it, you learn to embrace happiness and sorrow, successes and defeats, feelings of self-worth and worthlessness, a resolved and firm identity, and the experience of having layers of your identity slip away. Ultimately, we have to relinquish self-mastery and ourselves. Danny?

DANNY: People who lead others in some spiritual practices need to be aware of the risks of encouraging others to open themselves up to the great mysteries of this awesome universe because among those mysteries reside personal dragons and demons. They should be wise and experienced enough to know how to help people prepare to meet their dark side. Look what happened to our mother's artistic mentor, Mark Rothko. He committed suicide.

SARAH: Yes, that was sad. Many great spiritual figures have struggled with mental health issues.

★★★★★★★★★★★★★★★★★

RON: You and Danny have helped us to understand that besides our inner life, spirituality grows out of major changes in our culture as well as from generational and family experiences. And you've helped us examine how aging and development may deepen spirituality while still posing some risks and challenges. On behalf of our fellow symposium participants, I want to thank you for sharing your knowledge and life experiences. At lot has happened since you last appeared in the movies.

(Scraping of chairs. A teaspoon rattles against a cup.)

References

Baltes, P. and Smith (1990) "Towards a Psychology of Wisdom and Its Ontogenesis" in Robert J Sternberg (ed) *Wisdom: Its Nature, Origins and Development*. Cambridge: Cambridge University Press, 87–120.

Butler, Robert (1963). "The Life Review: An Interpretation of Reminiscence in the Aged." *Psychiatry* 26: 65–76.

Coleman, Peter G. (1986). *Ageing and Reminiscence Processes*. Chichester: John Wiley & Sons

Erikson, Erik (1968). *Identity, Youth and Crisis*. New York: Norton & Co.

Jeste, Dilip and Harris, James (2010). "Wisdom – A Neuroscience Perspective." *JAMA* 304(14): 1602–1603.

Jung, Carl (1928/1972). "Two Essays on Analytic Psychology." *Collected Works* 7. Cambridge, MA: Harvard University Press.

Kamenetz, Roger (1995). The Jew in the Lotus: A Poet's Re-Discovery of Jewish Identity in *Buddhist India*.

Kierkegaard, S. (1849/1983). *Sickness Unto Death. Translated by Howard and Edna Hong*. Princeton: Princeton University Press.

Koenig, Harold G. et al. (2001). *Handbook of Religion and Health*. New York: Oxford University Press.

Kaminsky, Marc (1984). *The Uses of Reminiscence: New Ways of Working With Older Adults*. New York: Springer.

McMahon, Arthur W. and Rhudick, Paul J. (1964). "Reminiscing: Adaptational Significance in the Aging." *Archives of General Psychiatry*. 10(3): 292–298.

Noddings, Nel (1984). *Caring: A Feminine Approach to Ethics and Moral Education*. Berkeley: University of California Press.

Puchalski, Christina M. and Ferrell, Betty (2010). *Making Health Care Whole*. West Conshohocken, PA: Templeton Press.

Roof, Wade Clark (1993). *A Generation of Seekers: the Spiritual Journeys of the Baby Boom Generation*. San Francisco: HarperSanFrancisco.

Schacter-Shalomi, Zalman (with Ronald Miller) (1995). *From Age-ing to Sage-ing*. New York: Grand Central Publishing.

Schwarz, Richard (2000). *Finding A Spiritual Home*. Woodstock, VT: Jewish Lights.

Tornstam, Lars (2005). *Gerotranscendence: A Developmental Theory of Positive Aging*. New York: Springer Publishing Co.

Wolfe, Tom (1968). *The Electric Kool-Aid Acid Test*. New York: Farrer, Straus, Giroux.

Part IV

Meeting Spiritual Needs in Older Age

14   Conversation Matters

Ann Morisy

Introduction

Research evidence supporting the positive contribution of spirituality to wellbeing in later life is now extensive. Likewise, the negative impact of loneliness on later life has been demonstrated by numerous research programmes. The clarity of such findings suggests that the issue is no longer that of unearthing more and more evidence, but rather identifying ways that such insights can be promoted and people encouraged to adopt the beneficial habits that counter loneliness and foster wellbeing. But more than this, the challenge is to enable such change to happen on a large scale.

The research evidence about what makes for a good and healthy old age is exemplified in the paradigm of 'active ageing'. The World Health Organisation defines active ageing as 'the process of optimising opportunities for health, participation and security in order to enhance quality of life' (2002, p. 6). This increasing emphasis on active ageing by policy makers arises because it provides an additional and positive response to the challenge of ageing populations. Instead of perpetuating anxiety by focusing solely on how to meet the immense and complex care needs of a rapidly increasing older population, active ageing provides an additional strategy. If people can be coaxed and coached into adopting the habits that make for a healthy old age, then not only do people maximise their chances of being active and healthy for longer, they are likely to make fewer demands on social and health care.

In Britain, a government 2010 White Paper (for discussion of policy prior to legislation), *Healthy Lives, Healthy People*, aimed to give momentum to a strategy for healthy ageing. This was followed by 2012 being designated the 'Year of Active Ageing' throughout the European Union. These steps seem puny in the face of the challenge to get people to review their lifestyle and undo years, if not decades, of less than healthy living. Furthermore, such change in behaviour has to be achieved on a massive scale. Both energy and imagination will be essential if healthy ageing is to be anything other than a pipedream.

The pressing task is to identify ways in which both insight and motivation can be engendered for harnessing healthy habits. It is in relation to this task that the contributions of conversation and reflection are commended. Additionally, they are offered as a route by which change in habits and practice can be achieved on a large scale.

PSALM and Conversation

A small UK charity called PSALM (Project for Seniors and Lifelong Ministry), of which I am an associate, has the strap line 'Taking ageing and faith seriously'. Our main activity is to host workshops that encourage conversation and reflection on issues associated with ageing and faith. It is the time spent talking with others that is frequently flagged up as the most valued aspect of the experience when participants are asked to complete an evaluation form at the end of a workshop.

This straightforward assessment of how conversation brings vitality to a subject, and to the participants, is endorsed by our own experience and observations as we facilitate the workshops. We are continuously impressed by the animation, sensitive turn taking, affirming body language and the use of *backchannels*[1] by participants who often are meeting for the first time. The evidence of good quality listening and engaging is strong, with participants eager, and even engrossed, in sharing their experiences and opinions. This is regularly confirmed by the difficulty in requesting the groups to return to plenary mode or take a break. Finally, we observe that the facial expressions change during the workshop, at the end of which participants are palpably more animated, faces appear enlivened and people's manner more cheery.

PSALM workshops are an example of informal education, where conversation is a trusted tool in fostering reflection. 'Informal education works through conversation and dialogue, and the exploration and enlargement of experience' (Smith 1997, 2005, 2011). Cultivating conversation lies at the centre of what informal educators do. 'It is not simply the form that their work takes, but also part of their purpose. In conversation, knowledge is not a fixed thing or commodity to be grasped. It is

---

[1] The term *backchannel* acknowledges that in any communication there are two 'channels' operating at the same time. The primary or predominant channel is the person who is speaking. The secondary channel (the backchannel) is the listener who will be providing clues that encourage continuation of the speaker's flow with, for example, 'Really?' or 'Wow!'. Substantive backchannels consist of more explicit turn-taking by the listener and might involve seeking clarification or repetitions.

not something 'out there' waiting to be discovered. Rather, it is an aspect of a process' (Smith 2001).

Conversation is an extraordinary achievement of the human species. For it to be conversation, rather than an inconsequential chat, mutual commitment is required to traverse the multiple differences between one universe of consciousness and that of another. Conversation also calls for an exceptional degree of trust because there can be no guarantee that what one tries to convey will be met with willing understanding, or be understood in the manner in which it was intended. To these achievements add the subliminal signs that are transmitted which indicate a commitment to sustain the conversation. Furthermore, all this is accomplished subconsciously in microseconds, so that our consciousness can give priority to attending both to the content of the conversation and to 'the other'.

Learning often takes place through conversation because, for many, it is helpful to be able to 'hear' oneself think, allowing the prompting and mutuality of an interlocutor to support the bringing of thoughts to birth. The framing of an issue by another, accompanied by the subliminal invitation to 'please come with me', provides the stretch which enables a person's insights to flow and be scrutinised, both by those who are party to the conversation and by themselves. In that moment, a person's horizon is enriched as insights from the past are tested in the encounter with the other, and this process goes on to inform and shape future perspectives and actions (Louden 1991, p. 106). Gadamer suggests that conversation enables the horizon of the present to become fluid as a person's notions are tested in the company of others. This melding of old notions and previous experiences with new insights Gadamer describes as a *fusion of horizons* (Gadamer 1979, p. 273). Ideas about later life in particular benefit from such sifting and reassessment, especially because what passes as common sense views of ageing will have been influenced by the manner in which previous generations grew old.

Ageing, perhaps more than any other process or phenomenon that we encounter, is remarkable in its capacity to generate private pondering, yet it is also a shared experience as others are likewise confronted by the manifold changes and challenges that are associated with growing ever older. It is perhaps no surprise, therefore, when given permission and encouragement to talk about this deeply personal yet shared process, that people are keen to embrace the opportunity. However, conversation can achieve more than solidarity in the face of change and challenge. Echoing Zeldin's recognition of the potency of conversation to prompt changes in attitudes and behaviour (Zeldin 1998), the dynamic and transformational capacity of conversation explains why conversation is a tool for informal educators. This understanding and confidence in the method is shared by the many proponents of 'talking therapies' that are the foundation of clinical psychology.

With such a full-blooded endorsement it is perhaps overdue that reflective conversation be encouraged as a means for those seeking to promote healthy and active ageing. In relation to 'active ageing' and the challenges of later life, PSALM, through its workshops, adopts a distinctive approach. This has four aspects:

1. Promoting 'structures of encouragement' in relation to conversation;
2. Alertness to the positive contribution of spirituality;
3. Encouraging skills and perspectives that can counter loneliness and the chronic undervaluing of self that diminishes resilience;
4. Recognition of the distinctive contribution that is to be called forth from older people.

These four aspects have been discerned through the reflection of PSALM associates who bring expertise in relation to the social sciences, theology, art and creativity and drama, as well as being students of ageing both academically and personally. This four-fold approach is underpinned by a hypothesis: Those who are becoming old, or are already old, are confronted by a new and unpredictable future, where previous assumptions about later life no longer provide a reliable map. In addition, the downward drag of pervasive negative attitudes towards old age, which at best promote the idea of later life being a story of diminishment and relinquishing, undermines the desired paradigm of 'active ageing'.

Workshops focus on themes specifically relevant to later life and these are sometimes suggested by participants, often in response to the evaluation form item that invites people to make suggestions. PSALM workshop facilitators also muse on possible themes and assess the potential viability of a theme by monitoring their own engagement. That is to say, the extent to which we find ourselves immersed in conversation about a theme, and having to discipline ourselves to focus on the design of the workshop, provides a good indication of the ease and enthusiasm with which participants are also likely to engage with it.

Examples of workshop themes include:

- Obligations in Later Life
- Decluttering – including sheds
- Difference and common ground (reflecting on the griefs and solidarity prompted by contemporary society)
- Gratitude (and its significance in relation to wellbeing and as a spiritual practice)

- Health, Healing and Eternity (including a forty minute conversation in groups about the nature and experience of 'time' and the sense that time speeds up in later life).

Sometimes the themes relate to an issue of the moment. For example, 2012 was marked in London by the Jubilee Celebrations for the monarch and the Olympic Games. It was appropriate therefore to host a workshop where conversation was directed towards the theme of celebration. That same year, the British media was close to a frenzy about its own ethics as 'phone hacking' was scrutinised by a judge-led Inquiry. In response, a workshop was hosted to encourage conversation about the media and its subtle and not so subtle impact on our attitudes.

The design of each workshop incorporates each of the four aspects (listed above) and these can be expressed through group work, a presentation, plenary discussion, case studies, guided meditation or artwork. PSALM workshops usually begin at 11.00 a.m. and conclude by 3.00 p.m. with forty-five minutes for lunch. The format of the workshop may involve an initial presentation of insights on the theme by one of the facilitators or a participant, and this presentation may be supported by a hand-out summarising research findings and encouraging further web-based exploration. The arena of positive psychology provides a helpful and engaging seam of material for this purpose of mapping or scoping the theme. The provision of such fact-based or 'expert' material is to ensure that participants are confident that some thought has gone into the theme and to legitimise *objective* as well as subjective and anecdotal contributions to the workshop.

The workshop leaders, usually two in number, are experienced in group facilitation, able to give reassurance of competence and safety for participants, and especially able to counter any impression of hierarchy, or status or expert knowledge. These dynamics of power can up-end the more important dynamics of concern, trust, respect, appreciation, affection and hope which Burbules (1993) suggests are vital to conversation that characterises informal education. As learning is the objective, the facilitators aim to heed guidance from Bohm and his colleagues to achieve this approach:

Their role should be to occasionally point out situations that might seem to be presenting sticking points for the group, in other words, to aid the process of collective proprioception, but these interventions should neither be manipulative nor obtrusive. Leaders are participants just like everybody else. Guidance, when it is felt to be necessary, should take the form of 'leading from behind,' and preserve the intention of making itself redundant as quickly as possible. (Bohm, Factor and Garrett 1991)

PSALM workshop themes are listed in a catalogue that is regularly updated. The aim of the catalogue is to enable churches (and other groups) to take up the art and skill of providing *a structure of encouragement* for conversations on themes for later life. However, the PSALM catalogue, the production of which was supported by a small grant from the UK National Lottery ('Awards for All' programme), does not just promote conversation amongst older people. It also emphasises that the workshops support people's ability and inclination to 'draw on the resources of *their* faith' in the face of the challenges that come in later life. The support from a rigorously non-religious funder such as the National Lottery, that explicitly prohibits proselytising, is a measure of the extent to which spirituality has been accepted as a vital pulse beat of the resilience needed to negotiate the hazards of later life and achieve healthy ageing.

PSALM and Spirituality

Whilst research makes the case for a link between spiritual practice and wellbeing in later life (Pandya 2010), the challenge remains that of encouraging and enabling people to 'limber up' in relation to their spiritual practice. There appears to be a subtle but strong taboo surrounding talk about prayer and closeness to God and other aspects of spirituality. However, experience suggests that people are eager for opportunities to explore, and to 'turn around' in conversation the religious experiences and things which weigh so heavily on their hearts that can only be uttered in something that approximates to prayer. In the United Kingdom, the extensiveness of religious experience, and people's ability and willingness to speak of it, has been repeatedly demonstrated through research by David Hay (2006), including the reluctant privacy in which many feel they have to enfold their experiences (Hay 1982, pp. 157–160).

PSALM workshops often give explicit permission to share religious or spiritual insights, and some themes lend themselves particularly to conversations about spirituality. For example, a workshop might involve coaching people in ways of praying and meditation as an antidote to ruminating and stress. For instance, a very popular session focuses solely on prayer, as people make a prayer bracelet 'Cairns for the Journey', with different beads representing particular issues, challenges and encouragements associated with later life. Workshop conversations often encourage people to speak from their own experience. For example the group might be invited to share about those times when they felt God to be particularly close to them, or how they handled a crisis and to what extent they found themselves drawing on inner resources. This encouragement to speak from experience enables participants to contribute their 'inklings' and hunches as well as knowledge, which for some will be drawn more directly from a Christian tradition. Importantly, whatever their source, such conversations enable a deeper self to be revealed to others, as the remembrance of things long forgotten are recalled and cherished by the attentiveness of others.

It was noted earlier that PSALM workshops often include insights from positive psychology, and this is particularly the case when the focus is on spiritual matters. This is not to deny the vast and diverse array of insights that are held within more formal religious domains, but rather to ensure accessibility for sceptics and non-religious believers. This reliance on positive psychology, including personal experience and insights, also serves to reduce the likelihood of truncated conversations (and truncated reflection) because it avoids *defeater beliefs*. These are beliefs and attitudes that Tim Keller, the Christian pastor and apologist, suggests are assumptions and beliefs that trump all other possibilities and thus close down dialogue (Keller 2004).

When encouraging conversation about personal spirituality, a problem can arise in our deeply secular context, where people often find they are limited by the language they have available. Finding language which enables us to cherish and express our inner lives is in short supply and people can be hesitant about putting words to what is in the process of coming to birth in their soul. This is amplified further because, as Richard Rohr observed: 'the language of the first half of life and the second half of life are almost two different vocabularies' (Rohr 2011, p. xxvii). He suggests that we live in a culture which is most at ease with the first half of life and its vocabulary of 'go getting' in contrast to a vocabulary of 'letting go' which is more apt for the second half of life. PSALM, in this context, has two aims: through conversation to enable people to widen their vocabulary in relation to the second half of life, and resist the temptation to disregard new ways and attitudes because of 'having become old'.

Resilience

Old age is likely to increase the frequency of *overwhelmings*, whether that be the light bulb that defies efforts to unscrew, the damp patch in the corner of the room that each week gets bigger, the note from the GP sending you to the local hospital for tests, the terminal illness of a close friend, or the impending divorce of one's youngest daughter. This list could easily grow, because the experience of *multiple overwhelmings* (Ford 1997) is one of the defining characteristics of later life. For active and healthy ageing to be maintained, resilience is needed in the face of all these potentially overwhelming hazards. What and how we think influences resilience and this, too, highlights the importance of conversation, because it gives us access to our thinking and feeling. Through conversation it is possible to reframe adverse events and, whilst it cannot be guaranteed to sort out the defiant light bulb (although indirectly it might), conversation can be a vital aid in the challenge of reframing one's perspective. The aim would be to locate a positive but not naïve standpoint from which to view that which threatens to overwhelm.

The expression 'come to terms with' is often used in relation to the multidirectional overwhelmings that happen in life. This colloquial articulation of the concept of resilience can be broken down helpfully into reflective conversational tasks. The theologian David Ford suggests that *to come to terms with* involves:

- Owning up to the state of one's being: 'I am overwhelmed'.
- Finding more precise words to describe one's state.
- Locating a perspective from which to view one's circumstances.
  (Ford 1997, p. 15)

Ford emphasises that the most important of these three stages 'is to stretch our minds, hearts and imaginations in trying to find and invent *shapes of living*' (Ford 1997, p. 18). Ford's expression 'shapes of living' accords well with one of the main objectives within positive psychology: that of enabling a person to achieve a positive perspective in relation to circumstances, and in particular to attain a greater level of intentionality (Lyubomirsky, Sheldon and Schkade 2005). In colloquial terms, this represents a move from bemoaning 'Why me?' or 'if only...' to that of 'This is what I intend (to do)'. Conversation, in its fullest sense, is the most available and accessible means of enabling this critical shift of reframing and embracing greater personal agency.

Research, especially from the field of positive psychology, now recognises the power of faith as a source of core strengths that contribute to resilience and unashamedly commend religious practices. Emmons writes: 'The religious traditions encourage us to do more than react with passivity and resignation to a loss or crisis; they advise us to change our perspective, so that our suffering is transformed into an opportunity for growth' (Emmons 2007, p. 160).

Emmons amplifies how this comes about:

Religious traditions ... articulate visions of how we should respond to the fact that life is full of suffering... People can adopt an attitude toward their suffering that allows it to be a meaningful component of life, perhaps opening the threshold to a deeper, more authentic existence. (Emmons 2007, p. 160)

Whilst resilience may be an appropriate goal for those promoting *active ageing*, there is a deeper challenge that emerges as we become older and older. The notion of active ageing is ultimately thwarted as we are overcome and overwhelmed by death. The ambition of active ageing brings a potential consequence of self-preoccupation, and this carries the existential hazard of *limitless self-expansion* (Freud 1959, pp. 316–317) which makes for 'a miserable animal, whose body decays, who will die, who will pass into dust and oblivion, disappear forever not only in this world but in all the possible dimensions of the universe, whose life serves no conceivable purpose.' (Becker 1973, p. 201)

Lars Tornstam in his theory of gerotranscendence also perceives naïvety associated with a notion of active ageing which is construed solely in terms of avoiding disease, remaining active and sustaining social relationships. Tornstam's theory and related research suggest that as we get older and become very old, we have the potential for a significant developmental stage. This enables a redefinition of the self and of relationships to others, as well as a new understanding of fundamental existential questions, including ascribing greater value to one's inner life and a greater capacity for solitude (Tornstam 2011).

Tornstam emphasises that gerotranscendence does not imply a state of withdrawal or disengagement. Rather, it is a theory proposing a developmental pattern that goes beyond the old dualism of activity and disengagement. There are echoes here of Erikson's concept of *grand generativity* as an antidote to the inclination towards limitless ego expansion despite the mounting overwhelmings of old age – an acceptance that these cannot be forever conquered and reframed. Erikson suggests that resilience and wellbeing are not enough and the task is rather, as Jung suggests, to outgrow the need for them. Erikson's notion of grand generativity puts emphasis on older people's vocation to care for the future, especially for the future of younger generations and ultimately, a concern for the flourishing of the world as a whole. This calling to grand generativity, 'Contributes to the sense of immortality that becomes so important in the individual's struggle to transcend realistic despair as the end of life approaches, inevitably' (Erikson 1986, p. 75).

Whilst Torstam suggests the capacity for solitude as an indicator of the deepest manifestation of resilience, Becker identifies religion, and Christianity in particular, as a way of achieving the profound resilience of late old age. Becker writes,

Religion alone keeps hope, because it holds open the dimension of the unknown and the unknowable, the fantastic mystery of creation that the human mind cannot even begin to approach, the possibility of a multidimensionality of existence, of heavens and possible embodiments that make a mockery of earthly logic – and in doing so, it relieves the absurdity of earthly life, all the impossible limitations and frustrations of living matter. (Becker 1973, pp. 203–204)

He notes that religion today (unlike earlier periods in human history) is a freely chosen dependency that provides shelter from narcissistic neurosis by enabling pre-occupation with personal power to be superseded by the power of the God in the cosmos. Becker notes, 'If God is hidden and intangible, all the better: that allows man to expand and develop by himself' (Becker 1973, p. 202). This expansiveness of being is not ego-centred, but rather involves the melting of ego because of the enfolding by a God in the cosmos, who can be real or imagined, but is sustained by myths and rituals and the fellowship of others who likewise seek to relinquish 'self' to God.

Becker acknowledges the difficulty of making this lonely leap of faith in a society that values what is measurable and has banished mystery as unreal, and is inclined to dismiss religious belief as naïveté. In a society that encourages 'cause and effect' thinking, the logical always trumps the mysterious and this creates a new dynamic: As research repeatedly highlights the health-giving nature of spiritual practice there is a risk that spirituality and spiritual practices will be embraced because of what they can do for us. In the light of this instrumentality, PSALM workshops, in coaching people in prayer and spirituality, and encouraging people to draw on the resources of their faith, could be seen to be reducing holy practices to self-serving purposes. However, evidence and observation suggest that what may start off as a selfish pursuit of happiness or holistic renewal, will indeed result in trans-formation. Regardless of our intentions, the pursuit of the holy, or the sacred, changes us. Tacey notes the insistence of Buddhist teachers who declare 'that even a spiritual journey begun with impure motives, such as the search for personal power, can actually serve a greater purpose, and can become transformed into an authentic spiritual quest' (Tacey 2004, p. 147).

A Cautionary Coda

Strategies for active ageing aim to ensure older people fulfil their personal capabilities and develop resilience to bounce back after setbacks. As was noted at the outset, the challenge is how to convey this new paradigm in such a way that the practices associated with active ageing are taken up on a larger scale. The case has been made here that the approach adopted in the PSALM workshops is able to make an exceptional contribution to this task of encouraging the large-scale adoption of habits that contribute to healthy ageing. Furthermore, the emphasis on one's faith applying to the ultimate challenges of dying and death make the PSALM approach worthy of consideration as a holistic approach.

The structure of encouragement that PSALM offers aims to help people to achieve a broader, more socially engaged identity and extend older people's sense of meaning and purpose in their lives. These are high ideals and it is reassuring that those who take part in PSALM workshops do report how they have begun to practise a new performance and new ways of being in the world. This could include whether greater prayerfulness, or greater awareness and thoughtfulness about how one engages with one's family, or a determination to seize the moment creatively when on the cusp of energy draining loneliness. However, despite the attractiveness and potential effectiveness of the PSALM workshop approach there is a major factor to consider: When we scrutinise who comes to a workshop, seventy percent of those who attend are women.

Ageing is a gendered issue in that it affects men and women differently. In Britain, for example, women continue to live, on average, almost six years longer than men. Conversation likewise is a gendered issue. There has been extensive research in relation to conversation and language usage by men and women, agreeing that men and women differ in the way they converse and how they use conversation, but the findings are far from straightforward. For example, there is evidence that women are more likely to be active listeners and harness a range of strategies to ensure that an interaction proceeds smoothly, and that others have opportunities to speak. By comparison, men are more likely to compete for the floor, and less likely to use strategies such as supportive feedback to signal their involvement or to encourage others to keep talking (Holmes and Stubbe, 1997). Such research, when applied to the big difference between the numbers of men and women who attend PSALM workshops, might suggest that men derive less personal satisfaction from conversation, and intuitively this insight has some merit.

There are other findings, however, that suggest there are reasons to review this intuitive explanation. For example, Coates (2004) details academic research undertaken by sociolinguists that suggests we should be less confident about consistent gender differences in relation to conversation patterns. Hyde (2005), having collated all relevant research and concluded that although men interrupt more than women, and women self-disclose more than men, the overall difference associated with gender is either small or close to zero. Moreover, the difference between average male and average female performance in relation to all aspects of conversation is small compared with the variations *among* women and *among* men.

This complex battery of research findings provides a further clue as to why so few men are interested in attending PSALM workshops. James and Drakich (1993) suggest there is an indirect relationship between gender and the amount and nature of talk. The more direct link between talk and gender is with status, which often combines with the formality of the setting. In formal and public contexts the pattern is for higher-status speakers to talk more than lower-status ones and, in such contexts, men are more likely than women to occupy high-status positions. Perhaps the informality of PSALM workshops is judged to be low status and therefore does not appeal as much to men as it does to women.

Even so, PSALM is not alone in experiencing a significant difference in participation rates of men and women. A similar issue affects the well-established and well-regarded University of the Third Age (U3A). Surveys of U3As indicate that participation rates are higher for women, with a ratio of 3:1 in the United Kingdom and Malta (Midwinter 1996; National Office of Statistics 2009) and 4:1 in Australia (Hebestreit 2006). Formosa (2014) also notes that not only is the membership mostly female, so too are the management committees and this would be also true for PSALM. These differential rates in participation are troubling because engaging in substantive conversations such as those PSALM seeks to promote, and likewise in U3A, is linked with increased levels of wellbeing (Mehl et al. 2010). Men may well be missing out on routes to wellbeing, especially as research suggests that when men (but not women) reach late-old age, their habits are likely to show a decline against measures of friendship, such as the number of new friends; desire for close friendships and involvement in beyond-family activities (Field 1999).

Evidence is growing that conversation can help people gain confidence in the inner skills that aid the development of spirituality, and which enable loneliness to become solitude. Conversation can also build resilience in relation to the challenges that are an inevitable part of later life. Moreover, conversation is not just easy to embark upon, it is a source of pleasure. With such a potent resource so easily to hand it is with some regret that PSALM notes its failure to attract and engage men. However, this limitation, rather than undermining the legitimacy of conversation as a means of fostering active ageing, highlights the importance of creative thinking and more research about ways of engaging older men, as well as remaining hopeful that the incoming older cohorts of men will be more adroit and enthusiastic about talking and joining-in.

References

Becker, E. (1973). *The Denial of Death*. New York: The Free Press.

Bohm, D., Factor, D. and Garrett, P. (1991). *Dialogue: A Proposal*. Available at www.infed.org/archives/e-texts/bohm_dialogue.htm

Burbules, N. (1993). *Dialogue in Teaching: Theory and Practice*. New York: Teachers College Press.

Coates, J. (2004). *Women, Men and Language* (3rd edition). Harlow: Pearson Education.

Emmons, R. (2007). *Thanks!* New York: Houghton Mifflin.

Erikson, E., Erikson, J. and Kivnick, H. (1986). *Vital Involvement in Old Age.* New York: W.W. Norton and Company.

Field, D. (1999). 'Continuity and Change in Friendships in Advanced Old Age: Findings from the Berkeley Older Generation Study', *The International Journal of Aging and Human Development* 48(4): 325–346.

Ford, D. F. (1997). *The Shape of Living.* Page references taken from the large print version (2002). Waterville, ME: Walker Large Print.

Formosa, M. (2014). 'Four Decades of Universities of the Third Age: Past, Present, Future', *Ageing and Society* 34(1): 42–66.

Freud, S. (1959). 'Thoughts for the Times on War and Death', in *Collected Papers*, Vol. 4, New York: Basic Books.

Hay, D. (1982). *Exploring Inner Space: Scientists and Religious Experience.* London: Penguin Books.

Hay, D. (2006). *Something There: The Biology of the Human Spirit.* London: Darton, Longman & Todd.

Hebestreit, L.K. 'An Evaluation of the Role of the University of the Third Age in the Provision of Lifelong Learning', Doctoral thesis, November 2006, University of South Africa.

Holmes, J. and Stubbe, M. (1997). 'Good Listeners: Gender Differences in New Zealand Conversation', *Women and Language* 20(2):7–14.

Hyde, J. S. (2005). 'The Gender Similarities Hypothesis', *American Psychologist* 60(6): 581–592.

Gadamer, H. G. (1979). *Truth and Method.* London: Sheed and Ward.

James, D. and Drakich, J. (1993). 'Understanding Gender Difference in Amount of Talk: A Critical review of Literature', in Tannen, D. (ed.) *Gender and Conversational Interaction.* Oxford: Oxford University Press, pp. 281–302.

Keller, T. (2004). *Deconstructing Defeater Beliefs.* Available at www.redeemer2.com/themovement/issues/2004/oct/deconstructing.html

Louden, W. (1991). *Understanding Teaching. Continuity and Change in Teachers' Knowledge.* London: Cassell.

Lyubomirsky, S., Sheldon, K. M. and Schkade, D. (2005). 'Pursuing Happiness: The Architecture of Sustainable Change', *Review of General Psychology (Special Issue: Positive Psychology)* 9(2): 111–131.

Mehl, M., Vazire, S., Holleran, E. and Shelby Clark, C. (2010). 'Eavesdropping on Happiness: Well-Being Is Related to Having Less Small Talk and More Substantive Conversations', *Psychological Science* 21(4): 539–541.

Midwinter, E. (1996). *U3A Thriving People.* London: Third Age Trust.

National Office of Statistics (2009). *Demographic Review 2008.* Valletta, Malta: National Statistics Office.

Pandya, S. (2010). *Ageing and Spirituality: Understanding the Construction, Engagement and Influences.* Saarbrücken: Lambert Academic Publishing.

Rohr, R. (2011). *Falling upward.* San Francisco: Jossey-Bass.

Smith, M. K. (1997, 2005, 2011). 'Introducing Informal Education', in *The Encyclopedia of Informal Education.* Available at www.infed.org/i-intro.htm.

Smith, M. K. (2001). 'Dialogue and Conversation', in *The Encyclopaedia of Informal Education*. Available at http://infed.org/mobi/dialogue-and-conversation/.

Tacey, D. (2004). *The Spirituality Revolution*. Hove: Routledge.

Tornstam, L. (2003). *Gerotranscendence from Young Old Age to Old Old Age*. Uppsala: The Social Gerontology Group. Available at www.soc.uu.se/publications/fulltext/gtransoldold.pdf.

Tornstam, L. (2011). 'Maturing into Gerotranscendence', *The Journal of TransPersonal Psychology* 43(2): 166–180.

World Health Organisation (2002). *Active Ageing: A Policy Framework*, p. 6. Available at www.who.int/ageing/publications/active_ageing/en/

Zeldin, T. (1998). *Conversation: How Talk Can Change Your Life*. London: Harvill Press.

15 Spiritual Development in Later Life
A Learning Experience?

Joanna Walker

Introduction

As we get older, challenging questions can arise concerning the meaning and purpose of life, especially as we move beyond the main phases of career and family building and look back on the mix of experiences that most lives encounter. There is a common-sense and culturally based understanding that the meaning of our life so far, and of its future, becomes more salient with age and that life review in various forms is an important means of exploring these issues. Faith and spirituality have traditionally been lenses through which people have explored existential matters such as identity, calling and purpose in life as well as their significance within the cosmos, relationship with an ultimate 'other', and other great mysteries of life and death.

This chapter explores ideas about spirituality in relation to ageing and learning and in particular how spirituality is experienced in later life. It focuses on the question of whether, and in what ways, learning in the later years can enhance a spiritual dimension to life. As a gerontologist who has a special interest in lifelong learning, I find that spirituality can be usefully discussed in terms of learning and development over the lifetime, and as part of mature identity (Walker 2010). The relevance of older people's faith and spirituality, often expressed in membership of a religion, is being rediscovered by social scientists as an important element in the meaning, experience and quality of later lives.

Faith and spirituality can enable older people to experience their lives as meaningful despite challenges to their quality of life; new meanings and purposes can replace those that experience has found wanting. Where physical or economic powers may diminish, a potential remains to reflect and make sense of things using the resources of faith and inner spiritual strength. Membership of a faith community can offer a valuable source of support, encouragement and identity. Participation in communal expressions of hope and belief, as well as in symbolically meaningful activities, are still significant aspects of many older people's lives.

Gerontological research across many disciplines and professional fields of practice increasingly links faith and spirituality in older people with higher levels of life satisfaction, better adjustment and coping with stressful life events, and recovery from illness and bereavement. Where faith or a spiritual dimension is absent or has become lost, the means for knowing who you really are and how you have lived your life have to be sought elsewhere. It is likely that these questions not only remain but also press for answers as people approach the end of their lives.

A significant part of scholarship in this field grapples with the topical concern to differentiate religion from spirituality, since research outcomes cannot be identified without conceptual clarity. Whereas the study of religion is well established within sociology and psychology, the research approach to spirituality is relatively new and ill defined. Religion and spirituality are clearly closely related, but debate continues about whether one includes the other and whether belief in a transcendent being or power (however defined) is critical. A working distinction is proposed between religion and spirituality for the purposes of this chapter: Religion can be understood as a sociocultural programme for developing spirituality and for bringing spiritual perspectives, beliefs and practices into a common framework for everyday and communal life. Spirituality refers more naturally to the inner experiences that may arise from practising a faith or following a particular spiritual path, often with connections to both the transcendent and the immanent. It can also refer to a variety of experiences not necessarily associated with an organised religion or recognised spiritual life, such as insights from everyday life or extraordinary experiences.

However, in order to put some sort of boundary around the idea of spirituality, it may be preferable to conclude that although spirituality is concerned with higher levels of meaning, insight, value and purpose in life, it is usually also associated with belief in a force beyond the material world. Other kinds of philosophical or political belief systems may also generate meaning, purpose and even elements of religiosity, but do not rely on a transcendent element, so should be excluded from ideas about spirituality. A better overall term for beliefs, values and goals that sustain meaning in life, whether derived from spiritual or humanistic sources, is 'existential meaning' (Coleman and O'Hanlon 2004, p. 136).

In terms of learning, religious belief, behaviour and practices are acquired and developed through formation within the faith community and socialisation within its institutions and culture, as well as in wider society and its prevailing culture of spirit (including family and community life). Spiritual understandings, practices and disciplines are also available outside particular faiths, and are more likely to be the outcomes of informal, self-directed or non-traditional forms of learning. Atchley (2009) addresses this in his observation that:

'Spiritual' is seen by the majority of people to be a broader term than 'religious' and to refer to an inside-out personal learning process rather than an outside-in socialisation process. (p. 16)

Since the millennium, the relevance of spirituality has increasingly interested researchers and professionals and, of course, the many adults who value a spiritual dimension to their lives. Interpreting the meaning and progress of our lives has traditionally been done through following a religion but now, in Western cultures at least, it is also being approached in alternative and less institutionalised ways. The practice of both religion and spirituality is said to reflect a fundamental cultural shift to greater individualisation, whilst the communal aspects of belonging to a faith or spiritual community are being re-negotiated to produce new forms.

What both members of faiths and spiritual seekers have in common is a desire to make sense of existence and to express and represent the truth discovered about meaningful human life. Religions offer systems and structures to bring people into contact with the sacred, involving beliefs, practices, symbols and a community life. More broadly, spirituality has come to symbolise the human quest for depth and values in people's lives. We attribute to the human spirit a vision for achieving our highest potential, through whatever lifestyle and practices are able to help this vision come about (Heelas and Woodhead 2005).

What Can We Know about Later Life Spiritual Learning and Development?

In the many fields of human enquiry involved, much research asserts that adults not only have the potential for spiritual learning, but that there appears to be an increased imperative to pursue it in later life (Bianchi 1984, Dalby 2006, Moberg 2008). However, the case is often argued from a theoretical or conceptual point of view, rather than on evidence. There are smaller amounts of empirical research, based on testing out such ideas, which lend support to this link between ageing and increased spirituality. The complexity of the methodological challenges means that these are mainly small-scale interpretive studies, often attempting to clarify concepts (Cohen et al 2008, McCann Mortimer et al 2008), with fewer large-scale or longitudinal studies (such as Wink and Dillon 2002).

The challenges for research can be characterised as the conceptual problem of defining and operationalising spirituality, and the methodological difficulty of separating ageing effects (all older people, everywhere) from cohort effects (this group at this time or place). Having said this, the relevance of humanistic and critical gerontological approaches is not in doubt. Ageing, spirituality and learning is essentially a human field of enquiry because relationship is at the heart of spirituality, rather than the content of beliefs, doctrines or practices. In spiritual learning, life experience is both the subject matter and the curriculum – the content and its means of apprehension.

Since observation and interpretation of the phenomena of both ageing and spirituality are a challenge for research, what kinds of evidence are useful or reliable to account for the changes that people do manifestly undergo over a lifetime? Without waiting to fully test the latent thesis that spirituality increases with age, much can be gathered from asking 'lower order' order questions such as what older people think, feel and do regarding spirituality and why, and in what circumstances. How and why do they pursue inner understandings and beliefs about 'ultimate reality' or a higher power (which they might call God), themselves and the world?

The established theme within social gerontology of meaning-making and making sense of life's experience implies a process by which people can and do transform their streams of reflective information, which comes from both internal and external sources. What enables some to develop a deeper level of insight about themselves and their world into spiritual beliefs, values and self-images? Why do some take it further, actively investing in learning to make these insights a conscious part of their self-identity? Why do others simply experience them as streams of consciousness, running through established mental routes without further review?

Throughout this chapter, it is implicit that learning to develop spiritually is essentially learning about oneself, including in relation to others. It is also about how one relates to society, to the cosmos and to an ultimate reality or higher power, however this might be conceived. Clearly individuals have a wide range of capabilities and dispositions to think spiritually. In order to conceptualise the ways in which older adults transform 'life-data' into constructed views of themselves and their life-worlds, a typology of older spiritual learners could be proposed:

> *Active learners:* Those who have entered the 'spiritual learning pathway', actively pursuing spiritual understanding or practices through formal studies; attendance at courses (with or without resulting credentials/qualifications), study days, summer schools, theological classes and engagement in

spiritual movements. A notable sub-set of people in membership of faith communities fall into this category but there are many others seeking beliefs, or holding none, who are also serious explorers. They may be at an early or advanced stage of their learning journey.

Self-directed learners: Those who are interested in and think about spiritual matters but do it in self-directed ways and not necessarily with others. They may develop their understanding of spirituality by focused reading of specialist literature in the form of books, magazines, blogs, websites; or through broadcast media such as radio, television and films. Increasingly, there are interactive and lifestyle-based e-communities, which may offer communication with others, but essentially still enable individual control of the learning journey. This group may also include those who have left faith communities to pursue their own path; those who are interested in spirituality as an aspect of self-development and conscious ageing; those who are reflecting deeply as a result of trauma or loss or other challenging life circumstances; those whose capacity for active learning has become limited through greater old age or disability.

Non-engaged learners: Those who are not specifically aware of spiritual learning but, if asked, could identify understanding or behaviours that served a spiritual purpose for them (e.g., appreciation of nature, music, art, service to others, sense of personal quest, etc.). This includes those who may hold more or less coherent views about the meaning of life but who take no evident actions to gain further information or insight. They may hold untested views influenced by mass media, parental or family mythologies, cultural or sub-cultural cosmologies, or based on positions learned at school, church or faith community, often in earlier life.

The most active area of research on later life and spirituality concerns how people who admit a spiritual dimension to life are better able to articulate meaning and purpose, which in turn has other beneficial effects. The ability to bring together all aspects of one's self, with a measure of tolerance for ambiguity and complexity, is considered the highest prize of both lifelong psychological development and of spiritual maturity. The term 'integrity' expresses this 'coming together' of the mature self. It is also seen as an expression of wisdom – the coalescence of understanding and experience, not just of accumulated knowledge.

Another key idea in the study of later life spirituality is that of 'generativity' or the urge to give back; to be outwardly orientated to the needs and concerns of others, not self-absorbed with one's own affairs and difficulties. The psychologist Dan McAdams has revived interest in the concept of generativity, which appeared as one of the developmental tasks for midlife in Erikson's original formulation of the life course (Erikson 1963). McAdams (2001) describes various features of generativity, arising in midlife, but continuing on into later life, and typifying older adults' concerns to care for others and for the future. Furthermore,

As they translate their concerns and beliefs into commitment and action designed to promote the well-being of the next generation, adults construct personal narrations of their generative efforts, which eventually become incorporated in to the larger, autobiographical tellings that comprise their life stories. (McAdams 2001, p. 407)

Social gerontologists (such as Atchley 2009) have coined the term 'serving from spirit' for this drive and it can be seen played out in voluntary organisations, faith communities, neighbourhoods and families.

Making a Case for Learning about Spirituality

The overall waning of religious authority of various kinds, in some parts of the world, has enabled a rise in individual, eclectic beliefs, membership of new movements and a reduced religious or spiritual 'literacy' among younger generations. How do adults of any age learn how to discern between competing spiritual claims for their attention or, indeed, whether they need a spiritual dimension to their lives at all? Huge cultural changes in the religious socialisation that today's older people experienced in their youth will have implications for future cohorts of elders (Coleman et al 2006).

What can developing a spiritual dimension to life offer to adults as they age? This can now be pursued both from a 'religiously-anchored' place and from more free-floating positions (Woodhead and Catto 2012). Spiritual learning outside of a religion probably takes different forms of learning or training from those one may pursue within a faith community. Within a faith or religion, people seek to become more advanced in its beliefs and practices and their application to life, or to take on a role within the organisation. Spirituality outside of the institution is more like a kind of personal development that takes seriously the need to grapple with issues of self-identity, purpose, integrity and so on.

Conversely, being put off spirituality because of one's negative view of religion might also explain why some never explore this aspect of their development. Coleman and O'Hanlon note Jung's view that the resistance to religion per se can hamper a 'search for the soul' and rob the second half of life of its meaning (Coleman and O'Hanlon 2004, p. 16). Perhaps the recent increase in spiritual searching beyond the confines of religion supports the development theorists' contentions that later life stages do have spiritual aspects that need attending to, regardless of someone's views on the substantive matters of faith and spirituality.

One way in which a spiritual dimension to life has been traditionally identified is through the idea of calling or vocation. This is clearly not restricted to religious life – many recognise the urge to find the purpose that relates to their talents and passions, and develop the courage to follow it. In human development terms, vocation would be mostly identified with the young adult discovering identity and a place in the world. Now we recognise that the greater prevalence of long life requires a sustained sense of purpose and role for many more people, for much longer. The great challenge of retirement, for instance, is to relocate a sense of vocation beyond the 'second age' structures of employment and family formation. Faith and spirituality can be sources of inspiration for working out what it is that our gifts and experience can continue to contribute. What kinds of learning will support this ability to identify, sustain or renew a calling throughout life?

The case for learning about spirituality is also increasingly being made by professionals, especially in the fields of health and social welfare, where the part played by spiritual factors in wellbeing, resilience and recovery is being noticed. 'Spiritual care' is now something that nurses, doctors and social workers, as well as chaplains, aspire to give. Policy makers have pursued with interest the research evidence that points to spiritually active older people being better able to cope with illness, disability, bereavement, stress and disability. For laypeople too, this opens up the potential of spiritual contributions to various situations as mentors and helpers and, not least, as grandparents. What kinds of 'training' or preparation would be useful to develop these extra dimensions to professional and citizenship roles?

Last, as spirituality enters more into public understanding as something separate from religion, learning about spirituality can be seen as offering people a natural and powerful metaphor for life's journey and for life planning in the broadest sense. Finding a direction, having a destination in mind, as well as enjoying the journey and relating to fellow travellers, are all readily understood ideas. Some may wish to read a map and follow directions, or share a vehicle with others. Others prefer to find their own way using intellectual or intuitive capacities and beating their own path. Learning to know oneself better, with one's strengths and preferences, will engender confidence for the journey as well as support practical skills such as planning and decision-making.

Greater acceptability of and interest in personal development of this kind is part of the secularisation process now well underway in most Western societies. Public discourse and provision of ways to pursue spiritual development without a religious or faith connection are increasing. However, both debate and provision are underdeveloped concerning the spirituality of much later life and its completion. We are happy for spirituality to contribute to 'successful' ageing or be a lifestyle choice, but have yet to appreciate its deeper value as strength in weakness for our diminishments and finitude, and for completing the journey of life. Yet these are the questions on the mind of many older adults.

Ways in Which Spiritual Learning Can Be Enabled in Later Life

In what ways can learning be seen as an integral part of spiritual ageing? Four areas in which learning might operate are proposed:

1. In the development of spiritual capacities and resources, especially when these are sought more consciously;
2. Learning as part of the movement between developmental life stages, for example in the completion of stage-related tasks;
3. Learning as central to the process of self-development and the continuing building of the self-system as part of mature identity;
4. The development of spiritual practices that contribute to a growing inner life and a 'practice-oriented spirituality'.

Developing Spiritual Capacities and Resources for Ageing

In this area, learning can operate to boost coping and resilience and be part of what has become defined as 'successful ageing'. As most social scientists will point out, a person's ability to shape the quality of later life has an inevitable materialistic, financial and class base, but it may also have a non-material spiritual one (Woodward 2008). Spirituality does seem to be linked empirically to coping, and some suggest that a spiritual perspective can enhance the concept of 'successful ageing' (Crowther et al. 2002, Sadler and Biggs 2006) but this risks reducing the spiritual dimension to some sort of super-coping mechanism. A better strategy would be to understand the meanings that older people attach to their lives, including their own notions of ageing well, and support them in developing these perceptions and capacities.

A number of researchers have noted the link between wellbeing and spirituality, which often operates through an increased sense of meaning and purpose in ageing as well as the perception of support and security that can sustain people in difficult times. (Fry 2000, Jewell 2004, Vahia 2011, von Humbolt et al. 2014) However, the development of spiritual capacities and resilience can be hampered by unhelpful cultural contexts such as consumerism, individualism and materialism. Woodward (2008) notes that such forces can prevent people from finding the space and inner strength to maintain a sense of a worthwhile life, even where their material or health resources appear to be adequate. To truly flourish we need to build up 'spiritual capital' as well as other kinds of resilience to confirm our position in relation to life and the world.

The development of spiritual capacities in later life may arise as part of maturation or normal ageing processes, but the spiritual learning that people need in order to develop a spiritual response to life's challenges may also require more active and conscious engagement. As with the typology suggested earlier, older learners can be active, opportunistic or inactive with regards to their spiritual learning. This is a more important matter than it sounds, since it can be argued that spiritually developed older people are not only managing their third and fourth ages better, but are also an asset to society, even if they appear relatively disabled. Understanding spiritual ageing therefore offers an alternative perspective on the societal contributions of older people. Civic or social contributions can be spiritual rather than economic – activities and roles that can be realised through spiritual development, such as counselling, mentoring, reconciling, advocating and so on (Schachter-Shalomi 1997).

Learning as Part of Developmental Life Stages and Tasks

The growth opportunities represented by adulthood and ageing have been described in terms of models, mostly by psychologists, who have identified a variety of ages and stages that have developmental tasks and transitions associated with them (Erikson 1997, Levinson 1978, Fisher and Simmons 2007). A number of gerontologists also propose developments associated with the latter part of the life journey. For instance, Moody (1998, reprinted 2015) cites six 'dimensions' or indicators of spiritual wellbeing that can be aimed for in later life:

1. Self-determined wisdom – encapsulating mature self-identity and a sense of one's capacities and competences
2. Self-transcendence – acknowledging and relating to something or someone greater than oneself

3. Discovery of meaning in ageing – making sense of one's current circumstances in the light of the past and future
4. Acceptance of the totality of life
5. Revival of spirituality
6. Preparation for death

In other models, growth opportunities are conceptualised more formally as life-stage tasks that must be addressed in order to move on. Erikson's adult developmental stages extend into mid-life and later-life. The mid-life task is to develop generativity, a move beyond oneself to help others to flourish and to avoid stagnation; the later life task is one of integrity, a coming together of the personality to achieve a fuller sense of the self as well as self-acceptance, to avoid despair (Erikson 1997). Elizabeth MacKinlay (2001, and Chapter 3 in this volume) offers a more recent model, comprising four major challenges that older people need to face and resolve in some way, to be worked out in relationship with others and with God. Older people should be supported as they struggle with these challenges: *self-sufficiency versus vulnerability; wisdom versus provisional understanding; relationship versus isolation; hope versus fear.*

Whilst most models of spiritual development involve trajectories or stages of age-related change, often involving learning in order to move forward, others invoke the passage of time as the main factor that calls us on, such as Jung's ideas on the second half of life (Rohr 2011). More general models of lifelong human development models nominate various drives in their later life phases that could be seen as spiritual, or can be applied to spiritual development. For example: the urge to reflect on and make sense of experience; to accept, deal with and move on from failures; to prepare and protect a 'legacy' (that is, one's mark in the world); to give back to the world or society and to develop a more rounded and integrated sense of self. (See Coleman and O'Hanlon 2004 for a good discussion of the spiritual aspects of human development.)

Alongside the 'ages and stages' models of human development, we may also wish to consider the stages of faith development, which aim to account for the development of spirituality over the lifetime. James Fowler's (1981) model is the best known and, whilst widely applied within faith communities, was primarily designed to address human development of 'faith' in general which he defined as

not always religious in its content or context (–) it is our way of finding coherence in and giving meaning to the multiple forces and relations that make up our lives. (Fowler 1981, p. 4)

Beyond the childhood stages (1 and 2) the adult stages that Fowler thought most people would experience were stages 3–5, which moved them from young adulthood to beyond mid-life: Most people move to stage three as emerging adults, when their life has grown to include several different circles of value and influence and there is a need to pull it all together. Any faith adopted is likely to be an all-encompassing belief system; faith can be strongly experienced and believed, and life changing. However, at this stage, people tend not to see outside their box or recognise that they are 'inside' a belief system. Authority is usually vested in individuals or groups that represent one's beliefs. Stage four takes over when the more mature adult starts seeing outside the box and realising that there are other 'boxes'. They begin to critically examine their beliefs and may become disillusioned with faith propositions formerly accepted. Their wrestling with belief results in a more explicit and personal responsibility and commitment to faith, usually with full participation in spiritual/faith community life.

Stage five is rarely reached before mid-life. This is the point when the 'reasonableness' of faith, developed in the previous stage, begins to run out and people start to accept the paradoxes in life. They increasingly appreciate that life contains greater complexity and mystery, and often return to sacred stories and symbols, but this time without being restricted to one theological box – allowing other symbols, voices and stories to speak by being open to spiritual guidance. The hallmarks of this stage are living consciously and creatively with ambiguity and provisional understanding.

Stokes (1990) provides an example of research that sought to test applicability of Fowler's proposed faith stages to spiritual maturity in later life. Studying several waves of adults of all ages, he did indeed find a clustering of faith changes that related to transitions to faith stage three (among 20+) and to stage four (among 40+). Faith development was also strongly related to major life events and times of change, and with participation within a faith community (although the idea of a 'changing' faith had negative connotations for some). The dynamic relationship between faith and the life course was held to have been demonstrated.

One of the strands of Fowler's model, over the years, has been its western, cognitive, male orientation. Slee (2004) offers a thoroughgoing critique of these aspects but, for the purposes of this discussion, a key issue is whether and to what extent developmental models alone can account for change and growth. Evidence of developmental stages proceeding in the manner of a biological process is hard to imagine let alone produce. A life-course context needs to be added to allow for variance in developmental pathways that comes from cultural norms, historical epoch and events, economic conditions, individual differences and so on (McAdams 2001).

Models should be viewed primarily as descriptive rather than predict-ive. The active ingredient that moves us on is more likely to be found in the dynamic of experience and the meanings we attribute to it. For mature adults to respond positively to the drives and challenges described by these various models, and not be overwhelmed or stalled by life's eventualities, there needs to be encouragement as well as means and opportunities; this is a role for spiritual learning in later life.

Self-development, Building the Self-system and Mature Identity

In contrast to the idea of stages of development, which are difficult to demonstrate evidentially, other approaches focus on the 'self' and its continuous development. Adult development takes place mostly through small incremental changes, although more significant or specific learning can take place through conscious effort or in response to crisis events. This idea is evidenced by the everyday, informal learning that takes place when a novel situation, however small, is encountered and the experience is integrated into existing understanding; or when changes provoke reflection and reassessment. A tradition of this 'learning cycle' based on experience and reflection can be found in classic adult education literature such as: Kolb (1984), Knowles (1990) and Jarvis (1995).

A similar idea is expressed in the continuity theory of ageing, which holds that people develop mental frameworks that represent life experi-ence, make decisions based on them, observe the results and respond by modifying the frameworks. This may explain why people reach certain conclusions or take particular actions, or see threads between things without the underlying connections necessarily being obvious to anyone else. It also illustrates something about the learning involved, which draws on life experience as the learning material. This private, personal world of internal understandings, values and preferences make up the 'self-system' (Atchley 2009). Such a world was thought only to be researchable through detailed phenomenological observation, or by using longitudinal methods to detect continuity of ideas and values over the lifespan, but is now being approached through narrative gerontology and methodologies involving life history and reminiscence.

Self-systems grow from decades of learning through life experience. They include values, which form some of the most enduring con-structs we have, fuelling both aspirations and controls. By middle age most people have developed confidence in a sense of themselves and their own agency. A prevalent personal goal among Atchley's subjects (Atchley 2009) was to accept the self 'as I am', and this became stronger over time. A shift from self-esteem based on feedback from others to one based on inner integration (what we make of ourselves) in turn lays a foundation for a greater concern for others or issues greater than those affecting the self.

Jungian theory describes a natural process (individuation) towards maturation and wisdom, the last stage of which he described as transcendence. This involves going beyond a current to a new understanding of the self, of relationships with others and of existential questions. Tornstam (2005) developed his theory of gerotranscendence where individuals in late life sought to combine insights from thinking (conceptualising), and their experience in terms of empirical evidence and practical applications. As part of the normal ageing process, he proposed that individuals would experience a shift in perspective from a materialistic and pragmatic view of the world to a more transcendent and cosmic one.

The outcomes were said to be less self-centredness, more selective participation in social engagement and a greater sense of life-satisfaction. Tornstam predicts that older people will therefore seek time and space for reflection, even solitary meditation, but that this is a positive and self-developing process, not the withdrawal and dependence predicted by the earlier disengagement theory. Discussion continues as to whether Tornstam's assertion of transcendence as the final state results from a lifelong and continuous process *as well as* from a transformational change to a qualitatively different mode of living (Thorsen 1998).

Spiritual Practices, Growing the Inner Life and Practice-Oriented Spirituality

A broad or humanistic approach to spirituality often includes recognition of the spiritual dimensions of all life journeys, implying that spiritual practices and a vibrant inner life are available to all. What forms these take are beginning to interest a renewed field of sociology and psychology of religion, which also seeks to investigate the impact of contemporary culture on more traditional expressions of faith and belief. The shift away from a religious to a spiritual discourse offers both challenges and opportunities to older people themselves.

On the one hand, an older person's failure to maintain practices and disciplines of earlier years (because their capacity or needs have changed, or the religious institution itself has changed) may feel like disloyalty. But on the other, encouragement to engage with new forms of spiritual practice, faith-based or otherwise, has the potential to bring about greater growth and a richer experience. Spiritual journeying teaches that persistence and progress are needed to sustain spiritual growth; older people may well have already learned that effort can bring results and that practices are worth sustaining to experience their benefit. They may also have the confidence to move on into imperfectly known territory on the basis of past experience (Albans and Johnson 2013).

A more conscious form of journeying is also possible, within faith communities or without. Life review can be done at any time to reconsider goals, purposes, relationships, values and so on. This form of learning is like self-appraisal, leading to self-directed learning. In order to nurture one's spiritual practice, Atchley (2009) recommends the following to develop 'conscious ageing':

- Have an enduring set of questions to ask of yourself to maintain spiritual awareness (he gives examples, to be addressed periodically, as a kind of self-appraisal).
- Identify and engage in spiritual activities that are meaningful and helpful for the inner journey, such as contemplative reading, meditation, prayer or movement practices such as yoga, or types of walking or breathing.
- Participate with others in a spiritual community and in programmes aimed at spiritual growth.
- Develop friendships or small groups for social support and opportunities for expression of spiritual experience and learning.

A key idea in discussions of contemporary spirituality is the 'spirituality of practice'. In a review of social change in spiritual thought in the latter half of the twentieth century, Wuthnow (1998) argued that (in the United States) spirituality had moved from a religion-centred 'spirituality of dwelling' to a person-centred 'spirituality of seeking'. It had most lately moved on to a personal 'spirituality of practice' – something that requires active attention and an ongoing creative response on the part of the individual. This broad thesis can be seen to have applicability across the developed world.

The *spirituality of dwelling* had offered stability and comfort: God in a definite place and humans enabled to share a sacred space, through doctrine, belief and practice, provided by organisational structure and order. In contrast, the *spirituality of seeking* began to offer journeying: learning and negotiation was required to travel a landscape of spiritual choices and confusing meanings. With no answers provided, people had to 'live the questions'. Wuthnow concluded that we are now in a period where people seek to balance both dwelling and seeking, to obtain security with openness. However, the currently emerging *practice-based spirituality* demands more by way of commitment to nurturing a spiritual life. An element of learning (in terms of knowledge, skills and attitude) is therefore required to actively manage a chosen and developing spiritual practice, of whatever derivation.

The new freedoms to define and pursue spirituality in later life may, of course, bring new social pressures to develop a meaningful, well-adjusted life and, by implication, a healthy mind and body. Laceulle (2012) describes this obligation of 'self-realisation' as a cultural and moral ideal. Older people will increasingly need to identify and follow 'the path through which one is supposed to create one's own "good", meaningful life' despite challenging contexts such as ageism and consumerism (p. 115). Processes of spiritual development do, however, still hold out the possibility of meaning in the conditions of vulnerable later life existence, Laceulle concludes, including in the face of structural inequalities and uneven life chances. However, the task of realising later life flourishing should be a joint project between individuals and societies they are part of, and attempts to shift the risk and responsibility to individuals alone should be resisted.

Conclusion

How can learning about later-life spirituality be made possible in practice? Whilst society catches up with its responsibilities to ageing populations, informal learning can be pursued by individuals and groups through self-directed reading, conversing and online browsing and by following up on resources and networks. Within spiritual communities there are hopefully more structured opportunities for both individual and group learning in later life, especially if the value of older members and the spiritual significance of ageing become increasingly recognised.

Although study material for spiritual learning is 'naturally occurring' in the sense that life experience is both the course content and the learning methodology, there is plenty of room for the development of more specific ideas and topics for spiritual learning in later life. One example would be recent study material for older learners from the Anglican and Methodist Churches in the United Kingdom: *Seasons of my Soul* nominates a range of relevant themes such as: identity; memories; transitions; wisdom; roles and relationships; reconciliation; death and dying; celebration of life (The Methodist Church and The Church of England 2014). More broadly, the increasingly privatised UK market in adult and continuing education provides a range of courses on spirituality, some of it applied to ageing, with many third agers prominent among their participants. Online learning is a growth area for spiritual development, with many programmes and learning communities on offer.[1]

In self-help or peer-learning modes, learning materials could be sourced and devised around some of the life and faith stage literature: For example, Harry Moody's 'five stages of the soul' *the call, the search, the struggle, the breakthrough, the return* (Moody and Carroll 1997) or Fisher and Simmons' *Journey of Aging* (2007) would make good bases for a curriculum. There is also a growing amount of popular literature on the spiritual aspects of ageing, written for and by older spiritual seekers, or those with a particular path to recommend, and mostly taking the line that there is a new quality of life available in older age. In this respect, they express similar sentiments to the sorts of books on retirement that were popular at the end of last century, urging their readers to embrace a new stage of life positively and draw on personal resources. See, for example: Chittister 2010; de Hennezel 2012; Hollis 2006. In addition to personal study, such literature could be part of the diet of community or faith groups operating in book club formats.

Research makes much of the educational value of talking and discussing together. This can be maximised in groups to create narratives that 'explain ourselves to ourselves', as it were, such as through autobiography or family or local history. In this way, life's experiences can be connected up and patterns seen. They can also be universalised, that is, set against a broader canvas of history, or of someone else's experience. Who are the teachers and the learners in these scenarios? Ideally older people are both, as participants and facilitators. The learning comes from listening and asking open questions that lead to reflection, as helpfully described and discussed by Ann Morisy in this volume.

In addition to the how, we should consider *what* people could learn to aid their spiritual development. Spiritual practices being re-discovered for the twenty-first century are mostly versions of classic ones.[2] For example, the discovery of silence and reflection are even more relevant now in a world of 24/7 media and sound-bite news. The revival of pilgrimage and retreats (by people of all faiths and none) are practices that increase awareness of today's spiritual learning deficits. We need to know how to attend to ourselves and to others, as well as to our deepest longings, guided by a sense of purpose and values. Spiritual 'skills' have inner and outer aspects. Contrary to a popular view of their being otherworldly or escapist, spiritual practices are about developing an inner life and sense of oneself *in order* to draw on these as the wellspring for our actions in the world. For many, this also involves a belief that they are listening and responding to God.

A particular context for developing later life spirituality is, of course, faith communities, where debate is growing on how they view the purpose of later life and engage with their older members. Indeed, churches, temples and mosques, for example, have great resources and need to apply them to a better understanding of ageing and older people. They have theologies of human and spiritual potential and calling; a strong value of inter-dependence; they recognise the importance of tolerance, forgiveness, reconciliation, life together, mutual support and many other positive things that contribute to later life.

Faith communities also have traditions and rituals that give shape to meaning over lifetimes and across generations, modelling behaviours that signify rich understandings. They can provide skills and support for the development of a life of prayer, contemplation, and meditation on sacred texts and spiritual writings. All of these are currently important to older followers of various faiths, whose views and participation should be increasingly and actively sought. Ministry with and for older people should be much higher on the training and policy concerns of faith communities.

The role of non-faith based intentional spiritual communities is also one of interest, as more individualised paths of spiritual development can lead to people coming together to create community and mutual support. For older spiritual seekers, such groups can offer a new stage on the journey and their experience could reveal more about what older people need and want in terms of spirituality. The US movement known as 'spiritual eldering' has no direct equivalent in the United Kingdom, but the seeds of it can be seen (in the Christian tradition at least) in the growth of ideas such as 'churchless faith' (spirituality beyond religion) and an increasing amount of web-based resources and interaction on later life spiritual matters

For any group wishing to enhance spiritual learning, opportunities will be needed to exchange life experiences and their meanings. This could include the development of narratives in various forms and media (written, spoken, depicted, filmed, etc.). Groups could also raise and discuss issues not often addressed, both positive and negative, about being and becoming in later life.[3] By utilising their own members' experience or drawing on others' expertise, there is a chance to practise the skills associated with inner journeying, such as reflection, meditation and mindfulness, as well as the techniques to improve them involving body, mind and spirit.

Last but not least, such groups could provide a means for combating ageism and the anti-age industry (that sells us products to ward off ageing), in order to help reclaim later life in all its fullness. Mature adults do not need to settle for prolonged middle age or to fear leaving their second or third age. Later-life spiritual development offers an alternative vision of human flourishing. Encouragement and learning should be available to respond to the spiritual call of ageing.

Acknowledgement

This chapter extends material presented in Walker, J. (2010) 'Learning from the Inside Out – Mapping Spirituality and Ageing', *International Journal of Education and Ageing* 1(2): 179–196.

Notes

1 Websites on older spirituality include:
www.centerforconsciouseldering.com
www.sage-ing.org
www.secondjourney.org
www.senioradultministry.com
www.spiritedexchanges.org.nz
www.spiritualityandaging.org
www.SpiritualityandPractice.com/ElderSpirituality

2 Spiritual disciplines and practices were recently described by Graham Tomlin (2006) as: *Silence* (to develop contentment), *sacrifice* (for generosity), *celebration* (for joy), *solitude* (to hear God's voice), *confession* (for honesty), *study* (for wisdom) and *fasting* (to increase focus and attention).

   For a secular perspective on spiritual practices, see Atchley (2009) who defines them as 'things we do on a regular basis to celebrate, appreciate, nurture and act on our experiences of presence, transcending the personal self and connecting directly with the sacred: Many types of mediation and prayer, devotional rituals and music, inspirational reading and reflection and movement-oriented spiritual disciplines can be mixed to support a contemplative, practice-oriented spirituality.' (p. 4)

3 The following ideas about later life spirituality were discussed with a regional grouping of Universities of the Third Age in South East England in 2014:

   Spirituality in later life involves:

   Reflecting on your experience and life so far; accepting the challenge and gifts of ageing

   Asking the big questions and working towards your answers; drawing on resources and help of others

   Maintaining your vehicle for the journey; your religion, your spiritual practice, your means of travelling on

Rewriting the rules for the second half - be liberated!

Filling your container, constructed in the first half of life; you worked hard to build it, what do you want to put in it?

Considering the end of the story; how do you want it to end? Any unfinished business? What legacy will you leave (not material ones, but creations, influence, relationships)?

References

Albans, K. and Johnson, M. (2013). *God, Me and Being Very Old: Stories and Spirituality in Later Life*. London: SCM Press Ltd.

Atchley, R.C. (2009). *Spirituality and Aging*. Baltimore: Johns Hopkins University Press.

Bianchi, E. (1984). *Aging as a Spiritual Journey*. New York: Crossroad Publishing Company.

Chittister, J. (2008). *The Gift of Years, Growing Old Gracefully*. New York: BlueBridge.

Cohen, H., Thomas, C. and Williamson, C. (2008). 'Religion and Spirituality as Defined by Older Adults', *Journal of Gerontological Social Work* 51(3–4): 284–299.

Coleman, P. and O'Hanlon, A. (2004). *Ageing and Development*. London: Arnold/Hodder.

Coleman, P., Mills, M. and Speck, P. (2006). 'Ageing and Belief – Between Tradition and Change', in Vincent, J., Phillipson, C. and Downs, M. (Eds.) *The Futures of Old Age*, pp. 125–134. London: Sage Publications.

Crowther, M.R., Parker, M.W., Achenbaum, W.A., Larimore, W.L. and Koenig, H.G. (2002). 'Rowe and Kahn's Model of Successful Aging Revisited: Positive Spirituality – the Forgotten Factor', *The Gerontologist* 42(5): 613–620.

Dalby, P. (2006). 'Is There a Process of Spiritual Change or Development Associated with Ageing? A Critical Review of Research', *Aging and Mental Health* 10(1): 4–12.

Erikson, E.H. (1963). *Childhood and Society*, 2nd edition. New York: Norton.

Erikson, J.M. (1997). *The Life Cycle Completed*. New York. Norton.

Fisher, J. and Simmons, H. (2007). *A Journey Called Aging: Challenges and Opportunities in Older Adulthood*. New York: Haworth Press.

Fowler, J. (1981). *Stages of Faith: The Psychology of Human Development and the Quest for Meaning*. London: Harper and Row.

Fowler, J. (2001). 'Faith Development Theory and the Postmodern Challenges', *International Journal for the Psychology of Religion* 11(3): 159–172.

Fry, P. (2000). 'Religious Involvement, Spirituality and Personal Meaning for Life: Existential Predictors of Psychological Wellbeing in Community-Residing and Institutional Care Elders', *Aging and Mental Health* 4(4): 375–387.

Heelas, P. and Woodhead, L. (2005). *The Spiritual Revolution: Why Religion Is Giving Way to Spirituality*. Oxford: Blackwell.

de Hennezel, M. (2011). *The Warmth of the Heart Prevents Your Body from Rusting*. London: Pan Macmillan.

Hollis, J. (2006). *Finding Meaning in the Second Half of Life*. New York: Gotham Books.

von Humbolt et al. (2014). 'Does Spirituality Really Matter? A Study of the Potential of Spirituality for Older Adults' Adjustment to Aging', *Japanese Psychological Research* 56(2): 114–125.

Jarvis, P. (1995). *Adult and Continuing Education: Theory and Practice*, 2nd edition. London: Routledge.

Jewell, A. (2004). *Report on Sisters Work*. London: Conference of Religious in England and Wales.

Kolb, D. (1984). *Experiential Learning: Experience as the Source of Learning and Development*. London: Prentice-Hall.

Knowles, M. (1990). *The Adult Learner: A Neglected Species*, 4th edition. Houston: Gulf Publishing.

Laceulle, H. (2012). 'Self-realisation and Ageing: A Spiritual Perspective', in Baars, J., Dohmen, J., Grenier, A. and Phillipson, C. (Eds.) *Ageing, Meaning and Social Structure: Connecting Humanistic and Critical Gerontology*, pp. 97–118. Bristol: Policy Press.

Levinson, D. (1978). *The Seasons of a Man's Life*. New York: Ballantine Books.

MacKinlay, E. (2001). *The Spiritual Dimensions of Ageing*. London: Jessica Kingsley Publishing.

McAdams, D. (2001). 'Generativity in Midlife' in Lachman, M. (Ed.) *Handbook of Midlife Development*. New York: Wiley.

McCann Mortimer, P., Ward, L. and Winefield, H. (2008). 'Successful Ageing by Whose Definition? Views of Older Spiritually Affiliated Women', *Australasian Journal on Ageing* 27(4): 200–204.

The Methodist Church and The Church of England (2014). *Seasons of my Soul: Conversations in the Second Half of Life*. London: Methodist Publishing.

Moberg, D. (2008). 'Spirituality and Aging: Research and Implications', *Journal of Religion, Spirituality and Aging* 20(1–2): 95–134.

Moody, H.R. and Carroll, D. (1997). *The Five Stages of the Soul*. New York: Anchor Books.

Moody, H. (1998, reprinted 2015). 'Does Old Age Have Meaning?' in Moody, H. and Sasser, J. (Eds.) *Aging; Concepts and Controversies*, 8th edition, pp. 29–39. Los Angeles: Sage Publications.

Rohr, R. (2011). *Falling upward: A Spirituality for the Two Halves of Life*. San Francisco: Jossey-Bass.

Sadler, E. and Biggs, S. (2006). 'Exploring the Links between Spirituality and "Successful Ageing"', *Journal of Social Work Practice* 20(3): 267–280.

Schachter-Shalomi, Z. (1997). *From Age-ing to Sage-ing: A Revolutionary Approach to Growing Older*. New York: Grand Central Publishing.

Slee, N. (2004). *Women's Faith Development: Patterns and Processes*. Farnham: Ashgate Publishing Limited.

Stokes, K. (1990). 'Faith Development in the Adult Life Cycle' in Seeber, J. J. (Ed.) *Spiritual Maturity in the Later Years*, pp. 167–184. New York: Howarth.

Thorsen, K. (1998). 'The Paradoxes of Gerotranscendence: The Theory of Gerotranscendence in a Cultural Gerontological and Post-modernist Perspective', *Norwegian Journal of Epidemiology* 8(2): 165–176.

Tomlin, G. (2009). *Spiritual Fitness*. London: Bloomsbury Continuum.

Tornstam. L. (2005). *Gerotranscendence: A Developmental Theory of Positive Aging*. New York: Springer.

Vahia, I. et al. (2011). 'Correlates of Spirituality in Older Women', *Aging and Mental Health* 15(1): 97–102.

Walker, J. (2010). 'Learning from the Inside Out – Mapping Spirituality and Ageing', *International Journal of Education and Ageing* 1(2): 179–196.

Wink, P. and Dillon, M. (2002). 'Spiritual Development Across the Adult Life Course: Findings from a Longitudinal Study', *Journal of Adult Development* 9(1): 79–94.

Woodhead, L. and Catto, R. (2012). *Religion and Change in Modern Britain*. Abingdon: Routledge.

Woodward, J. (2008). *Valuing Age: Pastoral Ministry with Older People*. London: SPCK.

Wuthnow, R. (1998). *After Heaven: Spirituality in America since the 1950s*. Berkeley: University of California Press.

16   Reimagining the Theology of Old Age

James Woodward

Introduction

In this chapter we shall explore how best to put theology to use when considering the nature of age and ageing in both ourselves and other people. The main body of this chapter consists of sketching out the shape of how theology might hold a number of important questions in order to both imagine age and seek a deeper and more insightful sense of the role of older people in both church and society (Woodward 2008). It continues a significant theme of this volume which is, that in imagining age, we cannot claim any complete or absolute framework of theology. Rather, these questions are scaffolding that support an exploration of how theology might be put to work in relation to our growing older. I begin with a story from my own experience. The reader is invited to enter imaginatively into this short narrative. This is followed by an intriguing extract from an interview with Carl Gustav Jung, which acts as a starting point for considering what we believe might help good ageing.

Who Is That in My Mirror?

I used to live in an affluent part of the West Midlands in the United Kingdom. Solihull was a borough full of affluent communities housing high achievers. The culture was busy, demanding and life could be stressful for these families. For some, the constant activity was chosen but for many it was deeply woven into the fabric of modern life. The constant flow of information and the need to be always on the move have the power to both satisfy and frustrate. In this culture, age and ageing have been marginalised such that older people seem not to be part of it.

Let me take you back to the local town where I shopped, or rather drove through, on my way to somewhere else. I am late for a meeting in Birmingham and I cannot find my mobile phone to let my colleagues know that I am behind. I negotiate a busy junction and then meet a pedestrian crossing. There are three cars in front of mine. My eyes catch the sight of an old man waiting to cross. He hesitates and then moves back while none of the cars ahead let him pass. I decide to let him cross even as my anxiety levels about the meeting continue to rise. I stop. He hesitates. Then slowly and laboriously he takes several steps from the curb. He is frail and the journey across the road seems to take forever.

The man seemed so alone and so vulnerable. I see his weakness and his pain. He had probably crossed that road for many years but suddenly that path had become treacherous and strange. How many minutes did I wait as he slowly placed one foot in front of another? How much longer would he be able to do this? Was he at the end of his life? Where was the man going? Who was he becoming? Was anyone helping him on his way?

As I drove off something very profound and disturbing struck me. He was me! The thought preoccupied me for the rest of my journey. The day would come when I, threatened by a jungle of cars, would hesitate and wonder how the familiar had become so foreign, how and why my body had become so heavy and difficult, and how my reactions had become so tranquilised. The old man had become a stark foreshadowing of what I would become. His vulnerability would become mine with all its dependence and imperfections. His appearance challenged the mask of my illusions. His ageing reflected my own. I both sympathised with that old man and hated him. His presence spoke about my passage through time, my own physical changes and my own inevitable death. I did not want to receive this message but it was written very clearly on the page of my busy day. It made me sad and gave me hope. He exhibited patience that reminded me that we all have to slow down.

This disposable person is the product of our culture, a bundle of experience, knowledge, life, concerns and wisdom. Who is he? I do not see him in my car wing mirror – he disappears strangely into the landscape. This man's story is important, as is your story. They belong together. These are the tales of unique human existence; fabric that took years to weave. We are all worth something.

What Do Older People Need in Order to Live Properly?

In 1959 John Freeman, the famous BBC journalist, interviewed Carl Gustav Jung when he was an old man of eighty-four, two years before his death in 1961. Jung was still working and his mind sharp, his concentration focussed. Here is an extract from the transcript:

FREEMAN: 'You have told us that we should regard death as the only goal.'
JUNG: 'Yes.'

FREEMAN: 'and to shrink away from it is to evade life and to make life
          purposeless?'
JUNG: 'Yes.'
FREEMAN: 'what advice would you give to people in later life to enable them to
          do this...?'
JUNG: 'I have treated many old people and it is quite interesting to watch
          what the unconscious is doing with the fact that it is apparently
          threatened with a complete end. It disregards it – life behaves as
          if it were going on, and I think it better for old people to live on –
          to look forward to the next day, as if he had to spend centuries,
          and then he lives properly. But when he is afraid he doesn't look
          forward, he looks back, he petrifies, he gets stiff and dies before
          his time; but when he is living on, looking forward to the great
          adventure that is ahead, then he lives ...' (Freeman 1989, p. 60)

Putting Theology to Work

Much of the research that has taken place in North America over the last
twenty to thirty years has indicated that people beyond mid-age (fifty-five
for sake of argument) become more spiritual, and therefore more open to
some of the religious questions that theology asks. Amongst the many
reasons for this increased 'religiosity' are two core realities. The first is
that beyond mid-age people are closer to their deaths than their births.
This increased sense of awareness of mortality is linked with a second
feature of the second half of life. This is preparedness to face up to one's
limitations, deficiencies and disappointments that both hurt and threaten
us. As individuals face their failures and mistakes, questions emerge
about what makes for human flourishing and well-being. Mid-age might
be viewed as a time of opportunity and even preparation for what shape
older age might take in us. What might these years look like as an
individual reflects on their experience of relationships made and lost,
the establishing of home and family, the nurture of children and career?
An intensified and deepening sense of the spiritual is forged out of life's
failures as well as its successes (Bianchi 1990, Coleman 2011).

   It is against this background that the remainder of this chapter explores
some of these theological themes. Though some of the questions that
follow are not limited to or confined by old age, they seem to take on a
particular significance during the processes of maturity. What follows are
eight sections of 'scaffolding' that form part of a theological exploration
of the process of ageing for others and ourselves. The reader might be
more drawn to some sections of this framework than others and should
be encouraged to consider how theology may help us to navigate this
particular stage of human experience.

What Is the Relationship between Being and Doing?

In an age where communication and information are fast and immediate it is sometimes difficult to keep up with the sheer activity, driven by tasks that so many of us are bound up with. Work for many people has become more demanding and less stable. It is a rare employer who values pace and perspective, time and relationship, as well as trust and some readiness to accept human vulnerability and even mistakes.

Add to this the demands of bringing up a family including perhaps looking after older parents, the responsibility of exercise, sensible eating and some balance between the public face of work and the private world of living and loving and it is easy to see why, despite the enormous benefits of modernisation, we seem to be less content.

Every human life might ask itself about the source of its worth and value. For many, our worth and sense of value itself is derived primarily from work and the work role. While we should acknowledge here that the shape of retirement is in the process of rapid change with many enjoying longer working lives, most people still aspire to a time of withdrawal from the pressures and demands of work to enjoy some freedom and space (Rohr 2011).

Older people then have to live with the inter-relationship between being and doing that reverberates so profoundly in all of our lives. Some cope with old age by 'just keeping on going on' and certainly a feature of good ageing can be the maintenance of an active, engaged and flexible living. For some older people there can be more space and time to reflect. This space offers an opportunity to have a richer sense of time and within that space to look at life more closely. Indeed many older people choose to give something back to the community through voluntary work. Some of this engagement takes place in the family in caring and supportive roles especially for grandchildren (Kroll 2006, p. 39).

Our Need for Redemption?

The place of both scripture and tradition in a reimagining of a theology of age remains problematic. Too much of the spiritual exploration of ageing has rested on simplistic dichotomies that stereotype older people, either as decrepit, dependent and demanding on the one hand, or as vigorous, autonomous and full of saintly wisdom, on the other. Surely older people need redemption as much as younger ones, and if this is true then questions of sin and judgement should find a place in any vision of ageing as well as wellbeing for the self. Put another way, in old age, as through the rest of the life space, humans are called to serve

God and not the self. Simply to be is not enough; being does not supplant doing in later life (Gunton 1988).

The family is a primary location for service to one another to be played out, but the relationship between children and parents is often complex. There are indications that many children feel much more ambivalent about their responsibility to care and support parents and older generations. This may be to do with past estrangements and also due to the reality that both generations may find it difficult to accept the role reversals that come about in the mature families. The adjustments and negotiations attendant on the new stages in family relationships can bring strain and conflict. The uncertainties of these transitions are natural but can give rise to misunderstandings and resentment. They can call up long forgotten grievances and lead to struggles for dominance.

From the perspective of theology, if family relations in later life are marked by failure it follows that a theology of ageing must take account, not only of the sinfulness that can mark family life, but also of the forgiveness and redemption that empower people to make new beginnings. In this sense the doctrine of redemption in Christ embraces both of these mysteries (Hauerwas 2003, p. 202).

Made in Whose Image?

A central focus of any theology of age must be the affirmation that human beings are created in the image of God. This does not refer to a physical representation; rather it goes beyond the physical by definition. Like God, the human species is able to create, albeit on a significantly more limited basis. Human beings are mortal but they approximate or imitate immortality and the ability to create through the act of creation and procreation (Baker 1970, p. 40).

Old age can sometimes be haunted by twin fears: fear of abandonment and fear of dependence. When Christians affirm that human beings are made in the image of God there is a declaration that all of God's creatures are dependent on the divine goodness for their existence. All creatures owe their being to God. Their very existence, all that sustains them, everything that helps them to flourish, all that they are and can be comes from God.

This belief is especially important to hold onto when the vulnerabilities of old age take the shape of the accumulation of losses. Dependence and disability are difficult to adapt to. Despite these losses and the even more challenging changes that age may bring to the memory through dementia there continues to be a unique value in every human being. Some older people have borne witness to the intuition of sheer gratuitousness, which discloses their belief about being made in the image of God, which speaks of the mystery of their lives as creatures of God. Even at their most dependent human beings are still receiving and being made. There is a spiritual maturity that comes from the realisation that existence is not in one's own hands (Koenig 1994; Tournier 1971).

The Power of Metaphor and Story

In the reimagining of age, I continue to be both committed to and energised by the importance of the integrative power of metaphor and story. If we are to take the work done in this area seriously then any reimagining of theology in the ageing process requires the convergence of multiple points of view.

We need stories of growing older, stories of transformation, self-transcendence, humility and wisdom not limited by a denial or physical decline and mortality. We need communities capable of hearing these stories, and of viewing these time-travellers not as fearful, alien old strangers but as pilgrims and children of hope, as ourselves. We need to revalue ageing, to also embrace the ageing body as a sacred space, and to emphasise the spirituality of nurturing in all the ways that this is both given and received through our lifetimes.

We need the books that flow from lived lives, in particular Christians need the elder tales of older Christians that reflect both the hope and the gift that are present in those narratives. Reinstating moral agents as concrete, embodied cells reasserts the inter-subjective nature of morality, thus redefining the second half of life as a moral category, not primarily a biological or psychological one.

Certainly the story, like all good stories, will require many tellings. The telling of any story will intersect in different ways with the grammar of the reader and the reader's tradition. Mired as we are in the modern tradition, captive to its images of ageing, and chained to its charting of life's course, is it possible to re-imagine age in a different narrative or with a different story?

We should remind ourselves that we do not learn to know God any other way than through the story. The story is the way we come to know the deeper meaning of living as expressed through the Christian tradition. The Bible as literature shares a range of stories. The teaching ministry of Jesus as narrated in the gospels is communicated through story (Burridge 1992).

In the Jewish tradition much has been made of a blessed old age. Amongst the features of such blessedness is a lack of infirmity, the presence of children and economic success but above all being afforded with respect. There is an assumption that an older person has learned a great deal from the wisdom of living and the Jewish tradition that therefore forms an ideal state of wisdom with old age. A Yiddish proverb says, 'Old age to the unlearned is winter. To the learned it is harvest time' (Chittister 2008).

With this perspective in mind it may follow that, if we are to learn the wisdom of old age, then older people themselves must become more visible and their voices, their stories and their experiences find expression. A practical example of this in my own experience relates to work in the Foundation of Lady Katherine Leveson, which embraced a church primary school and a centre for the care and housing of older people. We were keen to promote understanding between the generations and especially to find a role for older people in the nurture of children. Some of our older residents offered their time to support children who needed help with reading. A group of our residents engaged with learning about life during the war by sharing their own experiences and stories both from home and abroad. An old soldier talking about his medals and experiences in Italy; a farmer's wife sharing her experience of the bombing of the city centre of Coventry and others showing photographs, explaining rationing all served to bring the reality of war into the classroom in a vivid and moving way. This is one small example of the power of story.

If it were to be possible to reconstruct a more positive, inclusive narrative of ageing then this work must be done between and across the generations. Young people and those in middle age must consider what ageing means to them and be prepared to name some of the fears associated with older age. The language and metaphors used for this purpose will be a key means of embracing all of the possibilities of ageing and the shape of its meaning for us.

Nurturing the Possibilities of Wonder

It is interesting to ask how many individuals, particularly younger individuals, regard old age as a culmination of living – a highpoint. Consider this reflection by the theologian Karl Rahner: 'The real high point of my life is still to come. I mean the abyss of the mystery of God, into which one lets one's self fall in complete confidence of being caught up by God's love and mercy forever' (Rahner 1990, p. 38).

The challenge here is that it appears that technological society so insulates modern day people from the contingency of human life that they come to lose the capacity for wonder that moved earlier generations to search for God and surrender in worship. Perhaps in living we have become less accustomed to wonders because there seems to be very little space in this technological world where humans do not seem supremely in control. It may be for this reason that the sense for primal religious experience has been dulled. The occasions in which the intuition arises that human beings participate in a vast, complex world not of their making, one in which they play an exceedingly minor role but in which they are nonetheless highly valued, seem to have become more rare. Does it follow that technology obscures the mystery at the heart of human life? (Moody 1992)

Holding Fragility and Diminishment

We have noted that old age brings one face to face with mortality but we should also remind ourselves that the religious virtualities of old age are of a more subtle and intimate nature. As we grow older we experience a succession of transitions and crises at a whole number of different levels. Over time, these force the tension to consider ultimate realities. In this sense, the trajectory of ageing has changed. Traditional views of preparation for death have generally regarded death as the end of a process, either of ageing or illness. However, in more recent times ageing has changed for many older adults in so far as a relatively long period of active life is often followed by another long period of declining health and disability.

We should not underestimate the frailty of this period of life. Ageing tends to restrict mobility, diminish senses and impair speech and thinking. It can lead to a withdrawal from active public life forcing one, in time, to rely on the help of others to carry out most of the basic activities. The loss, suffering and diminishment of old age with its disengagement, isolation and dependence are opportunities to experience the precariousness of human existence – the graciousness of human life and the transcendent greatness of being. While to some this analysis may seem to place excessive emphasis on the negative aspects an infirm, late old age, one should not underestimate the opportunities that diminishment and dependence give to individuals which allows them the freedom, and possibly wisdom, to pose and explore very important ultimate questions of living and dying. We should question, then, in these circumstances whether our pastoral theology and practice provides a framework and a commitment to older people to assist them into a new and deeper human existence.

It may then be possible to support the view that the process of diminishment (which is the inward experience of loss undergone in old age) awakens the soul to the giftedness of life and makes it receptive to grace (Jewell 1999). For us to accept our limitation and, even more, diminishment, recognises a particular virtue of ageing that Erikson calls wisdom, and Ronald Blythe refers to as the willingness to bless life in the face of one's own suffering and mortality (Kimble et al. 1995).

From the point of view of Christian theology, dependence in old age, whether it takes the form of reliance on family members or on professional helpers, is an instance of the profound dependence at the heart of creative existence. When Christians confess their faith in the creed, they are declaring that all God's creatures are dependent on the divine goodness for their existence. All creatures owe their being to God. All that sustains them, everything that helps them flourish; all that they are and can be comes from God. The accumulation of losses persons suffer in old age, together with the deepening vulnerability that advanced ageing carries with it, opens the mind and heart to the sense of absolute dependence. As noted earlier, even at their least active, humans still have the potential to be recreated by life, by a hope in something beyond the material limitations of life and a sense that existence is not in one's own hands (Koenig 1994).

Modernity: Friend or Foe?

In the reimagining of age, it will, no doubt, be important to contextualise where and how theology is done in relation to old age. In other words, attention needs to be given to the way in which age is socially constructed in modern times. In the last analysis, some of these issues of construction should be firmly grounded in the realities that we ourselves face. Although, for example, I do not regard myself as especially old, the reality of my age is that I am coming into mid life and I am genuinely curious about what this period of my life will give birth to. Despite my prolonged exposure to older people and reflecting upon age, I cannot get away from a predominant sense that the gift of years is so often feared rather than revered. It is maybe to do with the losses of a certain sense of youth and a fear of encumbrance. Certainly the years do encumber us with wrinkles, sags and grey hair but we also have to recognise our complicated, peculiar and distinctive histories. As we face our histories, this is when the question of what kind of power we have to solve life's enigmas and complexities, through our own wisdom or life experience, comes back to confront us (Madsen et al. 2002).

What Are Older People For?

I want to make a plea to support the development of very different ways for speaking about what we struggle with, as we grow older. How ought we to grow old? Or what does it mean to grow old? How these particular questions overlap with families and generational relations and gender are also important. Like other aspects of our biological and social existence, ageing has been brought under the dominion of scientific management, which is primarily interested in how we age in order to explain and control the ageing process. How do we find a way of giving voice to the things that really matter? And if we can find a voice, who will listen to us? This is an arduous and at times frustrating task where we need to recall deep cultural assumptions radically into question. But in order to do that, we need to break out of ageing as an engineering problem to be solved or at least ameliorated. Even theologians who have focussed on ageing have often viewed it as simply a matter of social policy: unemployment, poverty, disease, health care, retirement and pensions (Vincent 2003). The point here is that Christian theology should have something more to offer.

The issue of ageing goes hand in hand with the cultural and symbolic impoverishment that has beset the last half of life since the late nineteenth century. Anyone who takes the time and effort to listen to the particular stories of ageing will understand that the phenomenon of ageing is not just a matter of making generalisations about the status of old age, attitudes towards ageing, class or gender differences or the treatment of the poor or frail old. While these are important issues, they will not be resolved through modernity's traditional dissociation of ideas, images and attitudes from the facts of ageing and an epistemological stance that denies the experience and cultural representation of human ageing. This dissociation makes ageing an abstraction and places us a comfortable distance away. It treats ideas, beliefs and feelings about ageing as if they were merely subjective reactions to an objective reality. The dissociation impedes a richer understanding of growing old. When internalised, it feels like a kind of false consciousness; a separation of body and self that is so common in our culture (Cruikshank 2003).

If the only narrative that we have for understanding the public discourse about ageing is that of statistics or science then we fail to develop a critical vision or a larger story within which people's experience makes sense. The narratives that surround our understanding of old age are many and complex. I write as a practical theologian but my understanding of ageing needs to be shaped by and appreciation of other faith traditions and their approach to older people; and understanding from science, gerontology, psychology and sociology. There needs to be a richer inter-professional approach to this subject where individuals and groups can make a contribution to our understanding of the meaning in the second half of life. Only through this kind of broader multidisciplinary approach might we be able to conquer the paradox that lies at the heart of a growing dominance of the mythology of scientific management (Woodward 2008, p. 116).

There can be no denying that in the last fifty years the central goal of the modern scientific enterprise – the conquest of premature death from acute disease and the prolongation of healthy vigorous life – has become a realistic expectation for most people (at least for white middle-class Westerners). Ironically, the very success of this enterprise has also created a new fate for the developed world: a longer old age and all that this might mean. Put rather crudely, what is the purpose of old age and what are older people for? This has in part something to do with how we all engage and embrace the unmanageable and ambiguous aspects of our existence (Small 2007).

As T.S. Eliot once remarked, 'There are two kinds of problems in life'. One kind provokes the question 'what are we going to do about it?' the other calls for different questions: 'what does it mean? How does one relate to it?' (Cole & Winkler 1994, p. 204) The first kind of problem is like a puzzle to be solved with appropriate technical resources and pragmatic responses. The second kind of problem poses a deeper range of challenges, which no particular strategy, policy or technique will overcome. This all points to a society that detaches persons from their own histories, from the meaningful performance of ageing within our bodies; an alienation and a kind of desperation which serve only the political economy in which we live.

This, then, is simply a plea to understand ageing in the context of moral and spiritual commitments, in the context of connectiveness and away from understanding it primarily as a scientific problem amenable to technical solution. Why strive to see the moral and spiritual possibilities of ageing when, given enough basic research and medical intervention, we can eliminate (or at least manage) physical decline? The modern shift cannot contain and does not allow the paradoxes of later life: ageing is a source of wisdom and suffering, spiritual growth and physical decline, honour and vulnerability (Atchley 2009).

Conclusion

We may ask our theological questions in different ways. This chapter has raised some of them and there certainly are others. I end with a reflection on one of the most obvious features of longevity – the shape of wrinkles as our skin ages as a symbol of moving beyond the superficial signs of old age to a more positive and imaginative view of the meanings of ageing.

The profit motive, the mass media's love affair with the new, and the anxiety provoked by growing old in a youth obsessed culture has led millions to surrender their faces to the war on wrinkles. We are being asked to unmake what we have spent a lifetime making. What do we receive in return for this sacrifice? Not youth. Instead we are given, at best, the facsimile of youth. Passion and history are pillaged in the pursuit of youth's fresh blankness. Do people fear wrinkles because of what they seem to say about us? They are the sum of all the days we have lived and will never live again. They tell us our story even when we do not want that story told. Even the attempt to erase them becomes part of what is written on our faces. We – the doers, the movers, the shakers, the achievers, the rocks of our families and communities – are being written upon. It shocks us to see ourselves, for the first time, as paper and not the pen we imagine ourselves to be.

Wrinkles are painless and harmless. They are us and we are them. What would it be like to live in a society that adored wrinkles? The idea may seem laughable at first, but for millennia, living to a ripe old age was an exceptional achievement and was often recognised as such by society. All this self-induced anguish might serve some purpose if it prodded us towards a re-examination of our longevity. Wrinkles give us a way to begin such a conversation, but it is just a start; plumbing the true nature of our longevity presents a much more exciting and demanding challenge.

This playing around with words asks us to imagine growing into an old age defined by full development, maturity, awareness, readiness and advancement – this really would be an opportune time. Instead we are mired in a highly negative view of ageing that envisions a one-way trip down the long road towards disease, dementia, disability and death. Peaches ripen, but human beings, it seems, cannot. Though we are all aware of the real and often unpleasant changes that come with advancing years, we lack a concept that fully recognises the positive elements of ageing. It is as if our longevity consists solely of deep, forbidding shadows. This emphasis is perhaps the most damaging consequence of contemporary society's glorification of youth. Those who seek a more complete understanding of longevity, an understanding capable of embracing both light and shadow, conduct their search within a culture that rarely misses an opportunity to emphasise the negative aspect of ageing. The positive dimensions of our longevity remain, for now, present but largely unseen.

References

Atchley, R. (2009). *Spirituality and Aging*. Baltimore: The Johns Hopkins University Press.

Baker, J. (1970). *The Foolishness of God*. London: Darton Longman & Todd.

Burridge, R. (1992). *What Are the Gospels?* Cambridge: Cambridge University Press.

Bianchi, E. (1990). *Aging as a Spiritual Journey.* New York: Crossroad Publishing Company.

Chittister, J. (2008). *The Gift of Years.* New York: BlueBridge.

Cole, T. & Winkler, M. (1994). *The Oxford Book of Aging.* New York: Oxford University Press.

Coleman, P. (2011). *Belief and Ageing.* Bristol: The Policy Press.

Cruikshank, M. (2003). *Learning to Be Old.* Oxford: Rowman & Littlefield.

Freeman, J. (1989). *Face to Face.* London: British Broadcasting Corporation.

Gunton, C. (1988). *The Actuality of Atonement.* Edinburgh: T&T Clark.

Hauerwas, S. et al. (2003). *Growing Old in Christ.* Grand Rapids: W.B. Eerdmans.

Jewell, A. (1999). *Spirituality and Ageing.* London: Jessica Kingsley Publishers.

Kimble, M., McFadden, S., Ellor, J. & Seeber, J. (eds.) (1995). *Aging, Spirituality and Religion: A Handbook.* Minneapolis: Fortress Press.

Kroll, U. (2006). *Living Life to the Full.* London: Continuum.

Koenig, H. (1994). *Aging and God.* New York: Haworth Press.

Madsen, R., Sullivan, W., Swidler, A. & Tipton, S. (eds.) (2002). *Meaning and Modernity: Religion, Polity and Self.* Berkeley: University of California Press.

Moody, H. (1992). *Ethics in an Aging Society.* Baltimore: The Johns Hopkins University Press.

Rahner, K. (1990). p. 38. in Imhof, P. and Biallowons, H. (eds.) *Faith in a Wintry Season: Conversations and Interviews with Karl Rahner in the Last Years of His Life.* Trans. H.D. Egan. New York: Crossroad Publishing Company.

Small, H. (2007). *The Long Life.* Oxford: Oxford University Press.

Rohr, R. (2011). *Falling upward.* San Francisco: Jossey-Bass.

Tournier, P. (1971). *Learning to Grow Old.* London: SCM Press.

Vincent, J. (2003). *Old Age.* London: Routledge.

Woodward, J. (2008). *Valuing Age.* London: SPCK Publishing.

Pressing towards the Finishing Line
Supporting Older People on Their Final Lap

Keith R. Albans

Introduction

The growing interest among the Western media in the ever-burgeoning numbers of older people has, by and large, ignored one crucial feature of the new ageing phenomenon, namely that death has increasingly become a feature of older age. In the United Kingdom during 1974, the 85+ age group made up 15.8% of all deaths, whereas by 2013 that figure had grown to 38.2%. For males only, during the same period, the figure more than trebled, from 9.3% to 28.7% (ONS, 2014). The factors behind this change are well understood, with better healthcare and the changing nature of employment being to the forefront. However, the consequences of the change, in terms of the existential experience of the older people themselves, have attracted far less attention. For those approaching the final stages of their life, even if that life has been long and fulfilled, the questions of what it has all been about and whether you will be remembered once you have gone operate at the heart of what we call their spiritual needs. Madeleine L'Engle's assertion that, '*The great thing about getting older is that you don't lose all the other ages you've been*', may be of comfort in middle age but it is at odds with the experience of many of those approaching death when loss looms (Anderson and Dunlap 1985). Likewise, Edward Abbey's assertion (Lamberton 2005) that, '*If my decomposing carcass helps nourish the roots of a juniper tree or the wings of a vulture – that is immortality enough for me*', sounds more plausible when the concerns of this life dominate than when we contemplate the imminence of the life beyond.

Many older people spend their final weeks and months living either alone or surrounded by their close family. For them, the issue of addressing their existential questions and their spiritual needs belongs to those in their immediate circle, which may or may not include a faith community. But for those older people who live in a residential aged care facility, these issues can and should be part of the on-going care that they receive. The image of the Final Lap comes from the Olympic Marathon where, having spent most of the race running around the streets of the host city, the runners enter the stadium for the final half kilometre. One final lap of the track after such a long race is, for many, only possible because of the support of the crowd who urge them to the finishing line. For older people approaching the end of life, those who share their journey can have exactly the same role.

In this chapter I will outline an approach to training social care staff which gives them the confidence to become accompanists to older people in their care, and advocates for them in working to ensure that their wishes are carried out. I will address the question of what might be considered to contribute to a 'Good Death' and I will also examine the role that Chaplains can play both for people of faith and those of no particular faith, in witnessing and working with the life stories of residents so as to better understand their spiritual journey. Finally, I will examine how remembering those who have died can be a significant means of reassuring residents that their own needs will be addressed when the time comes.

Older People and Dying in a Communal Setting

It is not simply the case that dying and death have become a feature of older age, for an obvious consequence is that residential care settings have also become places where death is more common. Indeed, the UK government has recently changed practice and now includes such deaths among the 'death in the usual place of residence' statistics. Of all deaths of those aged 75 and above in England during 2006–2008, just over 22% occurred in residential care homes. Of those aged 90 and above, the percentage rises to almost 37% (National End of Life Care Intelligence Network 2010, p. 23). It is also worth noting that the proportion of those dying in residential care, as opposed to nursing care, increases markedly with age. For these reasons, the oft-cited quotation from the founder of the modern hospice movement, Dame Cecily Saunders, seems particularly appropriate. She wrote that '*How people die remains in the memory of those who live on*', and there can be few places where this has a more poignant meaning than in the field of residential elder care. The presence of large numbers of people living communally in the fourth age of life should provide an end of life care environment where, because death is a regular occurrence, the tasks that belong to the final lap of a long life can be addressed to mutual benefit. However, the reality is that far too many care settings both in the United Kingdom and in many other countries, the task is beyond low-paid and often inexperienced and poorly trained care staff. This means that when the 'how people die' issue is handled poorly, the memory is not simply distressing to family, but to those residents whose end of life is approaching and to the staff who will support them.

It is still, sadly, not uncommon for care home staff to engage in a conspiracy of silence and pretence when a resident dies, seeking to ensure that no one catches sight of a hearse or an undertaker as a body is secretly removed from the premises via a back door. In such circumstances, the remaining residents are expected to barely notice that anything has happened and then welcome a newcomer, who fills the empty room, and carry on living. As a consequence, it must be hard for someone to reach any conclusion other than that this will happen when they die – they will disappear and be replaced, with no one knowing where they have gone.

Outlining bad practice and poor experience points towards the means by which they might be improved. In the United Kingdom, one consequence of the investment by government in the Department of Health's initiatives to improve end of life care was the publication of the first National End of Life Care Strategy (Department of Health 2008). A key recommendation was to encourage meaningful conversations about end of life wishes, and while this can be hard to achieve for older people living alone, those in residential settings are, at least in theory, better placed. Opportunities abound to discuss thoughts and feelings with their peers and with those outside their immediate family circle, but experience suggests that if these opportunities are to be grasped, a culture of openness is needed and staff in particular need training, encouragement and support.

Tasks for the Final Lap

Spiritual needs in older age, and particularly towards the end of life, vary from person to person, but in residential settings it is vital to encourage all staff to see that they have a role in addressing and meeting these needs. Indeed, care providers have a duty as well as an opportunity to ensure that residents are encouraged to explore their needs and wishes. Sadly, many organisations go no further than asking the question as to whether a resident has made a will, and whether or not they have made a directive regarding possible cardio-pulmonary resuscitation (DNACPR). By limiting their enquiries to such a cursory level they not only deny the older people in their care, but they also underestimate the benefit that staff can derive, once they have been given the opportunity to receive some instruction and training.

Before turning to look at the approach which we have developed, it is worth pausing to gather together the various tasks which are usually identified as being vital in the final lap of life, and to consider what might help to facilitate the 'good death' which many hope will await them at the finishing line.

Elizabeth MacKinlay (2012, p. 36) suggests that what she calls the 'final life career' has two parts, namely to hand over the baton to the next generation and to die well. Integral to the first of these is the notion of life review and spiritual reminiscence, whereby the construction and narration of a life story can help to bring about an understanding of its meaning and purpose. This can then become a crucial part of what is handed on to family and friends through an understanding of shared values, traditions and traits. For some, this process can be a religiously significant one – akin to that described at several points in the Old Testament (e.g., Genesis 48–50, Exodus 28–31, Deuteronomy 26:1–11) – but for everyone it is something which can go deep to the heart of what it is to be human. It is also something which is as significant for those left behind as it is for the one approaching death.

MacKinlay writes from an Australian perspective, and it is important to note that the study and practice of supporting older people on their final lap is truly international and multifaith. In this volume, Ellen Idler and Robert Atchley have written from a North American viewpoint, whilst elsewhere, Krishna Mohan, Linda Kristjanson and Ruwan Palapathwala reflect experiences from Uganda and Scandinavia as well as comparing insights from Buddhism and Christianity (Jewell 2004, p. 161; MacKinlay 2006, p. 153, 189).

There can be little doubt, therefore, that recognising the spiritual nature of the tasks to be faced on the final lap is vital if we are to ensure that people's final wishes are not simply approached in a functional manner. I have addressed this area elsewhere (Albans and Johnson 2013) in terms of five significant landmarks, and these give some important guidance not only for the older person themselves, but for all who accompany them on the final stages of their journey.

The first landmark is *Diminishment*, for a significant factor in the experience of ageing is the way in which the world can become increasingly small. For someone moving into a care home this is a physical reality, as everything they possess has to be contained within a single bedsitting room. This may well come on top of another experience of diminishment, as travelling or walking become more difficult, the space in which they live becomes more limited and, as a consequence, the feeling grows that their impact upon the world is reduced.

A second landmark is *Contemplation*. Most famous classical symphonies include a passage towards the end that recapitulates the principal themes around which the piece has been built. The experience of contemplation in later life is in many ways an opportunity and an invitation to do the same, but one that can require help and encouragement. For those who practise a religious faith, contemplation can have a further meaning that can help retain a sense of self-worth. In the Christian tradition, the shape of worship is designed to focus on the transformative nature of faith and to remember ourselves as made in the image of God and loved by God.

A third landmark is *Legacy*, which from a spiritual point of view, is tied up with the question of what impact we have made on those around us and how, if at all, we might be remembered after our death. Sadly, all too often, it is only at a person's funeral that we discover some vital fact about their story that would have completely altered our connection with them if only we had known it sooner. Helping an older person to identify and harvest their legacy is a great gift to offer, and in the current generation this can be particularly important to those who describe themselves as 'only a housewife'.

My fourth landmark is *Finitude*. Whereas one of the perils of youth is a tendency to think that you are indestructible, for the very old the opposite is true and the last years are lived in an on-going dialogue with the inevitability of death. This can give way to depression but, for others, it can be liberating, giving rise to a feeling that there is nothing to lose and that each day is a rather unexpected gift. For family and friends, accompanying those coming to terms with this experience of finitude can be frustrating and bewildering, as one day they are unwilling to entertain the possibility of making plans for the future because 'they may not still be here', while the next day the same person will be fussing as to what you want for Christmas!

The final landmark on the journey is the sense of *Completion* that can come in the final days and hours before death. While any dying leaves behind much that is incomplete and involves family and others in tidying up and, indeed, in all kinds of new beginnings, for the dying person themselves, the metaphor of approaching the finishing line is apt. St Paul uses precisely this image in describing his attitude to the rest of his life, 'I press towards the finishing line, to win the heavenly prize to which God has called me in Christ Jesus' (Phil. 3.14).

In thinking about the landmarks on the final lap of the journey, it becomes clear how important a role can be played by those able and willing to be accompanists on that journey. They highlight the significance of taking seriously an individual's story in order to help them retain a sense of identity and fulfil the spiritual tasks on the final lap. Listening to elders telling their stories used to be a feature of many communities, but it has, until recently, become increasingly rare. Thankfully, a recovery of the art has begun, and in particular through its application in both reminiscence work with older people and in narrative gerontology. For both the story-teller and the listener, the process of sharing enables connections to be made between the three dimensions of past, present and future. And it is the dynamic interplay between these dimensions that gives the stories of older people their particular richness, and offers helpful direction to those who accompany or support them.

Since 2001, it has been my privilege to listen to the stories of a great number of people on their final lap through my work with Methodist Homes (MHA). Founded by the Methodist Church in 1943, it is an independent charity with close links to the church, whose services are available to people of all faiths and none. As the largest not-for-profit provider of housing and care to older people in the United Kingdom, MHA supports around 16,000 individuals in a variety of settings, with around 10% of them receiving nursing care in specialist homes, while around half of those whom MHA serves live independently and are members of 'Live at Home' schemes. Since the turn of the millennium, there has been a significant growth in the organisation, and one of the major developments during that time has been in the role and scope of Chaplaincy, such that MHA now employs individual Chaplains in all of our residential care homes, to be available to residents and relatives as well as to staff and volunteers. By no means are all of our Chaplains ordained and few have had any specific training in elder care chaplaincy before being appointed. They come from a wide variety of backgrounds and religious traditions and through training, support and reflection many have become invaluable members of the local staff team.

One of the Chaplain's key roles is that of an accompanist. Andrew Norris (Albans and Johnson 2013, p. 72) outlines the part played by Chaplains in interacting with the older person's story, suggesting that 'as "facilitative listeners" the role is one of offering unconditional accept-ance, welcoming, affirming and being guided by the willingness and co-operation of the storyteller to share what they will.' In this they are both witnesses and catalysts, not just in their deep and meaningful conversa-tions but in the stuff of ordinary life. Norris also highlights the place of 'active listening' in the Chaplain's armoury, something which becomes particularly significant when older people are sharing stories of depth and personal vulnerability. These three key roles of the Chaplain as accom-panist, catalyst and witness make it all the more strange that, as Norris points out (op. cit., p. 204ff.), most reviews of the work of Chaplains ignore their place within the field of social care settings, particularly in relation to older people. In MHA, the availability of the Chaplain to listen, to reflect on what is heard and to deal creatively with the interaction means that they are able to address pastoral, spiritual and religious issues. This in turn offers the possibility of nurturing well-being and being a beacon of hope within a community where the transitions of older age can affect the whole community in a care home, and where the regular experience of loss and death can sap the energies of residents and of staff.

MHA now boasts a team of over 130 Chaplains, and their willingness to be witnesses to the sharing of deep confidences and life stories has also led to Chaplains becoming a key part of our end of life care work, not least in training and supporting the rest of the staff team.

A Good Death?

Having considered some of the tasks and landmarks which belong to the final lap, the approach of the finishing line brings into focus the concept of a 'good death'. Although the idea has been around for centuries, and debated by philosophers from Socrates to Hume, Wittgenstein and others, there has never been any real agreement either about what constitutes a 'good death' or, indeed, the whole question of whether or not a 'good death' is a meaningful concept. In the *Encyclopaedia of Death and Dying*, Donald Duclow (2009) outlines the development within the Christian tradition of the *ars moriendi* (art of dying) in the fifteenth century. He shows how it developed out of late medieval prayer and liturgy to become a manual of practical guidance for the dying and those who attend them. Such manuals informed the dying about what to expect, and prescribed prayers, actions, and attitudes that would lead to a 'good death' and salvation. Although practices have changed over time, many of the rituals and liturgies have found their way into contemporary prayer books, and the idea of the 'good death' continues to attract interest.

One area in particular where the idea holds sway is within the modern hospice movement, where many feel that what is promised is an idealised pain-free death. The term kalothanasia (beautiful death) is sometimes used in this connection, but Floriani and Schramm (2010, pp. 461–468) are among those who argue that in any medical setting and within a 'bio-techno-scientific paradigm' the hospice faces a challenge to deliver such a death. One might also question whether such an idealistic notion of a good-death is reasonable anyway, as it might be seen to limit the notion of pain to a purely physical idea and ignore the many other components of existential angst which are inevitably part of the dying process.

In our current context, it is in the area of elder care that the language of 'good death' is becoming more common, not least because it is then seen as part of the changing pattern of dying in later life. As talk about death has increasingly come to include talk about the dying process, then the notion of a 'good dying' becomes part of the vocabulary. In the United Kingdom, the Debate of the Age Health and Care Study Group included in its work some thinking around dying and death and published twelve principles of a good death (Smith 2000). These are:

- To know when death is coming, and to understand what can be expected.
- To be able to retain control of what happens.
- To be afforded dignity and privacy.
- To have control over pain relief and other symptom control.
- To have choice and control over where death occurs (at home or elsewhere).
- To have access to information and expertise of whatever kind is necessary.
- To have access to any spiritual or emotional support required.
- To have access to hospice care in any location, not only in hospital.
- To have control over who is present and who shares the end.
- To be able to issue advance directives which ensure wishes are respected.
- To have time to say goodbye, and control over other aspects of timing.
- To be able to leave when it is time to go, and not to have life prolonged pointlessly.

In many ways these principles highlight the central issues in trying to tease out both the theory and practice of a 'good death', particularly as it results to the care of older people. For a start it suggests that a 'good death' reflects the choice and preference of the dying person, rather than being something imposed by external pressure. Such preferences will inevitably vary from person to person, as well as reflecting different cultural, religious and national characteristics. But, as Steve Nolan observes, it fundamentally means 'accepting the person's right to die ("on their feet" if necessary; or with quiet acceptance; or with raging "against the dying of the light"), rather than the "good death" prescribed by palliative care' (Nolan 2012, p. 73). However, this immediately widens the discussion to include the place of autonomy in all aspects of care and particularly end of life care. The twelve principles frequently use words such as 'control', 'choice' and 'know' which, while they may or may not be desirable, cannot with any certainty be guaranteed. In particular, the extent to which any individual has 'control' over many aspects of the dying process can raise ethical questions which society has always struggled to answer, and which in the United Kingdom have been exercising minds recently as Parliament discusses legislation on Assisted Dying.

From a positive point of view, the twelve principles do emphasise the fact that an individual's dying involves and affects many people other than themselves. And whilst some of those people will be medical professionals going about their business, others will be family members and social carers who can take care of such things as maintaining a person's dignity and privacy. This is an important part of whatever we might mean by a 'good death' for all too often those who are nonmedically trained accompanists to someone's dying can feel that their role will be secondary at best. This can be debilitating to family members as well as to care staff in residential settings. However, it is well known that the presence of another human being, hearing their voice and knowing that their privacy is being preserved in the final moments rank high among their wishes. And the ability to offer this gift to a dying person call upon our basic humanity, not upon years of specialist medical training, and it is with a view to giving people the confidence to exercise this gift that we developed the programme for our staff and volunteers.

The Final Lap: Training the End of Life Accompanists

In developing our Final Lap programme, we have worked closely with Professor Malcolm Johnson and his team, who had worked with other care providers. In turn they have drawn on some of the work of the National Funerals College. In particular, the Dead Citizen's Charter emphasises the responsibility which the living have to the dying to ensure that their final wishes are carried out (National Funerals College 1999). Clearly if that is to be possible, then those wishes need to be expressed and known by someone involved in their end of life care.

The aim of our training programme was, 'To ensure that MHA Homes are places where dying and death are faced openly and positively, with support, and to explore what this might mean for Care Homes, for residents and their families, and for staff and volunteers' (MHA Care Group 2006, p. 3). Each aspect is important in promoting a holistic approach within a home and serves to remind everyone that the tasks of caring are shared and that the end of an individual's life affects the whole community. Our approach was based on four fundamental principles:

i. *Death is Part of Life* – there is an inevitability of dealing with death in caring for older people which all too often is ignored in staff recruitment. Equally, it is possible to approach end of life care in such a 'professionalised' way that it de-skills people and pushes away relatives and carers.

ii. *Death is not always a tragedy, particularly in Older Age* – one of the recurring difficulties that we face is finding ways of speaking about death. The death of a loved one will always be emotional, but many experience it as God's gift and as a natural conclusion to a long life. In Christianity, we also need to explore a new language for speaking about what we believe may lie beyond death.

iii. *Openness before and after Death is healthy, and wanted by Older People themselves.* This is a key principle both in encouraging staff to begin conversations with residents, and in reassuring relatives that such an approach is justified. Research from the University of Sheffield, published by Help the Aged, includes articles about seven older people's experiences which illustrate the veracity of this principle (Seymour et al. 2005; Owen 2005).

iv. *A Social Model of Care has a vital role in End of Life Care.* As I have said earlier, one of the recurring problems for those supporting others towards the end of life is the tendency to medicalise and professionalise dying. This lies behind some unnecessary hospitalisation and some pointless medication. For many older people in residential settings, having a member of staff who is known and trusted present in the final moments of life is the best gift that they can receive.

One key factor in developing an approach to staff training in this area is the great discrepancy between the lack of exposure the majority of people in contemporary society have to dying and death and the much greater familiarity with it that existed during the upbringing of today's older people. Things are beginning to change; there is some evidence of a greater willingness to mark death openly, particularly amongst the under thirties, and what may be the 'Princess Diana effect' seems to have created an acceptable public face of grief whenever a tragedy or accidental death occurs. However, the discrepancy remains and is particularly significant in residential settings for older people.

In Great Britain, right up to the 1950s, dying and its aftermath was something domestic and homely. Many deaths, particularly of older people, occurred in their own homes and communities. Neighbours knew when someone was dying, and when death happened a series of local people became actively involved – someone in helping lay out the body, someone in bringing round a coffin and others simply in visiting and helping out. The body did not generally leave the house until the day of the funeral and all visitors were expected to pay their respects by viewing the body of the deceased. Almost uniquely in contemporary

Britain, it is possible in residential aged care settings to go some way to recreating that culture for the generation for whom it was the norm.

Introducing staff to the practices around dying and death with which most of their residents grew up is one of the first areas covered in our Final Lap training. It serves to begin to bridge the cultural gap, emphasises the first three principles outlined above and gives people the confidence to be able to contemplate entering into discussions with residents about their own feelings.

A second vital area within our Final Lap training is to give staff an understanding of the funeral industry and to open their eyes as to what is possible, and perhaps desirable, when it comes to planning a funeral. It is often said that few people have to arrange more than three funerals during their lifetime – two parents and a partner or spouse. Consequently, most of us feel ourselves to be either passive recipients of what we are offered by a Funeral Director, or the re-enactor of what is considered to be the 'standard' funeral service by the local Crematorium's duty clergy. But for those involved in elder care the story can, and should, be different. For a start they need to see themselves as advocates for their residents in relation to Funeral Directors, and this means that the Home should take the initiative in defining when and how a body is removed. Many managers have good stories to tell of positive relationships built up between their care home and the local Funeral Directors. Sadly many others still recount horror stories where good end of life care offered by their own staff is undone by the crass insensitivity of those who come to collect the body.

Giving staff the confidence they need in this area comes from understanding their role as advocates in relation to other family members as well. This can involve sharing preferences that residents have expressed to staff, but couldn't speak about with family members, through to helping to plan, or even host, the funeral ceremony. This can be particularly helpful when a resident has few family members or has not lived locally before coming into the care home. I remember the first time I took a funeral service in a care home – it seemed strange beforehand and yet entirely appropriate on the day. The home was Jean's extended family and they wanted to be part of the service, which would not have been possible had it been held elsewhere.

Introducing staff to more imaginative and creative approaches to funerals can give rise to some very meaningful ceremonies, which in turn helps to create a sense of openness within the home and assists people in their own thinking and planning. Indeed funeral planning is one feature of our homes that has become far more prevalent and accepted since we began the Final Lap training. For some residents, expressing a choice of hymn or reading will be enough, while for others ensuring that their preference for burial or cremation is understood and recorded is vital. There are still others who wish to plan the whole ceremony and who gain a sense of comfort and relief from doing so. Such planning may not be easy for family members to listen to or participate in, but staff in residential homes can be trusted confidantes for such matters.

Another area of conversation which staff can be encouraged to initiate might come under the heading 'unfinished business'. At the deepest level this might include issues of reconciliation and restoration of broken relationships and friendships, where residents seek help in creating an opportunity for this to take place. Such things can only be undertaken after discussions amongst the senior team and, if appropriate, family members but being aware of the need is important in understanding the resident's needs at the end of life.

On another level the idea of unfinished business might include answers to the question, 'what is it important for you to do before you die?' It is not uncommon for children with a terminal illness to undertake special adventure holidays or trips, but with older people the wishes can be simpler and more mundane. That does not, however, underestimate their importance. One resident wanted to attend evensong at the local Cathedral where her great grandson was a choirboy, while another wanted to revisit a place of work which had been important to them in years gone by. The sense of completion which fulfilling these wishes can bring about is palpable.

This brings me to the most difficult part of the Final Lap training, and one without which none of the things I have outlined is possible. That is helping staff to feel able to participate in conversations with residents which might elicit their end of life care thoughts, feelings and aspirations. I referred earlier to the hesitancy with which most approach the topic of DNACPR directives, but that is only the beginning. The key aspect of training is around communication skills which give staff the confidence to stay with difficult emotional conversations with residents, and thus allow the older person to express their wishes. We do not serve either our staff or our residents if we have a culture whereby such conversations are discouraged or shut down with an attempt to cheer someone up with an inappropriate comment.

Many staff are naturally empathetic – it is part of why they are drawn to a caring profession – but plenty of staff are inexperienced and lack confidence in this area. However they usually find it easy to identify bad practice when it is demonstrated, and quickly learn to correct themselves without further prompting. And in this particular area of training it is important to include all types of staff within the home – not simply those involved in personal care. The domestic staff, for example, may be the ones who spend some significant time alone with a resident and who build up a relationship of confidence wherein these kinds of conversations might begin.

Some may feel that the training programme that I have outlined is back to front – dealing with issues of assessing needs and discussion of final wishes after dealing with funerals and the aftermath. Our experience however is that by doing it in this order helps to give staff the confidence to explore the more emotional and sensitive issues by first giving them a grounding in the more sociological and societal areas. I firmly believe that many find that the easiest way of talking about a difficult subject is to talk about talking about it! Many staff have reported back that they have introduced a discussion about dying and death with residents simply by telling them about the training course they have been on. That is often the only thing they have had to say – the residents have done the rest of the talking themselves.

The Needs of Those Left Behind

Death in a residential setting can inevitably have an effect on the whole community of staff and residents. Consequently good end of life care has to extend to them as well, whether that be through ensuring that those who wish to have an opportunity to say their own goodbyes, the way in which the news of a resident's death is communicated to others and the ways by which that death is marked within the on-going life of the home. Exploring ways of achieving this is an important aspect of the Final Lap training.

In particular, the area of memorialising – by which I do not mean a plaque on a bench or by a tree – is one which is perhaps least likely to have been addressed elsewhere. Encouraging residents to talk about the one who has died and share their stories can be a helpful experience. I recall witnessing this happening in one of our homes and listening as people shared memories both of what they liked about the deceased and some things which had annoyed them. The mixture of love, laughter and tears was a powerful testimony to the sense of community and loss, and I reflected that each resident there would have known that something similar would take place when their own death occurred.

Another aspect of memorialising is through the placing of a photograph of the person who has died in the entrance lobby of the home, together with their name and any funeral details once they are known. As well as informing people that a death has occurred, it also signals to visitors and relatives that a particular individual has died. In a care home, a resident will be known not only to their own visitors but to others as well.

A final aspect of memorialising which many find helpful is the remembering, within the context of an act of worship, of those residents who have died. In all of our homes this is done naturally in the next service after the death but many also hold special services on an annual basis to which relatives of those who have died are invited back. This is common in many hospices and as well as remembering the ones who have died it serves to extend the relationship between the care home and the family of residents. Once again it also helps the continuing residential community to have a foretaste of how their own death might be marked.

The Finishing Line and MHA's Five Values

In recruiting staff, Methodist Homes seeks those who are able and willing to work according to the values of the organisation. These are organised, as follows, under five headings:

- We *respect* every person as a unique individual.
- We treat others, especially the most frail and vulnerable, with the *dignity* we wish for ourselves.
- We are *open and fair* in all our dealings.
- We always seek to improve, to become the *best we can be.*
- We nurture each person's *body, mind and spirit* to promote a fulfilled life.

It is clear from what I have outlined earlier that in caring for those at the end of life, staff have the ideal opportunity to put each of these values into practice.

- Every resident's individuality must be respected – there is no 'one size fits all' approach to end of life care. Discovering a resident's wishes, and then helping all of the care team to work towards achieving them, is a key aspect of a carer's role and one which can bring about a great sense of achievement.
- A resident's dignity in the final hours of life can be hard to maintain, and they will rely entirely on others to ensure that it is. Helping staff to understand what would be important to them in these circumstances enables them to assist residents in this vital task.
- Building a culture of openness around end of life concerns has been central to the Final Lap. Helping staff to remain engaged in conversations around emotional topics is one aspect, as well as being open with all staff and residents before and after a death has occurred is helpful to everyone.

- For each individual we only get one chance to get it right in end of life care, but for the staff team there is the opportunity to learn and constantly improve. On many occasions I have seen staff discover that they have a particular aptitude for this aspect of their work, and this has led them both to become a mentor for their colleagues and to go the extra mile when a resident is dying.
- Recognising the interplay between physical, emotional and spiritual needs for an individual in their final days and hours is fundamental to good end of life care. Likewise, even when caring for someone at this stage, it is important to do everything possible to help them to achieve a sense of completion.

Conclusions

In much of the national media, the image of residential aged care facilities in Great Britain is almost universally negative. But for all that working with the most frail and vulnerable older people is fraught with difficulties, the possibility of delivering good end of life care and of creating a culture of openness and creativity around the issues of dying and death means that in one area at least, good news stories can be created. What is more, creating this culture gives staff a greater sense of purpose and achievement which, I believe, flows into the rest of their work and aids both staff retention and resident satisfaction. And ultimately, by putting Dame Cecily Saunders' words into practice in a care home, we begin to show the possibility of a wider cultural change which will be to the benefit of the whole society.

References

Albans, K. 2013. 'Supporting and Learning from the Oldest Old: The Spiritual Journey of Ageing', in K. Albans and M. Johnson (eds.) *God, Me and Being Very Old: Stories and Spirituality in Later Life*, pp. 20–36. London: SCM Press.

Anderson, S.H. and Dunlap, D.W. 1985. 'New York Day by Day; Author to Readers', *New York Times*, April 25, 1985.

Department of Health 2008. 'End of Life Care Strategy: Promoting High Quality Care for all Adults at the End of Life'. London: HMSO.

Duclow, D. 2009. 'Ars Moriendi', in *Encyclopedia of Death and Dying*, www.deathreference.com/A-Bi/Ars-Moriendi.html. Accessed August 3, 2014.

Floriani, C. and Schramm, F.R. 2010. 'Journey of Struggle: Kalothanasia and the Hospice Way of Dying', *Palliative Support Care* 8(4), 461–468.

Jewell, A. 2004. *Report on Sisters Work*. London: Conference of Religious in England and Wales.

Kristjanson, L. 2006. 'A Palliative Approach to Spirituality in Residential Aged Care', in E. MacKinlay (ed.) *Aging, Spirituality and Palliative Care*, pp. 189–205. Binghamton, NY: The Haworth Pastoral Press.

Lamberton, K. 2005. 'His Preferred Immortality', *Los Angeles Times*, September 20, 2005.

MacKinlay, E. 2006. *Spiritual Growth and Care in the Fourth Age of Life*. London: Jessica Kingsley Publishers.

MacKinlay, E. 2012. *Palliative Care, Ageing and Spirituality*. London: Jessica Kingsley Publishers.

MHA Care Group 2006. 'The Final Lap'. Derby: MHA.

Mohan, K. 2004. 'Eastern Perspectives and Implications for the West', in A. Jewell (ed.) *Ageing, Spirituality and Well-being*, pp. 161–179. London: Jessica Kingsley Publishers.

National End of Life Care Intelligence Network 2010. *Deaths in Older Adults in England*, pp. 23–24.

National Funerals College 1999. *Dead Citizens' Charter*.

Nolan, S. 2012. *Spiritual Care at the End of Life*. London: Jessica Kingsley Publishers.

Norris, A. 2013. 'Listening and Accompanying: The Essence of Later-Life Chaplaincy', in K. Albans and M. Johnson (eds.) *God, Me and Being Very Old: Stories and Spirituality in Later Life*, pp. 71–76. London: SCM Press.

Norris, A. 2013. 'Chaplaincy Among Older People: A Model for the Church's Ministry and Mission?', in K. Albans and M. Johnson (eds.) *God, Me and Being Very Old: Stories and Spirituality in Later Life*, pp. 200–213. London: SCM Press.

Office for National Statistics 2014. www.ons.gov.uk/ons/publications/re-reference-tables.html?edition=tcm%3A77-317522. Accessed August 13, 2014.

Owen, T. (ed.) 2005. *Dying in Older Age – reflections and experiences from an older person's perspective*. London: Help the Aged.

Palapathwala, R. 2006. 'Ageing and Death: A Buddhist-Christian Conceptual Framework for Spirituality in Later Life', in E. MacKinlay (ed.) *Aging, Spirituality and Palliative Care*, pp. 153–168. Binghamton, NY: The Haworth Pastoral Press.

Seymour, J., Witherspoon, R., Gott, M., Ross, H., Payne, S. and Owen, T. 2005. *End-of-Life-Care – Promoting Comfort, Choice and Well-being for Older People*. Bristol: Policy Press.

Smith, R. 2000. 'A Good Death', *British Medical Journal* 320, 129–130.

Index